D1032502

MARRIAGE, FAMILY, AND LAW IN MEDIEVAL EUROPE: COLLECTED STUDIES

MICHAEL M. SHEEHAN, CSB

MICHAEL M. SHEEHAN, CSB

Marriage, Family, and Law in Medieval Europe: Collected Studies

edited by James K. Farge

Introduction by Joel T. Rosenthal

UNIVERSITY OF TORONTO PRESS

Toronto Buffalo

© University of Toronto Press Incorporated 1996
Toronto Buffalo
Printed in Canada

ISBN 0-8020-0709-0 (cloth)

Printed on acid-free paper

Canadian Cataloguing in Publication Data

Sheehan, Michael M. (Michael McMahon), 1925–1992
Marriage, family, and law in medieval Europe :
collected studies

Includes bibliographical references.
ISBN 0-8020-0709-0

1. Marriage – Europe – History. 2. Marriage (Canon
law). 3. Family – Europe – History. 4. Wills –
Europe – History. 5. Wills (Canon law). 6. Europe –
Social conditions – To 1492. 1. Farge, James K.,
1938– . 11. Title.

HQ611.S54 1996   306.8'094'0902   C96-930068-9

University of Toronto Press acknowledges
the financial assistance to its publishing program of the
Canada Council and the Ontario Arts Council.

Contents

Foreword *by James K. Farge* vii

Introduction *by Joel T. Rosenthal* xiii

Acknowledgments xxix

Abbreviations xxxi

ONE
Report of a Thesis on the Will in Medieval England 3

TWO
A List of Thirteenth-Century English Wills 8

THREE
The Influence of Canon Law
on the Property Rights of Married Women in England 16

FOUR
Canon Law and English Institutions:
Some Notes on Current Research 31

FIVE
The Formation and Stability of Marriage
in Fourteenth-Century England: Evidence of an Ely Register 38

SIX
Marriage and Family
in English Conciliar and Synodal Legislation 77

SEVEN
Choice of Marriage Partner in the Middle Ages:
Development and Mode of Application of a Theory of Marriage 87

EIGHT
Marriage Theory and Practice
in the Conciliar Legislation
and Diocesan Statutes of Medieval England 118

NINE
The Wife of Bath and Her Four Sisters:
Reflections on a Woman's Life in the Age of Chaucer 177

TEN
English Wills and the Records
of the Ecclesiastical and Civil Jurisdictions 199

ELEVEN
Theory and Practice: Marriage
of the Unfree and the Poor in Medieval Society 211

TWELVE
The European Family and Canon Law 247

THIRTEEN
Maritalis affectio Revisited 262

FOURTEEN
The Bishop of Rome to a Barbarian King
on the Rituals of Marriage 278

FIFTEEN
Sexuality, Marriage, Celibacy, and the Family
in Central and Northern Italy:
Christian Legal and Moral Guides in the Early Middle Ages 292

SIXTEEN
The Bequest of Land in England
in the High Middle Ages: Testaments and the Law 311

Bibliography of Michael M. Sheehan, CSB 324
Compiled by Mary C. English and James K. Farge

Foreword

The death of Michael McMahon Sheehan in a cycling accident on 23 August 1992 brought to an untimely close the life of an innovative scholar, a dedicated teacher, a faithful priest, and a compassionate man. Failing health having reduced his heavy classroom commitments to a single seminar, Michael was hoping now to give greater attention to three long-delayed projects. The first, a comprehensive bibliography on marriage, the family, and related gender topics in the Middle Ages, he had steadily advanced over the years. Another, an edition of all the English wills analysed in his first book, had been on his agenda for thirty years. In the third and most ambitious project he hoped to produce a study of wills from 1300 to the end of the Middle Ages, in order to provide for this later period what he had already done for the earlier. The reels of microfilms and the editions of archival registers open on his desk the day he died show that he was working towards these ends.

Born on 29 January 1925 in the town of Renfrew in the Ottawa River valley in eastern Ontario, Michael Sheehan never lost his love for the elements of creation. Although his professional life drew him to urban areas of Canada and Europe, he loved finding time in the country to seek out unusual flora or to collect specimens of rock. He was fascinated with and curious about the being and workings of nature and manufacture alike.

In 1943, a year after enrolling in honours philosophy, English, and history at St Michael's College in the University of Toronto, Michael Sheehan joined the Basilian Fathers. He was ordained a priest in 1950. To confrères and colleagues he offered the steady presence of a mature personality and the honest interest of an undemanding companion.

After taking the master of arts in philosophy and matriculating in the licentiate programme of the Pontifical Institute of Mediaeval Studies,

Michael spent two years at the Ecole pratique des hautes études at the University of Paris, where he conceived the idea of his major thesis, *The Will in England: From the Conversion of the Anglo-Saxons to the End of the Thirteenth Century*. Its publication in 1963 earned him the rarely attained doctorate in mediaeval studies at the Pontifical Institute. A recent citation honouring him declared that this work 'remains a classic in its field.'

Michael had already begun, a decade earlier, his lifelong profession of teaching at the Institute and in the theological programme of St Michael's College. His lectures and seminars ranged from archaeology to the history of spirituality, from cathedral floor plans to the interaction of canon law and the realities of family life in the Middle Ages. Other courses included the mendicant orders, pastoral care, and the papacy. Cross-appointed to the University of Toronto's Centre for Medieval Studies and its Department of History, Michael supervised the doctoral theses of twenty students and the master's and licentiate theses of thirteen others. During the last ten years alone, he served on the examining boards of over forty doctoral candidates. Despite problems of health in later years, he persisted in teaching in the Faculty of Theology – so convinced was he that preparation for ministries in the Church is incomplete without a historical grounding in Catholic Tradition.

During his studies and travels in Europe and Asia Minor, Michael stored up in his exceptional visual memory an immense experience of the art and architecture of every era from the classical to the contemporary but especially of the early Byzantine and the later western medieval periods. From his first years of teaching he introduced both medievalists and theologians to this rich artistic expression by integrating it into the historical background he knew so well. He made frequent use of an extensive slide collection that he built up at the Institute.

Michael was curious too about buildings and artefacts which had disappeared over the ages. He believed that the process of sifting through the strata of past civilizations and interpreting the data they yield is as essential to the historian as are charters and codices. He twice spent sabbatical leaves digging in Asia Minor. His journey from France to one of the sites, carefully retracing the route taken by a Crusading army, is illustrative of Michael's multidisciplinary approach to studying the past.

Michael Sheehan's diverse competencies, evident wisdom, and sensible voice in matters academic and institutional marked him out for frequent nomination to boards and committees of the university, the Archdiocese of Toronto, and the Basilian Fathers dealing with such disparate interests as aging, art, ethics, family life, pastoral ministry, and revision of statutes.

Regular priestly ministry in one or another Toronto parish on weekends increased the demands on him for counselling and spiritual direction. He typically responded to such requests with a generosity that over the years lessened his time and energy for research and publication. Some might wish he had ordered his priorities differently; but anything else would not have been the instinctive, personal approach in charity which was characteristic of Michael.

The research and publication that he was able to accomplish established his reputation as an innovative, even path-finding scholar in several areas of medieval social and legal history. A recent formal citation, for example, described him as one of a handful of international pioneers of the last two decades who have contributed to our understanding of the family of Western Europe and the slowly evolving practice of marriage and socio-economic patterns over many centuries. Michael knew the canon and common law of England; but he also knew that close study and interpretation of the court records was often more important, since they chronicled patterns of living which formulated or influenced those laws. In demonstrating this relationship between theory and practice, Michael developed a methodology and example of research for others to follow. Both tyros and mature scholars return with profit to Michael Sheehan's work.

This record of achievements resulted in increasingly frequent invitations to speak at scholarly gatherings in North America and Europe and to serve as organizer or editor of conference proceedings and collections of essays in social and legal history. Just a few months before his death, poor health forced him reluctantly to cancel a talk in Ottawa. His last scholarly appearances were to deliver two papers in Germany, one on illegitimacy in the Middle Ages, the other in connection with the preparation of the multivolume *History of Medieval Canon Law* in which he had agreed to collaborate.

For many years Michael Sheehan produced an annual bibliography of materials for the study of Canadian church history. He held offices in the Canadian Catholic Historical Association and the American Catholic Historical Association and was an active member of several other historical societies. In 1985 he was named a visiting fellow of All Souls College, Oxford. He served on the editorial boards of five learned journals and steadily reviewed manuscripts for academic presses and journals. As vice-president of the Medieval Academy of America he would have acceded to its presidency in 1994.

All this service to institutions, associations, committees, and individuals flowed from Michael Sheehan's faith, his prayerful spiritual life, and his convicted hope in the reality of everlasting life. Like St Francis de Sales, on whose feast he was born and whose example he cherished, Michael gracefully channelled a strong temperament into a loving, active concern for each person he met. He never allowed differences of opinion to affect the duty and the desire to maintain friendly relationships with others.

After appraising the significance of Michael Sheehan's book *The Will in Medieval England* one reviewer concluded with this accolade: 'So complete and thorough an account ... of testamentary law and its application inevitably produced facts and conclusions that dictate corrections and revisions of earlier historians. Sheehan makes them, and, with a modesty not too common among revisionists, he neither flaunts his findings nor pillories his predecessors. Justly, he may take pride in the quality of his book, but he may take a greater pride in having written it with the humility that so becomes both his callings, the priest and the historian' (William H. Dunham, Jr, in *American Historical Review* 70 [1964] 426–7). Written in the early years of Michael Sheehan's career, this appraisal presaged his later academic achievements and his lifelong personal spirituality.

Michael Sheehan's unexpected death evoked deep feeling and many tributes. The memorial service at St Basil's Church in Toronto on 27 November 1992 included eulogies from colleagues at the Pontifical Institute of Mediaeval Studies and the University of Toronto, from the Archdiocese of Toronto, and from other universities. A canon law conference in Vancouver in November 1992 was dedicated to Michael's memory. Colleagues, family, and friends of Michael have undertaken to fund a student scholarship in his memory at the Pontifical Institute. A collection of studies on women, covering both legal and social approaches, *Wife and Widow in Medieval England* (Ann Arbor 1993), written by grateful friends and associates and edited by Sue Sheridan Walker, had originally been intended as a volume in Michael's honour. It appeared instead in his memory. The 1993 issue of *Florilegium* (Carleton University, Ottawa), edited by Douglas Wurtele, was dedicated to Michael Sheehan as a founding member of its editorial board. Still another volume, *Women, Marriage, and Family in Medieval Christendom: Essays in Memory of Michael M. Sheehan, CSB* (Kalamazoo 1995), planned and edited by Constance Rousseau and Joel Rosenthal, will contain the work of several of Michael's former doctoral students from Toronto. Through it, as through the present volume, the Sheehan influence, as well as the voice that is easily conjured up in the memory, will be with us for many years.

Written tributes have appeared in a spate of journals, notably the notice by Walter Principe, CSB (in *Mediaeval Studies* 55 [1993] vii–xi), the minute read by Jocelyn Hillgarth to the Medieval Academy (*Speculum* 68 [1993] 922), and the notice by Brian Hogan, CSB (*Toronto Journal of Theology* 9 [1993] 7–8) – on all of which I have freely drawn.

In the present edition, Michael Sheehan's original texts and presentation have been maintained with minimal changes. I have regularized the differing approaches to documentation in the sixteen articles. In only two cases (articles 10 and 15) did the original form of documentation necessitate changing the order and the numbers of the notes. For clarity's sake, I have amended slightly the title of article 1 (see the note at that place). To assist the reader, I have added the pagination of the present volume to Michael's own cross-references to his original articles. Typographical errors in the originals have been corrected whenever perceived; but the optical scanning of the articles may have introduced new flaws, for the presence of which I accept full responsibility.

The production of the present volume has been facilitated by a number of persons who share my conviction that Michael Sheehan's work relating to marriage, the family, and law, published over the space of thirty years, will best be appreciated and utilized when brought together in one volume. I am particularly grateful to Joel T. Rosenthal, who has skilfully drawn the threads of Michael's work together in the introduction. Suzanne Rancourt and the editorial board of the University of Toronto Press responded with enthusiasm when I proposed this book to them, and their referees acted with alacrity and offered helpful suggestions. The Centre for Medieval Studies of the University of Toronto, under its former director Jill R. Webster, underwrote the cost of the optical scanning of the articles and of preliminary checking of the results. Theresa Griffin, manuscript editor for the Press, worked with marvellous precision and care. David Wiljer helped to check the optical scanning of the originals. I am grateful to all of them. More than a mere tribute, the book we have produced together assures that Michael Sheehan's work will continue to teach and to guide the work of others.

JAMES K. FARGE, CSB
Pontifical Institute of Mediaeval Studies
29 January 1995

Introduction

Quality and consistency are the outstanding characteristics of the work of Michael Sheehan. From his publication of *The Will in Medieval England* in 1963 through 'The Bequest of Land in England in the High Middle Ages: Testaments and the Law' in 1992 he built steadily and persistently on the foundations of the work that had gone before. It is meant as an immense tribute to say that Michael rarely changed his mind, that he was a stubborn and determined scholar (which was the absolute opposite of his role as a friend and mentor), and that he relied heavily upon what he himself had already put in place as he moved on.

This intellectual intransigence was not owing to arrogance or a false estimation regarding either his own infallibility or the permanence of scholarly contributions in any given area of our ongoing intellectual/ historical discourse. It was owing rather to his concern, in the long run, with charting a difficult and individualistic path towards an end point that he always kept in sight. He drew up a list of problems for himself, almost as a mathematician or an engineer might do, and moved from one to the next as each answer enabled him to open the gate before which he had now arrived. Sometimes his progress was linear; at other times he might zigzag for several years as he thought out his next step forward. Nor is it surprising to his friends and readers to realize that his path, one which had often seemed obscure and tortuous before he had charted and sign-posted it, frequently turned out to be broad and almost self-evident once he had cleared the way.

To offer a thematic statement identifying the path that unifies so much of Michael Sheehan's work is a challenge. The response I venture here is that he sought to explicate the nature and evolution or development of three basic medieval institutions: the last will, in its emergence as a legal and social instrument whereby different and even competing social forces had their moment of expression; Christian marriage, as it became defined and codified in the high Middle Ages; and the secular family, especially as it was shaped by the same forces that argued for the definition of marriage. His approach or springboard for analysis and method of argument was largely by way of canon law, though from that point of entry he invariably was at pains to incorporate solid support for his scholarly brief from such sister fields as theology, the social and popular history of religion, and the history of sexuality and sexual behaviour. There was also an early recognition of the importance and centrality of what we usually sum up under the rubric of 'women's history.'

When we look at the full course of his scholarly career, we see that he turned to the history of Christian marriage as his main focal point more often than he did to any of his other areas of special interest, and it was perhaps in that particular field of inquiry that he left his most striking legacy. There are a number of salient characteristics of his formulation of the historical development of Christian marriage – as he moved to define the topic and the methods whereby it was best explicated – and perhaps the most basic was that it rested on the consent of the couple. In addition, it emphasized their centrality, along with that of the nuclear family, over both the extended family and the social and political hierarchy of medieval society. Furthermore, Christian wedlock only or ultimately came to full maturity when the involvement of the priest and of the local community – by assuming their various roles in the posting of banns, the public inquiry into impediments, and the sacramentalization of the ceremony – became integral units in the religious and the social process at some point in the high Middle Ages.

This summary does little justice to the complexity of his arguments or to the learning with which he supported them. Nor does it do full justice to his other interests, whether we think of him as a teacher or as an active member of many communities. Moreover, even when looking at the development of his views about marriage we must recognize how sensitive he was to the need to explicate the tensions created in the world by the shifting divisions of labour, of authority, and of legitimacy between the legal presence of the Church and that of the secular authority. Neither would he go for long, in his many articles on the subject, without wryly commenting on the tortuous balancing act we can follow within the Church itself, which often had to teeter between the institutional desideratum of social control and the theological and legal emphasis upon the role of individual volition. And if canon law was the effective tool whereby Sheehan entered the labyrinth of marital institutions and practices (in both their theoretical or Christian-normative aspects and their wide variations as practice), he reminded us that the key itself reached its singular level of effectiveness only because the canonists of the twelfth and thirteenth centuries had become adept at incorporating so much theology and patristic reflection into their legal writings. They had thereby succeeded in a coupling of ecclesiastical legislation and counsel so as to join together the act or ceremony of marriage, the physical and spiritual family, and the scope of personal freedom within (or into) one conjugal structure, noteworthy as much for its flexibility as for its sensitivity.

Thus Sheehan presented the social and legal realities that emerged to govern marriage in Europe from the second half of the twelfth century onwards as the result – albeit not always the smooth and predictable conclusion – of a process that could be unfolded (for us) as one of compromise, of a lot of give-and-take. It can be seen as a synthesis of the 'concordance of discordant canons' upon the topic, and of a need to accept a range of variations – in both ideology and practice – upon the question.

The singling out of the history of marriage as *the* main theme of Michael Sheehan's work does not reveal how he came to the topic, nor why, within its historical contours and boundaries, it came to represent the best centrepiece or fixed star of his many interests. We have noted that *The Will in Medieval England* was his first major scholarly contribution (appearing in 1963). Ostensibly, this path-breaking study – the outgrowth of his dissertation – was closer to the vein of legal history than it was to social and family history. In so far as we can make such a distinction for a large and complex book, norms were emphasized over 'real' behaviour and lived experience. However, we should remember that in 1963 'the new social history' was barely upon us, and though bridges were being built between the academic sub-disciplines, they were bridges mostly being opened without the cutting of ribbons, and they were traversed with little fanfare. Sheehan had been trained in the canonist tradition, and he just quietly moved, in his treatise on the history and development of the will, from the legal to the socio-economic and thence to a considerable focus on the status of women.

Furthermore, *The Will* largely concentrated on the early medieval period: the volume's subtitle was *From the Conversion of the Anglo-Saxons to the End of the Thirteenth Century*. In this choice of subtitle the author served notice that he would feel free – and it was a freedom he exercised – to return to the earlier centuries in the years to come, going back to what Marc Bloch would have applauded as that stage in Europe's history in which we could best search for roots and first signs. But despite the book's announced commitment to the Anglo-Saxon and the earlier post-Conquest centuries, most of us have continued to use *The Will* as an authoritative text that carries us to the Henrician Reformation and the legal reforms of the sixteenth century.

Many of the most important features that Michael Sheehan set forth in his treatment of the will also came to be adduced, in the years to come, as critical features in his iteration of the development and codification of medieval marriage and of the family. Though *The Will in Medieval England* was the only full-length monograph Sheehan ever published, his early study put him firmly on the road he was to follow for the rest of his scholarly career. He constantly drew from *The Will's* agenda of problems, and he returned to probe the topics he had initiated and that remained unsettled. Whether this return was owing to the internal logic of a scholar's career or to the power of analogy and of a tested and successful method that we hold on to as we turn to new problems and a reading of new texts is difficult to determine. As he was often to do in the later papers on these other topics, towards the beginning of *The Will* he stated a guiding premise that remained as both a personal and an academic testament; it was that the work he was now presenting was to be read as a case study, a further 'example of the part played by Christianity in the growth of western civilization ... [and of] how the injection of a religious notion into a society was able to enrich and develop several secular institutions.'[1]

Of course, this observation about thematic persistence comes from a reading of *The Will* in hindsight. Some years passed after he published that landmark volume before Sheehan was ready to push ahead in what seems, looking back, to be the obvious and logical direction for his future work. His formulated statements on the history of marriage and the family were still some years ahead, and at the far end Michael died without ever offering us his own retrospective view covering the entire body of his scholarly work. Nevertheless, his early statement about the Church's contribution to the structure and function of secular society

---

1 *The Will in Medieval England: From the Conversion of the Anglo-Saxons to the End of the Thirteenth Century*, Studies and Texts 6 (Toronto 1963) 3. Two early articles, 'A List of Thirteenth-Century English Wills' (1961) and 'Report of a Thesis Defended at the Pontifical Institute of Mediaeval Studies' (1961; entitled here 'Report of a Thesis on the Will in Medieval England'), are direct offshoots of the dissertation research.

stands as a guiding beacon. It would illuminate and unify much of the work he was to publish in the next three decades as he went from institution to institution, from century to century, and from the British Isles to the Continent and back.

As he argued in *The Will* – and elsewhere, in comparable statements – the development and power of the will in medieval England grew out of a need to mediate between the clash of powerful if competing interests: those seeking to predetermine and govern the descent of property through impersonalized rules and legal practices and those striving to offer some scope (or 'space') for the exercise of personal volition, particularly as that volition was shaped in considerable part by the Church's teachings revolving around the duty to give alms. But beyond these particulars, the similarities of exposition and of method that link Sheehan's study of the English will and his later writings on (primarily English) marriage are striking – far beyond the coincidences of style and 'voice.' In both bodies of his scholarly writing – in so far as we can separate them – we can gauge the importance he assigned to such phenomena as the role of witnesses, the centrality of the priest's presence in bestowing and representing sanctity and legitimacy, the power of oral disposition when no written text had been generated, the irrevocable and contractual nature of the transaction under consideration, and the persistent medieval inclination to steer volitional matters towards church courts and those affecting real property towards secular ones. He might well have responded, to this complimentary summation, that if the views of Gratian and Innocent III and Innocent IV were sewn together into a single garment of historical interpretation, why should we be taken aback that Sheehan too would argue for and build a case upon convergence and systematization?

When Michael Sheehan turned towards the history of Christian marriage, he was going to pick up, sooner or later, virtually all these themes that first emerge so prominently in his treatment of the will. Such themes continued to appear, often as the prime movers, in his explanatory strategy for his new fields of inquiry. Other themes came in as well, of course, since the development of 'a theory of marriage' was comparable to the development of wills in some ways, different in some striking and basic respects. When he turned to marriage, he now had to focus on the importance of celibacy for Christianity, both as a concept and as a practice; on how its challenges to familial and/or extra-familial sexuality had to be incorporated into patristic and canonical views of marriage and social relations. Betwixt marriage and celibacy – emerging in the early

Church as a peculiarly Christian alternative to marriage – were any number of halfway points, intermediate steps in behaviour and rest stops on the chronological journey from non-Christian and pre-Christian practices towards the mature medieval institution with its full sacramental definition and blessing, and, in some instances, with its critical milestones as they might be distributed along the individual life line.[2]

In keeping with Sheehan's treatment of the development of the will, the elements that ultimately comprised his interpretation of the Christian definition of marriage – for those parties or groups just named, as well as for all others – were presented as the end products and fine-tunings of a complex harmonic of legal and historical evolution and of conflict resolution. From the wide expanse of territory between theory and practice and case law and human behavioural patterns there eventually emerged a major institution, armed to do battle and yet socialized to accommodate new elements and precedents. The process whereby varying and sometimes directly conflicting views on marriage were eventually synthesized was an integral part of its institutional development, as it was of the long, trial-and-error search for a correctness of both doctrine and practice.

It is hardly necessary, in the course of this introduction, to lead the reader through each of the papers reprinted in this collection. It will suffice if some of the basic steps along the road are marked out and some significant transitions noted. The reading of the Sheehan corpus, as offered in these comments, is but the interpretation and assessment of one colleague (and admirer), and my treatment is neither comprehensive nor equally at home in all the areas covered by the full span of scholarly writings that we are fortunate enough to have from this learned and gifted man. The papers selected for publication have been arranged in chronological order, in large part because Sheehan's intellectual approach to his own agenda was accretionary. Such an arrangement enables us to trace his backtracking and his own concern to refine and refocus what he had already said about the topics he found of such enduring interest, as well as the way in which he moved along his path. A thematic arrangement, one that would separate his main research contributions from the more synthetic and reflective ones and contrast the two kinds, could well have been used; it would have clarified his desire to reach different audiences and to tie his historical work to contemporary issues that continued to be of great concern.

---

2 'Marriage and Family in English Conciliar and Synodal Legislation' (1974) is probably the paper that deals at greatest length with the problems posed for the family, marriage, and sexuality by the institution and practice of celibacy.

In a chronological discussion of Michael Sheehan's work, we should note that his early endeavours after *The Will* were mostly devoted to tracing the influence of canon law on married women's property rights, rather than on marriage per se. For the next eight years (1963–71) topics that arose more or less directly from *The Will* – focusing on property and women's rights – were the main scope of Michael's printed work. But in looking at the topics he chose to work on we see a consistent interest in returning to and expanding upon some particular spin-off topics from *The Will* that steadily and logically moved him towards the study of women, of marriage, and of the family. Did he know, from the start, the direction in which he wished to move, or was it a case of one set of problems, when addressed, just leading inexorably to the next? Regardless of our answer to this question, when taken as a single body of work the writing of these years gives us a good idea of how his scholarly agenda was evolving. They were his years of exploration and discovery, years in which he directed and anchored himself, after the major journey that gave us his only full-length monograph.

In a sense he was seeking to unravel and clarify the process whereby the Church codified its views on marriage (and related topics) while he also worked to define the way in which 'the two spheres' of medieval society determined what, concerning these topics, belonged to Caesar and what to Christ. The argued stance of twelfth- and thirteenth-century ecclesiastical pronouncements that militated in favour of gender equality and a single standard between the sexes and across (most) social divisions was set as a foil against secular assertions of jurisdiction – over people, property, and behaviour – as they emanated from those whose role it was to make 'the feudal system' work. This line of analysis had been important in his treatment of the will, and it was to prove just as useful and enlightening when he turned to marriage and the family.

However, Michael Sheehan did not see himself as a defender of the historical Church against the onslaughts and insensitivities of secular society per se, whether the attacks were then or now. He had little urge to bully his way across contested turf in order to claim that the prize invariably went – or should have gone – to the Church. If he personally believed in ultimate or transcendental truths, he never failed to have a keen eye for ecclesiastical fallibility, atop ecclesiastical discord and contradiction. On the other hand, when, in a particular context relating to thirteenth-century English practice, he had to acknowledge that 'the position of the ecclesiastical courts was not accepted,' he was at the same time not reluctant to remind us that the costs were going to be paid, and usually by those of limited resources and power. 'This rejection [of the

Church's position] involved a serious set-back to the property rights of the married women of England.'[3]

Sheehan did not emerge as a major and focused contributor on marriage until he published his 1971 article in *Mediaeval Studies* entitled 'The Formation and Stability of Marriage in Fourteenth-Century England: Evidence of an Ely Register.' In this essay – a classic case study that helped launch a field of inquiry – he presented an elaborate examination of the data he extracted from the Ely Register. By setting the Register's material within the scope of canonical practices, of local custom or lived experience, and of theological disputation, he offered an analysis of hard information regarding the frequency with which some routes – to the creation of the marital bond, to its sanctification, and to its dissolution – were followed, some ignored or abandoned. In this early paper on marriage he set out what would pretty much remain the core of his statement on its historical development. As he reconstructed the tale, the formulation or codification of Christian marriage really matured and moved towards an acceptable synthesis/definition around 1150, and it was largely set in place by 1300.[4]

Sheehan emphasized the complex web of problems – for ecclesiastical as well as for secular authorities – that were compounded, if not actually

3 This comes at the very end of his 1963 'The Influence of Canon Law on the Property Rights of Married Women in England.' Actually, in the corpus there are two papers that are written in defence of the Church's position. One is his 1985 'Christian Marriage: An Historical Perspective,' written as a background piece to explain the Church's decision to withdraw the Catholic Charities from United Community Fund of Toronto. The other is the 1991 'The European Family and Canon Law,' where Sheehan seems to have felt a need to answer Jack Goody's views (in *The Development of the Family and Marriage in Europe*, 1983, and *The Oriental, the Ancient, and the Primitive: Systems of Marriage and the Family in Preindustrial Societies of Eurasia*, 1990) regarding the motivations behind the ecclesiastical interest and involvement in the development of marriage. The review essay on homosexuality, discussed below, n13, also has an eye on refuting some views that seem, to Sheehan, insufficiently nuanced regarding ongoing debate and varieties of interpretation within the historical Church.

4 This paper was singled out by Jocelyn Hillgarth (*Speculum* 68 [1993] 922), referring to Charles Donahue's comment on it as 'the first modern work to use English church court records to try to discover how canon law was *applied* to actual medieval marriages.' The article seems to have been Sheehan's only brush with quantitative analysis, and his efforts to count the population of Ely and the rate of resort to the court for marital cases must have exhausted his interest in such tallies and calculations. He was, however, invariably interested in quantitative approaches as pursued by colleagues and students.

created, by the Church's insistence on choice and personal commitment, forced in good part by the logic of the canonists' emphasis on consent. Clandestine marriage – or the troublesome claim that there had been clandestine marriage or a private agreement to enter into marriage – had to be balanced or compensated for by the growing emphasis on the posting of the marital banns and the concomitant appeal to public and community knowledge regarding prior commitments or impediments.

His subsequent work on English marriage broadened the scope of the treatment. In a series of important papers that followed his 1971 statement, Sheehan extended his research to embrace such issues as the interaction between conciliar legislation and behaviour and the downward social extension of ideas and prescriptions that were, in the first instance, usually formulated with men and women of property in mind.[5] In a model article, adaptable for almost any graduate seminar on historical methodology, he explained how the legal or social historian can reassemble the discordant pieces of a historical jigsaw puzzle to uncover both process and pattern. By the end even the least initiated of readers can understand 'the long effort by canonists to give legal structure to the institution [of marriage] that resulted and to guide society in the secular process of accepting it.'[6] In this essay he matched and compared the unresolved and even contradictory dictates of councils, synods, and canonists on the key elements of marriage. The twin themes that he showed to be woven into a single fabric are the disparate views of the many authorities and the development of coherent doctrine over time (mostly between 1050 and the early thirteenth century). From these, as we have seen, Sheehan explained how synthesis and uniformity emerged and became accepted.

5 Between 1974 and 1978 Sheehan published three major papers on the topic and really established himself as standing at, or even as being, the centre of the question: 'Marriage and Family in English Conciliar and Synodal Legislation' (1974); 'Choice of Marriage Partner in the Middle Ages: Development and Mode of Application of a Theory of Marriage' (1978); 'Marriage Theory and Practice in the Conciliar Legislation and Diocesan Statutes of Medieval England' (1978).
6 'Marriage Theory and Practice' 457 (here p 174). A personal note: this was the Sheehan paper that told me the most about things I should have known but did not. As I have discovered to be the case with many of my friends in the profession, I keep saying to myself that *next* summer will be the one in which I get around to reading more about medieval law. The availability of Michael Sheehan's papers has – for better or for worse – made it possible to postpone 'next summer' into an indefinite future.

Once he had established the English framework for the definition and regulation of marriage – at least to the point of establishing a grid onto which more data and theory could be added – Michael indicated (in his work, as well as in conversation) that it was time to branch out a bit. England was fine, but it was hardly Western Christendom. Furthermore, a definition of marriage and family for/from the high Middle Ages seemed to call for an inquiry into institutional roots and precedents that ran back to the days of the Fathers and the early Church, nor should it rest too heavily on English contributions. Accordingly, the best single compact statement of Michael Sheehan's view of marriage, as a historical phenomenon, is to be found in his article 'Family and Marriage, Western European,' written for the *Dictionary of the Middle Ages*. Here, in a piece drafted in 1984 and designed to be applicable to all of Western Christendom, he offered the essence of the arguments that he had worked to test and to document for many years.[7]

At about the same time, Sheehan produced another synthetic article, 'Christian Marriage: An Historical Perspective,'[8] which extended his survey into modern times and also connected it with contemporary moral and ethical issues. As the single published example of the pastoral dimension of Michael Sheehan's scholarship, we had hoped to include it in this volume. The original publisher's refusal to extend permission, however, has precluded its appearance here.

In the article for the *Dictionary of the Middle Ages*, as in many of the papers of his last decade, Michael ranged far beyond the original insular matrix of his work, as well as away from its high medieval focus. In 1991 he looked at the way in which an unusual opportunity to give advice on a variety of subjects to Boris, khan of the Bulgars, moved Pope Nicholas I in the ninth century to codify the Church's current views on marriage.

---

7 *Dictionary of the Middle Ages*, ed Joseph R. Strayer, 13 vols (New York 1982–9) IV 608–12. Sheehan also contributed the valuable article 'Dispensation' (IV 216–18) for the same *Dictionary*; these short essays are not republished in this collection. Perhaps the best really short summary of his views on Christian marriage is given on p 484 of his 1988 'Theory and Practice: Marriage of the Unfree and the Poor in Medieval Society' (here p 242): 'there is clear evidence in the thinking of the time that, in principle, their exercise of sexual powers should be within the framework of a marriage that, essentially, was common to all Christians. This teaching was developed by the elements in society that were to produce the synthesis on sexuality, marriage, and the celibate life that was one of the principal achievements in the social thinking of the high Middle Ages.'

8 In *Christian Marriage Today: Growth or Breakdown? Interdisciplinary Essays*, ed Joseph A. Buijs (Lewiston, N.Y. 1985) 15–32.

The matter of papal leadership, expressed by way of correspondence to the leaders of the barbarian kingdoms, is a topic with which most of us are familiar from the responses that Pope Gregory I sent to Augustine of Canterbury and from the relations between the kings of the Franks and Rome. Sheehan's command of the sources and his confidence in his expository power allowed him to shed light on this issue while looking towards Eastern Europe. Another paper of 1991 dealt with the transition in the early Christian centuries, in Italy, from an eclectic model of marriage and family, with pagan precedents and a diversity of practices and conventions, towards one in keeping with a new culture that meant new styles of family and private life.[9]

The last paper published here, 'The Bequest of Land in England,' serves as a reinforcement of the idea that Michael Sheehan maintained his interest in all his areas of primary concern, at least at intervals, throughout his career. The last will, read as an instrument of social and individual activity, continued to be a topic that held his attention; he published on it in 1988 ('English Wills and the Records of the Ecclesiastical and Civil Jurisdictions') and again in 1992, as he continued to play with the conflict between freedom to dispose of land and legal restraints upon such freedom. Towards the end of his life he was talking with great pleasure about having time to get back to his early and still unfinished work on this topic. He was excited by the prospect of having a lot more to say and the prospect of saying it with his unflagging combination of conviction and enthusiasm.

This brief appreciation of Michael Sheehan's scholarship cannot end without testifying to his impact as a scholar, a teacher, and an immensely generous and supportive colleague. There is indeed a 'Sheehan School.' Some of it is expressed in and continued by his students, and this voice will be heard for many years to come. Much of it rests on Michael's completed work, and a fair portion of this (excluding *The Will in Medieval England*) is included below. Today our interpretation of marriage in the Middle Ages usually begins with the idea that *consent* was the critical element; Sheehan was an early leader in elevating this specific point to

---

9 There is a 1989 paper, not published here, that gives another view of Sheehan's interest in what we might call the foreign policy of the papacy, in this case Anglo-papal relations: 'Archbishop John Pecham's Perception of the Papacy,' in *The Religious Roles of the Papacy: Ideals and Realities, 1150–1300*, ed Christopher Ryan, Papers in Mediaeval Studies 8 (Toronto 1989) 299–320.

the privileged position it now holds. Furthermore, when he began to ana-lyse case studies and to hold them up to theory, neither historical demography nor the social history of marriage (as revealed by theories about secular activity, like those of Georges Duby, and in the wealth of local and defined case studies we now have) was there to help guide his hand. If calling him a pioneer seems a little dramatic, he certainly was a bold leader who knew how to lead in a way that others would be eager to follow.

This assessment of Michael Sheehan's contributions does no justice to the very considerable body of material he wrote in fields other than medieval history; all his writings are listed in the bibliography, published first in *Mediaeval Studies*[10] and reprinted in an updated version in the present volume.[11] The span of the full bibliography is almost as impressive for its diversity as for its uniform quality. Michael regularly produced a bibliography of Canadian church history for the *Canadian Catholic Historical Association, Study Sessions*. He wrote on ecclesiastical architecture in Europe and on churches in Canada, he wrote tributes to and obituaries for (and about) his colleagues (Bertie Wilkinson in 1979, George Bernard Cardinal Flahiff in 1990, Dom Jean Leclercq in 1991), and he produced working papers on canon law and contemporary Catholic moral issues and debates. An abiding interest in archaeology resulted in a paper on an early Christian site in Turkey which he had helped to excavate and study.

Michael Sheehan had a reputation for being a caring teacher. In addition he was known for his willingness to teach almost any subject to which he thought students at Toronto should be exposed; the high price of having to master new material 'just' to teach it is one not many research scholars are eager to pay as they get older and more focused on their own concerns. As an outgrowth of his identification with teaching and collegial research we have two bibliographies that he launched and helped to compile. In 1976, while a visiting professor at the University of British Columbia, he worked with Kathy D. Scardallato on *Family and Marriage in Medieval Europe: A Working Bibliography*. This was so well received that he then worked with Jacqueline Murray (and Heather Phillips and Constance M. Rousseau) to produce an enlarged version of the booklet in 1990, intended as part of an ongoing series of such contributions: *Domestic Society in Medieval Europe: A Select Bibliography*.[12]

10 Compiled by Mary C. English and James K. Farge, CSB, in *Mediaeval Studies* 55 (1993) xi–xvi (including reviews).
11 See below, pp 324–30.
12 Toronto: Pontifical Institute of Mediaeval Studies, 1990; repr 1995.

These working tools helped focus scholarly attention on emerging fields of social history, as well as offering a precise guide to recent publications. Beyond this, the publication of the bibliographies enabled the students who worked on them to emerge into the world of publishing under the tutelage of a sure-handed and generous mentor.

Like most working scholars, Michael Sheehan reviewed many books. Most of the reviews were brief affairs, and they are listed in the full bibliography at the end of this volume. A few reviews, however, engaged his serious attention; their greater length attests to the freedom he was given to have his say. As well as being interested in what his colleagues said about the history of western marriage, he was very interested in the growing attention being paid to the history of sexuality and homosexuality.[13] He thought that the Church's record regarding tolerance and a willingness to accept diversity was at least respectable and defensible. Simple lines on the graph that seemed to lead, inexorably, towards an inflexible posture of repression or of denial struck him as reductionist and even misleading as these topics become more serious ones in our own

13 The extended review essay – Sheehan's longest such endeavour – written in 1982, 'Christianity and Homosexuality,' is not included in this volume, on the grounds that it mostly looked at the work of other scholars. However, not only did Sheehan consider the books he covered in the review (Michael Goodich, *The Unmentionable Vice: Homosexuality in the Later Medieval Period*; Peter Coleman, *Christian Attitudes to Homosexuality*; John Boswell, *Christianity, Social Tolerance, and Homosexuality: Gay People in Western Europe from the Beginning of the Christian Era to the Fourteenth Century*) to be of singular importance, but he also clearly wanted to get on record his own say about the Church's historical position on homosexuality and to insist that, like any subject, it be approached with meticulous scholarship and cautious interpretation. In addition to this important review essay, there are five longish reviews, relevant to Sheehan's main themes, that seem of some enduring value and that are closely related to the areas of Sheehan's own writing: Richard H. Helmholz, *Marriage Litigation in Medieval England*, reviewed in *Speculum* 52 (1977) 983–7; Henry Ansgar Kelly, *The Matrimonial Trials of Henry VIII*, reviewed in *Renaissance and Reformation / Renaissance et Réforme* o s 16 (1980) 105–7; Georges Duby, *Medieval Marriage: Two Models from Twelfth-Century France*, reviewed in *Catholic Historical Review* 66 (1980) 647–9; Norma Adams and Charles Donahue, Jr, eds, *Select Cases from the Ecclesiastical Courts of the Province of Canterbury, c. 1200–1301*, reviewed in *Speculum* 59 (1984) 106–9; and James A. Brundage, *Law, Sex, and Christian Society in Medieval Europe*, reviewed in *Catholic Historical Review* 76 (1990) 334–6. As well as expressing his opinion of each book under review, Sheehan was concerned to establish whether the book's argument was so difficult that students would have trouble reading it or, conversely, whether the topic was made to seem simpler than it really was. Though both books were praised, the Kelly book worried him on the former score, the Brundage on the latter.

dialogue about how to construct a functioning civil society. The complexities of western history were too vast and too important to be presented merely in terms of positions that were locked into place.

An appreciation of a single scholar tends to isolate him, to make him stand out as a lonely and solitary traveller. In some ways there is always an element of truth to such a view; to a considerable degree we all work on our own. On the other hand, we simultaneously are partners in many dialogues, and it is important to call attention to the way in which Michael Sheehan's work can be set in different contexts, all of them vital and ongoing. In so far as Michael was a leader in the effort to combine legal and social history, he constantly talked to, with, and about the work of such colleagues as James Brundage, Richard Helmholz, Charles Donahue, Jr, and Sue Sheridan Walker. He borrowed and glossed and relied upon a huge network of men and women in North America and in Europe, as they did upon him; the intellectual circle has neither beginning nor end. I do not know what his relations with David Herlihy were, but to many of us the two men were the North American bookends within which (or between whom) so much of the medieval social history of the last twenty years is held in place. Work that neither man lived to complete includes, for Michael, the second volume on the will, intended to carry his detailed analysis through the later Middle Ages. This work was well under way before his death. In addition a computerized project, designed to put all the extant English medieval wills on a database, was projected and partially carried out.

We have tried to identify some of the themes that gave Michael Sheehan's productive scholarly work coherence and consistency by setting forth three main categories: the last will, Christian marriage, and the family. But his singular interest in and contributions to women's history must also be given the full or explicit credit due to them. Perhaps we would do better to think of women's history as a subtext or sub-field running through much of the body of Sheehan scholarship, sometimes surfacing and sometimes staying just out of sight but never drifting very far away and always remaining among his major interests. Again like David Herlihy, Michael Sheehan was both an active scholar, a teacher, and a friend and an evangelist of the new field. His delightful B.K. Smith Lecture at the University of St Thomas in Houston[14] (published as 'The

---

14 Michael Sheehan and David Herlihy spoke there on the same evening under the joint title 'Did Women Have a Renaissance?'

Wife of Bath and Her Four Sisters: Reflections on a Woman's Life in the Age of Chaucer') is a simple-seeming paper from an old master. With obvious debts to Eileen Power's *Medieval People* and with his prosy references to such prototypical constructs as 'Poor Widow' and 'Rose Foreign,' he introduces the complexities of a woman's life cycle, of her social class, and of some of the permissible individual variations within the other categories. Nor do his published papers tell anything approaching the whole story of Sheehan's contributions to women's history as an emerging field that still is not always given equal status and equal time. There is the long saga of students' seminar papers and dissertations, of years of deep sympathy with and support for women graduate students and young colleagues, and of a steady insistence that women's history be made an integral part of the mainstream in both our research and our classroom agendas.

Persistence, I have asserted, was not only a salient characteristic of Sheehan as a scholar and colleague but also a trait that emerged early and that never wavered. Another characteristic was generosity. It shows in the printed work, and it lives in the memories and the tales of his colleagues and students. Michael was eager to share the excitement of his work with others, and he was equally enthusiastic about the joy and excitement that their work brought him. From almost the beginning of his writing he was unusually sensitive to the realization that there would be historical problems, bodies of sources, and variations of interpretation that called out for further work. In his writings, as in his teaching, he regularly paused, stepped back, and invited any and all who so chose to join in. Unfinished tasks were most profitable and most pleasurable when they could be made into collective tasks. The team could be in his own seminar, or it could be spread out across two or three continents and over two or three decades. Only dedication, a serious interest in the problems of historical research and exposition, and a not so serious interest in talking them over were needed to qualify for citizenship in the world of scholarship as it was defined and practised by Michael Sheehan.

I wish to acknowledge the generosity and support of others in the composition of this introduction. James K. Farge of the Pontifical Institute of Mediaeval Studies honoured me by asking me to try my hand at such an enterprise. Constance M. Rousseau has done much to see that Michael Sheehan's work and spirit remain with us. Sue Sheridan Walker has shared her thoughts and has helped to refine some of mine. Frank Walker made some valuable points about my prose and the clarity of this text. Richard Helmholz was extremely generous in his comments about an earlier version of this introduction, and I hope I have caught the essence of his suggestions. And to the many others with whom I have discussed Michael over the years – both in the context of friendship and in that of his scholarly work – my thanks and my hope that they find this short essay worthy of its subject.

JOEL T. ROSENTHAL
State University of New York at Stony Brook

Acknowledgments

'Report of a Thesis on the Will in Medieval England,' originally entitled 'Report of a Thesis Defended at the Pontifical Institute of Mediaeval Studies,' is reprinted by permission of the publisher, *Mediaeval Studies* 23 (1961) 368–71. © 1961 by the Pontifical Institute of Mediaeval Studies, Toronto.

'A List of Thirteenth-Century English Wills' is reprinted from *Genealogists' Magazine* 13:9 (March 1961) 259–65, with the permission of the Society of Genealogists.

'The Influence of Canon Law on the Property Rights of Married Women in England' is reprinted from *Mediaeval Studies* 25 (1963) 109–24, by permission of the publisher. © 1963 by the Pontifical Institute of Mediaeval Studies, Toronto.

'Canon Law and English Institutions: Some Notes on Current Research' is reprinted from *Proceedings of the Second International Congress of Medieval Canon Law*, Monumenta iuris canonici, Series C: Subsidia 1, ed Stephan Kuttner and J. Joseph Ryan (Vatican City 1965) 391–7, with permission of the Congregation for Catholic Education.

'The Formation and Stability of Marriage in Fourteenth-Century England: Evidence of an Ely Register' is reprinted from *Mediaeval Studies* 33 (1971) 228–63 by permission of the publisher. © 1971 by the Pontifical Institute of Mediaeval Studies, Toronto.

'Marriage and Family in English Conciliar and Synodal Legislation' is reprinted from *Essays in Honour of Anton Charles Pegis*, ed J. Reginald O'Donnell, 205–14, by permission of the publisher. © 1974 by the Pontifical Institute of Mediaeval Studies, Toronto.

'Choice of Marriage Partner in the Middle Ages: Development and Mode of Application of a Theory of Marriage' is reprinted from *Studies in*

Medieval and Renaissance History n s 1 (1978) 1–33. © 1978 by AMS Press, Inc. Reprinted with permission.

'Marriage Theory and Practice in the Conciliar Legislation and Diocesan Statutes of Medieval England' is reprinted from *Mediaeval Studies* 40 (1978) 408–60, by permission of the publisher. © 1978 by the Pontifical Institute of Mediaeval Studies, Toronto.

'The Wife of Bath and Her Four Sisters: Reflections on a Woman's Life in the Age of Chaucer' is reprinted with permission from *Medievalia et Humanistica*, ed Paul Maurice Clogan, n s 13 (Totowa, N.J. 1985) 23–42.

'English Wills and the Records of the Ecclesiastical and Civil Jurisdictions' is reprinted with permission from *Journal of Medieval History* 14 (1988) 3–12. © 1988 Elsevier Science Publishers B.V., Amsterdam Publishing Division.

'Theory and Practice: Marriage of the Unfree and the Poor in Medieval Society' is reprinted from *Mediaeval Studies* 50 [1988] 457–87, by permission of the publisher. © 1988 by the Pontifical Institute of Mediaeval Studies, Toronto.

'The European Family and Canon Law' is reprinted from *Continuity and Change* 6 (1991) 347–60, by permission of the publisher. © 1991 by Cambridge University Press.

'*Maritalis affectio* Revisited' is reprinted from *The Olde Daunce*, ed Robert R. Edwards and Stephen Spector. © 1991 State University of New York Press. Reprinted with permission.

'The Bishop of Rome to a Barbarian King on the Rituals of Marriage' is reprinted from *In iure veritas: Studies in Canon Law in Memory of Schafer Williams*, ed Steven B. Bowman and Blanche E. Cody (Cincinnati: University of Cincinnati College of Law 1991) 187–99. © 1991 by Steven B. Bowman and Blanche E. Cody. Reprinted with permission.

'Sexuality, Marriage, Celibacy, and the Family in Central and Northern Italy: Christian Legal and Moral Guides in the Early Middle Ages' is reprinted from *The Family in Italy from Antiquity to the Present*, ed David I. Kertzer and Richard P. Saller (New Haven and London 1991) 168–83, with the permission of the publisher. © 1991 Yale University Press.

'The Bequest of Land in England in the High Middle Ages: Testaments and the Law' is reprinted from *Marriage, Property, and Succession*, ed Lloyd Bonfield, Comparative Studies in Continental and Anglo-American Legal History 10 (Berlin 1992) 326–38, with permission of the publisher. © 1992 Duncker & Humblot GmbH, Berlin.

Abbreviations

BL	British Library, London
BN	Bibliothèque nationale, Paris
C	Causa [in Gratian, *Decretum*, pars II]
c, cc	canon, canons
ca	circa
D	Distinctio [in Gratian, *Decretum*, pars I]
DDC	*Dictionnaire de droit canonique*, ed A. Villein, E. Gagnin, and R. Naz, 7 vols (Paris 1935–65)
DTC	*Dictionnaire de théologie catholique*, ed. A. Vacant, E. Mangenot, and E. Amman, 15 vols (Paris 1899–1950)
ed	edition or edited by
Ep, Epp	Epistola, Epistolae
MGH	*Monumenta Germaniae Historica*
PG	*Patrologiae cursus completus*, series graeca
PL	*Patrologiae cursus completus*, series latina
PRO	Public Record Office, London
q	quaestio
repr	reprint
RS	Rerum Britannicarum medii aevi scriptores (Rolls Series)
X	*Extravagantes*

The siglum × between two dates denotes the plausible chronological limits of an event of uncertain date.

MARRIAGE, FAMILY, AND LAW IN MEDIEVAL EUROPE:
COLLECTED STUDIES

1

Report of a Thesis on the Will in Medieval England

*The Last Will in England from the Conversion to
the End of the Thirteenth Century*

The last will or testament in English common law provides an interesting example of the meeting of the three great cultural streams of medieval Europe. The Christian desire to give alms at death and legal notions derived from Roman law gradually modified the Germanic customs of succession in use among the Anglo-Saxons and their Norman conquerors; but certain Germanic qualities survived to produce the unique legal institution that still plays an important role in contemporary society.

The present thesis undertakes to study the rather long historical evolution that produced the last will of English law. It follows the development of this institution from the time when the Anglo-Saxons first came under the influence of Christian missionaries until the last years of the thirteenth century, and considers the legal nature of the will, its enforcement, the persons who were allowed to use it, and the property of which it disposed.

As the distribution of wealth at death developed among the Anglo-Saxons, it followed a pattern common to the invading peoples in northern Europe. The Germans were already accustomed, in some areas at least, to provide for the future needs of the deceased by burying or destroying part of his property with his body. When a family was threatened by extinction, the estate of the owner could be bequeathed by a legal process

This brief report was originally entitled 'Report of a Thesis Defended at the Pontifical Institute of Mediaeval Studies.' As an abstract of Michael Sheehan's thesis presented for the degree of Doctor of Mediaeval Studies, it is not representative of his later work. However, because it provides a synopsis of his important monograph *The Will in Medieval England: From the Conversion of the Anglo-Saxons to the End of the Thirteenth Century*, Studies and Texts 6 (Toronto 1963), which led him to further investigations into the law, marriage, and the family, we have thought it appropriate to include it here. – Editor

similar to adoption. With the coming of Christianity another and more general motive for asserting a right of bequest appeared. It was already an established Christian practice that a dying man should give part of his property in alms for the good of his soul. This practice came to England with the Christian missionaries and remained the chief motive for exercising a power of bequest throughout the period treated in this dissertation. There were other motives as well: for example, the expression of affection, the reward of service, the rectification of past injustice.

Bequests were made by three different legal acts, namely, the *post obit* gift, the deathbed gift, and the *cwide*. In the completion of these gifts a third party was sometimes used to deliver the testator's property to the legatee. The first two forms of the will were contractual, irrevocable donations; but the *cwide*, though most of its elements were possessed of these qualities, included some legacies that were not contractual and could be revoked. The *cwide* was a special form of will, limited to members of the upper class, and usually dependent on the support of a protector for its completion. In external appearance, though not in effect, it was similar to the canonical will that developed late in the twelfth century.

These acts were performed in accord with the demands of Germanic law. They were formal, oral transactions, and often included the delivery of a token or a *wedd*. Though a written witness of wills was often made, the preparation and signing of the document were not part of the formalities of the donation. The written wills of Anglo-Saxon England are unique in Western Europe at that time. Most are in the vernacular, and when they relate to *cwides* they sometimes provide a remarkably detailed account of the possessions of the deceased.

By Cnut's day, the notion was already current that it was a crime to die intestate. Male freemen were expected to make a will; bishops, priests, widows, and unmarried women were also free to bequeath their property. Of other members of society there is less information: married women could own property and they made wills, but in all surviving examples their husbands were associated with them in the act; religious were not normally allowed to bequeath property, though superiors sometimes did so as a means of protecting the endowment of the house of which they were head.

Of the types of property bequeathed, chattels, including slaves, farmstock, and rights of every description, were the most common legacies. There were also many donations of land by will, but these bequests were privileged; they were either donations of bookland, or land whose bequest was permitted by the lord or by the heir. The bequest of land was probably introduced as a means of protecting the endowment of churches and monasteries from the families of deceased bishops and abbots.

The Norman Conquest produced many changes in English political and social institutions but did not cause a profound modification in the theory and practice of the will. The most important change was the disappearance of the *cwide* and of the vernacular English will. But the persons who exercised a power of bequest remained much as before, and the *post obit* gift and the deathbed gift continued in use until late in the second half of the twelfth century. Then a new theory of the will came to the fore.

This important change is related to the renaissance of Roman law that occurred during the twelfth century. Included within the Roman legal system were a theory and jurisprudence of the testament, an act disposing of property at death that possessed several advantages over the different forms of will that were in use throughout northern Europe. This Roman testament influenced the English will; the special quality of that influence was determined by the fact that it came to England by way of canon law.

The essential purpose of the Roman testament was the appointment of an heir, although it could include the donation of legacies and usually did so. The canonists, on the other hand, were interested in the testament as an instrument whereby donations were made in alms; the legacy was their chief concern. The testament found a place in the developing call on law of the twelfth century, but it was a testament seen from a special point of view, one that ignored the appointment of an heir and concentrated on the legacies it included. This was called *ultima voluntas* and was similar to the codicil of Roman law. It was revocable, unilateral, and ambulatory, as was the Roman testament. It could be made either orally or in writing, and required the presence of only two or three witnesses. Late in the twelfth century this simplified testament began to be used in England. In the following years it almost completely replaced the older forms of donation at the time of death. The executor, named by the testator in his will and empowered to act in his place, grew in importance until, by 1285, he was considered to be the ordinary representative of the deceased.

The most important stages in this development occurred during the years when the supervision of the will in England passed to the courts of the Church. Glanvill (ca 1187) tells us that where there was question of the validity of a will or of its contents, decisions were to be obtained in the courts Christian. Thus these courts were able to fix the rules for the validity of the will and establish its revocability. In addition to this internal

jurisdiction over the will, the church courts acquired an external jurisdiction as well. This power to enforce bequests was obtained during the
last years of the reign of King John. By the middle of the thirteenth
century, probate, the taking of inventory and the rendering of an account
by the executor, had become regular procedure. In the boroughs, probate
of wills bequeathing land developed at about the same time. The courts
Christian enforced the delivery of legacies and began to assist in collecting
the debts owed the deceased and in the acquittal of claims against his
estate. Early in the reign of Edward I the executor was recognized as the
representative of the deceased by the courts of common law, so that all
cases rising from the collection or payment of debts passed to this jurisdiction.

The religious motive for the making of wills continued to be a powerful force after the Conquest and was one of the causes of an effort to
extend the right of bequest to a larger portion of the population. According to the theory of common law, the married woman and the villein
owned no chattels and therefore could not dispose of them by will without
the consent of the husband or the lord. But both groups were accustomed
to use possessions as though they were their own, and both were as
anxious to provide for their souls as were other members of society. Many
forces in thirteenth-century England sought to extend a testamentary right
to the wife and the villein. These pressures were successfully resisted by
the common lawyers, but it is evident that, in practice, many members of
both groups made wills which were successfully executed.

The distinction between movable and immovable property, already evident in Anglo-Saxon wills, became even more clear in the period after the
Conquest. The bequest of land did not become a general practice. In spite
of a tendency to remove obstacles to the alienation of land during the
lifetime of the owner, the development of a similar freedom of alienation
by will was prevented. There were many motives for this decision, but it
seems best to conclude that the most enduring cause of the restriction
was a procedural one: the requirements for livery of seisin, as developed
by common law, made the transfer of land by will technically impossible.
In the boroughs and other areas not subject to common law, a right of
devise of land slowly developed, so that by the second half of the thirteenth century the bequest of land was of common occurrence.

Wills were especially concerned with legacies of movable property.
Chattels of every sort were included. By the early years of the reign of
Henry III, grain growing in the field, the right to marriages and ward-
ships, and even leased land were freely distributed by will. Except in a few

cases, the villein did not appear in post-Conquest wills either as a bequest or as a legatee to whom freedom was given.

The Anglo-Saxon testator seems to have made reasonable provision for the future needs of his wife and children, but, so far as can be seen, the part of his property over which he had full right of alienation was not limited to a precise portion. After the Conquest it became a general, though not universal, custom that the testator with dependents could dispose of one-third of his chattels. The remaining two-thirds were reserved to his wife and children. Those who died without dependents were free to dispose of all their chattels except those claimed as a mortuary or as a heriot.

As was remarked at the beginning of this report, all the wills of the period under consideration were characterized by a profound concern for the good of the testator's soul. Thus the donation in alms was of prime importance. However, in this medieval context, 'alms' must be understood in a very wide sense. It included offerings for liturgical services, gifts to churches, hospitals, and the poor, as would be expected. But education, the building of roads and bridges, and equipment for the defence of a country or of Christendom found a place there as well. The will thus provided a voluntary source of income for the well-developed social services of medieval England.

2

A List of Thirteenth-Century
English Wills

For several years I have been collecting wills made in England or by Englishmen during the period from the death of Henry II to 1300. Most of these documents will be published in the near future.[1] But it will be worthwhile in the mean time to publish a list of the testators who made these wills, with the hope that students of history will find it of use and that they will inform me of other wills or additional copies of wills with which they are acquainted.

The majority of the documents described below are complete wills, but there are many fragments from cartularies and court rolls. The most important collection of enrolments of selected bequests is that which was made on the husting roll in London beginning in 1258. These documents have been calendared,[2] and no mention of them is made here except in a few cases where the enrolment has been published *in extenso* or exists in a second copy. Wills were proved and enrolled in the mayor's court at Exeter. Since a description of these documents is not readily available, they are included here.

In the following list, no attempt has been made to modernize the forms of names. They are printed as they appear in the wills. Most dates are certain, although in some cases it has been necessary to give rather wide limits. A few dates are still open to question and are indicated as

---

1 Michael Sheehan never fulfilled this resolve. His monograph, *The Will in Medieval England: From the Conversion of the Anglo-Saxons to the End of the Thirteenth Century*, Studies and Texts 6 (Toronto 1963), constituted a careful analysis of their contents and meaning. In his last years, he was working on the analysis of late medieval English wills. – Editor

2 By Reginald R. Sharpe in *A Calendar of Wills Proved and Enrolled in the Court of Husting, London, A.D. 1258 – A.D. 1688*, 2 vols (London 1889–90).

such. Where a will has already been published with adequate information as to its manuscript source, I have been content to indicate where the printed text is available. But where the document has changed hands or, for some other reason, the information supplied in the earlier edition is misleading, the manuscript source is indicated. Wills which have already been published and of which the manuscript source is now lost are designated by an asterisk.

The gathering of these texts has been facilitated by the collections made by historians in the past and by the generous assistance of those archivists and librarians who are now in charge of the various muniments which have been used. No attempt will be made to acknowledge my obligation to them beyond this general mention of their help. Later, and in another place, it will be possible to thank them more adequately.

Abbreviations:

BL	British Library [formerly BM British Museum – Editor]
D & C	Dean and Chapter
f	folio
Formulare	*Formulare Anglicanum*, ed T. Madox (London 1702)
fr	fragment
Giffard	The Register of Bishop Godfrey Giffard of Worcester, calendared and published in part by J.W. Willis Bund, 2 vols (Worcestershire Historical Society 1900–2)
Liber Y	*The Chartulary of the High Church of Chichester*, ed W.D. Peckham (Sussex Record Society 46, 1942–3)
MCR	Exeter, Mayor's Court Roll
PRO	Public Record Office, London
Sharpe	R.R. Sharpe, *A Calendar of Wills* etc

Abingdon, Robert de, 1266; Salisbury, D & C muniments, Press IV Box W

Annian II, bishop of St Asaph, 1288; Canterbury, D & C Library, *Sede Vacante* Scrap Book II 187

Aquablanca, Peter de, bishop of Hereford, 1269; *Camden Miscellany* 14 (Camden Society, 3rd ser 37, 1926)

Arundel, William de, shortly before 1256; *Liber Y* f 184v

Arundel, William de, 1295; *Formulare* 425 no DCCLXXI; PRO E 327/771

Aumbrisbury, Geoffrey de, 1273; *Cartulary of St Mary Clerkenwell*, ed W.O. Hassal (Camden Society, 3rd ser 71, 1949) 273–4; cf Sharpe I 14

Austin, Walter, 1289/90; fr, MCR 17–18 Edward I, m 51d

Awberland, vicar of the church of, 1296; fr, MCR 24–5 Edward I, m 5d

Barentone, Nicolas de, 1262/3; London, BL Add Ch 28493

Baudeney, Henry, 1296; *Lincoln Wills* I 4–5 (Lincoln Record Society 5, 1914)

Beauveir, Robert de, canon of Salisbury, 1261; Salisbury, D & C muniments, Press IV Box W

Beche, Avelina ate, 1293; London, BL Harl Ch 45 H 21

Beggeberi, Geoffrey de, 1293; London, BL Harl Ch 76 B 22

Bellocampo, William de, 1268; *Giffard* f IIv

Bellocampo, William de, earl of Warwick, 1297; *Giffard* f 428r

Bellomonte, Ricard de, 1291; Durham, D & C muniments, I 5, Ebor 30

Bennington, Christiana, relict of John, 1283; *Lincoln Wills* I 2–4

Berkeleye, Giles de, ca 1294; *Giffard* f 384v

Bigot, Roger, earl of Norfolk, 1258; fr, London, BL Harl MS 5019 f 7

Bologna, Johanna de, 1260/70; *St Frideswide's Cartulary* I 334 (Oxford Historical Society 28, 1894)

Brommere, John, 1299; London, BL Cott Ch VIII/23

*Budlecs, Hengerom de, ca 1235 (?); *Formulare* 424 no DCCLXIX

Carville, Robert de, treasurer of Salisbury, 1264; Salisbury, D & C muniments, Press IV Box W

Chamberleyn, John, 1291; fr, MCR 19–20 Edward I, m 7d

Chamberleyn, Nicholas le, 1296; *Giffard* f 407v

Chelesham, William de, 1300; Oxford, Merton College Ch 266

Clifford, Roger de, 1285; *Giffard* f 250r

Coccyng, William, 1297; fr, MCR 24–5 Edward I, m 28d

Cocus, John, *ante* 1241; fr, *Liber Y* f 182v

Cokeseye, Walter de, 1294; *Giffard* f 410r

Colebi, Henry de, of Lincoln, 1271; *Lincoln Wills* II 215–17 (Lincoln Record Society 10, 1918)

Collecote, Adam de, 1269; Exeter, Cathedral Library, VC 3053

Collecote, Henry de, son of the preceding, 1295; *The Episcopal Registers of the Diocese of Exeter (1257–1307)*, ed F.C. Hingeston-Randolph (London 1889) I 435–6

Condet, Agnes de, wife of Walter Clifford, ca 1222/3; *Registrum antiquissimum* of Lincoln I 293–5 (Lincoln Record Society 27, 1931); London, BL Harl Ch 48 C 25

Cornwaleys, Adam, 1271; London, St Paul's, D & C, Box A 66 no 2

Cosin, Peter, citizen of London, 1290; London, BL Harl Ch 48 H 17

Crandon, Thomas de, 1290; fr, MCR 17–18 Edward I, m 31d

Creke, Margery de, 1282; London, BL Camp Ch III/1
Croom, Geoffrey de, ca 1250; fr, Malton Cartulary f 145r, London,
    BL MS Cott Claud D XI
Donion, Ralph, canon of St Paul's, 1282; London, St Paul's, D & C,
    Box A 66 no 7
Doulys, John de, 1267; London, BL Add Ch 27523
Dumbelton, Nicholas de, 1295; *Giffard* f 396r
Eastry, Agnes de, 1277; Canterbury, D & C Library, *Sede Vacante* Scrap
    Book II 184
Edelmeton, Henry de, 1276; London, St Paul's, D & C, Box A 68 no 79
Edward I, king of England, 1272; *Foedera*, ed Rymer (London 1816–69)
    I 495
Elmham, Richard, 1228; *Archaeological Journal* 24 (1867) 343–4
Enfield, Henry de, 1290; *Cartulary of St Mary Clerkenwell* 256–7
Espic, Richard le, 1290; fr, MCR 17–18 Edward I, m 27d
Evesham, Cardinal Hugh of, 1286; *Giffard* f 345v
*Exeter, William de, 1291; fr, MCR 19–20 Edward I, m 12d
Fabro, Clarice, wife of Aregon, 1288; fr, MCR 15–16 Edward I, m 29d
Flameng, Walter de, 1258; Oxford, Bodleian, Queen's College Ch 1071
Fordham, Robert, son of Alan de, 1190–1200 (?); Oxford, Bodleian,
    MS Charters, Norfolk a 6 (614)
Foresthulle, Richard de, 1287; *Giffard* f 273r
Fosse, Matilda de la, 1290; fr, MCR 18–19 Edward I, m 5d
Fot, Matilda, 1296; fr, MCR 23–4 Edward I, m 24d
Freville, James de, 1286; Cambridge, Fitzwilliam Museum, MS 329,
    f 109r
Frowik, Henry de, citizen of London, 1284; London, St Paul's, D & C,
    Box A 66 no 8
Gaschoyng, Peter, 1291; fr, MCR 18–19 Edward I, m 15d
Germeyn, Adam, 1296; fr, MCR 23–4 Edward I, m 28d
Gernun, Thomas, 1248; Durham, D & C muniments, 3, 5, Spec 6
Gervas, Walter, son of Nicholas, 1257; Exeter, Cathedral Library,
    VC 3345
Geyton, Richard de, 1276; Kings Lynn, Town Hall, Charter Ae 34
Giffard, Bertha, wife of Ely, ca 1179; fr, *Historia et cartularium
    monasterii Gloucestriae* I 188 (RS 33, 1863–7)
Gilbert, son of Fulk, ca 1215; PRO E 40/11559
Godard, Geoffrey, proved 1273; fr, London, St Paul's, D & C, Box A 66
    no 3; cf Sharpe I 17
Gordet, Walter, 1290; fr, MCR 17–18 Edward I, m 15d

Gravesend, Richard de, bishop of London, 1289; London, St Paul's,
D & C, Box A 66 no 14

Gurney, Sir Anselm, 1286; *Giffard* f 259r

Hamond, John, 1265; *St Frideswide's Cartulary* I 233–4

Heleweton, Henry de, 1274; Oxford, Bodleian, MS Charters, Suffolk
a 1 (75)

Henry II, king of England, 1182; *Recueil des actes de Henri II*, ed L.
Delisle and E. Berger (Paris 1909) no DCXII, II 219–21

Henry III, king of England, 1253; *Foedera*, ed Rymer I 496

Herbert, son of Peter, ca 1248; fr, Reading Cartulary f 114v, London,
BL Harl MS 1708

Hog, William, 1288; fr, MCR 15–16 Edward I, m 36d

Hole, William de la, vicar of Exeter, ca 1282; fr, Peckham's Register
f 183r, London, Lambeth Palace Library

*Holy Cross, Martin, master of, 1259; Surtees Society 2 (1835) 6–11

Huse, Cecily, wife of Geoffrey, 1269; PRO E 210/291

John, king of England, 1216; *Foedera*, ed Rymer I 144

Juvene, Isabel la, 1272; London, Corporation Records, Bridge House
Deeds, F 16

Juvenis, Thomas, husband of the preceding, *ante* 1272; London,
Corporation Records, Bridge House Deeds, A 9

Kilrington, John de, 1291; fr, MCR 18–19 Edward I, m 43d

Kunelond, Emma de, 1290; fr, MCR 18–19 Edward I, m 2d

Kymmyng, Rosemunda wife of John Smurch, 1295; *The Episcopal Registers of the Diocese of Exeter (1257–1307)*, ed F.C. Hingeston-Randolph
(cf the reference to the will of Henry de Collecote, above) I 433–4

Legh, Bartholomew de, ca 1230; *Formulare* 432–4 no DCCLXVIII; PRO E
315/42 (246)

Lincoln, Agnes de, wife of Reginald ad Fontem, ca 1297; Lincoln,
D & C muniments, D ij 77 3 69

Lincolnia, Henry de, 1275; fr, *Cartulary of the Hospital of St John the
Baptist* I 270–1 (Oxford Historical Society 66, 68, 69, 1914–16)

Longespee, Nicholas, bishop of Salisbury, 1297; *English Historical
Review* 15 (1900) 523–8

Longespee, William de, earl of Salisbury, 1225; *Rotuli litterarum clau-
sarum* II 71 (Record Comm, London 1833–44)

Lorimer, Philip le, 1271; fr, MCR 48 Henry III–2 Edward I, m 19

Loudelowe, William de, 1298 or shortly before; London, St Paul's,
D & C, Box A 66 no 42

Lovecok, Roger, 1295; fr, MCR 23–4 Edward I, m 3d

Lundreys, Lucy, 1296; Wells, D & C Library, *Liber Albus* I 128

Lyden, Adam de, 1278; Canterbury, D & C Library, *Sede Vacante* Scrap Book II 185

Marg, Henry le, 1291; fr, MCR 18–19 Edward I, m 15d

Mason, Reginald le, 1270–5; *St Frideswide's Cartulary* I 375–6

Melkere, William le, proved 1273; London, St Paul's, D & C, Box A 66 no 4

Merton, Walter de, bishop of Rochester, 1277; Oxford, Merton College Ch 4234a

Mitton, Nicholas de, 1290; *Giffard* f 334v

Molendinis, William de, 1296; *Giffard* f 406v

Montfort, Simon de, 1259; *Simon de Montfort*, ed C. Belmont, English trans (Oxford 1930) 276–8

Mundeville, Richard de, 1298; *Giffard* f 439v

Neville, Sir Hugh de, 1267; *Archaeologia* 56 (1899) 357–70

Page, William, 1286; fr, MCR 14 Edward I, m 4d

Panebrok, Hugh de, 1293; Canterbury, D & C Library, *Sede Vacante* Scrap Book II 189

Paris, William, 1272; PRO E 40/2296

Pavelli, William de, 1241; *Formulare* 424 no DCCLXX; PRO E 327/770

Peliparii, Richard, 1273; fr, MCR 48 Henry III–2 Edward I, m 28

Pere, Robert le, of Rommey, 1278; Canterbury, D & C Library, Ch Ant W 237a

Perle, Henry, 1260; *Cartulary of the Hospital of St John the Baptist* I 466–7

Peverel, Sir Hugh, 1296; fr, MCR 23–4 Edward I, m 41d

Peverel, Sir Thomas, 1300; fr, MCR 27–8 Edward I, m 28d

Plesset, Sir Hugh de, 1292; *Giffard* f 364v

Poer, Eva, of Tylne, 1276; London, BL Harl Ch 112 C 17

Ponte, Amery de, 1291; fr, MCR 18–19 Edward I, m 14d

Ponte, Gilbert de, 1220 (?); Durham, D & C muniments, Ch Misc 2305

Punchard, Agnes, 1281; *Cartulary of the Hospital of St John the Baptist* I 320–1

Pynghe, Robert, 1296; fr, MCR 23–4 Edward I, m 27d

Ralph II, bishop of Chichester, 1244; fr, *Liber Y* f 162r

Richard, son of Robert, rector of Insnac, Kilkenny, 1267; London, BL Eger Ch 528

Rupibus, Luke de, 1230–9; PRO E 210/11304

Rus, Richard le, 1279; Cambridge, Fitzwilliam Museum, MS 329 f 94v

St David, Bartholomew de, 1221–5; London, BL Cott Ch II 11 (21)

St John, John de, 1231; *Oseney Cartulary* I 135–6 (Oxford Historical
  Society 89, 1929)
St Marie Ecclesia, Philip de, 1226; London, St Paul's, D & C,
  Box A 66 no 1
St Martin, Abel de, proved 1276; London, St Paul's, D & C,
  Box A 66 no 5
St Michael, Laurence, 1282; PRO E 315/46
Sandwich, John de, 1293; Canterbury, D & C Library, *Sede Vacante*
  Scrap Book II 190
Scarborough, Roger, son of Haldan of, 1202–29; *Early Yorkshire Chart-
  ers*, ed W. Farrer (Edinburgh 1914) I 288
Seneschal, Robert le, canon of St Paul's, 1298; London, St Paul's,
  D & C, Box A 66 no 10
Skelmerskerth, William de, 1247; *Furness Cartulary* I 411 (Chetham
  Society n s 2, 1887)
Southover, Richard, 1300; Wells Museum, Ch 7
Spagard, Stephen, 1300 (?); PRO C 146/9493
Stappe, Ralph de la, 1292; fr, MCR 19–20 Edward I, m 34d
Sude, Benedict, 1298; fr, MCR 25–6 Edward I, m 26d
Suffield, Walter, bishop of Norwich, 1256; *Topographical History of the
  County of Norfolk*, ed F. Blomefield (1739–75) II 345–6
Suthcherch, John de, 1293; Canterbury, D & C Library, Ch Ant W 209
Swaby, John de, 1279; Oxford, Magdalen College Ch Swaby 150a
Swapham, Henry de; *see* Lincolnia, Henry de, above
Swyn, Simon, 1274; Oxford, Bodleian, MS Rolls, Norfolk 13 (b)
Tailor, John le, ca 1295; *St Frideswide's Cartulary* I 126–8
Tailor, Philip le, 1293; fr, *Cartulary of St Mary Clerkenwell* 259–60;
  cf Sharpe I 107
Thomas, son of Peter, 1272; PRO E 40/11569
Thorkil, Gilbert dictus, 1215–50; *Historia et cartularium monasterii Glou-
  cestriae* III cxii, from volume B f 270r, Gloucester, D & C Library
Totintone, John de, 1278; Canterbury, D & C Library, *Sede Vacante*
  Scrap Book II 186
Vaus, Walter de, 1277; London, St Paul's, D & C, Box A 66 no 6
Watford, Edmund de, of Northampton, 1291; PRO E 40/11568
Wele, Matilda, 1295; fr, MCR 23–4 Edward I, m 1d
Wells, Hugh of, bishop of Lincoln: 1st will, 1212, Wells, D & C Library,
  Liber Albus R III f 248v; 2nd will, *Registrum antiquissimum* of Lincoln
  II 70–5 (Lincoln Record Society 28, 1933)
Weston, Alice de, 1294; Oxford, Bodleian, MS Charters, Oxon a 7 (14b)

Weston, Nicholas de, 1271; *Oseney Cartulary* II 562–5 (Oxford Historical Society 90, 1930)

William, constable of Wirneris, ca 1220; Oxford, Bodleian, MS Charters, Essex a 2 (37)

William, rector of West Tilbury, proved 1298; fr, London, St Paul's, D & C, Box A 66 no 9

William, son of Richard, 1269; PRO LR 14/16

Wobourn, William de, 1299; London, St Paul's, D & C, Box A 66 no 12

Wockesweye, Stephen de, 1290; fr, MCR 18–19 Edward I, m 9d

Woodstock, John, son of Thomas, 1286; Oxford, Magdalen College Ch Hospital in Gen 6

Worcester, John de, 1291; *Giffard* 363r

Wretham, Reginald de, canon of St Martin's, 1233–44; London, Westminster Abbey muniments, 13373

Wych, Richard, bishop of Chichester, ca 1253; *Sussex Archaeological Collections* I 164–92 (1858), Chichester, Diocesan Record Office, County Hall, *Liber E* f 169

Wyth, Juliana, 1282; *Oseney Cartulary* I 411–13

3

The Influence of Canon Law on the Property Rights of Married Women in England

The canon law of marriage was primarily concerned with the matrimonial bond. But in the elaboration of the conditions required for validity, and in the consideration of secondary questions such as the termination of marriage, certain doctrines were advanced that went beyond the regulation of the sacrament itself. Some of these doctrines involved a partial state-ment and defence of the property rights of women during and after their marriage.

Thus in the analysis of the solemnity of matrimony canonists tended to relate the financial arrangements between the spouses to the *celebratio in facie ecclesiae*. Roman law had considered the constitution of dowry[1] to be a sign of regular marriage, and Gratian, as did other canonists before him, tended to attach much importance to it.[2] In fact, one text which he ascribed to a Council of Arles seemed to require the grant in dowry for the validity of the marriage.[3] A literal interpretation of this text did not

This is an expanded version of a paper read during the session 'Canon Law and Social Change in Medieval Europe' at the seventy-seventh annual meeting of the American Historical Association in Chicago, 30 December 1962. – Editor
1 Throughout the present study the word 'dowry' will be used for the gift to the husband on the part of the wife. It will correspond to the marriage portion (*mari-tagium*) of the English law courts and writers and to *dos* as commonly employed by the canonists and civilians. The word 'dower' will be used for the husband's endow-ment of his wife. It will correspond to the *dos* of English writers and to the *donatio propter nuptias* of the canonists and civilians.
2 Gratian, *Decretum* C3 q4 c4; C27 q2 c31; C30 q5 cc 1, 3, 4, 6. For the appearance of these texts in earlier collections see the notes to A. Friedberg's edition of the *Decretum*, in *Corpus iuris canonici*, 2nd ed (Leipzig 1879; repr Graz 1955).
3 'Nullum sine dote fiat conjugium' (C30 q5 c6). The source of the canon is the *False Capitularies* of Benedict the Levite, *Benedicti Capitularia liber II*, cap. 133, ed G.H.

agree with the accepted notion of the essential conditions for marriage, and the decretists were quick to disallow it.[4] But their law contained an important series of texts associating *dos* and *donatio propter nuptias* with the proper constitution of the marital bond, and this association was to have consequences of importance.

The canonists were also concerned with the devolution of property owned by a married couple when their marriage came to an end by separation or death. Their views on this problem were based on a series of papal letters, several of which were sent to addressees in Great Britain. In these decretals it was claimed that, since the dissolution of the marriage by declaration of nullity or separation pertained to the ecclesiastical courts, the supervision of an equitable division of property, accessory to the main decision, also pertained to this jurisdiction.[5] As to substantive rulings: where the causes of separation were licit, the spouses were to have what each had contributed to the marriage; the adulterous wife was unable to recover her dowry.[6] These decretals were collected, organized with the title *De dote post divortium restituenda* of the *Compilatio prima*, found a place in most of the subsequent systematic collections, and, with the publication of the *Decretals* of Gregory IX, became part of the common law of the Church.[7] In the glosses and treatises on these collections the recovery of donations between spouses is usually treated. It will suffice for our present purpose to stress three important qualities of this literature: first, it was accepted that the jurisdiction of the courts Christian should extend beyond the declaration of nullity or separation to the division of property between spouses;[8] second, the discussion was usually carried on within

Pertz, MGH Leges II (Hannover 1837; repr Leipzig 1925) pars altera 80. On the earlier history of this rule and on the gradual shift of the meaning of the word *dos*, so that well before Gratian's time it often meant the husband's gift to his wife (dower), see A. Lemaire, 'Origine de la règle "Nullum sine dote fiat conjugium",' in *Mélanges Paul Fournier* (Paris 1929) 415–24.

4 Decretists' teaching is presented in Adhémar Esmein, *Le mariage en droit canonique*, ed Robert Génestal and Jean Dauvillier, 2nd ed (Paris 1929–35) I 209–11.

5 Clement III (1187–91), *Regesta pontificum Romanorum*, ed P. Jaffé, 2nd ed S. Loewenfeld, F. Kaltenbrunner, and P. Ewald (Leipzig 1885–8) 16589 [henceforth JL]. This decretal became X IV 20 3.

6 X IV 20 1, 2, 4, 5.

7 *Compilatio Ia* IV 21; *Compilatio IIa* IV 14; *Compilatio IIIa* IV 15; *Compilatio Va* IV 3; *Collectio Lipsiensis*, tit LXIII, etc; see *Quinque compilationes antiquae*, ed A. Friedberg (Leipzig 1882).

8 *Bernardi Papiensis Summa decretalium*, ed Ernst A.T. Laspeyres (Regensburg 1860; repr Graz 1956) 193; *Tancredi Summa de matrimonio*, ed A. Wunderlich (Göttingen

the terms of a dotal system (the main preoccupation was the recovery of the property of the wife); third, both papal decretals and the canonists were careful to recognize local custom.[9]

Closely allied to this concern of the canon law with the property of the wife when marriage was terminated was the special position it gave to the widow. This portion of ecclesiastical law was not accessory to the law of marriage, but was based on an entirely different principle. It will be recalled that even in apostolic times the widow was the object of special solicitude. As the centuries passed, various customs and institutions were developed to protect her and regulate her activity; in time, canon law included certain rules in her regard.[10] These are of interest to us from two points of view: first, they afforded general protection to the widow as a *miserabilis persona*; second, they provided precise rules for the defence of her free choice of state in either widowhood or remarriage. Considered as a *miserabilis persona*, she could claim the special protection of both the bishop and the king (of God and the king as the Anglo-Saxons expressed it). The principle was clear enough, but the extent of its practical application was not. In fact it posed a dilemma to the canonist. Did the widow have the right of recourse to ecclesiastical protection only when justice was refused her? The canonist claimed this right for every Christian. Or did she have the right of recourse to the courts of the Church, direct and immediate, in any plea? This understanding of her privilege was unacceptable to the lay jurisdiction and contradicted the royal duty to protect the widow, a duty that was stated within the *Decretum* itself.[11] Professor Brian Tierney has recently described how these conflicting claims were resolved in an equitable fashion by the canonists of the first half of the thirteenth century.[12]

Of a more immediately practical application were the canonists' ideas on the widow's freedom to choose her state. Their position was a nice

---

1841) 107–12; Raymund of Peñafort, *Summa de poenitentia et matrimonio* IV 25 (Rome 1503) 481–4; *Glossa ordinaria ad* X IV 20 3, *incidens accessorie*.

9 Eg a letter of Alexander III to the bishop of Bath: he is to enforce restoration of dowry, 'aut secundum consuetudinem terrae in presentia tua iustitiae plenitudinem exhibeat' (JL 13766; *Compilatio Ia* IV 21 2, ed Friedberg). Cf *Glossa ordinaria ad* X IV 20 2.

10 See A. Rosambert, *La veuve en droit canonique jusqu'au XIVe siècle* (Paris 1923) 39–92, 154–201.

11 C23 q5 c23.

12 *Medieval Poor Law: A Sketch of Canonical Theory and Its Application to England* (Berkeley 1959) 15–19: the widow who was really poor and helpless was allowed to bring her plea before the courts of the Church even though she had not exhausted the possibilities of the secular tribunals.

resolution of two principles, namely, that the state of continence was in itself the better state and that marriage was a good which the widow was free to choose. They defended and favoured her right to live in widow-hood, while at the same time they insisted that she was free to marry, that her spouse should be of her own choice, and that she was not bound by the rule of mourning, the *tempus luctus* of Roman law, so that her re-marriage could take place as soon as she wished. This statement of her freedom was completed by Gratian's time.[13] Its bearing on the position of the widow in a feudal society was not without important practical results.

Finally, canon law exerted influence on the property rights of married women through its treatment of the testament. It would take the present study too far afield to attempt a description of the rather complex process whereby the canonists and ecclesiastical courts became involved in the supervision of bequests.[14] Let it be sufficient to state the following facts: first, from the beginning Christian teaching emphasized the importance of the donation in alms;[15] second, in time the pious gift became associated with the testament – so much so, in fact, that in some areas of the West the testament became known as the *eleemosyna*;[16] third, bishops acquired a right of supervision over the delivery of legacies in alms.[17] By the last years of the twelfth century, as is clear in treatises like Bernard of Pavia's *Summa decretalium*, a sophisticated theory of the testament was being de-veloped by the canonists.[18] In this they were deeply indebted to Roman civil law, though they were subject to other influences as well. Their doctrine incorporated a theory of the testament, notions on the personal

13 *Decretum* C27 qı cc 38, 42; C31 qı cc 10–13 and q2; C32 q2 c16. With regard to the widow's freedom to remarry immediately, Gratian remarks (*dict. ad* C2 q3 c7) that some secular laws still attached infamy to failure to observe the *tempus luctus*. This was the case in late Anglo-Saxon law: the widow was not allowed to marry for one year after her husband's death; see 5 Æthelred 21, 6 Æthelred 26.1, and II Cnut 75, *The Laws of the Kings of England from Edmund to Henry I*, ed A.J. Robert-son (Cambridge 1925) 85, 99, 211, 329n. See Rosambert, *La veuve en droit canonique* 121–7.

14 See H. Auffroy, *Evolution du testament en France des origines au XIIIe siècle* (Paris 1899) 384–98 for a brief description of the canon law of the testament. The growth of this jurisdiction is described more fully by the present writer in *The Will in Medieval England: From the Conversion of the Anglo-Saxons to the End of the Thirteenth Century*, Studies and Texts 6 (Toronto 1963) 120–35.

15 'Quia eleemosyna morte liberat' (Tob 4:11), cited by St Polycarp of Smyrna in his *Letter to the Philippians* ch 10, was a favourite dictum.

16 A. Perraud, *Etude sur le testament en Bretagne* (Rennes 1921) 33n.

17 Sheehan, *The Will in Medieval England* 11 and passim.

18 Ibid 132–3.

material extent of testamentary freedom, and a procedure of implementation and supervision. It included a consideration of the testamentary capacity of the married woman.

The common law of England was taking shape in the last years of the twelfth century. By that time, as has been seen, the canon law of the Western Church included a complete if not systematic treatment of the property rights of the married woman. This canonical teaching was to have considerable consequences in English law and practice. The understanding of the development that is now to be sketched will be facilitated by recalling several general tendencies that appeared in the rules governing property in England as they became explicit in common law. There was, first of all, the insistence that any plea of land must be held before the secular courts. Perhaps more important from the point of view of the present study was the tendency to limit the proprietary capacity of the married woman: lands of her dowry or inheritance were controlled by her husband so far as administration and fruits were concerned. The wife retained ownership and, on termination of the marriage, ordinarily could recover. With regard to chattels her position was even weaker: movable property received in dowry or that came to her after marriage fell to the husband. This was not merely a case of the control of movable property by the husband as in some of the community systems on the Continent; it was a case of outright ownership. Another tendency that weakened the claims of the married woman was the gradual breakdown of the customs protecting family rights in the property of the husband and father. During the late twelfth and thirteenth centuries his right to alienate land by *donatio inter vivos* or sale was asserted against the claims of the heir and the lord.[19] Only the wife's dower resisted this movement. The same tendency is evident in the husband's disposition of movable property (which, it will be remembered, included the chattels brought to the marriage by the wife). At first he exercised his testamentary freedom to dispose of chattels within a quota system, which reserved a portion of his movable property to wife and children. But this restriction was gradually removed so that, by the end of the Middle Ages, throughout much of England he could alienate all chattels in his last will. Thus if the needs of the wife were respected it was by the choice of her husband rather than by requirement of law.

19 Cf F. Pollock and F.W. Maitland, *The History of English Law*, 2nd ed (Cambridge 1911) I 329–49; II 308–11; also S. Painter, 'The Family and the Feudal System in Twelfth-Century England,' *Speculum* 35 (1960) 11–12.

We shall first investigate the influence of canon law on the English practice of dower. It is not intended to explore the early history of this institution;[20] we shall begin, rather, with its appearance in Glanvill. As was mentioned above, the preoccupation of the canonists was with dowry, the wife's gift to the husband. In England, it was dower, the husband's gift to the wife, that was of chief concern. Glanvill began his treatment of this subject with the statement that dower was demanded by both ecclesiastical and secular law.[21] For reasons that we have seen, the canonists could not make a donation of any sort a requirement for the validity of marriage. However, they favoured it, for the publicity of the gift helped to establish the publicity of the marriage itself. In England the endowment of the bride at the door of the church was incorporated into the sacramental liturgy.[22] Glanvill's remark is some indication of the effectiveness of this support of the system of dower. However, it is significant that, although questions touching the validity of a marriage were normally referred to the courts Christian, questions as to the constitution of dower at the door of the church were not. This information was sought from a jury of neighbours. The jury might include the priest who had questioned the groom about the provision for his wife, but his presence was not necessary. The law of the Church and its concretization in the ritual encouraged the gift of dower and, what is very important, gave it a place within a public religious act. But it did not demand it for the validity of marriage.

It was admitted in England that judgment of nullity of marriage or separation pertained to the spiritual forum. But the extent to which accessory proprietary pleas belonged to this jurisdiction is one of the

20 For orientation in this problem see F. Joüon des Longrais, *La conception anglaise de la saisine du XIIe au XIVe siècle* (Paris 1925) 315–17.

21 'Tenetur autem unusquisque tam iure ecclesiastico quam iure seculari' (VI 1): see above, n3, where it is pointed out that *dos* in *Decretum* C30 q5 c6 was interpreted as dower.

22 'Ordo ad facienda sponsalia incipit. Statuantur vir et mulier ad hostium ecclesie coram presbitero et dicatur a viro dos mulieris et ponatur super scutum vel super aliud sive aurum sive argentum seu cetera. Deinde detur femina a patre suo,' *The Sarum Missal Edited from Three Early Manuscripts*, ed J. Wickham Legg (Oxford 1916) 413. There are interesting variants of the rubric, ibid n2. For the ceremony in the fourteenth century see *Manuale ad usum percelebris ecclesie Sarisburiensis*, ed A. Jefferies Collins, Henry Bradshaw Society 91 (London 1960) 44–6. Detailed examples are cited by Cyril T. Flower, *Introduction to the Curia Regis Rolls, 1199–1230 A.D.*, Selden Society 62 (London 1944) 236–7; cf Cecile S. Margulies, 'The Marriages and the Wealth of the Wife of Bath,' *Mediaeval Studies* 24 (1962) 210–16.

problems that still require clarification. A decretal of Alexander III that was probably addressed to the bishop of Bath ordered that a husband who had been separated from his wife by the bishop's judgment be compelled to return her dowry.[23] Yet other letters of the same pope imply that he did not press the right of the courts Christian to judge of lay fee even though the plea began as a matrimonial case before this jurisdiction.[24] On investigation, the lay courts are found to be enforcing a division of land following the separation of a couple similar to that sought by canon law. Like it they were especially concerned with the wife's dowry. On declaration of the nullity of her marriage, she could recover landed property from her former husband by a writ of novel disseisin.[25] Similarly, her husband's heirs could bar her claim of dower.[26] As in the canon law it was held that the adulterous wife should be punished by loss of property. The generally held opinion that she forfeited her claim to dower was reinforced by the Second Statute of Westminster, canon 34 (1285), in which it was denied her unless the husband had freely received her back before his death.[27] Cases concerning the movable portion of the wife's dowry pertained to the courts of the Church, being one of two pleas *de catallis et debitis* that were permitted them.[28] But the extent of this jurisdiction as exercised by the courts Christian remains largely unexplored. From the first years of the thirteenth century it is evident that the husband can come before this court to demand payment of dowry in movable property by the donor or his heir.[29] But did this jurisdiction seek to supervise the return of the movable part of a wife's dowry that remained after the dissolution of her marriage? After separation could it force her husband to support his children by her? Would it even seek to enforce the return of the wife's dowry lands by ecclesiastical sanctions? There are

23 Cited above, n9. In 1224, Henry III obtained the support of the pope in his efforts to recover the dowry given with his sister Joan to Hugh de Lusignan, who had married Queen Isabella instead, *Regesta pontificum Romanorum*, ed A. Potthast (Berlin 1874–5) 7293; *Compilatio Va* IV 3 1 (ed Friedberg 180–1).
24 X IV 17 4–5; cf Adrian Morey, *Bartholomew of Exeter, Bishop and Canonist: A Study in the Twelfth Century* (Cambridge 1937) 68–70.
25 Eg *Curia Regis Rolls* [henceforth CRR] II 267, 298 (1203); V 251; XIV no 1387; cf Flower, *Introduction to the Curia Regis Rolls* 102–3.
26 Eg CRR XI no 1852 (AD 1224).
27 See Pollock and Maitland, *The History of English Law* II 394–6.
28 Flower, *Introduction to the Curia Regis Rolls* 246–7; G.B. Flahiff, 'The Writ of Prohibition to Court Christian in the Thirteenth Century,' *Mediaeval Studies* 6 (1944) 277–9.
29 'cognitio de maritagio pertinet ad forum ecclesiasticum de denariis' (CRR XIV no 575, dated 1230). Similarly, London, PRO KB 26/124 m 18d (Michaelmas 1242).

many indications in episcopal registers of the late thirteenth and early fourteenth centuries that the answer will be yes to all of these questions.[30] As yet, however, an answer is not possible. It is hoped that current studies of the ecclesiastical courts of England will provide the information that is needed. For the moment it can safely be maintained that at least an important moral pressure was exerted by the bishops and their courts in defence of all the property rights of women, following declaration of nullity of marriage or separation from their husbands.

When we turn to the position of the widow in common law, we find that her legal defence came to rest normally with the secular courts. Her rights had tended to suffer during the power struggles within feudal society, so that by King John's time the lot of the widow of the upper classes was a rather hard one. She had become an asset of king or lord; her right to marry or not to marry was largely dictated by financial and political needs.[31] Late in John's reign a powerful current in the opposite direction set in. The Barnwell chronicle tells us that the king was already moved to improve the widow's position in the concessions made late in 1212 after his withdrawal from the Welsh campaign.[32] As is well known, the widow's rights to dower, dowry and inheritance, a share in her husband's chattels, and reasonable necessities and shelter during the period pending award of dower were expressed with increasing care in a series of clauses extending from the 'Unknown Charter' through the Articles of the Barons to their final statement in the Charter of 1217.[33] When court records resume once more after the advent of Henry III, they

30 Eg in *Registrum Roberti Winchelsey*, ed Rose Graham, Canterbury and York Society (Oxford 1952–6) I 163–4, 256, judges are ordered to see that 'omniaque bona mobilia et immobilia ipsius mulieris' are returned to the plaintiff following the declaration of the nullity of her marriage (1297); a similar case is in *Registrum Henrici Woodlock diocesis Wintoniensis A.D. 1305–16*, ed A.W. Goodman, Canterbury and York Society 43–4 (Oxford 1940–1) II 556. In 1348 Reginald Webbe appeared before the court of the bishop of Rochester and agreed to support his children by Joan Akerman, *Registrum Hamonis Hethe diocesis Roffensis A.D. 1318–52*, ed C. Johnson, Canterbury and York Society 49 (Oxford 1948) II 1004.
31 Sidney Painter, *The Reign of King John* (Baltimore 1949) 218–19; Doris M. Stenton, *The English Woman in History* (London 1947) 36–9.
32 *Memoriale fratris Walteri de Coventria*, ed W. Stubbs, RS 58 (London 1872–3) II 207: 'sed et viduis dicitur propitius exstitisse.' See J.C. Holt, *The Northerners* (Oxford 1961) 84–6.
33 'Unknown Charter,' cc 4, 6, *Studies and Notes Supplementary to Stubbs' Constitutional History*, ed Charles Petit-Dutaillis, trans W.E. Rhodes (Manchester 1908–29) I 117–18; Articles of the Barons, cc 4, 17, 35; Magna Carta (1215) cc 7, 8, 11, 26; Reissue of 1216, cc 7, 8, 20; Reissue of 1217, cc 7, 8, 22; Reissue of 1225, cc 7, 8, 18 (*Select Charters*, ed W. Stubbs, 9th ed H.W.C. Davis, 286–9, 294–6, 327–8, 341–2, 350).

convey the impression not only that the royal courts were well equipped to defend the widow's right to dower and marriage portion[34] but also that her pleas enjoyed certain procedural advantages as well.[35] It is evident that the final statement of the widow's right to choose her state, to marry when and whom she would, and of her property rights was almost exactly that which the canonists had sought for her seventy-five years before.[36] I have no evidence that canonical teaching was explicitly invoked in the preparation of this portion of Magna Carta. It was undoubtedly well known to Archbishop Langton and the other bishops, and it seems reasonable to conclude that it contributed to the climate of opinion in which such notions about the widow could be stated and enforced.[37] King John himself had undoubtedly acquired more than passing acquaintance with the papal notions of the widow's rights in the long struggle with Innocent III over the dower of Queen Berengaria.[38]

It becomes apparent even in this brief examination of dower and the rights of women on the termination of their marriage that, in the period during which the main principles governing married women's property in English common law were stated, the canonists provided some of the legal notions, and their law served as a support and occasionally as a development of the common law. One has a strong impression that the two jurisdictions had a remarkable identity of purpose. This impression disappears when attention is turned to the testamentary rights of the married woman. In some ways the most profound influence of the canonists on common law was through their contribution to the law of wills. The general law of the Church with regard to the testament was not only

34 For the later history of dower see William S. Holdsworth, *A History of English Law*, 3rd ed (London 1923) III 189–92; and T.F.T. Plucknett, *A Concise History of the Common Law*, 5th ed (London 1956) 566–8.

35 Essoins of bed-sickness and royal business were disallowed in pleas of dower in CRR VIII 137 (1219); XII nos 176, 1026; XIV no 4. See Flower, *Introduction to the Curia Regis Rolls* 238.

36 For a consideration of the state of widowhood by a twelfth-century English author see Morey, *Bartholomew of Exeter, Bishop and Canonist* 67 and *Augustinus de bono viduitatis*, c LXII in Bartholomew's *Penitential*, printed ibid 228–9.

37 Roger of Wendover mentions that during the meeting of the barons in London, August 1213, Archbishop Stephen Langton showed them the Coronation Charter of Henry I and suggested that they use it to recover their lost liberties. This charter guaranteed the rights of widows in chapters 3 and 4 (*Select Charters*, ed Stubbs 118); see F.M. Powicke, *Stephen Langton*, Ford Lectures, 1927 (Oxford 1928) 113–16.

38 See 'Two Royal Surveys of Wiltshire during the Interdict,' ed W. Raymond Powell, Publications of the Pipe Roll Society, n s 34 (1958) 4–5; and *Selected Letters of Pope Innocent III Concerning England*, ed C.R. Cheney and W.H. Semple (London 1957) xxxv n3.

applied in England but also developed there to an extent unknown elsewhere. By Glanvill's time the courts Christian had acquired an intrinsic jurisdiction over the will; they dealt with questions touching the validity and contents of the act. During the last years of King John's reign an extrinsic jurisdiction was admitted in the same courts so that their powers were extended to include supervision of the execution and enforcement of most wills.[39] Finally, during the middle years of the thirteenth century, the bishops consolidated their position as supervisors of the distribution of the movable property of the intestate.[40]

This unique jurisdiction influenced the property rights of the wife in three ways. The first and most enduring consequence was not derived from the theory of the canon law nor from the intention of those officers of the courts Christian who accepted jurisdiction in testamentary cases, but it was to prove of major importance. Given the complete control of pleas of land by the civil courts, the assumption of testamentary jurisdiction by the ecclesiastical courts meant that succession to movable and immovable property came under different authorities. A general and consistent view of the property rights of husband and wife became difficult, if not impossible. This division is probably one of the main reasons for the wife's unfavourable position before common law with regard to chattels.[41] The second and third influences of the canon law of wills tended to compensate for the first effect. They are to be seen in the attempt to establish and defend rights of the wife in the chattels of the family. On the one hand an effort was made to give her a power of bequest, while on the other hand the testamentary freedom of her husband was subjected to limitations so that a portion of his movable property would be reserved to her.

The power of bequest exercised by the married woman is described by Glanvill in a chapter that immediately reveals the tension between that which was enforceable by law and that which was fitting (*pium esset et merito valde honestum*). Since the wife can own no chattels, she does not have the right to make a will. However, Glanvill considers it to be fitting that her husband permit her to bequeath that part of his property that would fall to her if she survived him.[42] We now know that the 'fitting' responded to the desires of a large part of the population. The same

---

39 Sheehan, *The Will in Medieval England* 164–9.
40 Ibid 169–76.
41 See Pollock and Maitland, *The History of English Law* II 432–3; and Holdsworth, *A History of English Law* III 525–8.
42 *De legibus* VII 5.

tension between the legal and the suitable appears again in Bracton and
Fleta with an even stronger note of suitability attached to the bequest of
clothing and jewels that were especially associated with the wife's personal
use.[43] But during the next two hundred years the common law would unfold the implications of its initial decision that the wife could own no
chattels. This process, carried through to completion in the teeth of strong
resistance, has been described in the great histories of English law and
can be read there.[44] However, there was resistance to this process, and it
is to one part of it that we must now turn.

In synodal decrees of the thirteenth century English bishops claimed
a right of bequest for all adults. By this time, of course, canonists were
fully aware of the Roman law touching the persons to whom testamentary
freedom was extended (a group that included the married woman), and
they were able to draw on it. However, it should be remembered that the
roots of the ecclesiastical jurisdiction in testamentary matters did not lie
in a canonical theory of family property but in a theory of alms; within
the framework of that theory, the freedom to bequeath was as much the
need of the wife as of the husband or the widow. Glanvill witnesses to
this point of view when he makes a distinction between the *testamentum*
and the *ultima voluntas*, pointing out that even the latter, which was
especially associated with the final gift in alms, was not permitted the wife
without her husband's permission. Beginning with the statutes of Bishop
Walter de Cantilupe of Worcester in 1240 the bishops stated again and
again the wife's right of bequest.[45] However, the synodal statement of the
wife's testamentary capacity as customary (Lambeth, 1261) or as a right to
bequeath her own property (Exeter, 1287) was easily met by the common
lawyers. They pointed out that the wife had no such customary right and
that she could not be expected to bequeath the property that, by her state,
she was excluded from owning.[46] A last great effort to state and defend
the wife's position was made in the provincial statutes of Archbishop
Stratford in 1342. This occasioned a protest in Parliament two years later,
which strengthens the impression of a deterioration of the situation.

43 Bracton f 6ob; *Fleta* II 57.
44 Cf Pollock and Maitland, *The History of English Law* II 400ff; and Holdsworth, *A
    History of English Law* III 521–30.
45 Cap. 67, De testamento pauperis, *Concilia Magnae Britanniae et Hiberniae, 446–1718,*
    ed David Wilkins (London 1737) I 675. The wife's right of bequest was stated in
    statutes at Lambeth (1261), Salisbury (probably 1257–62), Winchester (1262–5), Exeter
    (1287); see *Concilia,* ed Wilkins I 754, 714; II 298, 155–6.
46 See Sheehan, *The Will in Medieval England* 238–9.

There would be further efforts, but the common law stood firm.[47] It is perhaps an indication of the decline of the Church's hopes for the testamentary capacity of the wife that in 1287 Bishop Quivil could speak of the wife's clothing and other personal effects as being so much her own that they were not included in the division of property in thirds on her death or that of her husband, while, in the middle of the fifteenth century, Lyndwood pleaded that at least the wife's paraphernalia should be freely bequeathed.[48]

So far as can be seen the pressure exerted by the courts Christian throughout this debate remained on the level of persuasion. I have discovered no example where it is certain that the husband was excommunicated for hindering execution of his wife's will.[49] Nor is there any example of a bishop declaring a wife deceased without a will to be intestate.[50] He could then proceed as her bishop to appoint an administrator to distribute her goods.[51]

47 See *Provinciale (seu constitutiones Angliae)*, ed W. Lyndwood (Oxford 1679) 173; cf Holdsworth, *A History of English Law* III 543.

48 Exeter (1287) cap. 50, De testamentis: 'Quae autem ad usum testatoris specialiter sunt parata, utputa equi et arma, et caetera hujusmodi; vel quae ad usum uxoris, utputa supellectilia, vestes muliebres, monilia, annuli, absque divisione utrique eorum praecipua reserventur' (*Concilia*, ed Wilkins II 156); *Provinciale*, ed Lyndwood: 'Et sic patet quod licet in rebus dotalibus maritus sit dominus, non tamen sic in rebus paraphernalibus. Nam res paraphernales sunt propriae ipsius mulieris, etiam stante matrimonio, ut legitur et notatur C. *de pact. conven. l. fi. et l. hac. l.* de quibus uxor libere testari potest, ut ibi innuitur (173b, *gl. ad verb. "propriarum uxorum"*).' Cf Pollock and Maitland, *The History of English Law* II 429–30 and notes.

49 Episcopal registers include excommunications of those who interfere with wills of married women, but in the examples that have been identified the husband has not been identified as an offender; eg in 1291 Bishop Sutton of Lincoln excommunicated those who hindered execution of the will of Lecia, wife of Robert de Marays, *The Rolls and Register of Bishop Oliver Sutton, 1280–1299*, ed R.M.T. Hill, Lincoln Record Society 48 (Hereford 1954) III 125.

50 This fact was noted in the Year Book of 5 Edward II: 'E d'autrepart si femme devie intestat l'ordinarie s'entremettera point' (ed G.J. Turner, Selden Society 63 [London 1947] 241). An interesting case of the year 1347 appears in the register of Bishop Hamo de Hethe of Rochester: William Miller is charged with unlawful disposal of the goods of his wife, who died intestate. He appears and swears that 'dicta Alicia bona aliqua non dimisit de quibus testari potuit.' The entry concludes with the remark 'unde nos officialis predictus prefatum Willelmum ab officio nostro dimittimus propter paupertatem Alicie prenotate,' implying the possibility that there could have been intestate succession in Alice's case; see *Registrum Hamonis Hethe*, ed Johnson II 972.

51 On episcopal supervision of distribution of the property of the intestate see Plucknett, *A Concise History of the Common Law* 729–31.

Such was the law. But the law was not the whole story. In fact, documents of practice during the thirteenth and fourteenth centuries indicate that many wives made wills and that they were successfully implemented. Pollock and Maitland illustrated this fact for the fourteenth century.[52] The same can be done for the thirteenth century. From the distinctions of property bequeathed in the wills of these women, it becomes clear how strong was the resistance to the system of chattel ownership described by Glanvill, Bracton, and others. A good example is provided by the will of Agnes de Condet, which can be dated 1223 or a little earlier. The testatrix indicates the sources from which her legacies were to be drawn, and reveals an attitude towards married women's property far removed from that described by Glanvill. The husband granted her one-half of the chattels on his lands. The income of a manor was to be devoted for one year after her death to the completion of her will, as was the income from a wardship that she had purchased from her husband. Finally, those chattels that were her own (*omnium que mea sunt*) were to be sold for the same purpose. The residue of her property was to be distributed for the good of her soul at the discretion of her executors.[53] Many other examples of this sort of document could be given, starting with the early years of the reign of Henry III and extending well into the fifteenth century.[54]

It is very difficult to know how frequently married women in the Middle Ages made bequests. Most early wills have come down to us because they included a legacy of land. But, since wives did not normally control the devolution of real estate, only a small proportion of their wills has survived. Occasionally, however, one can establish proportions between the number of wills made by men and women. Thus in the diocese of Rochester, during the Black Death, circumstances were such that

---

52 *The History of English Law* II 428–9.

53 London, BL, Harl Ch 48 C 25; a slightly different version is published by C.W. Forster, *The Registrum antiquissimum of the Cathedral Church of Lincoln*, Lincoln Record Society 27 (Hereford 1931) I 293–5.

54 Eg the will of Cecily, wife of Geoffrey Huse, 1267 (London, PRO E 210/291); the will of Lucy Lundreys, 1299 (Wells, Library of the Dean and Chapter, Liber Albus R I f 128), summarized in *Historical Manuscripts Commission Report* 28 (1907) I 165–6. For the fourteenth century see the examples from York discussed in Pollock and Maitland, *The History of English Law* II 428–9. Good fifteenth-century examples are printed by E.F. Jacob and H.C. Johnson in *The Register of Henry Chichele, Archbishop of Canterbury, 1414–1443*, 2: *Wills Proved before the Archbishop or His Commissaries* (Oxford 1938); note especially the will of Elizabeth de Clynton, 266–8. For the later period see the studies of Professor W.K. Jordan, especially *The Charities of Rural England* (London 1961) 27.

some comparative figures can be established.[55] In 1347 in a small group of villages the wills of fifty-one men and twenty women were proved. Of the women's wills twelve were presented for probate by the husbands of the deceased, two were the wills of unmarried women, and five were the wills of women of undetermined status, of which at least one was probably married at the time of death. The following year the wills of seventy-eight men and thirty-seven women are mentioned. Of the latter, fourteen were presented for probate by the husband of the deceased, two were the wills of unmarried women, and twenty-one the wills of women of undetermined status, of which at least four were almost certainly married at the time of death. Thus it seems possible to conclude that, although the common law of England steadfastly refused to enforce the will of the married woman, in fact she very often managed to distribute property at death. I do not wish to give the impression that canon law was the unique or even the most important cause of this practice of bequest among married women. The desire to give alms at death and to manifest affection in this way was prior to any law.[56] Yet it seems beyond question that the efforts of the bishops and their courts were partially responsible for the continued attempts by married women to exercise a testamentary capacity. Due to this influence many wives made wills, and these wills were executed. As a result two-thirds rather than one-half of a family's chattels were distributed. These facts are of importance to the social and economic historian as well as to the historian of law.

During the twelfth and thirteenth centuries the husband exercised his right of bequest within a quota system. There were various arrangements, according to local custom, though by far the most common provided a third of the movable property for husband, wife, and children.[57] The courts of the Church supervised this distribution. They do not seem to have advanced a position of their own as to the portion to be bequeathed, but were content to honour the custom of the locality.[58] The exercise of a testamentary power within a quota system poses many problems. Even in the wills of the thirteenth century it is sometimes evident that husbands were deciding which pieces of equipment, animals, etc would constitute the portion reserved to their wives and children. Soon they can be seen extending their freedom of alienation over larger and larger

---

55 See *Registrum Hamonis Hethe*, ed Johnson II 1270, Index, s v 'Wills–Probate'.
56 Cf *Borough Customs*, ed Mary Bateson, Selden Society 18, 21 (London 1904–6) II civ.
57 Pollock and Maitland, *The History of English Law* II 350–6.
58 Ibid.

portions of their movable property. During the fourteenth century this tendency apparently reached its term. The provincial statutes of 1342 condemned those who alienated all their property on their deathbeds by gift *inter vivos*, to the neglect of wife, children, and others.[59] Twenty-five years later, a statute of Archbishop Thoresby of York mentioned that men were using their wills for the same purpose and condemned the practice.[60] Pleas before the royal courts show that wives and children were occasionally seeking their portions before this jurisdiction.[61] Though the bishops were opposed to this neglect of obligations, their courts could not or would not prevent it. Husbands were drawing out the implications of the system of chattel ownership that had been announced by Glanvill; if they had outright ownership of all the movable property of the family, it seemed reasonable that they should be able to dispose of it all in their own way. The details of this important and uneven development remain to be investigated.[62] But the results are clear: by Elizabeth's time, in much of the province of Canterbury, the wife's claim was denied. It was only in the distribution of the property of the intestate, a distribution supervised by the bishop, that a portion of the husband's movable goods was reserved to his wife.[63]

It is in the law of wills that the canonists made one of their chief substantive contributions to English common law. But in two important areas of this law of wills, namely, the persons to whom testamentary freedom was extended and the portion of a husband's movable property over which his power might be exercised, the canonists supported a position that was opposed to those principles of chattel ownership that were adopted by the common law. The position of the ecclesiastical courts was not accepted. This rejection involved a serious set-back to the property rights of the married women of England.

---

59 *Concilia*, ed Wilkins II 706, cap. 8, 9. An example of this procedure is mentioned in *Registrum Hamonis Hethe*, ed Johnson II 988: Thomas, son of John Amfrey, appears before the court and says that his father did not make a will but 'diu ante mortem suam bona sua omnia alienavit' (1348).

60 *Concilia*, ed Wilkins III 70.

61 For an account of these pleas before royal courts see Pollock and Maitland, *The History of English Law* II 351–2; and the supplementary information in Plucknett, *A Concise History of the Common Law* 743–5.

62 Holdsworth, *A History of English Law* III 550–5.

63 Plucknett, *A Concise History of the Common Law* 729–31. The widow was often made administrator of the estate of the intestate husband.

4

Canon Law and English Institutions: Some Notes on Current Research

In this communication I wish to relate canon law to two rather important elements in the life of medieval England, indicating its influence on social institutions and on some of the theory and practice of English common law as well. I shall try, in brief compass, to set out conclusions that flow from my own study of the last will and marriage and to indicate certain problems and lines of future investigations that have been suggested there.

First, a word on the testament. It is well known that Christian teaching and custom attached considerable importance to the gift of alms, especially at the end of life. Eventually the regulation of this matter found a place in canon law; that law exerted a powerful influence on the testamentary usages of all of Christendom. This fact has been investigated in general, and there are in addition many monographs dealing with institutions governing succession and inheritance in local areas which demonstrate the impact of canonical teaching.[1] The influence of the law of the Church on the English will is of considerable interest, not only because its result is still part of a living legal system but also because of the remarkable degree to which that influence was received. The main lines of this development have been known for some time. My own studies have made it possible to establish certain facts with greater precision and have revealed problems to which answers have yet to be given.[2]

---

1 Recent examples of local studies are L. de Charrin, *Les testaments dans la région de Montpellier au moyen âge* (Ambilly 1961) 28, 48, 51–3, 134ff; and L.F. Poudret, *La succession testamentaire dans le pays de Vaud à l'époque savoyarde (XIIIe–XVe siècles)*, Bibliothèque historique vaudoise (Lausanne 1955) 53, 65–7, and passim.

2 Michael M. Sheehan, *The Will in Medieval England: From the Conversion of the Anglo-Saxons to the End of the Thirteenth Century*, Studies and Texts 6 (Toronto 1963).

In twelfth-century England the implications of the separation of civil and ecclesiastical jurisdictions by William the Conqueror were made explicit as a boundary was drawn through the group of pleas that were at once civil and religious. In this division, internal jurisdiction over the will fell to the courts of the Church. They proceeded to apply the law they knew; thus a theory of bequest, drawn from Roman civil law, and the simplified canonical requirements for validity became the bases of the English will. Later, during the reign of King John (1199–1216), the courts Christian assumed an extrinsic jurisdiction over the will;[3] in their efforts to make execution as effective as possible[4] they were setting out on a road that would lead to many conflicts with the courts of common law. In the process, the whole system of implementation – probate, inventory, letters of administration, the rendering of account, and the dismissal of the executors – was perfected. Thus the law of the Church came to exercise an important influence in this sector of the legal, social, and economic life of England, an influence that would eventually lead church courts into areas of activity that were never intended when they assumed a supervision of the bequest for pious causes. Much later, the will was to pass from the control of the courts Christian, but it would remain basically the same, a permanent contribution of canon law to the legal structure of the English-speaking world.

Within the historical evolution that has just been sketched there are three features that will, I think, be of interest here. First, it has been pointed out that as the canonical defence of the *miserabiles personae* was perfected, these weaker members of society assumed the privileges of the cleric, became possessed of a sort of *privilegium fori*.[5] In the long development of the English will during the twelfth and thirteenth centuries, there was, I think, a similar process. The regular supervision of the execution of bequests, non-contentious probate, the systematic taking of inventory, and permission to assume control of property for purposes of administration were first used in dealing with the estates of the clergy and then applied to the wills of laymen as well.[6]

A second point of interest is the fact that those lay courts possessed of an internal and external supervision of wills were subject to considerable

3 Ibid 171–6.
4 Ibid 220–30.
5 Gabriel Le Bras, 'Le droit classique de l'Eglise au service de l'homme,' *Congrès de droit canonique médiéval, Louvain et Bruxelles, 22–26 juillet 1958* (Louvain 1959) 108–9.
6 Sheehan, *The Will in Medieval England* 233–4, 195–220 passim. The suggestion that a similar development occurred among the Anglo-Saxons is made ibid 89–96.

influence by canon law. The courts Christian were not allowed to receive pleas dealing with lay fee, so the bequest of land, permitted in most towns, was supervised by the borough court.[7] The refusal of the London Hustings to honour the ecclesiastical probate of the portion of a will dealing with the bequest of land led to a sharp exchange in the 1260s, but the Hustings and the courts of other boroughs continued to exercise a jurisdiction over the will of land, deciding as to validity, issuing probate, etc.[8] Even though there was this friction, there are strong indications that here, as in so many other ways, English borough law was especially receptive of canonical influence. As a general rule, the procedure of probate and, with some minor exceptions, the requirements for validity were in accord with those of the courts Christian.

There is a problem here, however, to which further study must be devoted. By the theory of the canonical will, the act was unilateral, ambulatory, and revocable. For conveyance of land by English common law, there had to be a real transfer of seisin during the lifetime of the donor, a condition of donation that made the bequest of land impossible. These two theories of donation met in the courts supervising the devise of burgage tenements. The conflict that resulted and its probable influence on the theory of the bequest of land in common law have not yet received the investigation that is warranted.[9]

There is evidence that, by the fourteenth century, some manorial courts gave probate to the wills of villeins. It is not yet clear whether the theory of the will and the procedure of probate received in these courts were derived from canon law. Certainly many of those owing suit to the manorial court would be familiar with the procedure of the archdeacon's court, so that, even in the manors of laymen, the canonical influence could be expected.[10] However, the matter remains to be investigated in detail.

One further point about the English will should be mentioned, a point involving a serious opposition between canon law and English common

7 *Borough Customs*, ed Mary Bateson, Selden Society 18, 21 (London 1904–6) I 243–69, II lxxxv–c, 90–102; and M. de W. Hemmeon, *Burgage Tenure in Mediaeval England* (Cambridge, Mass. 1914) 4–5, 130–53, 183–4.

8 Sheehan, *The Will in Medieval England* 207–10.

9 For a preliminary orientation in the problem see William S. Holdsworth, *A History of English Law*, 3rd ed (London 1923) III 273–4; and E.W. Veale, Introduction: 'Burgage Tenure in Mediaeval Bristol,' in *The Great Red Book of Bristol*, Bristol Record Society 2 (Bristol 1931) 62–3, 66.

10 A. Elizabeth Levett, *Studies in Manorial History*, ed Helen M. Cam et al (Oxford 1938) 208–34.

law.[11] It is concerned with the right of bequest of the married woman and the villein, and reached well beyond the merely legal problem to consequences of considerable importance in the social and economic spheres. By common law, as stated in Glanvill and developed in later treatises and decisions, the married woman could own no chattels. Similarly, by manorial law (supported where necessary by the common law), the villein owned nothing, all property belonging to his lord. These theories of property collided with the theory of alms that sought freedom for all adults to give a pious gift for the good of their souls at death. In spite of considerable and remarkably constant pressure from the bishops, English common law did not yield on this matter during the period that concerns us here. This, however, is one of those cases where the mere statement of law is not a satisfactory description of the social situation that it regulates. On investigating the documents of practice, we find that, in fact, many wives and villeins made wills and these acts were executed. Inasmuch as canon law reinforced this desire to make a will, and the petition to the Parliament of 1344 shows how effective this support was, its contribution was important, not only in the long term (the right of the wife and the villager would eventually be supported by law) but immediately in the social and economic spheres.

The second topic of this discussion touches the matter just treated at several points. It was the concern of canon law to support and enforce the property rights of women during and after marriage. This influence was felt in England at each step of the married woman's career.[12] On her wedding day it was invoked to support endowment by her husband, and the transfer of the property was even included in the sacramental ritual.[13] Canon law also lent its support to the *maritagium*, the property brought to the marriage by the wife. Glanvill, writing late in the twelfth century, gives the rather astonishing information that the groom, his wife, or his heir could demand delivery of a *maritagium* in land from the donor or his heir before either lay or ecclesiastical courts. If the demand were made of other parties, the plea fell to the lay jurisdiction. Certainly in the following century the plea of land was a matter for the lay court, but the claim for delivery of movable property was received by the court Christian.[14] The

11 See Michael M. Sheehan, 'The Influence of Canon Law on the Property Rights of Married Women in England,' *Mediaeval Studies* 25 (1963) 118–21 (here pp 25–7).

12 Ibid 109–24 (here pp 16–30).

13 Examples are cited ibid 114 n22 (here p 21).

14 On the *maritagium* or dowry see F. Makower, *A Constitutional History and Constitution of the Church of England* (London 1895) 424–5; the texts of Glanvill, Bracton, etc

frequency of these cases before the spiritual jurisdiction as well as the speed and efficiency of the remedy remain to be investigated.

If a woman died before her husband, she was not allowed to make a will unless he permitted it. As we have seen, canon law held a different position, and the bishops tried to bring about its acceptance.

When a marriage failed and separation of spouses occurred, it was necessary to divide their property. Decree of separation and declaration of nullity pertained to the courts of the Church, and it was a widely held opinion among canonists that the subsequent division of property was accessory to the main cause and, as such, pertained to their jurisdiction. So far as land is concerned, there is no indication that the English ecclesiastical courts often insisted on this matter. In fact, common law developed procedures for recovery of dower and dowry by husband and wife respectively that brought about the equitable arrangement sought by canon law. Occasionally bishops supplemented the activity of the lay courts by ecclesiastical sanctions or acted where these courts failed to do so.[15] But what of the division of chattels? Once again, there are indications in bishops' registers that disputes on this important matter fell within the purview of the courts Christian; but, until the subject is investigated in detail, it will not be possible to estimate the extent and the effectiveness of this part of the ecclesiastical jurisdiction.[16]

Canon law showed a special interest in the defence of a woman's rights after the death of her husband. The widow, a *miserabilis persona*, had been a concern of the Church from apostolic times. Her freedom to choose her state, her property rights, and her claim to special legal protection were carefully stated by Gratian and were reinforced by the decretal literature of the following century. The form which the widow's rights received in Magna Carta (1215) is remarkably close to that stated earlier in canon law. Given the important part played by Archbishop Stephen Langton and Bishop Eustace of Ely in the preparation of the

are assembled p 424 n104. On the pleas of chattels given in *maritagium* before the courts Christian see Sheehan, 'The Influence of Canon Law' 115 (here p 22). This plea was accepted in the courts of common law under certain conditions in the fourteenth century; see Makower, *A Constitutional History* 424.

15 Examples are cited in Sheehan, 'The Influence of Canon Law' 116 n30 and 115 n23 (here pp 23 and 22).

16 Cf the examples cited in the previous note. In 1291 husbands are required to provide for their wives after separation, Register of Godfrey Giffard, bishop of Worcester, Worcestershire Record Office MS 713 f 339v; also in 1348, *Registrum Hamonis Hethe diocesis Roffensis A.D. 1318–52*, ed C. Johnson, Canterbury and York Society 48–9 (Oxford 1948) II 1004.

Charter, it does not seem rash to conclude that in these matters the teaching of the canonists exerted a considerable influence.[17] Certainly the thirteenth and fourteenth centuries witnessed an improvement of the widow's position in society. There are many indications that, among the free classes, she enjoyed increased freedom to remain unmarried or in her choice of husband. As for the peasantry, the widows of villeins were often instructed to marry so that they might better provide the labour services required of their holdings. This seems to have been an economic matter, without the political overtones so often part of the marriage of the widow of the upper class, so that her choice of husband was not often dictated to her.[18] A colleague who is currently investigating this matter informs me that, beginning about 1300 in some areas, directions to widows to marry tend to disappear from the rolls of the manorial court.[19] It is obvious that late in the fourteenth century the diminishing demand for land lessened the likelihood that she would be required either to marry against her preference or to give up her property; but there is a strong possibility that the earlier appearance of this freedom found at least a partial cause in the more refined view of the widow's needs and rights, of which canon law was the vehicle.

As for the property rights of the widow, the delivery of dower lands was enforced by the courts of common law in processes that developed to a reasonably high level of competence in the middle years of the reign of Henry III. But what of the *dos in denariis*, the dower in chattels? We hear very little of it either in legal treatises or in histories of common law.[20] It soon became apparent that recovery after alienation by the husband was difficult. In fact the very notion opposed the tendency of English common law to put all chattels that came to the wife entirely in the husband's control. Yet liturgical treatises normally speak in terms of dower in movable property.[21] If one reflects on the problem, it immediately becomes apparent that, even among the free, there must have been a fairly large number of husbands who could not hope to offer their brides

---

17 Sheehan, 'The Influence of Canon Law' 116–17 (here pp 23–4).

18 George C. Homans, *English Villagers of the Thirteenth Century* (Cambridge, Mass. 1960; repr 1970, 1975) 160–73; H.S. Bennett, *Life on the English Manor*, Cambridge Studies in Medieval Life and Thought (Cambridge 1948) 243–5.

19 See J. Ambrose Raftis, *Tenure and Mobility: Studies in the Social History of the Mediaeval English Village*, Studies and Texts 8 (Toronto 1964) ch 2 and 9.

20 Glanvill 6 1 2; Bracton, *De legibus* f 94; see Holdsworth, *A History of English Law* II 615, III 189–90.

21 Examples are cited in Sheehan, 'The Influence of Canon Law' 114 n22 (here p 21).

either present or future rights in land. What then became of the dower in chattels? Was it, in fact, so completely absorbed in the movable property of the family, and therefore owned by the husband, that it could not be distinguished at his death? Or was there here an area of activity by the ecclesiastical courts that has not yet been isolated and analysed? Could it even be that there is some connection between the dower of chattels and legitim – the third part of a husband's chattels reserved to his widow by custom – and that the disappearance of legitim throughout much of England is connected in some way with the refusal of the courts of common law to enforce payment of dower in movable property?[22] It may be that from the twelfth until the late fourteenth century these matters were considered by ecclesiastical courts, not as a jurisdiction accessory to matrimony but as part of the law of wills.

From all of these problems it becomes apparent that a satisfactory understanding of the statement and defence of married women's property by canon law and an assessment of its effectiveness are not yet possible, because most investigations have been cast in terms of land, an area in which the courts Christian could only be supplementary to the lay jurisdiction. What is needed is a systematic investigation of the activity of the courts of the Church in the area that was proper to them, namely, pleas of chattels flowing from matrimony.

Enough has been said, however, to make it clear that the canon law of the will and marriage exerted profound and permanent influence on English law touching family property and on the economic and social structure that underlay it. In some cases this influence resulted in defence of rights within the law of the land; in others it never penetrated beyond the level of moral suasion. As yet, some influences can only be suggested as possibilities. Finally, it becomes evident that, before many of the important problems touched on can be solved, before we shall be able to state the effectiveness of the Church and her law in the society on this matter of family property, there must be a careful scrutiny of the documents of practice. The investigation should extend not only to the documents of ecclesiastical courts but also to those of other jurisdictions – royal, manorial, and private; and it should be carried out in such a way that records of the different courts control and supplement each other.

22 On the later history of legitim see Holdsworth, *A History of English Law* III 550–5; and T.F.T. Plucknett, *A Concise History of the Common Law*, 5th ed (London 1956) 745–6. Dower of chattels is declared legally impossible in the Year Book of 7 Henry IV; see Holdsworth, *A History of English Law* III 190 n7.

5

The Formation and Stability of Marriage in Fourteenth-Century England: Evidence of an Ely Register

Among the records that survive from Thomas Arundel's reign as bishop of Ely is a register showing the activities of his consistory court from March 1374 to March 1382. This volume is a rich source of information on the personnel, procedure, and efficiency of diocesan administration, as Margaret Aston's recent and excellent study of Arundel makes clear.[1] It is also possible to use the information supplied by this register to penetrate beneath the machinery of ecclesiastical government, which it describes so well, to the lives of the men and women of the diocese, to see to what extent this government served and guided the faithful and, occasionally, demanded their obedience. Considerable light is thrown on several areas where belief stated itself in daily life; one of them, the marriage practices of the time, is to be examined here. The register makes it possible to draw several useful conclusions on the effect of the theory and the canon law of marriage within the diocese of Ely late in the fourteenth century. Occasionally it becomes possible to move beyond the text of the law to see how it was interpreted by court and people and thus to find rare but valuable indications of the way in which this law was influencing the direction of society's development.

The matter that is to be discussed will be better understood if it is located in the broader historical and cultural panorama of which it is but a tiny part. Moral aspects of family life and marriage were matters of

The collection and interpretation of source material for this article was made possible by a Nuffield Foundation Travel Grant.

1 Cambridge, University Library, Ely Diocesan Records D 2 (1). See D.M. Owen, 'Ely Diocesan Records,' in *Studies in Church History*, ed C.W. Dugmore and C. Duggan (London 1964) I 177–8; and Margaret Aston, *Thomas Arundel: A Study of Church Life in the Reign of Richard II* (Oxford 1967) 52 n3.

serious consideration by Christians from the beginning. Already in the apostolic age certain doctrines and resulting practices were stated. As time went on and broader experience was gained by the Christian community, the consequences of these doctrines were revealed in greater detail. This process of examination and of explication reached a high point in the work of canonists and theologians from the twelfth through the fourteenth centuries. By the late fourteenth century, the Western Church had arrived at a general theory and description of the ends and practice of marriage that can be accepted as the background for all that is written here. These included an understanding of the purposes and agreement on the main qualities of marriage, a set of regulations establishing the capacity of the individual and the couple, extremely important notions on consent as that which constituted the marital bond, and formalities for the public exchange of this consent. Furthermore, the ecclesiastical courts had a highly developed jurisprudence for dealing with questions of law, a less perfect set of procedures for dealing with questions of fact, and means for the defence and support of the valid marriage.

This doctrine of marriage was slowly incorporated in the local law of the Western Church among peoples of widely varied traditions. Some of these traditions had contributed to the formation of the general law; others were more or less seriously threatened by its application. The process of adjustment was continuous and sometimes marred by bitter conflicts. In the long run the most important development was the adoption of the consensual theory of marriage by Alexander III and Innocent III and the exploitation of its consequences in the following decades. Not only was the consent of the spouses necessary for valid marriage, but in time it became evident that the consent of no other person was required. However much theologians and canonists stressed the importance of the social controls and supports of marriage, they had launched a new set of ideas whereby marriage would be considered from the point of view of the couple rather than from that of the extended family. The potential for an individualistic view of marriage in these ideas might not have been realized if the situation had permitted social controls to intervene later and force withdrawal from the union.[2] But since the consensual theory was linked with the teaching that a valid marriage was

---

2 This is the way the nurse reacted in *Romeo and Juliet* when Romeo had fled and Count Paris asked for Juliet's hand. She knew of the marriage of the young couple, but she said: 'Romeo is banished ... / Then since the case so stands as now it doth / I think it best you married with the Count' (III v 215, 218–19).

indissoluble, the possibilities were immense. It meant that medieval society had developed a theory of matrimony which enabled the individual to escape the control of family, feudal lord, and even the king in a choice of marriage partner.[3] The extent and the rate at which the understanding of this freedom spread through medieval society, the extent to which the freedom was used, are problems that remain to be answered. But when viewed in secular terms the consequences of this development are seen to be immense. It is true that there has been considerable ebb and flow as now individualism, now a broader social view of marriage have asserted themselves,[4] but the overall tendency has been in the direction of the individual's freedom. It is unlikely that all the consequences of those twelfth-century decisions have yet been realized in the West, though a new contest seems to be prepared as hitherto undreamed of social controls begin to appear among us.

Closely related to the development of the consensual theory was the conclusion that the private or clandestine marriage was valid. In part it was the logical if not very wise consequence of the theologian's teaching that the couple gave the sacrament to each other. Perhaps the canonists' tendency to simplify the required formalities of a legal act contributed to its acceptance. It is very likely that a way was prepared for it among different peoples by the survival of customs whereby men and women entered rather lightly into relationships considerably less serious in consequences and durability than Christian marriage. The danger of abuse was obvious; all through the Middle Ages councils, synods, and teachers at every level of instruction thundered against it. But it is significant that, however severe the penalties against the principals and all others associated with these marriages, there was no serious, long-term questioning of the validity of the act.[5] It would be several centuries before

---

3 A Juliet might not understand the strength of her position. Though her father could have prevented her from living with Romeo, her conscience, the Church, and society as a whole would not let her be Paris' wife. Of course she might be too frightened to try to maintain her position. Margery Paston resisted her mother, brothers, chaplain, and bishop to preserve her marriage to Richard Calle, *The Paston Letters*, nos 607, 617, ed J. Gairdner (London 1872–5, suppl 1901; repr Edinburgh 1910) II 347, 363–6.

4 Eg Catherine E. Holmes, *L'éloquence judiciaire de 1620 à 1660: Reflet des problèmes sociaux, religieux, et politiques de l'époque* (Paris 1967) 72–119. Cf DTC 9 II (1927) 2224–2316, s v 'Mariage'.

5 The teaching of English synods on this matter is studied in my article 'Marriage Theory and Practice in the Conciliar Legislation and Diocesan Statutes of Medieval England,' *Mediaeval Studies* 40 (1978) 408–60 (here pp 118–76).

the dilemma of the forbidden possibility would be resolved in a way that respected the unique right to consent by the spouses yet guaranteed sufficient publicity to provide a minimum of social control and support of the marriage.

The history of the theology and the general law of marriage in the Middle Ages has been the subject of careful study during the past two generations.[6] Already much is known of the application of the general law at the provincial and diocesan levels. The publishing of collections of sermons and, most recently, the beginnings of the study and edition of the *Summae confessorum* have made it possible to observe teaching and moral instruction on marriage at the level of pastoral care.[7] There remains the question of the extent of the influence of this teaching in society; one line of investigation contributing towards the answer is provided by the records of the ecclesiastical courts. It is true that these courts dealt with contentious matters and that their records were accordingly limited to those marriages that were in difficulties. However, it is possible to compensate for this bias and extract much valuable information: the scholar makes contact not only with the theory and general rules of marriage and with the more practically oriented advice of the moral guide but also with individual men and women, the problems they met in their marriages, and the way in which those problems were resolved. Several recent studies have analysed marriage practice as it appears in court records.[8] These analyses have been soundings, closely limited in time and space but yielding important information on the application of canon law, illustrating those areas where its rules were an easily accepted organiza-

6 See the bibliography assembled by Jean Dauvillier, *Le mariage dans le droit classique de l'Eglise depuis le Décret de Gratien (1140) jusqu'à la mort de Clément V (1314)* (Paris 1933) 491–540. Cf Gabriel Le Bras, 'Mariage: La doctrine du mariage chez les théologiens et les canonistes depuis l'an mille,' DTC 9 II 2123–2223, and 'Le mariage dans la théologie et le droit de l'Eglise du XIe au XIIIe siècle,' *Cahiers de civilisation médiévale* II (1968) 191–202; Claude Schahl, *La doctrine des fins du mariage dans la théologie scolastique*, Etudes de sciences religieuses 6 (Paris 1948).

7 See *Thomae de Chobham Summa confessorum*, ed F. Broomfield, Analecta mediaevalia Namurcensia 25 (Louvain 1968) 144–91; and Robert of Flamborough, *Liber poenitentialis: A Critical Edition with Introduction and Notes*, ed J.J. Francis Firth, Studies and Texts 18 (Toronto 1971) 63–9.

8 See Juliette M. Turlan, 'Recherches sur le mariage dans la pratique coutumière (XIIe–XVIe s.),' *Revue historique de droit français et étranger*, 4th ser, 35 (1957) 477–528; and Jean-Philippe Lévy, 'L'officialité de Paris et les questions familiales à la fin du XIVe siècle,' in *Etudes d'histoire du droit canonique dédiées à Gabriel Le Bras* (Paris 1965) II 1265–94.

tion of life as well as other areas where the law met serious opposition. The Ely register provides information on marital practice over an eight-year period in one of the smaller dioceses of England.

The evidence of the register takes on more meaning if an effort is made to sketch the size and quality of the population involved in the activity of the consistory court. The diocese of Ely corresponded almost exactly with the county of Cambridgeshire. Thirteen parishes on the eastern edge of the county north of Newmarket were an exception. They belonged to the deanery of Fordham in the diocese of Norwich.[9] The surviving poll-tax returns of 1377 are excellent for Cambridgeshire. They indicate a population of 30,974 persons, fourteen years old or over, for that year. J.C. Russell, arriving at a figure of about 50 per cent for those below the age of fourteen, projects a total of 46,461 laymen.[10] In addition there were 1,006 clerics, with a fairly high concentration of them at Cambridge and Ely, the only large centres of population in the county. Russell has carefully estimated the degree of under-enumeration and concludes that the tax of 1377 is nearest of all taxes of that period to a true estimate of population. He limits under-enumeration to 5 per cent. This amount would be offset – perhaps slightly more than offset – by the loss of the thirteen parishes in the deanery of Fordham mentioned above. Thus the court, whose register is under study here, dealt with a population of about 47,500 persons. From the point of view of marriage, the actual figure of the poll tax, 30,974, is a useful one, since fourteen was the cut-off age for the survey. The figure of 1,006 for the clergy is somewhat uncertain, since it is not possible to say how many of them were married. However, the proportion overall would be small, so a round figure of 31,000 for those married or eligible to marry can be accepted.

Unfortunately for the purposes of this study, the bishop's consistory was not the only court of the diocese that brought in judgments in marriage disputes. The other tribunal of the bishop, his court of audience, heard cases occasionally, and some of them dealt with problems touching matrimony and divorce.[11] Usually such disputes passed at some stage of the proceedings to the bishop's official and thus came to be included in his register. There are in addition a few disputes which, although the bishop carried them through to judgment, are recorded by the official.[12]

9 *The Victoria County History of Suffolk*, ed William Page (London 1907) II 12–13.
10 J.C. Russell, *British Medieval Population* (Albuquerque, N. Mex. 1948) 132ff.
11 Aston, *Arundel* 39–42.
12 Ibid 41; eg *Fisher* f 140r. [Note: the name of one of the principals in marginal rubrics

But Miss Aston notes one case where the bishop's exercise of jurisdiction is mentioned by accident;[13] she concludes that there were probably others of which there is record neither in the register of the official nor in that of the bishop himself. However, even though this did occur from time to time, direct exercise of jurisdiction by Bishop Arundel seems to have been comparatively rare. Thus the number of unreported marriage cases before the court of audience is not likely to have been large.

The court of the official of the archdeacon of Ely, however, is quite another matter. Thirteen of the 122 matrimonial suits that appear in the register involved the revision of sentences by this tribunal.[14] From early in the thirteenth century, in England as on the Continent, efforts had been made to withdraw matrimonial jurisdiction from the archdeacon; but it was not until the settlement made in 1401 by Arundel, when he was archbishop of Canterbury, that this ruling was effectively applied at Ely.[15] No records survive for the archdeacon's court, so that it is impossible to know the number or the types of matrimonial cases that came before it. Given the fact that for some at least this jurisdiction had the advantage of proximity, and – as the official of the bishop stated more than once – of a rather impressionistic sense of justice, it may have received many cases. In fact most of the appeals to the consistory from the archdeacon's court were in marriage disputes.[16] It seems necessary to conclude that these matters appeared frequently before the court of the archdeacon and that some of them have not been reflected in the register; their number must remain unknown.

indicates each appearance of a suit in the register; throughout this article, cases will be indicated by the rubric – as *Fisher* – with the number of the folio on which the case first appears. Additional references will be included as necessary.]

13 Aston, *Arundel* 41; *Gobat* f 143v: 'non curat ducere in uxorem Julianam Bigot ... prout alias iuravit et cui fuerat adiudicatus per venerabilem patrem et dominum, dominum Thomam.'

14 The following suits were appeals from the court of the archdeacon: *Grantesden* [*Gransden*] f 5v, *Deye* f 101, *Bonde* f 111, *Bargon* f 46v, *Wyldeman* f 61r, *Deynes* f 61r, *Niel* f 63v, *Arneld* f 85v, *Worlich* f 96v, *Martin* f 113v, *Tydd* f 119r; in addition *Chilterne* f 103r/v was an *ex officio* investigation of a decree of annulment by the archdeacon's court, and *Sterre* f 35v, which began as an instance case, involved the quashing of an earlier decision by the same court. Cf Aston, *Arundel* 98–109, 129–30; the author mentions twelve appeals, 98–9.

15 Aston, *Arundel* 88, 106–10. On the broader aspects of the problem see Paul Fournier, *Les officialités au moyen âge* (Paris 1880) 136; A. Amanieu, 'Archidiacre,' DDC 1 (1935) 948–1004; A.H. Thompson, *Diocesan Organization in the Middle Ages: Archdeacons and Rural Deans*, The Raleigh Lecture (London 1943); repr Proceedings of the British Academy 29 (London 1943).

16 Aston, *Arundel* 99 n2.

Finally, there were the jurisdictions exercised by the sacristan of Ely and the chancellor of the University of Cambridge. The court register includes an appeal from the sacristan's sentence in a matrimonial case and a statement of April 1376 by the official in which not only was the sentence confirmed but also the jurisdiction was approved.[17] However, the number of suits of this sort does not seem to have been significant. Very little is known of the jurisdiction of the chancellor of the university at this time, though it may be presumed to have had no more than incidental interest in matrimonial cases. Thus it can be concluded that, from the point of view of marriage disputes, the consistory had only one serious competitor, namely, the court of the archdeacon. If the records of this latter jurisdiction had survived, it is likely that marriage cases not accounted for otherwise would be found in considerable numbers. Therefore it is necessary to postulate an increase, perhaps a significant increase, in the number of cases of the type that will be studied in what follows.

The object of investigation, then, is a population of about 31,000 people of marriageable age seen in terms of the most important local court regulating and applying marriage law. One hundred and twenty-two cases, approximately one-quarter of the business that came before the consistory, dealt with inquiries and disputes about the marriage bond.[18] Directly concerned in these cases were 273 persons. The register ignores question of status completely except in one case where the information that the husband was of servile condition was a fact at issue.[19] However, eighteen of the principals are identified as household servants. Artisans, tavern-keepers, and clerks are found in considerable numbers. Scores seem to be peasants attached to manors in the countryside. (Until comparison with manorial court rolls has been made, it will not be possible to prove this surmise.) If any social group is likely to be underrepresented, it is the well-to-do. Such persons had more direct access to the bishop and would likely avail themselves of the advantage.[20] On the

---

17 *Clerk* f 26v; see Aston, *Arundel* 84–5.
18 Five hundred and nineteen separate items came before the court; this number includes many non-contentious causes, testament executions, interlocutory appeals, etc. Brian Woodcock found that about one-third of the cases before the consistory court at Canterbury during the years 1373–4 were matrimonial suits, *Medieval Ecclesiastical Courts of the Diocese of Canterbury* (London 1952) 85.
19 *Everard* f 55Bv: 'idem Johannes tempore dicti contractus ante et post fuit et adhuc est servus et nativus et servilis conditionis.'
20 Eg John Wedon's suit of marriage and divorce against Eleanor Francis and Geoffrey Cobbe, her *de facto* husband. The suit began before Arundel's commissaries in

other hand, the consequences of this fact should not be over-stressed, for there were powerful reasons urging them to see that decisions touching their cases should be enrolled. The provision of processes in cases of appeal, later questions touching validity, legitimacy of children, and the transfer of property at the time of marriage all demanded that a written record survive. Thus it seems not unreasonable to conclude that the principals of the marriage suits that appear in the register form a spectrum that, with the possible under-representation of the upper class, accurately reflects non-clerical Cambridgeshire society as a whole.

Clandestine marriage had long been a problem in the West. In fact, bishops and councils as well as other teachers had been forbidding it for centuries before the period of the Ely register.[21] Beginning late in the twelfth century local attempts to improve the situation were made by supplementing the oft-repeated prohibition by a positive requirement.[22] These arrangements were characterized by a demand that the local priest make a public announcement of a proposed marriage sufficiently in advance so that anyone who saw reason for objecting to the union would have time to do so. This procedure became of general application with canon 51 of the Fourth Lateran Council. The priest was required to announce the marriage and to investigate the couple's freedom from impediment. Detailed implementation of this ruling was worked out in subsequent years on a local basis. In England the reading of the banns on three Sundays or major feasts had been long in use by the period of interest here. This procedure served two broad purposes: it required the friends and neighbours of the couple to examine the past and report any impediment that prevented marriage; it protected the marriage in the future by increasing its publicity.[23] Thus the reading of the banns not only tended to prevent the duplicity to which the couple might be tempted; it also helped them to avoid the dangers of ignorance and the self-deception to which they were prone before marriage and after it.

December 1378 (*Wedon* f 79v), but the bishop summoned the parties and named the commission on 10 September, Register of Thomas Arundel, Cambridge, University Library, Ely Diocesan Records G 1 f 24v. On Geoffrey Cobbe see Aston, *Arundel* 39, 142.

21 See DDC 3 (1942) 795–801, s v 'Clandestinité'; Adhémar Esmein, *Le mariage en droit canonique*, ed Robert Génestal and Jean Dauvillier, 2nd ed (Paris 1929–35) I 205–7.

22 Ibid I 25–6, 202–4; and *Thomae de Chobham*, ed Broomfield 146 n6.

23 Thomas of Chobham adds that those who hear the banns should speak against the marriage immediately; afterwards they may not object (146–7); cf X IV 18 6.

The implementation of this system is illustrated in detail in the Ely register. Occasionally, objection to a proposed marriage seems to have been made on the spot. The point is illustrated by the following:[24] 'In the publication of banns in the chapel of March between John Dany and Alice Lenton of March, in the diocese of Ely, a certain Joan Gibbe, also of March, opposed the banns, making a claim. Because of this, she was cited before us ... the Thursday after the feast of St Hilary [15 January] 1377, in the church of the Holy Trinity in the city of Ely, to propose and show the cause of her claim in legal form. The said day and place she appeared before us personally and proposed as the cause of her claim that she and John had contracted marriage.[25] Therefore she asked that John be judged her husband.' In other words, Alice alleged pre-contract with John and, in effect, accused him of attempting bigamy. In such cases, as here, the court proceeded to hear her claim as in an instance suit. At other times, objection to a proposed marriage was delayed. The information conveyed in the banns would spread beyond the circle of hearers to others who might be aware of an impediment. Eventually the pastor would be informed; he was expected to refuse to solemnize the marriage.[26]

The register includes twelve suits that rose from objections to marriage following the reading of the banns. In six cases, the objectors (two men and four women) claimed pre-contract. Five failed to prove their allegation.[27] In another case that did not come to sentence in the period of the register, a proposed marriage was met by several objections, including pre-contract of the woman and affinity arising from her sexual union with a man related to her proposed husband within the forbidden degree.[28] The impediment of affinity appears in four other cases as well. In three of the four the allegation was proved, so the parties were not allowed to marry.[29] The same result occurred in a single example of an

---

24 *Dany Gibbe* f 61v.
25 Contract is expressed: 'per verba de presenti mutuum consensum eorum exprimentia, seu per verba de futuro, carnali copula subsecuta.' This clause is discussed below, 244 (here p 55).
26 Eg in January 1379 John Slory and Joan, daughter of John Feltwell, both of Chesterton, claimed that their banns were read three times without objection. Later, having learned of affinity within the forbidden degree, the vicar and chaplain of Chesterton refused to solemnize the marriage, *Slory* f 108r.
27 *Sadelere* f 47r, *Pateshull* f 57v, *Dany Gibbe* f 61v–62r, *Blofeld* f 90r, *Myntemor* f 137v. The objection was successful in *Fisher* f 82v, 111r.
28 *Andrew* f 149v.
29 Marriage was forbidden in *Slory* f 108r, *Page* f 113r, and *Byleye* [*Biley*] f 136v–137r. It was allowed in *Barbour* f 152r. Penance was given to Alice Cok, who seems to have

objection based on the consanguinity of the couple.[30] Thus it appears from this small sampling that objections to proposed marriages on the basis of an impediment of consanguinity or affinity were more likely to prove effective than those based on a claim of pre-contract. Since claims of the latter type led to suits before the court, it is probable that all or nearly all objections based on pre-contract were included in the register. On the other hand, the discovery of impediments of consanguinity and affinity resulting from the publications of the banns may well be under-reported, since it is likely that such revelation sometimes led to a decision to abandon the marriage, ending the matter without leaving a trace.[31]

If no objection were raised to a proposed union announced in the banns, the couple solemnized their marriage by an exchange of consent before the Church (*coram facie ecclesie*). The reading of the banns and this public religious act constituted the duly solemnized marriage; all other unions were clandestine. This distinction between the solemn and the clandestine is a commonplace in the history of the canon law of marriage. However, it is a drastic simplification, one which can easily lead to misunderstanding, not only of the law but especially of the social history and the sacramental theology of the time.[32] The term 'clandestine' includes a bewildering variety of forms for exchanging consent, and rather hard questions have to be asked of the accepted notion of a solemn marriage. As it happens, the opening stages of most of the marriage cases in the Ely register were pleaded orally. Much of the discussion of the way in which couples proceeded to marriage survives there. Thus it is possible to illustrate the various procedures whereby the nuptial bond was established.

been responsible for the objection. It should be noted that the register usually mentions earlier marriages; there is no indication of this in these affinity cases. Thus there is reason to conclude that the impediment arose from fornication. On the other hand, no penances were assigned.

30 *Stanhard* f 95v.
31 Thus *Stanhard* could easily have disappeared from view. It came before the court because the couple considered the vicar of Bourn to have refused to solemnize after reading the banns 'absque causa rationabili quacumque'; cf f 108r, 130v.
32 Note the use of the term in the following: in May 1376 John, son of Thomas Lister, and Margaret, stepdaughter of Robert Ballard, were cited 'super contractu matrimoniali inter eosdem, ut dicitur, clandestine inito.' They replied that they were married 'per verba de presenti ... non tamen clandestine, sed publice, testibus adhibitis, premissa debita bannorum editione.' The court decided for the marriage and ordered it to be solemnized, *Lister* f 47v.

At one extreme was the marriage exactly in accord with the demands of canon law and local custom. After financial arrangements had been made by the families concerned, the betrothal took place. This consisted of a promise to marry (*per verba de futuro*) and often was expressed as a form of words before witnesses. Next the banns were read in the parish church. If no objection to the marriage resulted, or if objections had been dealt with in a satisfactory way, the couple publicly solemnized their union by an exchange of consent (*per verba de presenti*) at the church door. This would be seen as the moment when the sacrament was given by the couple to each other. The ceremonies before witnesses included the endowment of the bride, her delivery by her father to her husband, and various rituals, including a form of words and the giving of a ring. Finally, the bridal party entered the church for the nuptial mass.[33]

Such was the duly performed marriage. But, given the distinction between requirements for liceity and those for validity, a profound, though not necessarily a visible, change could be introduced into this pattern at any point. Betrothal followed by intercourse became marriage. The contract *per verba de presenti* could be entered into before the public event at the door of the church whenever the couple chose. However difficult such acts might be to defend or prove in the public forum, they were considered to be valid, and theologians as well as others of informed and refined conscience would insist that they were so. Furthermore, conditions of family consent, financial arrangements, etc could be inserted in the proceedings, and the realization of the condition might not be possible until after the event at the church door. In fact, in one sense the banns themselves became a condition. Thus in seven of the cases mentioned above, where the reading of the banns led to a challenge of the proposed marriage, the notes on the case reveal that the contract *per verba de presenti* had occurred before the banns were read.[34] In two other cases

33 The stages of marriage are described in episcopal statutes and in liturgical books. See, among many, Statutes of London II (1245×59) c43, *Councils and Synods with Other Documents Relating to the English Church, 2: A.D. 1205–1313*, ed F.M. Powicke and C.R. Cheney (Oxford 1964) I 643; Statutes of Exeter II (1287) c7, ibid II 996–9; *The Sarum Missal Edited from Three Early Manuscripts*, ed J. Wickham Legg (Oxford 1916) 413–18. Cf George C. Homans, *English Villagers of the Thirteenth Century* (Cambridge, Mass. 1942) 160–76; Michael M. Sheehan, 'The Influence of Canon Law on the Property Rights of Married Women in England,' *Mediaeval Studies* 25 (1963) 114 n22 (here p 21).

34 The court's clear understanding of this fact is illustrated by *Stanhard* f 95v. The record begins: 'Ad nostrum nuper pervenit auditum quod Thomas, filius Johannis Stanhard, et Agnes, filia Johannis Molt de Brunne, matrimonium ad invicem per

where the completion of solemnization was delayed after the banns, the cause of delay seems to have been second thoughts on the part of one of the principals. But the development of the suits shows that the court considered the marriages to have been validly contracted already. In the first of these suits, Joan sought to avoid completing the marriage after the banns were read, having discovered that John Everard, with whom she had exchanged consent, was a serf. The formula of consent repeated to the court by Joan is somewhat vague and could be interpreted as a promise *per verba de futuro*.[35] But John's description, though it lacks the freshness of Joan's words, being expressed in the general formula, makes it clear that he considered the contract to have been *per verba de presenti*.[36] This reading of the text is supported by the fact that, having satisfied itself that John's status was known before the exchange of consent, the court declared the couple man and wife, ordering them to solemnize their marriage.[37] In a similar situation, though one with different ramifications, William de Potton and Agnes Knotte were said to have exchanged consent before witnesses and to have had intercourse; but after the banns were read, William entered the hospital of St John, Cambridge, was professed, and received the subdiaconate. The court pronounced for their marriage, declaring William's religious profession and reception of order to have been invalid.[38]

From examples such as these – and there are many more – it becomes evident that in some cases the reading of the banns and the solemn exchange of consent before the Church, acts that in sequence and form may have seemed correct realizations of the canon law of marriage, were actually the publicity of an act that, so far as validity was concerned, was

verba de presenti mutuum consensum eorundem exprimentia legitime contraxerunt.' The court judged that the vicar of Bourn acted correctly in refusing to solemnize the marriage and concluded 'ideo matrimonium inter vos contractum, si quis initus fuerat, non posse subsistere nec debere' (f 119v). Also *Blofeld* f 90r, *Slory* f 108r, *Page* f 113r, *Byleye* f 136v, *Myntemor* f 137v, *Barbour* f 152v.

35 *Everard* f 55Bv: 'Johanna ... fatebatur quod contraxerunt sub forma que sequitur et non alio modo; dictus Johannes quesivit ab eadem sub ista forma: "Vis te habere me in virum"; et ipsa respondit "Sic"; et quod placuit sibi. Fatetur etiam dicta Johanna quod postea procurarunt banna edi in facie ecclesie.'

36 John claimed 'matrimonium ad invicem per verba de presenti mutuum consensum eorundem exprimentia contraxerunt, quem quidem contractum utrique eorum in alterius et aliorum fidedignorum presencia fatebantur et recognoverunt et super quibus publica fama dinoscitur laborare' (ibid).

37 See f 58v–59r.

38 *Potton Knotte* f 139r.

already complete.[39] There are certain analogies here with transfers of land in the twelfth century, where the ritual attending the preparation and transfer of a charter was but the preparation of an undying memory of a legal act that had occurred some time before.

Although some of the defendants summoned before the Ely consistory showed a rather nonchalant attitude to the banns,[40] the general impression is that when they were used they proved to be an effective weapon against the abuses to which the clandestine union lent itself. For that reason many sought to avoid the banns. This was true not only of the large group that avoided religious ceremonies entirely but also of some of those who for various reasons chose to exchange consent solemnly before the Church. This effectiveness of the publication of the banns as contrasted with the solemn exchange of consent – an act which proved more amenable of convenient adjustment – is revealed not only in local English law but also in the day-by-day activity of the Ely court.

Cum inhibitio, canon 51 of the Fourth Lateran Council, prescribed the publication of a couple's intent to marry – the procedure that became known as the publication of banns. In this canon the new provision was situated within the broader context of a general prohibition of clandestine marriage (including the punishment of those who presumed to marry secretly or in spite of objection to the announcement of their intention), the legal status of their children, and the suspension of clergy who disobeyed the ruling of the Council. In 1328, *Cum inhibitio* was cited in a statute of Archbishop Simon Mepham.[41] But here all interest was focused on the banns as the means of avoiding the dangers of clandestine marriage; thus though the Lateran canon was to be explained to the people in the vernacular, what was specified was the reading of the banns and the punishment of priests who took part in marriage contracts not preceded by publication. One further precision was included: marriages

---

39 See Esmein, *Le mariage en droit canonique* I 207–9. Homans, *English Villagers* 164 cited examples of this form of marriage in the sixteenth century and suggested that it might have been found in thirteenth-century England as well.

40 *Lovechild* f 137v: the couple agreed that they had contracted *de presenti* and the husband said the banns were read, though the wife denied it; *Halfpeny* f 29r: the couple admitted contract *de presenti* and intercourse and that 'iuraverunt de dictum matrimonium sollemnizando in facie ecclesie,' but four years had elapsed without their doing so; *Page* f 113r: the couple contracted marriage in May 1377, and objection to the reading of their banns reached the court in March 1379.

41 *Concilia Magnae Britanniae et Hiberniae, 446–1718,* ed David Wilkins (London 1737) II 554.

were to be celebrated in churches or chapels of parochial right. Otherwise, the priest, whether secular or religious, had to obtain the licence of the bishop. The implication, that those planning marriage were sometimes moving the solemnization of their union away from their parish church, became explicit in *Humana concupiscentia*, a canon of Archbishop John Stratford's provincial council of London, 1342. In a remarkable introduction to this canon several interesting reflections were made on the effectiveness of public control of marriage through the banns and on the desirability of solemnization before the Church. It is stated that many persons, seeking the respectability that the solemn act gave their union but aware of an impediment and of the fact that local publication of their intent would render solemnization impossible, went to a distant place where they were unknown and there married before a priest, without banns and at unsuitable times and seasons. They would then live as man and wife either in the place of marriage or in their original parish. Admitting that court procedures had proved unable to deal with the problem, the council decreed major excommunication, *ipso facto*, of those who proceeded in this manner and of priests who assisted at such unions. The same penalty was applied to any priest who solemnized the marriage of non-parishioners without permission of those charged with their care; this penalty was to be incurred even if the marriage were licit.[42]

Violation of *Humana concupiscentia* was a main point at issue in ten of the marriage cases that came before the Ely consistory. The unworthy motive for solemnization mentioned by the canon is found, though the obstacles it was used to overcome were sometimes quite different: marriages were solemnized in this way in an attempt to override an objection made explicit after the publication of banns or to present the court with a fait accompli, when a marriage was under its scrutiny. One case in the register, that of John Anegold and Joan Andrew, seems to have been exactly as described in the introduction to *Humana concupiscentia*. When summoned, they admitted that, although they were aware of the impediment between them, they left the diocese and, in a place where they were unknown, solemnized their marriage without a licence. They were declared excommunicated and, when they sought reconciliation, were assigned penance. The penance was performed.[43] The case of John Slory and Joan, widow of John Feltwell, began in exactly the same way. However, as the suit developed, it became clear that the banns had been

---

42 Ibid II 707. Mepham's rule on marriage in churches of parochial right was repeated.
43 *Anegold* f 108v.

published and that it was only after some time that the vicar of Chesterton learned that there seemed to be an impediment of affinity between
them. Acting as *Humana concupiscentia* said they should, the vicar and his
chaplain refused to solemnize the marriage. The couple then left the
diocese, were married in contravention of the statute, and returned home
to live as man and wife until summoned by the court.[44] What seems to
be involved in this case is less a desire to comply with the requirements
of canon law than an attempt to use them to obtain a form of public
approval for their marriage which could override the opposition to it that
became explicit with the reading of the banns.

A somewhat different purpose may lie behind a series of events
involving Hugh Candlesby, registrar of the archdeacon of Ely. When the
banns of his marriage to Alice, widow of James le Eyr (alias, James
Fisher) were published, Agnes Pateshull objected.[45] Summoned before the
court she claimed pre-contract with Hugh and added that he intended to
complete the publication of banns in the privacy that an unusual time –
vespers of a feast – allowed, and then solemnize his marriage in spite of
her claim. Agnes asked the court to inhibit solemnization or any other
contract.[46] This was done under pain of major excommunication. Agnes
was given her day in court, but Hugh denied her claim. She had to admit
that there was no proof, and the case went against her. In spite of all,
Hugh and Alice had gone ahead with their plans, finding an available
priest in Hugh's friend, John Grebby, commissary of the archdeacon's
official.[47] There are many unanswered problems in this case, but some
points can be made. First, Hugh seems to have tried to achieve something
close to a proper publication of banns by the adjustment mentioned
above. Further, it is likely that he tried to strengthen his position against
Agnes by presenting the court with a fait accompli, his solemnized union
with Alice. As matters developed, this was unnecessary; but there is a hint
that Agnes presented a weaker case than was possible to her, so that the

44 *Slory* f 108r. The chaplain of the parish church of Wilberton solemnized the mar-
    riage of John Frost and Amy, widow of Robert Brid, in spite of objection by John
    Fisher, *Wilberton Mustell* f 82v–83r. See Aston, *Arundel* 123–4.
45 *Pateshull* f 57v–58r.
46 Here there is an intimation that if Hugh and Alice solemnized their marriage, Ag-
    nes' position would be weaker. This notion that the fact of solemnization strength-
    ened the case for a marriage occurs frequently. In *Kele* f 149v, where William Kele
    sought the annulment of his marriage to his wife Helen, claiming pre-contract and
    intercourse with Alice Burgoyne, Helen presented a single defence: 'idem Robertus
    ipsam duxit in facie ecclesie in uxorem secuta debita sollemnitate.' The case was not
    carried further in the register.
47 *Candlesby* f 58r; on Hugh see Aston, *Arundel* 77–9, 97, 121–6, 142–3.

solemnization of the marriage may have been but one of Hugh's lines of defence.[48]

Whatever the motives of this rather sinister man may have been, the attempt to use the fact of solemnization to influence the decision of the court is well illustrated by the troubles of John Draper of Cambridge in the summer of 1375. Agnes Durant and Alice Cakebred launched two suits claiming him as husband on 6 June.[49] Agnes claimed contract *de presenti*, which John denied. Alice claimed contract and intercourse; to this John agreed. Alice then went with John to her home parish in the diocese of London and there they solemnized marriage, contravening the statute 'ut sub matrimonii velamine possent carnis copulam perniciosam et illicitam liberius adimplere.'[50] After an interval they returned to Cambridge and lived as husband and wife. They must have enjoyed their new status only a few days, for on 5 July they were brought before the bishop's official, to whom they confessed what they had done. On 21 July excommunication was pronounced; five days later the court brought in a decision in favour of the marriage of Agnes Durant and John.[51]

A variation of this abuse of solemnization is found in a few cases where the intervention of the court threatened to enforce a contract of dubious status. Thus early in July 1375, John Saffrey and Alice, daughter of Richard Molt, were cited *ex officio* about a clandestine marriage of which there was rumour.[52] John claimed contract; Alice proved difficult to bring into court and was declared contumacious. Finally after a month she appeared, promised obedience to the decisions of the consistory, and was absolved. The fifth of October was set as the date of her reply to John's claim, but in the interval she solemnized marriage with William Martin. Her father seems to have arranged the wedding; he, as well as the

---

48 Agnes said that she could not prove her marriage to Hugh; the register continues: 'iuratisque partibus predictis de malicia et de collusione vitanda; idem dicunt sicut prius' (f 58r). The oaths *de calumpnia et de veritate dicenda* were taken at the usual place in proceedings, after the *litis contestatio*. The oaths *de malicia* and *de collusione* were required during Agnes' first term after she announced her inability to prove her claim. Hugh had already married Alice by this time. Miss Aston rightly surmised that Hugh's escapade is to be related to the decision at the synod of May 1377 to republish *Humana concupiscentia* (76).

49 *Cakebred* f 48r, *Durant* f 48r. The suits coalesced at the moment of sentence, f 52v.

50 *Draper Cakebred* f 53r. In *Concilia*, ed Wilkins II 707 the phrase from the introduction to *Humana concupiscentia* is 'ut sub matrimonii contecti velamine possint carnis operam perniciosam et illicitam liberius adimplere.'

51 Cf *Grantesden* f 5r and *Bonde* f 11r.

52 *Saffrey* f 27r.

couple, was excommunicated.[53] Another form of this type of case first appears in the register in July 1380, as an inquiry of Stephan Gobat: why did he not take Juliana Bigod as wife as he had sworn to do after a sentence by the bishop?[54] Gobat replied that he could not marry her because of affinity between them, resulting from Juliana's earlier carnal union with William Attemor, to whom he was related within the forbidden degree. The case took a new turn in March 1381, when Stephan Pertefeu claimed contract *de presenti* with Juliana, asking that she be judged his wife.[55] Whether Juliana found some way of winning Gobat's heart is unclear; but on 5 April, when the suit next appeared before the court, he withdrew his statement that he was related to Attemor within the forbidden degree and claimed that his marriage to Juliana was prior to her contract with Pertefeu. On 3 May they left Sawston and went to the parish of Westley, where their marriage was solemnized before witnesses. Three weeks later they admitted the fact before the court and were declared excommunicated in virtue of *Humana concupiscentia*. Finally, on 12 November, the court brought in its sentence: the earlier objection of an impediment of affinity was vindicated and Pertefeu was declared Juliana's husband.[56]

Thus the abuse of solemnization went considerably beyond that indicated in the introduction to *Humana concupiscentia*, occurring not only where the publication of banns would make impediments explicit but especially where the impossibility of marriage had become public knowledge or was under examination by the court. Given the rapid and strict manner with which these ceremonies were treated by the Ely consistory, it is not easy to see why they were attempted. One fact remains clear, however: though many men and women of that age sought to avoid marriage before the Church, there were more than a few who tried to use the ceremony to avoid the very control of marriage that solemnization was intended to provide.

Complete or partial performance of the formalities required by the Church is characteristic of the marriages discussed thus far. The couples

---

53 They claimed that the case was pending before the archdeacon's court. John Saffrey's suit continued for six months, but Alice never appeared. The case then disappeared from the register, f 40v.

54 *Gobat* f 143r.

55 *Pertefeu* f 148r.

56 *Pertefeu* f 149r, 150v, 155v. Neither Juliana nor Gobat was present in court for sentence. A note for execution continued in the register until February 1382, when an inhibition was received from the court of Canterbury (*Gobat* f 160v). The register ends with the entry for the next consistory so it is not possible to trace the suit further.

in question may have published their banns and exchanged consent solemnly before the Church in the ordinary course of their courtship, or they may have been driven by circumstances to a solemnization that they would have preferred to avoid. In either case public canonical formalities were executed. Many other suits before the consistory revealed marriages in which such procedures were completely absent. This is the large and rather complex category of the clandestine marriage. When these unions are examined in the light of the Ely register, it is found that, while they indeed lacked the formalities required by canon law, it would be a serious error to conclude that they were performed without ceremony or ritual. In fact, many were formal public acts which satisfied the couple that they had entered a contract, assured them of witnesses, and made it possible for the marriage to be generally known in the neighbourhood.

In the cases involving clandestine marriages which came before the Ely consistory the contract between the couple was sometimes described with considerable care. The most common type was the contract *per verba de presenti*.[57] The register indicated that about half of these unions were consummated.[58] The betrothal or promise to marry, rendered a binding, permanent union by intercourse, is found less frequently.[59] In about thirty cases an omnibus phrase was used that guaranteed the existence of contract in one form or another: 'matrimonium ad invicem per verba de presenti, mutuum consensum eorundem exprimentia, seu per verba de futuro, carnali copula subsecuta, legitime contraxerunt.'[60] Fourteen of the contracts examined by the court were conditional.[61]

---

57 Eg *Lister* f 47v: 'fatebantur se matrimonium ad invicem contraxisse per verba de presenti.'

58 Eg *Symond* f 28v: 'fatentur quod contraxerunt matrimonium ad invicem per verba de presenti, mutuum consensum eorundem exprimentia, carnali copula subsecuta.'

59 The usual expression, as in *Colne* f 161r, is 'contraxerunt ad invicem per verba de futuro, carnali copula subsecuta.' Cf *Leicester* f 55Ar: 'fatebantur quod promiserunt se mutuo se invicem habituros in virum et uxorem et quod postmodum inter eos carnalis copula sepius intervenit.' The term 'sponsalia' occurs occasionally, as in *Sadelere* f 47r.

60 *Band* f 39r, cf *Sterre* f 35v. A similar clause is often used in reporting the opening stage of *ex officio* suits in the register. Thus in *Saffrey* f 27r: 'Fama publica referente, ad nostrum pervenit auditum quod Johannes Saffrey de Wynepol et Alicia, filia Ricardi Molt de Wendeye, diocesis Eliensis, matrimonium ad invicem clandestine contraxerunt per verba de presenti seu per verba de futuro, carnali copula subsecuta, nec curant dictum matrimonium in facie ecclesie, iuxta ritum ecclesie facere solempnizari.' The more common form employed in the register is '[N] citatus super contractu matrimoniali ... fama publica referente'; eg *Bocher* f 11v.

61 Examples are given below, 246 (here pp 57–8). On the special group of cases where the condition was future intercourse, see below, 254–5 (here pp 66–7).

In many cases it can be shown that the clandestine contract was made in a series of acts involving forms of words and ritual actions. A good example is provided in the evidence of Alexander Wrighte and Isabel, daughter of Joan of Wisbech, when they appeared to answer an inquiry about their reputed marriage: 'fatebantur quod vir dixit mulieri ista verba, "Vis tu esse uxor mea?" et ipsa respondit quod sic. Et tunc dictus Alexander affidavit dictam Isabellam quod ipsam duceret in uxorem et strinxerunt manum in manu, et fatentur quod dictus Alexander dedit eidem Isabelle munera, videlicet, unum flameolum et unum loculum.'[62] Several moments can be distinguished in the proceedings described here. First, there was Alexander's question of Isabel and her indication of a desire to marry him. Next, Alexander pledged to marry her, probably in a form of words that is omitted; at the same time there was a ritual joining of hands. The third moment involved the endowment of Isabel with a kerchief and a little chest.

Several forms of words are given in the register; with minor variations most of them can be reduced to two types, those stating a promise of marriage and those indicating contract *de presenti*. The former, the evidence of those all-too-fragile agreements followed by sexual union, are the most frequently reported in detail. Such are the words 'Hic fides mea: habebo te in uxorem et nullam aliam' that Katherine, daughter of Geoffrey Bugge, alleged were said to her by John Rigges.[63] A form of words expressing contract *de presenti* is found in the evidence that John Page and Margery Chapman gave during the suit that began as a result of their belated publication of banns: 'contraxerunt ad invicem matrimonium per ista verba: "Accipio te in virum et ad hoc do tibi fidem meam"; et "Ego accipio te in uxorem et ad hoc do tibi fidem meam"; et quod posuit dicte Margerie annulum in digito; et postmodum eam carnaliter cognovit.'[64] In some cases it is difficult to decide to what type of contract a form of words belongs. In the Lovechild case, for example, Tilla Taillor's version of the contract *de presenti* was explicit: 'contraxerunt ad

---

62 *Wrighte* f 25v.

63 *Rigges* f 8r. Some variations: *Fordham* f 69r: 'fatentur quod promiserunt se invicem ducturos in virum et uxorem sub ista forma "Ego volo habere te in virum", et "Ego volo habere te in uxorem"; fatebantur etiam quod postea se invicem carnaliter cognoverunt'; *Snow* f 98v: Agnes claimed 'quod ipsi Johannes et Agnes matrimonium ad invicem contraxerunt per ista verba "Numquam ducam aliam nisi te," nec capellanus [?] pro me, et ad hoc do tibi fidem meam, carnali copula subsecuta.' The meaning of 'nec capellanus pro me' is not clear.

64 *Page* f 113r.

invicem matrimonium per ista verba "Ego accipio te in uxorem meam";
et "Ego accipio te in virum meum."' But John Lovechild's information
was less clear: 'Johannes fatetur quod ipse dixit eidem Tille ista verba
"Volo te habere in uxorem" et quod ipsa consentiit.'[65] Is 'Volo' in John's
phrase meant to imply a promise to marry in the future or, as is more
likely, does it mean 'I want you to be my wife now'? A similar difficulty
appears in the *ex officio* inquiry about the clandestine marriage of John
Saffrey and Alice, daughter of Richard Molt. John described the formalities: 'contraxerunt per ista, videlicet, verba: "Volo te habere in virum"; et
"Ego volo te habere in uxorem"; et adhuc mutuo dederunt fidem, tenendo
manum in manu.'[66] Here as in the account of the Wrighte case, quoted
in the previous paragraph, the form of words and ritual acts are described,
but it is not clear whether the joining of hands related to a promise to
marry or to a plighting of troth *de presenti*. This uncertainty must have
been fairly widespread where unsophisticated men and women, moved by
who knows what desires and pressures, tried to establish a relationship
within the categories and the procedures demanded by a custom which
in part was the debris of a culture that no longer existed and in part was
a ritual statement of a new and vastly different view of marriage.[67]

The form of words used in conditional contracts also maintained the
distinction between the promise to marry and the contract *de presenti*. As
the logic of the situation would lead one to expect, conditional contracts
de futuro were the more common.[68] Thus in one of the rare cases where
family consent was involved, John Borewelle informed the court 'quod
promisit ipsam Margaretam ducere in uxorem sub ista condicione et

65 *Lovechild* f 137v.
66 *Saffrey* f 27r.
67 This is illustrated by the questioning of Margery Paston by the bishop of Norwich
    about her agreement with Richard Calle. The bishop 'said that he would understand
    the words that she had said to him [Calle], whether it made matrimony or not.' The
    letter continues: 'And she rehearsed what she had said, and said if tho words made
    it not sure she said boldly that she would make it surer ere than she went thence;
    for she said she thought in her conscience she was bound, whatsoever the words
    wern.' See *The Paston Letters: A Selection in Modern Spelling*, ed Norman Davis
    (London 1963) 182; in Gairdner's edition, the letter is no 617, II 364. The court's
    activity itself illustrates the difficulty. The Wrighte case entered the register 24 May
    1375. The court was to pronounce on the couple's confession the next day. Though
    the suit was noted in each consistory until it disappeared after 25 October 1380, it
    made no further progress. In many cases the present or future meaning of 'volo' is
    clear from the context.
68 Cf Esmein, *Le mariage en droit canonique* I 191–8.

forma "Volo habere te in uxorem meam si parentes mei consentiant."
Fatetur etiam quod ipsa respondit "Volo te habere in virum meum."'[69] A
similar condition appears in the Bradenho case, though this time it was
attached to a contract that is called *de presenti*. Philip, son of Richard
Bradenho, informed the court 'quod ipse et prefata Johanna matrimonium
ad invicem contraxerunt per verba de presenti mutuum consensum
eorum exprimentia, videlicet, per ista verba "Ego volo habere te in
uxorem"; et super hoc posuit fidem suam in manus cuiusdam Johannis
filii Thome de March; et "Ego volo habere te in virum."' Joan did not
object to the form of words but pointed out that the contract was
conditioned by her parents' consent.[70]

As will be evident from the above quotations, the register contains
information on the use of formal actions as well as forms of words in
clandestine marriages. The oath or pledge, which in most cases[71] was part
of the contract *de presenti*, seems to have included the joining of hands,[72]
and, in two cases, the pledge was delivered by a third person.[73] In the
Page suit the pledging is associated with the gift and reception of a ring.[74]
Finally, as in the gift of a kerchief and a coffer by Alexander Wrighte, the
ancient ritual that survived in the liturgy as the endowment of the bride

---

69 *Borewelle* f 73v–74r. Cf *Lyngewode* f 154v: 'Volo te ducere in uxorem si bene facias.' In
the Lungedon case the condition was the bride's freedom to marry. Two slightly
different versions of the form were given; they provide the same information and
give reason for thinking that the forms of words were reported carefully. John
Lungedon said that he contracted with the words 'Si sis libera ab omni viro, volo te
habere in uxorem.' In Margaret's version he said: 'Hic fides mea, volo ducere te in
uxorem meam et nunquam ducam aliam nisi te, si sis libera ab aliis.' John added
'quod ipsa nihil respondit.' They had intercourse; but Margaret was not free,
Lungedon f 71v.

70 'Johanna ... fatebatur contractum matrimoniale inter eos initum sub ista conditione,
si parentes illius Johanne consenserint,' *Bradenho* f 119v.

71 But the Wrighte case, cited above, n62, might have been a contract *de futuro*. It
included an *affidatio*.

72 In Jan van Eyck's painting in the National Gallery, London (no 186), the gesture of
Giovanni Arnolfini and Jeanne de Chenamy may indicate this moment in a clandestine contract. The place and formality of the scene, the single candle, and the
presence of third parties support the interpretation of the painting. Cf Erwin Panof-
sky, 'Jan van Eyck's *Arnolfini* Portrait,' *Burlington Magazine* 64 (1934) 117–27.

73 *Bradenho* f 119v, *Bradenham* f 144r. Homans associated the *manu media* with the
betrothal (*English Villagers* 161), but both these contracts were specifically stated to be
de presenti. Note, however, that they were conditioned contracts.

74 *Page* f 119v.

at the church door continued to find a place in some clandestine ceremonies.

Descriptions of the contracts establishing clandestine marriages
sometimes included information on the circumstances in which the
exchange of consent occurred. A good example is provided by the description of proceedings in the Band case, where the circumstances of the
contract and their consequences are set out in detail: 'Thomas et Isabella
matrimonium ad invicem per verba de presenti mutuum consensum eorundem exprimentia, seu per verba de futuro, carnali copula subsecuta,
legitime contraxerunt, quem quidem contractum uterque eorum in alterius et aliorum fidedignorum presencia ex certa sciencia fatebatur, recognovit, innovavit et publicavit, super quibus labor at publica vox et fama in
villis de Chestreford, Trippelawe et locis aliis convicinis.'[75] Several
important points should be noticed in this text. First, a consensual notion
of marriage is apparently involved: it is made clear that both principals
were present and that each of them spoke the words of contract, understanding their import. Second, the act was performed in the presence of
witnesses. Finally, the fact of the contract between the couple was
successfully communicated to their circle of acquaintance.

Enough has been written above to explain the role of the couple in the
ritual of the marital contract. However, one clause from the account of the
Band marriage requires comment. The words 'fatebatur, recognovit, innovavit et publicavit' are redolent of the acts of purchase and donation found
in land charters; it would not be unreasonable to suspect that such clauses
had become *de cursu* and that they should not be stressed as an indication
of the publicity of the marriage in question.[76] On the other hand, when
the clause is examined in the accounts of other contracts, it becomes
evident that there is a variety in the verbs chosen, a possible indication of
a variety of modes of publicity.[77] Furthermore it can be shown that the

---

75 *Band* f 39r; cf variant form in *Sterre* f 35r.
76 This is clear in the claim of pre-contract with John Russel launched by Alice,
    daughter of Robert Borewell. She admitted 'se non posse dictum precontractum
    aliunde quam per confessiones partium probare, quia non interfuerunt testes.'
    Eighteen months later she began another instance. This time her libellus employed
    phrases implying exchange of consent before witnesses: 'quem quidem precontrac-
    tum uterque eorum, videlicet Johannes et Alicia, in alterius et aliorum fidedignorum
    presencia fatebatur et recognovit, publicavit, innovavit etc.' The claim was rejected
    with costs against her. She appealed. See *Borewell* f 67v, 98v, 134r.
77 *Sterre* f 35r reads: 'ex certa sciencia fatebatur et recognovit et super quibus etc.'

notions of repetition, acknowledgment, confirmation, and publication are not unfittingly applied to some of the clandestine contracts, for the process is described. The notion of repetition of a contract *de futuro* appears with pathetic clarity in the case of John Borewelle and Margaret Stistede, discussed above among the conditional contracts. John said that he promised marriage with Margaret if his family (*parentes*) consented, and that afterwards they had intercourse. Margaret maintained the promise and sexual union but denied the condition. More information became available the following day when John admitted that they had exchanged promises several times and that, on one of these occasions, before seeking the consent of his circle (*amicorum*), he and Margaret had intercourse.[78] An even more clear demonstration of this point is found in the case of John Webster and Isabel, daughter of John Herbert. The couple informed the consistory that they contracted *de presenti* and had intercourse on the feast of St Michael, 1380, and that later they confirmed, published, and repeated the contract in the presence of witnesses.[79] Here we find a secret exchange of consent and a later, public repetition of it that is very much like the process illustrated above, where it was shown that the reading of the banns and the ceremony before the Church were sometimes the publishing of a marriage that already existed.

The presence of witnesses was valued by the couple for many reasons, not least of all as proof of the fact that they had exchanged consent. The frequent successful defence of a clandestine marriage before the Ely consistory is clear evidence of the role played by witnesses in this regard. Furthermore, the witnesses were the route whereby knowledge of the union of the couple passed to relatives and neighbours, so that their circle considered them to be man and wife. The court itself admitted the cogency of this *publica vox et fama*; many of the office inquiries came before the court on the basis of such information. Couples used this common opinion about them as an argument for the existence and the

---

78 *Borewelle* f 74r: 'dictus Johannes iterum fatebatur quod diversis vicibus sicut premittitur ad invicem contraxerunt, et dicit quod una vice sic contraxit et ante requisitionem consensus amicorum ipsam Margaretam carnaliter cognovit.' The court found for the marriage and ordered solemnization.

79 *Webster* f 149r: 'matrimonium ad invicem contraxerunt per verba de presenti mutuum consensum eorundem exprimentia, carnali copula subsecuta, et dicit quod sic contraxerunt in festo Sancti Michaelis, AD 1380, et ipsum contractum postea innovarunt, publicarunt et recitarunt ac fatebantur et recognoverunt, utrique, videlicet, in alterius et aliorum presentia, et super premissa laborat publica vox et fama.'

validity of the contract they sought to defend.[80] In one case the litigants were careful to point out that public knowledge of their marriage existed before there was any questioning of the contract.[81]

In the Wrighte case, analysed in some detail above, we are told of a form of words, the joining of hands, and the endowment of the woman, but there is no mention of witnesses. This may be an example of a fully clandestine contract. The case does not develop further, however, so it is impossible to be certain. In many other cases the exchange of consent was admitted to have been a purely private affair. If both parties admitted the union it was usually accepted by the court.[82] Occasionally a means was found to vindicate such a contract even in face of a denial,[83] but usually such cases ended with the admission by the claimant that contract could not be proved because no witnesses were present.[84]

From the many examples that have been assembled above, it will be evident that clandestine marriages occurred frequently in the area and period under study. Yet it may prove surprising to learn how numerous they were. There were 122 cases dealing with the existence or creation of the marriage bond in the Ely register. Of these, eighty-nine involved a union, real or alleged, that was clandestine. So far as can be seen, seventy of these marriages would not have received religious formalities if they had not been brought before the court. In thirteen cases, the parties proceeded to solemnize either by publication of banns alone or by banns and an exchange of consent *coram facie ecclesie* after they had already become man and wife by a clandestine union the validity of which was vouched for by the court itself. Finally, there were six cases where formalities were observed in opposition to the statute *Humana concupiscentia* and which were invalid, whatever the intentions of the couple might

---

80 As in the Band case cited above, n75. On *fama* as proof of marriage in the common law of the Church see Esmein, *Le mariage en droit canonique* I 224–5.

81 *Sterre* f 35r: 'ante omnem litem in hac parte motam.'

82 Eg *Fordham* f 69r; but in *Borewell* f 67v, a claim of pre-contract, claimant and defendant admitted consent and sexual union, but the court decided against the marriage. See above, n76.

83 In *Braunche* f 132r Joan Braunche claimed contract *de presenti* and sexual union, while John, son of Thomas Dellay, denied contract though he admitted intercourse. The parties agreed to the examination of their chaplains even on matter touching the internal forum. Three weeks later they agreed to marry before the Church.

84 Eg *Dany Gibbe* f 61v–62r: 'quia dicta Johanna dixit se non habere testes ad dictum contractum probandum nec aliunde posse probare quia non interfuerunt testes tempore contractus.'

have been.[85] It should be remembered that many of these cases involved bigamy and that among them a second, a third, or even more clandestine unions of all types were alleged and often proved. Fourteen of the cases that came before the courts involved appeals or other matters where the mode of contract was not indicated; seven other cases were inquiries into concubinary relationships where there was no question of contract.[86] Thus eighty-nine of the 101 marriages about which there is relevant information – considerably more than four-fifths – are discovered to have been clandestine unions. As will be shown, the official of Ely made serious efforts to investigate reputed marriages and, if they were free of impediment, to see to their solemnization. However, it should be noted that there is no example where the couple was penalized for failing to arrange their marriage in accord with canon law. They were not required to separate pending solemnization, nor was there special urgency in arranging for it to be done. Usually they were instructed to do so, *pro loco et tempore opportunis*.[87] On the other hand, contravention of *Humana concupiscentia* was punished severely: the couple involved, friends who encouraged them, and the clergy who assisted were excommunicated.[88] It can usually be shown that the culprits were absolved only when penance was accepted. The solemnization forbidden by the statute was seen as an attempt to give colour of respectability to a union that was known to be impossible. As such it was the perversion of a sacrament and was dealt with accordingly. But when the court turned to deal with a true but clandestine marriage, its attitude was different. One has the impression from the register that it was well understood that such unions were worthy of respect.[89] The court insisted that what was lacking be supplied, but it knew that the essential was already present.

85 At least four other weddings contrary to the statute involved couples who had already contracted in private: *Grantesden* f 5r, *Draper Cakebred* f 53r, *Wilberton Frost* f 83v–84r, *Gobat* f 143v (to be related to *Pertefeu* f 148r, 155v). These are included among the seventy.

86 See below, p 66.

87 On 28 February 1377 John Frebern was required to solemnize his marriage with Alice Attepool within three weeks after Easter (29 March). They had been judged husband and wife by the official of Ely, but were not living together: *Frebern* f 64v. In *Leicester* f 55Av the couple promised to solemnize within six weeks.

88 Eg the excommunications of the *Candlesby* case, f 57v–58r, 62v and the *Fisher, Wilberton, Frost* group of cases, f 82v–83r, 83v–84r, 85v.

89 The tone of the episcopal statutes, conciliar canons, and homiletic literature is much more severe.

Given the large number of clandestine marriages it is not surprising that there were many bigamous unions. Here the word 'bigamous' is intended to apply to a marriage involving an individual simultaneously united to two or more spouses, admitted or merely alleged.[90] Sixty-one cases dealt with claims that involved bigamous situations; twenty-two of them were concerned with several claims on the same individuals. As these coalesce into ten decisions by the court, we are dealing with forty-nine cases where a defendant was alleged to be a bigamist or to be on the point of becoming one.[91] Thus considerably more than two-fifths of the marriage suits before the court were concerned with the problem of bigamy.

Certain information on the relation of clandestinity to bigamy can be obtained from an analysis of the place of origin of the principals in the suits. First, it is seen that in the four cases where both marriages were solemnized before the Church, the ceremonies occurred in different dioceses.[92] Second, even in those cases where the unions were clandestine to a greater or lesser degree, bigamists showed a marked tendency to choose their partners in different villages. As can be seen from Table 1, about two-thirds of the bigamous marriages involved persons from different villages, a figure significantly different from the non-bigamous cases, two-thirds of which involved persons from the same villages.

If the private quality of so many marriages increased the possibility of bigamy, it also created a situation in which a person might 'remember' an earlier union and, concluding that his present marriage was bigamous, request the court to annul it. The possibility of collusion – and even of self-deception – was considerable here. A particularly blatant example which came to light when a collusive witness behaved stupidly and cast doubts on her earlier activities is described in detail in the register.[93] William Chilterne and Amicia Nene were married before the Church and

---

90 Relationships such as the *Saffrey* case (f 27r), where John claimed marriage to Alice and she claimed to be the wife of William Martin, are included here as well as the more common type, where two men claim the hand of the same woman or two women claimed to be the wife of the same man.

91 As in the cases where the publication of banns resulted in a claim of pre-contract; eg *Sadelere* f 47r.

92 *Brodyng* f 94v (Lincoln and Ely), *Wolleman* f 110v (Norwich and Ely), *Bakewhyt* f 138v (Salisbury and Ely), *Galion* f 138v (Norwich and Ely). The places of origin shown here as well as those indicated in the table which follows reveal a remarkable degree of mobility among the principals involved.

93 *Chilterne* f 103r–104r.

TABLE 1

	Village unknown	One village	Two villages	Three villages	Four villages	Total
Bigamy of 3 persons	3	12	27	4	0	46
Bigamy of 4 persons	0	1	0	1	0	2
Bigamy of 5 persons	0	0	0	0	1	1
Bigamy cases, TOTAL	3	13	27	5	1	49
Non-bigamous cases	5	41	15	0	0	61

had lived together for two years when William, 'acting,' as he was later to confess, 'to the injury of Amicia, his wife, from malice towards her that had grown in him,'[94] entered into collusion with Joan Squire. They went before the official of the archdeacon claiming pre-contract and children. The court, scandalously inept or corrupt, or both, annulled the marriage of William and Amicia, declaring William and Joan to be husband and wife. Joan soon went off and married another man. On learning of this, Bishop Arundel ordered the case reopened. The corruption of the court and William's crime were revealed and the marriage to Amicia declared valid from the first.[95]

It need hardly be said that the consistory was not always able to expose collusion in this way. It seems, however, to have been very careful to seek objective proof to supplement the evidence of those who claimed pre-contract. Thus when Alice, daughter of Robert Borewell, claimed an earlier marriage with John Russel, de facto husband of Katherine Selvald, John agreed. But Alice had to admit that 'she could not prove the said pre-contract other than by the confession of the parties to the suit, since there were no witnesses'; her claim was dismissed.[96] In cases such as this, all three contestants were required to swear that they had not entered into collusion. A similar demand was made where the temptation was not to 'remember' an earlier contract but to 'forget' it. Thus there are several suits where the court seems to have thought that claimants to pre-contract did not prosecute their case as well as they might: when John Haukyn and Margaret, daughter of John Wrong, claimed that they had married

94 Ibid f 103v: 'erga dictam Amiciam uxorem suam moleste gerens ex malicia quam erga eam conceperat.'
95 The suit is discussed in detail with special reference to the archdeacon's marriage jurisdiction in Aston, *Arundel* 104–6.
96 See above, n76.

clandestinely, the court objected that there was a rumour of pre-contract between John and Mariot Foote.[97] John denied it, so Mariot was summoned before the court. She said that she was married to John but that there was no way of proving it. The court required her to swear that it was not through malice nor by collusion that she failed to prove her claim, and the case was dismissed.[98] In this, as in several other disputes, the register gives the impression that the court felt that evidence did not correspond to fact. The evidence of the principals was respected, but the entry in the register ends with the eloquent phrase 'the court leaves them to their consciences.'[99]

The individualistic theory of marriage taught by the Church, coupled with an informal conception of contract that she opposed but considered valid, seems to have contributed to a situation in the period of the Ely register where such marriages occurred frequently and under conditions that tended to weaken the bond for the permanence of which the Church had struggled for so long. A zealous bishop would be expected to do all in his power to see that his flock married within the norms of canon law or, failing that, to solemnize their marriages when possible. At Ely, his official launched an investigation where a couple was said to be living together or to have contracted marriage without proper solemnization. He acted on information provided by *vox publica et fama*, at the suggestion of neighbours, and occasionally, one would think, at the request of one of the parties who could not easily bring an instance suit before the court. When the couple came before the consistory, almost any kind of relationship might be revealed. If they claimed a contract of marriage, though a clandestine one, the court proceeded to investigate their freedom to marry and, if there were no impediment, declared them husband and wife and ordered them to celebrate their marriage before the Church.[100] This procedure was a rapid one, sometimes accomplished in a single day. As was shown above, the public act before the Church was usually left to the convenience of the couple.

97 *Wrong* f 129r.
98 'Mariota Foot de Trumpiton personaliter comparuit: asseruit quod non habet testes ad probandum contractum matrimoniale inter ipsam et prefatum Johannem Haukyn initum, nec alio modo potuit dictum contractum probare. Ideo facta fide per dictam Mariotam quod non maliciose nec collusorie omittit dictum contractum probare, ipsum Johannem ab impetitione dicte Mariote dimittimus, eorum consienciis relinquendo.' See *Wrong* f 136v.
99 *Bonde* f 15v; *Dany Gibbe* f 61v–62r.
100 *Humbelton* f 35r.

The inquiry often revealed an illicit ménage. In this situation the
couple was asked to separate or, if they were free and willing to do so, to
marry. On occasion, if their freedom were evident, they exchanged consent then and there before the court.[101] In other cases where the couple
did not intend to marry but where the court feared that they would not
separate, a different procedure was used. The couple's decision not to
marry was respected, but the court required them to make a conditional
contract so that further sexual union would *ipso facto* constitute marriage.[102] Theirs was a promise *de futuro* from which it was impossible to
withdraw except by taking steps to marry another person. An example
with rather touching overtones is reported in detail in the register.[103] The
entry begins with the statement that on 10 March 1376 Thomas Barbo of
St Benedict's parish, Cambridge, and Joan Seustere, who had been his
mistress, were summoned before Thomas of Gloucester, the official's
commissary, for inquiry about a contract of marriage and subsequent
intercourse. Joan replied first. She said that they married the Sunday after
the feast of the Exaltation of the Holy Cross the previous year (14
September 1375) at the Stourbridge fair, and asked that the court declare
Thomas her husband. But Thomas had a different story to tell. He said
that before the feast he had decided to dismiss her, so he told her that he
would have nothing more to do with her. But later, when he learned that
she was going away, he was so sad that he wanted to kill himself. 'So
about the time of the feast of the Exaltation, during the above-mentioned
fair at Stourbridge, he came and in tears spoke to Joan as follows: "Joan,
if you will stay here, I will be true to you"; Joan replied that she wished
to stay. Then Thomas said to her, "Joan, I give you my word that I wish
to have you," and Joan immediately said, "I am content." Thomas went
on to say that afterwards, as before, he had intercourse with Joan. He
said, however, that it was not and is not his intention to marry her, that

---

101 *Bokesworth* f 55Ar: 'Unde de eorum mutuo consensu et expresso coram nobis iudicia-
liter prestito, pro matrimonio inter eos sententialiter et diffinitive pronunciamus.'
102 In England the procedure goes back to a series of constitutions of the middle years
of the thirteenth century. The final form seen in action in the Ely register appears at
Wells about 1258 and at Winchester a little later. See *Councils and Synods 2*, ed
Powicke and Cheney I 598 (Wells c13) and 707 (Winchester c29). In *Pikerel* f 125v
and *Rous* f 136r the contract is termed *iuxta formam constitutionis*. On similar practice
at Cerisy in Normandy see Esmein, *Le mariage en droit canonique* I 158; and Lévy,
'L'officialité de Paris' II 1274 n59.
103 *Seustere* f 39v–40r.

he only meant to keep her as his mistress as before.'[104] Joan immediately called a witness and was given until 20 March to produce others. But the register continues: 'However, then and there, before us sitting in judgment in court, Thomas and Joan were required to contract marriage in the following form: Thomas said to Joan, "I accept you as my wife if, from now on, I have carnal knowledge of you." And Joan at once replied "I accept you as my husband if, from now on, you have carnal knowledge of me."'[105] Then follow date, place, the names of witnesses, and an indication of the registrar's notarial sign.

Joan continued her suit, and twenty-five months later the court decided that she was indeed the wife of Thomas.[106] This almost Draconian form of contract was not used lightly;[107] it occurs six times during the eight years of the register. While it may have helped men and women to understand the seriousness of their acts, it was a procedure that was fraught with difficulty. Although further sexual relationship created a permanent marriage bond, it might be impossible to prove its existence in the public forum if one of the parties chose to deny it: in March 1379 Isabel Pikers brought Thomas Bacon into court, claiming marriage *sub forma constitu-*

104 'Dictus Thomas, circa festum Exaltationis predictum tempore nundinarum predictarum apud Storesbrugh, accessit et lacrimabiliter eidem Johanne dixit ista verba: "Johanna si velis morari in partibus, volo te affidare"; et dicta Johanna respondebat se velle morari. Et tunc dictus Thomas dixit eidem Johanne, "Hic securo tibi fidem meam quod volo te habere" et quod [sic] dicta Johanna respondebat incontinenti "Placet mihi". Fatebatur insuper dictus Thomas quod post dictum tempus et etiam ante prefatam Johannam carnaliter cognovit; dicit tamen quod non fuit nec est intentionis sue quod ipsam duceret in uxorem sed dumtaxat quod ipsam detineret in concubinam sicut prius detinuit' (f 39v–40r).

105 'Et nihilominus dicti Thomas et Johanna tunc ibidem coram nobis in judicio pro tribunali sedentes, videlicet, die lune proxima ante festum Sancti Gregorii papae, loco quo supra, matrimonium ad invicem contraxerunt sub forma infrascripta, videlicet, prefatus Thomas dixit eidem Johanne ista verba: "Hic accipio te in uxorem meam si ex nunc cognoscam te carnaliter". Et prefata Johanna eidem statim respondit: "Hic accipio te in virum meum, si ex nunc cognoscam me carnaliter"' (f 40r).

106 *Seustere* f 91v.

107 When John Robinson and Joan, daughter of Geoffrey Morice, came before the court in March 1373, they admitted that they had practised fornication for three years, were often convicted by the official, and, admitting further sexual activity at their last conviction, were required to contract conditionally before the court, *Robynesson* f 12v; in *Wolron* f 55Ar the couple had lived in concubinage for two years before the court used the contract in their case. [See in this respect Richard H. Helmholz, 'Abjuration *sub pena nubendi* in the Church Courts of Medieval England,' *Jurist* 32 (1972) 80–90; repr in his *Canon Law and the Law of England* (London 1987) 145–55. – Editor]

tionis and subsequent sexual union, and asked that he be declared her husband. Thomas admitted the conditional contract but denied intercourse, and Isabel lost her case.[108] On the other hand, much like the contract *de futuro* though it was, parties could not withdraw from it: in March 1380, Adam, servant of John Smith, admitted both the contract and subsequent sexual union with Roisey Rous, but claimed that before intercourse he stated that he did not want her as wife. The court thought otherwise and, having failed to find any canonical impediment, declared them to be married.[109]

There is a certain irony in the fact that the promise *per verba de futuro*, the most fragile bond in conscience and law, should have been adapted to create this formidable instrument for dealing with concubinage. With it, the Ely information on the modes by which men and women were united in matrimony is complete. It becomes evident that in addition to the proper canonical marriage there was a spectrum of clandestine unions ranging from those that were close civil parallels of solemnization before the Church to others that were strictly private exchanges of consent and, beyond them, to those that, stable or ephemeral, were not intended to create a marriage bond. It was the duty of pastor and preacher to instruct the people and instil in them the desire to enter into marriages that were religious, public, and stable. Under a bishop like Arundel moral suasion was supported by the steady pressure of a consistory court that examined dubious unions, brought those that were legitimate to the level of formality required by canon law, and tried to end those that were morally or legally impossible.

The analysis of the different modes whereby men and women of the diocese of Ely formed their marriage bonds necessarily involved many indirect references to disputes with which the consistory dealt. It is now proposed to turn to these disputes – in other words, to examine the register in its own terms as a record of suits that came before the court. Here it is possible to discover the special difficulties of marital practices of the time and to investigate the role of the bishop's official in dealing with them.

108 *Pikerel* f 125v.
109 *Rous* f 136r; the decision of the official's commissary was appealed and confirmed by the official, f 155r. In *Robynesson* f 12v the couple admitted conditional marriage and to spending two nights together, *solus cum sola, nudus cum nuda*. Both denied carnal union. They were to hear sentence on their confession the following week but did not appear. Judgment is unknown.

When this approach is used, one fact becomes evident immediately: the *sponsalia* – the mere promise of marriage that assumed such importance in canonical treatises and in the activity of ecclesiastical courts on the Continent – is absent.[110] With two possible exceptions there is no case where the principals of such a contract sought to enforce it or to be freed from it.[111] It is instead the reading of the banns and contracts based on betrothal followed by intercourse or contracts *per verba de presenti* that are found to be in dispute. It will be recalled that in the analysis of the use of the banns it was shown that twelve cases were brought before the consistory because of objections to proposed marriages and that five of these objections were based on an impediment of affinity, one on an impediment of consanguinity, and six on the objector's assertion that he or she was already married to one of those preparing to solemnize their union. As it happened, this last, the claim of previous contract, was vindicated in only one case, but its high proportion among objections to proposed marriages is an indication of the role it will be found to play in the matrimonial suits brought before the court.

During the eight years covered by the register, sixty instance cases and appeals touching marriage disputes were heard by the consistory. In forty-eight of them the actor asked the court to judge that the defendant was his spouse; in the other twelve he sought a declaration that his marriage was invalid. Judgments favouring the claim of marriage were brought down in eighteen cases. To attain their success claimants had to overcome a variety of objections: four were simple denials of contract by the defendant; four were counter-claims where the same spouse was sought by another in a bigamy case;[112] one was the admission of contract with the

110 See Esmein, *Le mariage en droit canonique* I 151–84; Lévy, 'L'officialité de Paris' II 1265–76.
111 When Agnes Durant and John Draper were summoned to show why they should not be compelled to obey an earlier decision of the court regarding their marriage, Agnes said that before contracting with John she agreed to marry another: 'Henricus Walter de Crewell et ipsa, ante omnem contractum inter ipsam et Johannem initum, fuerant concordes de matrimonio inter eos contrahendo, et post contractum inter ipsos Johannem et Agnetam initum, etiam post sententiam diffinitivam in ea parte latam et non ante, predicti Henricus et Agnes matrimonium ad invicem contraxerunt' (*Draper Durant* f 136v, 138r). On the bigamy case in which John was judged Agnes' husband see above, 242 (here p 53). Agnes' early relationship to Henry seems to have been a simple contract *per verba de futuro*. Note that this is an office case. Agnes did not seek to use the court to claim freedom from John Draper. The other possibility is *Saffrey* f 27r; it too is an office case. See the discussion of the formula of contract above, 245 (here pp 56–7).
112 In one of these bigamy suits the successfully claimed spouse denied the contract.

rider that it included an unfulfilled condition; and the remainder involved pre-contract. In three suits of this group the claimant had to overcome the objection of an earlier marriage advanced by the defendant or the court.[113] Previous contract was also involved in the Geffrey case, but it was used to meet the objection of vows and holy orders: John Myntemoor, priest and Austin Canon of Anglesey, was brought before the court by Alice Geffrey, who successfully claimed him as husband.[114] The same claim was advanced in five other cases, not to overcome the objection of orders but to bring about the separation of the defendant from his *de facto* spouse.[115]

On the other hand, twenty instance and appeal cases saw the claimant fail to vindicate his marriage; seven claims collapsed before denial of contract by the alleged spouse; four were the unsuccessful claims in bigamy cases;[116] two failed because of unfulfilled conditions; and one was met by proof of fear in making the contract and of the impediment of consanguinity between the parties.[117] In two cases the defendants admitted the claim but proved previous contract with other women, and four were unsuccessful attempts to claim as spouses persons who were already married – here at least three of the claimants said that theirs was the earlier marriage.[118]

Ten suits were not brought to sentence in the period covered by the register. The reasons for opposing the claim was unspecified in three of them. Objections in the other suits were as follows: one unfulfilled condition, four bigamy claims, two prior contracts.[119]

Thus, although Agnes Durant won over Alice Cakebred in her claim of John Draper, it was in spite of John's denial of marriage with her and his affirmation of marriage with Alice, *Durant* f 48r. As was seen above, n111, this sentence proved difficult to enforce; see *Draper* f 69r and *Draper Durant* f 136v, 149v.

113 *Pertefeu* f 148r, *Sterre* f 35r, *Webster* f 149r.
114 *Geffrey* f 78r.
115 Three of these judgments were in appeals against earlier decisions for marriage. The couples were required to separate and the pre-contract of appellant and appealed declared valid, *Grantesden* f 133v, *Drenge* f 33v, *Worlych Mason* f 133v–134r. All were appealed. In *Cattefos* f 79r, 115v and *Brodyng* f 94v, 143v marriages solemnized before the Church were successfully challenged by women claiming pre-contract with the husband. The Cattefos decision was appealed.
116 The Cakebred claim was the complement of that discussed above, n112.
117 *Pope* f 95r, 123v.
118 *Wardeyn* f 36v–37r, *Borewell* f 67v (another instance, equally unsuccessful, is found, f 98v, 134r; it was followed by an appeal), *Wedene* f 79v, 104v. The basis of claim of Joan Peyntor against Richard Lister and Emma, his wife, is not clear: *Lister* f 5v, 21r.
119 In *Vyneter* f 67r the defendant admitted the marriage to the claimant but said that she had a previous contract; *Crisp* f 122r proceeded in writing immediately so the

The second group of instance and appeal suits sought decrees of annulment against existing marriages. Five of the twelve were successful. Of these, three were appeals from judgments of the archdeacon's official in favour of marriages from which the appellants wished to escape.[120] Robert Marion had his marriage to Agnes, his wife, annulled when he showed that there was an impediment of affinity between them, resulting from his relations with Katherine Bird, related to Agnes within the forbidden degree.[121] In the fifth case, one in which the consistory seems to have had some reason to fear collusion, Alice Bakewhyt brought Hugh Mayheu and Isabel Loot into court and proved that, though she and Hugh had been married before the Church, the marriage was invalid because Hugh and Isabel had solemnized their union thirty years before.[122]

Failure to bring about annulment was the result in an equal number of suits, all five of them appeals against sentences in favour of the marriages in which the appellants were involved. Finally, there were two cases which were left incomplete. Both involved pre-contract; both have an unpleasant odour about them. In one, William Kele claimed that his union with Helen, his wife, was invalid because before this marriage he had contracted with Alice Burgoyne, who later married Philip Disse.[123] In the other, John Malyn, Sr, was brought before the court by his wife, Margaret, who asked for a divorce from him, claiming that both of them had previous contracts with persons still living.[124]

It was shown in the earlier section dealing with the establishment of the marriage bond that office inquiries in rumoured clandestine unions uncovered a variety of marital situations. Thirty-nine of these inquiries became suits where an effort was made, sometimes against heavy opposition, to prove that a valid marriage existed. Twenty of them were successful. Of the successes, five were attained without dispute: the couple agreed that they had entered a clandestine union; there was no impediment, so the court instructed them to solemnize their marriage. Two other inquiries seemed to be leading to the same easy conclusion, when third parties appeared claiming to have married one of the persons

basis of claim is unspecified. The form of reporting, however, gives reason for concluding that Juliana, daughter of Walter Crisp, claimed that her marriage to Lawrence Taillor was prior to his marriage to Catherine, his *de facto* wife.

120 *Niel* f 63v, 159v, *Martin* f 113v, 141v (appealed), *Tydd* f 119r, 126r.
121 *Marion* f 80r.
122 *Bakewhyt* f 138v.
123 *Kele* f 149v.
124 *Malyn* f 150r.

involved in the inquiry. In both cases the defendants admitted the claim
– thus confessing bigamy – but maintained with success that the contracts which were being investigated by the court were prior to those with
the claimants. A similar decision resulted in a third case of this type
where the opposition at first came from the court itself: John Haukyn and
Margaret, daughter of John Wrong, claimed valid union when summoned,
but the court confronted John with the rumour that he had a prior contract with Mariot Foote. As was seen above, Mariot failed to prove her
position against John's denial.[125] In addition, marriage was successfully
asserted against three denials of the partner, three objections of unfulfilled condition, two counter-claims in bigamy suits, and two objections
of fear in making the contract.[126] Finally, *ex officio* investigations uncovered two anomalies, which the court proceeded to correct. The first
was the Chilterne case, analysed in some detail above.[127] Here a collusive
claim of pre-contract had resulted in a declaration of nullity; the original
couple was reunited. The second was the discovery that William de
Potton, subdeacon and brother of St John's, Cambridge, had entered into
clandestine union with Agnes Knotte before receiving orders. Here, too,
the marriage was vindicated.[128]

Attempts to prove the existence of the marriage bond failed in nine of
the cases following office inquiries. The objections that stood in the way
of success were denial of contract by the alleged spouse in three cases,
counter-claims in three bigamy suits, an impediment of consanguinity
revealed by the father of a *de facto* husband,[129] an unspecified impediment
that the couple sought to hide by solemnization against the prohibition
of *Humana concupiscentia*, and a previous contract.[130]

Nine other suits developed along similar lines but were left incomplete.

125 *Wrong* f 129r; see above, 252–3 (here pp 64–5).
126 *Pulter* f 93r presents the reader with an account of a fourteenth-century 'shotgun
    marriage' with all the speed of execution that the informality of the clandestine
    contract made possible. John Castre and Marion Pulter were summoned *ex officio*;
    John denied marriage, adding that if there were a contract between them it was
    extracted from him by threats. He went on to describe how he was spending the
    night with Marion when servants of Sir Hugh Zouche broke down the door of their
    room, beat him, and threatened mutilation if he did not promise marriage. He
    admitted that he and Marion had continued to have carnal relations for more than a
    year. The court decided for the marriage and ordered solemnization, *Pulter* f 114r.
127 See 252 (here pp 63–4).
128 *Potton Knotte* f 139r.
129 *Symond* f 28v.
130 *Lungedon* f 71v: see above, 246 n69 (here p 58).

In two of them, objections to the contract are uncertain;[131] one saw a vigorous denial by the alleged wife,[132] two were dealing with the opposed claims of a bigamy case, and four involved couples whose union was threatened by previous contracts.[133]

The consistory was also active in supporting and enforcing contracts of marriage. Thus when couples failed to cohabit the court investigated. Six enquiries of this sort revealed a variety of difficulties. John Frebern and Alice Attepool were obviously displeased with a judgment in favour of their marriage and had delayed its solemnization. They were told to see to it within a limited time.[134] But more serious legal problems appeared in the other cases. One woman, having won a husband in a bigamy suit, began to have scruples about an earlier promise of marriage.[135] Two husbands refused to live with their wives because of impediments of affinity.[136] One refused to do so because of a previous contract.[137] Another inquiry showed that Joan, daughter of Robert Pencot, had lived with John Maddyngle for some time after their wedding, but had eventually left him because he was impotent. She asked that their marriage be annulled. However, proof of John's condition was not easily accomplished. Finally, after more than two years, she entered a second objection to their marriage, namely the impediment of consanguinity. A declaration of nullity based on this impediment was brought in more than a year later.[138]

---

131 *Andrew* f 5v: office proceedings involving Richard Andrew and Agnes, his *de facto* wife, had come to sentence when the register opens. They were never brought into court nor was sentence brought down though the suit remained on the docket until October 1380. The Wrighte case is discussed above, 244–5 (here p 56).

132 *Saffrey* f 27r.

133 *Arneys* f 117r: Etheldreda countered John Arney's claim that she was his wife with the allegation that he had two earlier contracts. In *Wolleman* f 110v, *Kirkeby* f 129r, and *Galion* f 138v allegations of pre-contract were introduced *ex officio*.

134 *Frebern* f 64v: the official of Ely had judged John and Alice Attepol to be husband and wife several years before. John had run the gamut of contumacy, excommunication, a request to the king for his *captio*, and appeal to Canterbury in his effort to resist. The appeal had not been prosecuted; and finally, after three years, he submitted and came before the court. He was instructed to solemnize marriage with Alice before the third week after Easter, ie within eight weeks. Nothing more is · heard of the case.

135 *Durant Draper* f 136r, 138r; discussed above, 256 niii (here p 69).

136 *Gobat* f 143v (see above, 243 [here p 54]); *Lile* f 155v was not brought to sentence.

137 Robert Puf said that he did not live with Inetta, his wife of thirty years, because of his pre-contract with Margaret Benet, then living in London, *Puf* f 153v. The suit was not brought to sentence.

138 *Maddyngle* f 91r, 154r.

A similar situation, but with more serious consequences, was revealed by an inquiry into the marital situation of John Poynant. He and Joan Swan had married and, after some time together, had their marriage annulled because of John's impotence. Joan married again and John took up with Isabel Pybbel, who became pregnant. He was on the point of marrying her when the court began its investigations.[139] It was proposed that since John was not impotent he should be restored to his original spouse. John interposed the interesting objection that, since Joan and Isabel were related within the forbidden degree, an impediment of affinity would preclude his return to Joan. But two years later, the court, satisfied as to John's capacity and that the impediment did not obtain, corrected the earlier error, quashed the divorce, and restored the original marriage.[140]

The above analysis of contentious proceedings before the Ely consistory reveals many interesting facts about marriage and its problems in fourteenth-century Cambridgeshire; but above all it establishes two important patterns, one touching the activity of the court itself, the other the point at which marriage was most vulnerable. As for the first: the court's principal activity was the vindication and defence of the marriage bond; pleas of annulment occurred infrequently. This is true not only of office proceedings, where the court set out to investigate the bond linking reputed couples and usually found itself deciding between alleged spouses who could not agree or between them and others who opposed their marriages, but also in instance suits, where the court was asked to vindicate a claim to marriage – usually against the objections of a reluctant spouse. Behind many of these suits lay clandestine marriage and the confusion as to act and intention that it tended to foster.

Clandestinity also contributed to the second pattern, the point at which marriage, as revealed by the register, was most vulnerable. It is something of a commonplace to suppose that the conscientious statement or the manipulation of the impediments of consanguinity and affinity were the main threats to the stability of the bond in the Middle Ages. The Ely evidence leads to a different conclusion. If the information from the suits discussed in the previous pages is compiled, the result is as shown in Table 2.[141]

---

139 Isabel said that she and John had already contracted marriage, *Poynant* f 100r.
140 Ibid.
141 Simple denials of contract are not included in this table. Many of the bigamy cases probably turned on the question of which union was prior; since the reporting of these suits was not stated in these terms, they are not numbered among the

TABLE 2
Objections to marriages that were proposed, claimed, admitted, but alleged to be invalid

	Pre-contract (ligamen)	Vows and orders	Consanguinity	Affinity	Crimen (adultery)	Crimen (murder)	Ignorance	Fear	Impotence	Condition	Unknown
MARRIAGES ANNOUNCED IN BANNS											
Objection successful	1		1	3							
Objection unsuccessful	5			1							
Objection in incomplete case	1			1	1	1					
MARRIAGE CLAIMED IN OFFICE SUITS AGAINST OBJECTION											
Successfully, against	4	1		1			1	2	1	2	
Unsuccessfully, against	2		2	1					1	1	1
Objection in incomplete case	5			1						1	3
MARRIAGE CLAIMED IN INSTANCE SUITS AGAINST OBJECTION											
Successfully, against	3	1								1	
Unsuccessfully, against	2		2					1		2	
Objection in incomplete case	2									1	3
OBJECTION TO BOND IN INSTANCE SUITS											
Objection successful	6			1							3
Objection unsuccessful	4										5
Objection in incomplete case	2										
TOTALS	37	2	5	9	1	1	1	3	2	8	15

It becomes evident that marriages were not especially threatened by impediments of consanguinity and affinity. Revelation of a previous marriage was the greater danger. Here, where the possibilities of self-

objections based on pre-contract. Where several objections to a marriage are advanced, they are included; thus the four objections to the proposed marriage of Robert Andrew and Alice Solfa are those indicated as incomplete among the 'objections to marriages announced in banns'; cf *Andrew* f 149v.

deception, error, dishonesty, and collusion were especially strong, the fundamental weakness of the system seems to be indicated. It helps the historian to grasp why so much effort was expended to help men and women understand the necessity of due solemnization: the frequent occurrence of pre-contract was directly related to the possibility of clandestine marriage.

A few conclusions – conclusions that at this stage of investigation must be sharply limited in their application to both time and place – can be drawn from the analysis of the Ely register. It is evident, first of all, that where difficulties led to court proceedings most of the marriages were clandestine and more than a third had a hint of bigamy about them. Second, the court was primarily a body for the proof and defence of marriage rather than an instrument of easy annulment. The third conclusion is much less precise; it is based on an impression rather than on a series of statistics. Yet, from the point of view of long-term social change, it may be the most important. The reporting of matrimonial suits in the Ely register reveals an astonishingly individualistic attitude to marriage and its problems. Familial and seigniorial decision as to the time of betrothal and the choice of spouse, practices that are always associated with medieval society, are simply not found in the register. The exertion of this kind of pressure by feudal or manorial lord is never mentioned. Parental consent appears in a few cases but merely as a condition added, or said to have been added, by one of the alleged spouses. Financial arrangements seem of minimal importance, appearing, if they appear at all, as conditions attached by the spouses to the contract. Even the children were ignored except in a few cases where their birth seems to have been mentioned as an argument in favour of a claim. Older norms – those of family, village, and upper-class society – remained powerful. Of that there is no doubt; but we know that even among the upper classes it was possible for a determined person to escape these norms by the rather simple process of entering a canonically acceptable marriage of his own choosing. The question posed at the beginning of this article remains: it is still impossible to say how rapidly the understanding and the use of freedom of choice of a marriage partner spread through medieval society as a whole. But perhaps some of the information that will contribute to an answer is here: the point of view manifested by the Ely register is an indication of a pressure in late medieval society that was pushing men and women towards the more individualistic view of marriage that was implicit in decisions made two hundred years before.

6

Marriage and Family
in English Conciliar and
Synodal Legislation

In the chapter of his *Feudal Society* entitled 'Character and Vicissitudes of the Tie of Kinship,' Marc Bloch quotes a *chanson de geste*: '"Be quiet," is the rough response of Garin le Lorrain to the widow of his murdered brother, who is weeping over the body and bemoaning her lot, "a noble knight will take you up again ... it is I who must go on deep in mourning".'[1] Most of us will have read this anecdote; some many times. But I, for one, am still pulled up sharply by the glimpse it affords of a world in which a marital relationship could be established and destroyed with such ease, almost with insouciance, a world in which kinship provided the permanent and serious bond.

The element of surprise felt by the modern reader is especially strong in one who has for some time been studying the canonical, the pastoral and, to a certain extent, the theological sources touching the history of marriage. In fact, it is in a moment like this, when the historian sees the general tone of that type of source material in perspective, that he realizes how different is its point of view from that of the *chanson de geste* just quoted. Sources for the history of marriage are concerned with relationship of the spouses, often paying little attention to the familial group from which they came and into which they would be drawn, or even to their duties to the children they were expected to bring into the world. No doubt, the broad social context in which this literature was written is to be presumed. But sometimes it is quite clear that it presents a view of marriage that is in conflict with that social context. Marriage, after all, was

---

1 Marc Bloch, *La société féodale*, L'évolution de l'humanité 24 (Paris 1939–40) II 212. Cf Marc Bloch, *Feudal Society*, trans L.A. Manyon (Chicago 1961) 136. See *Li roman de Garin le Loherain*, ed P. Paris (Paris 1835) II 268.

the key to family recruitment. Christian teaching came, in time, to define marriage, and that definition did not always fit well with older usages. The question of concern here is to learn how, if at all, the family evolved under that pressure.

On the whole, historians of canon law, even those who have published major studies on marriage, have paid little attention to the family as such. On the other hand, historians of civil institutions and, more recently, anthropologists have turned to early canonical sources in their investigations of family and kinship.[2] I suggest that once the traditional point of view of the historian of marriage is widened he will not only make significant contributions to the study of the family but also deepen his understanding of marriage itself.

Simply stated, the Christian conception of marriage included three complementary sets of ideas: 1) Marriage was seen as a sacred relationship, one that provided the ordinary means to the full Christian life. Because of its importance, the Church came eventually to state and defend the conditions that made marriage possible. 2) The ideal sought in the full Christian life was one in which there would be no erotic activity outside marriage. 3) A viable alternative to marriage in religious life and in the clerical state was elaborated. Each of these ideals had an impact on the evolution of the family. I propose, within the limits possible here, to indicate examples of their influence in England and suggest lines of further investigation. The Church's moral teaching and theological investigations usually moved ahead of its law. Here, however, we shall be content to examine two of the sources of that law, the local council and the synod. Whatever their limitations, they indicate the moment at which one can be reasonably certain that an effort was being made to enforce a given mode of behaviour in society. Marriage directly involved the principals of the nuclear group. The word 'family' will be used of them but will also include the group united by blood, though no attempt will be made here to enter the discussion of its effective extent in different parts of England or at different times in English history.[3]

Let us begin with a consideration of the impact of the Church's conception of religious life as a viable alternative to marriage. There were to be

2 Eg Lorrain Lancaster, 'Kinship in Anglo-Saxon Society,' *British Journal of Sociology* 9 (1958) 230–50, 359–77; D.A. Bullough, 'Early Medieval Social Groupings: The Terminology of Kinship,' *Past and Present* 45 (1969) 3–18.
3 See Lancaster, 'Kinship' 373–6.

important refinements and developments over the years, but the ideal and the realization of dedicated chastity were already established by the time the missionaries – and they were monks – arrived among the Anglo-Saxons. A brief acquaintance with the insular Penitentials makes it clear that Christian leaders were no less realistic about the possibilities of religious life than they were about marriage. But it is also clear that a powerful movement of teaching and example was launched, one that led to a widespread conviction that the former was the superior state.

The implementation of such an ideal had considerable impact on the family. In principle the religious renounced the possibility of establishing a nuclear family and withdrew from the obligations and rights of kinship. The kin had no further rights or duties in his regard. Should a child be born to such a person, it was without rights in the kin or in the voluntary association that had replaced the kin. The main stages of this interesting process, a process in which religious and their families slowly came to realize the consequences of a choice that had been made, occurred during the Anglo-Saxon period.

Boniface associated a prohibition of the nun's marriage with a synod in Augustine's time.[4] Such a rule is extant in the report of the legates to Adrian I (787) and in the constitutions of archbishop Oda (ca 945).[5] A somewhat different approach is seen in Alfred's law forbidding such marriage without the permission of king or bishop. The kin was ignored in the penalty that was attached; payment was to those whose permission had not been sought.[6] The general prohibition was repeated in the ecclesiastical codes of Ethelred and Cnut. These seem to be the last sets of regulations seeking to establish that nuns could not marry. When Anglo-Norman councils turned to the matter, as in the case of those women who had fled to monasteries during the Norman invasion and the investigation of Matilda's freedom to marry Henry I, the bishops were concerned with questions of fact: were these women bound by vows or not?[7]

---

4 Ep 50, *S. Bonifatii et Lullii Epistolae*, ed Michael Tangl, MGH Epistolae selectae I (Berlin 1916) 83–4.

5 *Councils and Ecclesiastical Documents Relating to Great Britain and Ireland*, ed A.W. Haddan and W. Stubbs (Oxford 1871) III 455; and *Concilia Magnae Britanniae et Hiberniae, 446–1718*, ed David Wilkins (London 1737) I 213.

6 Af 8, *Die Gesetze der Angelsachsen*, ed Felix Liebermann [henceforth *Gesetze*; Liebermann's abbreviations for the codes are used throughout] (Halle 1903–16) I 54–5. Cf I Em 4 (942–6) and Northu 63 (probably 1020–3), *Gesetze* I 184–5, 384.

7 *Concilia*, ed Wilkins I 362; and *Eadmeri Historia novorum in Anglia*, ed Martin Rule, RS 81 (London 1884) 121–5.

As early as the legatine synods of 787 the child of the nun was equated with the child of adultery, in this case the adultery of her who 'se Deo voverit, et ... sponsam Christi vocitare non dubitamus.'[8] The child was denied rights of inheritance. A further consequence is revealed in the law of Alfred mentioned above in which the nun's marriage without permission was forbidden: the child, like his mother, was to have no rights in his father's property; if he were killed, the king was to have the mother's part of the wergild while the paternal kin received its share.[9]

It is interesting to note that there is no similar set of regulations touching the monk. It seemed to have been understood that the nun, more than the monk, needed to be protected: from herself, no doubt, but especially from the importunate suitor or the pressure from the family that would not forget its old prerogative of arranging the marriages of its daughters. On the other hand, VIII Ethelred stated that the monk was not to be involved in the feud, since he had left the obligations of kinship when he submitted to the rule.[10]

Literary sources reveal the initial difficulty of the Anglo-Saxons in understanding that the property administered by abbots or abbesses did not pass to their families when they died.[11] On the Continent, councils had been careful to protect ecclesiastical property from alienation, and their regulations were probably known in England, though they are not to be found there except in general terms.[12]

The process whereby the ties of family weakened before the claims of lordship, its chronology and extent, are among the important problems that require an answer of the historian of the Anglo-Saxons. From the foregoing sketch it should be clear that the intrusion of a way of life that did not include marriage was another force in early medieval English society that required an adjustment of the family's conception of itself and a limitation of its role.

8 *Councils*, ed Haddan and Stubbs III 455.
9 Af 8 2, 8 3, *Gesetze* I 54–5. Ine 27 (688–91) awarded the wergild of an unacknowledged child to lord and king, ibid I 100–1.
10 VIII Atr 25, ibid I 266–7: 'he gaeð of his maeglage, ponne he gebihd to regollage.'
11 See E. John, 'The Social and Political Problems of the Early English Church,' in *Land, Church, and People: Essays Presented to H.P.R. Finberg*, ed J. Thirsk, *Agriculture History Review* 18 (1970) suppl 60–2; and Michael M. Sheehan, *The Will in Medieval England: From the Conversion of the Anglo-Saxons to the End of the Thirteenth Century*, Studies and Texts 6 (Toronto 1963) 91–4.
12 Ibid 91 n6. Cf Abt 1, *Gesetze* I 3.

The ideal that there should be no sexual activity outside of marriage was elaborated and refined in theological, moral, and pastoral writings throughout the centuries. Aspects of human sexuality that involved more than one person, especially those causing injustice or damage to a third party, were regulated by canon law and frequently came before the ecclesiastical courts. Some of these matters have had an important part to play in the evolution of the family in the West. By way of illustration, I would like to present one development in England. It should be seen in the context of the remarkable effort at reform that characterized the late twelfth and thirteenth centuries, a movement that was especially strong in the period after the Fourth Lateran Council.

The development in question is to be related to the problem of the couple who were unmarried but who lived together or frequented each other's company to the scandal of all. Perhaps in some cases descriptions of this relationship mask the survival of an older form of inferior union with some analogies to the Roman *contubernium*.[13] That matter need not be pursued here. In the context of reform it was a case of public scandal in that, though the couple was free to marry, yet, in spite of their obvious attachment, they refused to do so. It was discussed in Peter the Chanter's *Summa de sacramentis* (ca 1192) and appeared towards 1216 in England in Thomas of Chobham's *Summa confessorum*.[14] Discussing sins reserved to the bishop or his penitentiary, Chobham points out that the criteria of reservation are the seriousness and public nature of the actions in question. He indicates that it is customary that those who have a concubine and are free to marry are required either to abjure or to marry her. The abjuration is more than a simple promise to avoid the woman in question, but it takes the form of a promise that, should there be any further carnal relation, the couple will marry. If, having taken such an oath, a recidivist refuses to do so, he is to be summoned before the bishop and charged not with fornication but with perjury.

In less than ten years a developed form of this doctrine in which conditional contract replaced promise appeared in episcopal statutes. Its

13 There is a series of references to unacceptable unions through the Anglo-Saxon period: Council of Hertford c10, *Councils*, ed Haddan and Stubbs III 120; *Judicium Clementis* c15, ibid 227; *Dialogue of Egbert* 13, ibid 409; Constitutiones Odonis c7 W 1 213; Wi 3, 4, 4 1, 5, *Gesetze* I 12; V Atr 10, ibid 240–1; VI Atr 11, ibid 250–1.

14 *Summa de sacramentis et anime consiliis*, ed Jean-Albert Dugauquier, Analecta mediaevalia Namurcensia 4, 7, 11, 16, 21 (Louvain and Lille 1954–67) II 449; *Thomae de Chobham Summa confessorum*, ed F. Broomfield, Analecta mediaevalia Namurcensia 25 (Louvain and Paris 1968) 214.

first statement by Peter des Roches at Winchester allowed for several situations. The layman who publicly lived with a concubine was compelled to betroth her or enter into a conditional contract whereby further sexual union would constitute marriage.[15] In the case of him whose intercourse was public and frequent but casual, both he and the woman were to swear a similar oath before witnesses or, if they refused to do so, to promise with sureties that they would be subject to a fine if, henceforth, they were found together.[16] A few years later similar legislation was included in the Coventry statutes. Here, in a context of the correction of public mortal sin, it is stated that the fornicator who has forsworn his paramour then returned to her must face the penalty of marrying her or paying a large part of his property in fine.[17] In the second set of Salisbury statutes (1238–44) the legislation was directly related to the proposition 'quod omnis carnalis commixtio inter virum et mulierem extra legitimum matrimonium mortale peccatum existit.' A developed procedure was outlined: public fornicators and their concubines were to be reported by local clergy to rural deans, who would bring them before the archdeacon. If there were no impediment, the couple were to be compelled by ecclesiastical censures to swear in each other's presence that further sexual union would constitute marriage. The form of the oath was given.[18] The second Winchester statutes took up the matter once more in 1247. This time, abjuration under penalty of fine was rejected.[19] An attempt was made to render the procedure more humane: canon 52 begins with the statement that marriage must be free and between those capable of contracting it. Clergy with pastoral charge of a couple involved in an extra-marital relationship were instructed to inquire as to impediments and, if the couple were free, to try to induce them to marry. If there were an impediment, they were to abjure each other with prescription of penance should they fall again. But if they were free yet refused to marry, the conditional contract was to be imposed on them.[20] Similar, occasionally more detailed rules were to appear in episcopal statutes of the last half of the thirteenth

---

15 c54, *Councils and Synods with Other Documents Relating to the English Church, 2: A.D. 1205–1313*, ed F.M. Powicke and C.R. Cheney (Oxford 1964) I 134.

16 c58, ibid I 135.

17 c15: 'indicatur talis pena ei si eandem cognoverit, quod eam desponset, vel magnum portionem substantie sue, secundum quod facultates sue competunt, nobis tribuat sub sacramento,' ibid I 213.

18 c53, ibid I 385.

19 c55, ibid I 411. On the date, probably 1247, ibid I 403.

20 c52, ibid I 410–11.

century.[21] They were not without opposition. Professor Cheney included a gloss in his edition of the second Exeter statutes (1287): 'Nota quod hec constitutio est contra iura et naturalem equitatem, quia de jure libera debent esse matrimonia et sponsalia ...'[22] Be that as it may, there is sufficient evidence to show that that these statutes were enforced.[23]

Thus, in tracing this development through thirteenth-century statutes, we discover an attempt to implement an ideal of sexual activity that obtruded on the more important doctrine of the dignity of marriage – a doctrine that was often stated in these very statutes.[24] The context of this position is entirely different from that of the *chanson de geste* cited above; but, from one point of view, the two attitudes are surprisingly similar. Garin le Lorrain implied that the replacement of a husband was a slight matter; one of the statutes, in an unhappy phrase, presented marriage as a penalty for fornication. In the former case the needs of the extended family were dominant. In the case of the statutes it was the protection of the public from scandal and the protection of the couple from sin that mattered. It was the needs of the couple, understood in terms of an ultimate good, and of the wider society rather than those of the family that prevailed. On the other hand, the pressures that would cause a couple to enter a marriage that one at least did not desire[25] should be related to other, quite different forces which for centuries have led to the forced marriage. The history of this phenomenon is, to my knowledge, not yet written. When it is, this English legislation of the thirteenth century should have a place there. Finally, if there were a type of imperfect union still extant in English society, this legislation may well have helped lift it to the level of regular marriage, with the permanence and the rights and duties that the notion implies. The long-range consequences might well be very important, but they too remain to be investigated.

21 Wells 13 (1258?) includes a written account of proceedings, as does 3 Winchester 29 (1262–5) and 2 Exeter 7 (1287); see ibid I 598, 707, and II 999. The form of the oath is given in 1 London 3 (1245–59), where it is referred to Bishop Roger Niger (1229–41), and in 2 London 80 (1245–59), ibid I 631, 650.
22 Ibid I 999 n4.
23 See Richard H. Helmholz, 'Abjuration *sub pena nubendi* in the Church courts of Medieval England,' *Jurist* 32 (1972) 81–90; and Michael M. Sheehan, 'The Formation and Stability of Marriage in Fourteenth-Century England,' *Mediaeval Studies* 33 (1971) 253–6 (here pp 38–76).
24 See 1 Salisbury 83 and derivatives: 2 Canterbury, Durham Peculiars 50, 1 Chichester 27, *Councils and Synods 2*, ed Powicke and Cheney I 87, 116, 443, 456–7.
25 See Sheehan, 'The Formation and Stability of Marriage,' 254–6 (here pp 66–8), the account of Thomas Barbo and Joan Seustere. Thomas was opposed to the marriage.

Though the direction taken by episcopal statutes in the attempt to support a moral position may in some ways have been detrimental to it, marriage was of major importance in the Church's view of human life. A consultation of the statutes in question will remove all doubt on this score. In fact, between the beginning of the twelfth-century revival and the end of the thirteenth century, in an intellectual effort that has probably had no equal in western tradition except possibly today, marriage was examined at all levels of thought ranging from theology, through moral guidance and law, to confessional practice. The ends of marriage, its qualities, and the conditions for its validity were discussed and stated in detail. Many aspects of the history of the family in the West must, in my opinion, be related to this process if they are to be understood.

Perhaps the most obvious impact on the evolution of the family came from the Church's conclusions on the persons who were free to marry. As the conceptions of consanguinity, affinity, and spiritual relationship were refined, the network of forbidden marriage partners first enlarged, then diminished. In spite of a hoary tradition in English historiography that the rules in question provided a convenient bolt-hole for those who sought divorce, the question has not been studied with care, either in itself or in its effect on the kindred. To what extent families were denied the possibility of reinforcing intergroup ties, to what extent lower-class mobility and the resulting restriction of active kinship were consequences of these developments still need careful examination. Beyond this indication of need, it is not possible to pursue the topic here. I propose, instead, to reflect on a dilemma that was implicit in the Church's theory of consent, indicate the way in which it was resolved, and suggest implications of that solution from the point of view of marriage and family.

The effect of the Church's position on the consent of the couple appeared quite late in the legislation of the Anglo-Saxons. Ecclesiastical codes of Ethelred (1008) ruled that a year after the death of her husband a widow could do what she willed.[26] The rule was repeated in II Cnut[27] with the addition that neither widow nor maiden was to be forced to marry a man she disliked.[28] By 1175 a Council of Westminster would have

26 V Atr 21 1: 'ceose syððan, þhat heo sylf wille,' *Gesetze* I 242–3. The text is repeated in Atr 26 1. The Latin paraphrase makes it clear that choice is about marrying or not marrying: 'libero utantur arbitrio vel nubendi vel in continentia permanendi,' ibid I 254–5.

27 II Cn 73; in the *Quadripartitus* it is translated 'elegat postea quem velit,' thus transferring the choice from marriage to the person married, ibid I 360–1.

28 II Cn 73–4, ibid. Cf Wif 1, ibid I 442–3; Liebermann dated the treatise 975×1030, preferring a date towards the end of that period.

carried the requirement of consent much further: 'ubi non est consensus utriusque, non est conjugium.'[29] By this time, theory had progressed still further, the opinion becoming explicit that neither presence nor consent of anyone other than the couple was required. By 1216 Thomas of Chobham could write: 'It is clear however that a man and a woman can contract marriage by themselves, without a priest or anyone else, in any place, so long as they agree to live together forever.'[30] When this point had been reached the dilemma was clear. The stressing of consent made it all too easy for couples to be ignorant of or to choose to forget impediments that rendered their marriage impossible. Later, discovering the impediment or becoming dubious about their original intent or simply unhappy, it would be a simple matter for them to deny their union.[31] Easy marriage, without external controls, meant easy separation. Thus the practical implications of a theory of consent threatened the permanence of marriage.

It is interesting to note that the statutes of the thirteenth century avoided stating the possibility of the clandestine marriage. Thus the first Canterbury statutes (1213–14) and their derivatives forbade such unions and carefully prescribed proper public forms. If the marriage occurred in spite of the prohibition, it was not to be admitted without the special authority of the archbishop.[32] It is unlikely that this ruling denied the validity of the contract, but it is clear that the weight of the statute was against such proceedings.[33] It is only with the Statutes of Wells (1258?) that it is explicitly stated that the clandestine marriage was valid, a point that would not often be made again.[34]

29 *Concilia*, ed Wilkins I 477. Cf Gratian, C30 q2 c1.
30 'Pater igitur quod vir et mulier possunt contrahere matrimonium per se sine sacerdote et sine omnibus aliis in quocumque loco, dummodo consentiant in perpetuam vite consuetudinem,' *Summa confessorum*, ed Broomfield 146.
31 On the frequency of marriages invalid by pre-contract as revealed by a small sample in the late fourteenth century, see Sheehan, 'The Formation and Stability of Marriage,' 262–3 (here pp 74–6).
32 1 Canterbury 54, 1 Salisbury 85, Constitutiones cuiusdam episcopi 59, and Durham Peculiars 52, *Councils and Synods 2*, ed Powicke and Cheney I 34, 88, 190, 444.
33 The text, 'Si vero secus factum fuerit, non admittatur in ecclesia nisi de speciali auctoritate domini archiepiscopi,' has been interpreted to mean that the marriage was invalid, *Councils and Synods 2*, ed Powicke and Cheney II 1429, s v 'Marriage, clandestine, invalidity of'. There is no indication that exchange of consent had to be repeated. It would seem, rather, that the text is intended to discourage clandestine marriages, requiring that each case come before the archbishop for judgment and, no doubt, for punishment.
34 c11, *Councils and Synods 2*, ed Powicke and Cheney I 597–8; 2 Exeter 7 is similar, ibid II 999.

The solution to the problem, however, lay along different lines. The main thrust of legislation was to guarantee permanence by the social control of information. In a long series of rules extending from Hubert Walter's council at Westminster in 1200 to that of John of Stratford in London in 1342, more than thirty sets of canons and statutes dealt with the problem of clandestine marriage. They worked out the well-known two-stage system whereby proper marriage required an announcement of intent so that parish information about the suitability of the couple could be consulted, followed by a public exchange of consent to ensure that general knowledge of the event might be preserved. In none of these proceedings was the family as such introduced. In fact, it would be one of the main sources and preservers of information about its members, but it was as part of the parish or the vicinage that it was to be consulted. Heads of families were not required to give consent or even to be present at the public ceremony. On the other hand, the priest, the head of the parish community, was to play a role: first, seeking, receiving, and interpreting information as to the couple's capacity, second, by his presence at the betrothal or at least at the marriage.[35]

Such a solution tended to emphasize the principals of the nuclear family at the expense of the extended group. It neither denied nor limited the emphasis on consent by the couple and, in spite of secular tradition of family controls, did not turn to the kin for a solution to the abuse of this consent. The implications of this approach have taken centuries to unfold, but I suggest that in it is one of the keys to the history of the family in the English-speaking world during the last seven centuries.

35 On the replacement of the father in the marriage ceremony by the priest, see the discussions of Edward C. Schillebeeckx, *Marriage: Human Reality and Saving Mystery*, trans N.D. Smith (New York 1965) 272–9.

7

Choice of Marriage Partner
in the Middle Ages:
Development and Mode of Application
of a Theory of Marriage

In the discussion of the family during the past fifteen years, four publications in English can be taken as an index of progress in this area of research. They are 1) a special number of the *International Social Science Journal* of 1962; 2) *Household and Family in Past Time*, edited a decade later by Peter Haslett and Richard Wall; 3) a special number of the *Journal of Marriage and Family* in 1973, dealing with the history of the family; and 4) a series entitled 'The Family in History' by Christopher Lasch in the *New York Review of Books*, November–December 1975.[1]

These publications reveal a considerable broadening of the instruments of research applied to the study of the family. From the point of view of results, they show some disarray: data touching change in the ideology as well as in the structure of the family not only suggest variety in the tempo and quality of that change but also indicate that, as conditions required, it shifted its direction. One of the more obvious signs of the broadening of approach is the rapid increase in the number of historical studies of the family. This discipline, in fact, has provided much of the data that has

The research for this article was completed during tenure of the Cecil and Ida Green Visiting Professorship at the University of British Columbia, Vancouver. An earlier version was presented to the Shelby Cullom Davis Center seminar, Princeton University, in 1977; the discussion that occurred there contributed much to what follows.

1 *International Social Science Journal* 14:3 (1962), published the same year under the UNESCO imprint as *Changes in the Family*; Peter Laslett and Richard Wall, *Household and Family in Past Time* (Cambridge 1972); *Journal of Marriage and Family* 25 (1973); Christopher Lasch, 'The Family and History,' *New York Review of Books* 18 (13 Nov 1975) 33–8; continued, ibid, as 'The Emotions of Family Life,' 19 (27 Nov 1975) 37–41, and 'What the Doctor Ordered,' 20 (11 Dec 1975) 50–4; cf the critique of Lasch's position in Barbara J. Harris, 'Recent Work in the History of the Family: A Review Article,' *Feminist Studies* 3 (1976) 159–72.

upset the long-held, if somewhat simplistic, understanding of the passage from the extended to the nuclear family and, in the process, has suggested the refinement, even the abandonment, of the notions of industrialization and urbanization as the theoretical explanation of the change. Perhaps more than any other group the students of the family in medieval Europe have made the theory of unilinear progress from the extended to the nuclear family untenable. These scholars have developed and applied new methods in their research, and the results have been remarkable. Local studies such as those of Georges Duby for the Mâconnais, David Herlihy for Florence, Diane Hughes for Genoa, J. Ambrose Raftis for East Midland villages in England, and Jacques Heers' recent synthetic analysis of the structures of individual cities show a rich variety of family patterns and a bewildering series of changes within them.[2]

Such variety comes as no surprise to one with even a general knowledge of medieval law. On the Continent, the rich and remarkably tenacious diversity of local usage is obvious. Even in England, such a diversity becomes more and more discernible as the limited application of the common law is better understood. The West, after all, was formed after many groups of peoples established themselves in new areas in the Empire and in northeastern Europe. Given different backgrounds and the differing conditions of life in their new homes, the variety of family customs to which their laws give access is not surprising. It is true that the variety in question most often touched details, but even on fundamental matters there were significant differences. Change beginning from such a complex base could hardly be expected to be either a simple or a common process.

However, there were several institutions of general influence in the medieval world that confronted the welter of family patterns and tended to induce some common elements. One of those institutions was the

2 Among the writings of these scholars see especially Georges Duby, *La société au XIe et XIIe siècles dans la région mâconnaise* (Paris 1952), and 'Systèmes familiaux: Lignage, noblesse, et chevalerie au XIIe siècle dans la région mâconnaise: Une révision,' *Annales: Economies, sociétés, civilisations* 27 (1972) 803–23; David Herlihy, 'Family Solidarity in Medieval Italian History,' in *Economy, Society, and Government in Medieval Italy: Essays in Memory of Robert L. Reynolds*, ed David Herlihy et al (Kent, Ohio 1969) 175–84; Diane O. Hughes, 'Urban Growth and Family Structure in Medieval Genoa,' *Past and Present* 66 (1975) 3–28; J. Ambrose Raftis, *Tenure and Mobility: Studies in the Social History of the Mediaeval English Village*, Studies and Texts 8 (Toronto 1964) 33–62, and *Warboys: Two Hundred Years in the Life of an English Mediaeval Village*, Studies and Texts 29 (Toronto 1974) 225–40; Jacques Heers, *Le clan familial* (Paris 1974).

Church. Its action was primarily in the realm of ideas and moral guidance – areas that, for the most part, historians of the medieval family have tended to avoid. This limitation of the historian's approach is understandable. His main sources have been surveys of various kinds: the polyptique, tax roll, court roll, etc. In them, it is the household, sex-ratios, lifespan, domicile, and geographic and social mobility that are open to analysis. In a few cases, by a systematic organization of randomly occurring data, it has been possible to establish networks involving kin, neighbourhood, and occupational as well as political contacts that reveal the actual set of relationships operative in the lives of individuals. But if family is approached less from the point of view of the groups of persons of which it consists or of the power structure within it and is examined instead from the point of view of one of its procedures for recruiting new members, namely marriage, then there is a special place for the role of ideas. This is true not only in the sense that spouses often developed through different processes of socialization but also because the very notion of marriage, its mode of establishment, and its purpose were capable of analysis and development. Furthermore, while it was characteristic of Europe to consist of many areas with different family customs and different marriage usages, matrimony came to an ever greater extent under the control of the religion that was common to Europe. In that situation a common ideology of marriage was developed. However that ideology may have been refracted in the practical order, it is important to realize that, along with the variety of customs touching the family and marriage, there was to appear a common set of ideas that concerned an essential mode of family recruitment; and that, we may theorize, was an important influence on family itself.

These ideas, often part of a larger set, developed at different tempos. A suitable point of entry for their examination is the end of the eleventh century. By that time, we find the peoples of Europe in the areas that, with minor changes, they would inhabit until the great migrations of the nineteenth century. This same period saw the beginnings of notable developments in the intellectual order and the appearance of structures capable of applying the conclusions of that intellectual activity. In less abstract terms, the reference is to the simultaneous beginnings of legal studies and scholastic theology and the implementation of the administrative side of the Gregorian movement of reform. One of the objects of that intellectual activity was an examination of marriage. The result was an ideology of immense social consequence; it is our intention to examine it and to investigate the question of its application.

This investigation will lead us to examine a theory of marriage developed during the high Middle Ages and to suggest at least some of its operative ideas – in several cases, quite new ideas – that gradually came to be accepted by society. At that point it may be possible to sketch, with varying degrees of probability, what the principals of a marriage were expected to seek in it.[3] It has been said in jest, though not without a serious overtone, that Christianity destroyed the family. If this sentence has any meaning, it is in this investigation that it should be discovered. Marriage has been studied by the historians of canon law very thoroughly; one need only mention the works of Esmein (1891), Freisen (1893), Le Bras (1926 and passim), and Dauvillier (1933). Historians of theology have not yet investigated medieval marriage with the same care, though current studies are promising.[4] It is worth noting that these scholars have tended to ignore the family in their discussions. Thus the paradox: medieval social historians have usually paid insufficient attention to marriage as a relationship, while historians of canon law and theology have almost overlooked the family, the institution that provided the raison d'être of the sacrament that they studied.

Investigation of the beginnings of Christianity has shown that it held no special position on family nor, by and large, on marriage: the earliest Christians were accustomed to Jewish usages; as the new religion spread through the Roman Empire and beyond, it accepted the local forms of these institutions, forms that varied from the rather sophisticated usages of Rome to the customs of the provincial peoples. The first thousand years of the Church's life can be seen as a period during which Christian doctrine, confronted by a bewildering profusion of marriage customs, concentrated its efforts on defending and enhancing the moral value of matrimony. Steady insistence on the permanence and sanctity of the relationship of husband and wife, and on the limitation of erotic sexuality to that relationship, gained significant acceptance by society, even though

---

3 Cf William J. Goode, *World Revolution and Family Patterns* (New York 1963) 1–26, 365–80.
4 The fundamental study remains that of L. Godefroy and Gabriel Le Bras in DTC 9 II (1927) 2043–2123, s v 'Mariage'. Valuable more recent studies include Henri Rondet, *Introduction à l'étude de la théologie du mariage*, Théologie pastorale et spiritualité, Recherches et synthèses 6 (Paris 1960); Edward C. Schillebeeckx, *Marriage: Human Reality and Saving Mystery*, trans N.D. Smith (London 1965); Gabriel Le Bras, 'Le mariage dans la théologie et le droit de l'Eglise du XIe au XIIIe siècle,' *Cahiers de civilisation médiévale* 11 (1968) 191–202; John F. Quinn, 'Saint Bonaventure and the Sacrament of Matrimony,' *Franciscan Studies* 12 (1974) 103–43.

individual practice and the different civil customs and laws lagged well behind. The Church's position was often locally stated, was not always consistent, nor was it organized and complete.[5]

As the first millennium came to an end, however, a significant change occurred in the West. Europe recovered from the second period of invasions, and a profound reorganization began. The older vagueness of distinction between the civil and religious orders was found wanting; the process of division was begun. Marriage, hitherto essentially an institution regulated by family custom and, to a certain extent, by Roman and barbarian civil law, passed more and more into the jurisdiction of the bishop. The older pastoral attitude towards marriage, one involving instruction, blessing, exhortation, and the occasional excommunication when abuse became intolerable, was no longer considered adequate. Instead, as part of a general re-examination of Christian life by canonists and theologians, marriage was analysed in detail: the creation of the marriage bond, the role of consent, the qualifications of the principals of the relationship, the ends and the qualities of the married state all were subject to careful scrutiny. A collecting and sorting, ordering and interpretation of patristic literature went on through the late eleventh and twelfth centuries. The process was assisted mightily by the discovery of the texts of Roman law and the impetus that it gave to the development of legal science. By the 1150s, the first syntheses, the one canonistic, the other theological, were available in the *Decretum Gratiani* and the *Libri IV Sententiarum* of Peter Lombard.[6] In these works and in the legislation and jurisprudence of the next three generations, a theory of marital consent was elaborated, the practical implications of which were to have immense social consequences – implications that may not be entirely unfolded to the present day.

In broad terms, the resulting view of marriage can be set out as follows: 1) The matrimonial bond was created by consent; neither consummation nor formality of any kind was required for validity. 2) It was the consent of the couple that created the marriage bond. Whatever the role of the family or the lord may have been, it was secondary and dispensable. 3) It was preferred that the marriage bond be created in a

---

5 As a general introduction to these very complex matters see Henri Crouzel, *L'Eglise primitive face au divorce du premier au cinquième siècle* (Paris 1970); and Korbinian Ritzer, *Formen, Riten, und religiöses Brauchtum der Eheschliessung in den christlichen Kirchen des ersten Jahrtausends*, Liturgiewissenschaftliche Quellen und Forschungen 38 (Münster 1962); references are to the French translation, *Le mariage dans les églises chrétiennes du Ier au XIe siècle* (Paris 1970).

6 DTC 9 II 2129–55.

public setting; but, inasmuch as external formalities were developed and imposed, they were located within neither familial nor seigniorial structures but in the local community considered in its religious or parochial capacity. 4) There was a desire to internalize the marriage relationship. Theologians emphasized the bond of charity between the spouses and the possibility of its growth as a reason for their choice of each other. 5) Throughout the discussion by both canonists and theologians the point of view was one that focused on the couple: by and large, lordship was ignored; the wider family circle and even the children born to the couple received little attention.

In what follows it is proposed to set out the broad lines of the development sketched in the previous paragraph, then to approach the question of the application of the ideal that resulted.

It is with the *Concordia discordantium canonum* of Gratian (ca 1140) that we propose to begin. The text is usually referred to as the *Decretum*, but this briefer title should never mask the original implication that the volume was intended to bring divergent positions into agreement.[7] The dialectical quality of the work is especially evident in its middle section, a series of cases; *Causae* 27–36 contain the bulk of Gratian's doctrine on marriage. From the point of view of the present study, it is his treatment of the mode of establishing the marriage bond that is most important.[8] He espoused the *concubitus* theory: the married state was begun by an exchange of consent (*matrimonium initiatum*), but the union was completed (*matrimonium ratum*) only by consummation.[9] Another position, the consent theory, based on the older view of Roman law, saw the marriage bond established by the simple consent to live as husband and wife. This Gratian rejected – though, as it happened, it was to hold the future.

It was on the related topic of the persons whose consent was necessary for the creation of the marriage bond that Gratian's teaching is of special

---

7 See Stanley Chodorow, *Christian Political Theory and Church Politics in the Mid-Twelfth Century: The Ecclesiology of Gratian's Decretum* (Berkeley 1972) 1–16. Standard reference forms to the *Decretum* are used throughout; thus Causa 26, quaestio 1, canon 1 is rendered C26 q1 c1. All quotations are from *Decretum magistri Gratiani* in *Corpus iuris canonici*, 1, ed A. Friedberg, 2nd ed (Leipzig 1879; repr Graz 1955).

8 See Gérard Fransen, 'La formation du lien matrimonial au moyen âge,' in *Le lien matrimonial*, Colloque du Cerdic, Strasbourg, 21–3 mai 1970, ed René Metz and Jean Schlick (Strasbourg 1970) 106–26.

9 C27 q2 c29.

interest here. There is no need to dwell on the powerful influence of lord and family in the choice of marriage partner at all levels of society. It would continue for centuries and would often tend to ignore the choice or even the agreement of the couple involved.[10] At the same time, it should be remembered that through the early Middle Ages there was interest in preserving the spouses' freedom of choice, interest that seems to have been quickening during the eleventh century.[11] However, with Gratian's *Decretum* the role of the principals of the marriage received decisive re-evaluation. This matter was set out in detail by John Noonan, Jr in 'Power to Choose' at the meeting of the Medieval Academy of America in 1972 at Los Angeles.[12] The debt to Professor Noonan's presentation in what follows will be obvious.

Causa 31, *quaestio* 2 of the *Decretum* is entitled '*An filia sit tradenda inuita alicui?*' ('May a daughter be given in marriage against her will?').[13] In the introduction to the question Gratian refers to a fourth-century gloss on the Pauline text 'Let a widow marry whom she wills, only in the Lord' (1 Cor 7:39), ascribed to Ambrosiaster. It reads: 'Unwilling marriages usually have bad results.'[14] 'Ambrosius testifies,' Gratian writes, 'that a woman may not be compelled to marry a man ... because unwilling marriages usually have bad results.'[15] As was pointed out, the gloss refers to

10 In the *Summa* of Peter the Chanter (1191–7) and the *Summa* of Robert of Curson (1208–13), where the tension between individual and family rights and feudal claims in the marriage of an heir is discussed, the problem is put largely in terms of financial loss and gain; the matter of the choice of the person, the arrangement of whose marriage is in question, is largely ignored; see John W. Baldwin, *Masters, Princes, and Merchants: The Social Views of Peter the Chanter and His Circle* (Princeton 1970) I 248–9.

11 On the recurring theme of free consent in the Roman legal tradition, see Ritzer, *Formen* 167–8, 211, 212, 218–19, and passim; in literature, ibid 361–4; among the Anglo-Saxons, see Michael M. Sheehan, 'Marriage and Family in English Conciliar and Synodal Legislation,' in *Essays in Honour of Anton Charles Pegis*, ed J. Reginald O'Donnell (Toronto 1974) 212 and nn 26, 27 (here p 84). The efforts to regulate the marriages of the unpropertied classes, marriages in which dynastic or family strategies would be unimportant, may well have contributed to a more acute awareness of the importance of consent to the union; cf the suggestions of James A. Brundage, 'Concubinage and Marriage in Medieval Canon Law,' *Journal of Medieval History* 1 (April 1975) 1–17.

12 *Viator* 4 (1973) 419–34. The article is part of the series 'Marriage in the Middle Ages'; see the Introduction by John Leyerle, ibid 413–14.

13 The title of q2 in the introduction to C31.

14 On the author of the gloss see Noonan, 'Power to Choose' 419 n1.

15 'Quod autem aliqua non sit cogenda nubere alicui, Ambrosius testatur super primam epistolam ad Chorinthios: "Nubat uidua cui uult: tantum in Domino"; id est quem

widows: Gratian enlarged its application to a general prohibition. Thus the first five lines of the question suggest the direction of its solution.

The first canon is a decretal of Urban II (1088–99) touching the marriage of the daughter of Jourdain I, prince of Capua, to Renaud Ridel, duke of Gaeta. Jourdain had been forced to espouse his daughter to Renaud and was unhappy about it. The little girl – she is called *infantula* – was in tears, and her mother and relations were also opposed to the match. The pope judged that the authority of the canons and the laws did not approve of such a union; but, lest those ignorant of such matters consider his decision too harsh, he tempered it. If the prince, the child, her mother, and relatives assented to the marriage, it was to go forward. If (as seemed likely) they did not, the papal legate was to ascertain that the facts of the case were as presented and declare the girl free of the disputed union so that she might marry as she chose.[16] Note that in the case the opposition to the marriage was presented as general within the girl's family; there is nothing to suggest that more importance should be attached to her objection than to that of others.[17] Yet Gratian's rubric to the canon carried the matter much further, focusing attention on the daughter: 'A father's oath cannot compel a girl to marry one to whom she has never assented.'[18]

The discord within the question was provided by the second canon, a *palea* that was probably added to the *Decretum* after it left Gratian's

---

sibi aptum putauerit, illi nubat; quia inuitae nuptiae solent malos prouentus habere. "Tantum autem in Domino": Id est, ut sine suspicione turpitudinis nubat, et uiro suae religionis nubat' (C31 q2 *dict. ad* c1).

16 'Si uerum esse constiterit, quod nobis legati Iordanis principis retulerunt, scilicet, quod ipse coactus et dolens filiam suam infantulam nolentem, flentem, et pro uiribus renitentem, non assentientibus sed ualde dolentibus matre et parentela, Rainaldo Rodelli filio desponsauerit, quonian canonum et legum auctoritas, talia sponsalia (ut infra ostenditur) non approbat, ne ignorantibus leges et canones nimis durum quod dicimus uideatur, ita sentenciam temperamus, ut, si princeps cum filiae, matris, et parentelae assensu id, quod ceptum est, perficere uoluerit, concedamus. Sin autem, legatus noster utrasque partes audiat, et si nichil fuerit ex parte supradicti Rainaldi amplius, quod inpediat, ab ipso Iordane sacramentum, quod ita constent hec, ut dicta sunt, accipiat, et nos canonum ac legum scita sequentes deinceps non prohibemus, quin alii uiro, si uoluerit, predicta filia eius tantum in Domino nubat' (C31 q2 c1).

17 Noonan, 'Power to Choose' 420 notes that the child was not identified by name.

18 'Iuramento patris non cogitur puella nubere, cui numquam assensum prebuit.' On the problem of Gratian's authorship of the rubrics see Gabriel Le Bras, Charles Lefebvre, and Jacqueline Rimbaud, *L'âge classique, 1140–1378: Sources et théorie du droit*, Histoire du droit et des institutions de l'Eglise en Occident 7 (Paris 1965) 59–74.

hands.[19] Here, in a decretal ascribed to Pope Hormisdas (514–23), the position that a father cannot force his adult son to marry against his will was maintained. However, the decretal went on to assert that a father could give a minor son in marriage and that the boy, having come to man's estate, was to honour the agreement.

In the next canon, the text returned to its main argument, using a second decision of Urban II.[20] The case was set out as follows: Sancho Ramirez, king of Aragon-Navarre, in a time of difficulty had pledged a niece in marriage. She refused and persisted in her refusal. The king, who clearly desired to be freed from an embarrassing promise, was instructed not to force her compliance. On this occasion the pope gave a reason for his decision: 'Those one in body ought to be one in spirit.' He went further to warn those who would do otherwise: '... lest when, against the command of the Lord and the Apostle, the woman will have been un-willingly united to some man, she incur the guilt of divorce or the crime of fornication.'[21] (Note that the authority of Christ and Paul was set out

19 'Econtra Hormisda Papa scribit Eusebio Episcopo. "Tua sanctitas nos requisiuit, frater uenerande, de filio adulto, quem pater matrimonium contrahere uult, si sine uoluntate filii adulti facere potest. Ad quod dicimus, si aliquo modo non consentit filius, fieri non posse. Potest autem de filio nondum adulto, uoluntas cuius nondum discerni potest, pater eum, cui uult, in matrimonium tradere, et post, quam filius peruenerit ad perfectam etatem, omnino obseruare et adimplere debet. Hoc ab omnibus orthodoxae fidei cultoribus sancitum a nobis tenendum mandamus"' (C31 q2 c2). On the *palea* see Le Bras et al, *L'âge classique* 100–29; and Jacqueline Rimbaud, 'Les paleae dans le Décret de Gratien,' in *Proceedings of the Second International Congress of Medieval Canon Law*, ed ed Stephan Kuttner and J. Joseph Ryan, Monumenta iuris canonici, Series C: Subsidia 1 (Vatican City 1965) 23–44.

20 'De neptis tuae coniugio, quam te cuidam militi daturum necessitatis instante articulo sub fidei pollicitatione firmasti, hoc equitate dictante decernimus, ut, si illa uirum illum, ut dicitur, omnino rennuit, et in eadem uoluntatis auctoritate persistit, ut uiro illi prorsus se deneget nupturam, nequaquam eam inuitam et renitentem eiusdem uiri cogas sociari coniugio. Quorum enim unum corpus est, unus debet esse et animus, ne forte, cum uirgo fuerit alicui inuita copulata, contra Domini Apostolique preceptum aut reatum discidii, aut crimen fornicationis incurrat. Cuius uidelicet peccati malum in eum redundare constat, qui eam coniunxit inuitam. Quod pari tenore de uiro est sentiendum' (C31 q2 c3).

21 The punctuation of the phrase 'ne forte ... incurrat' in Friedberg's edition (see n20) requires a different translation, namely, 'Lest when the woman will have been unwillingly united to some man she incur the guilt of divorce or the crime of fornication against the command of the Lord and the Apostle.' This translation would considerably weaken the force of Gratian's argument. However, the punctuation 'ne forte, cum uirgo fuerit alicui inuite copulata contra Domini apostolique preceptum, aut reatum discidii aut crimen fornicationis incurrat,' which relates the

in opposition to such a union!) The text went on to say that where this occurred the sin would redound on those who had brought about the marriage of the woman, and ended with the remark that the ruling also applied to men. The internalization of the act between the couple was far advanced in the motives for this papal judgment, and it was on precisely this that Gratian seized in the rubric of the canon, lifting the desire for unity of spirit to the level of a principle standing in the way of any forced marriage: 'Where there is to be union of bodies there ought to be union of spirits, and therefore no unwilling person is to be joined to another.'[22]

After a final canon dealing with a coerced confession used in an attempt to bring about a divorce, Gratian summed up his doctrine: to the question 'May a daughter be given in marriage against her will?' there is a clear answer, 'By these authorities it is evident that no woman should be married to anyone except by her free will.'[23]

It will perhaps have been noted that in each canon of *quaestio* 2 the context was such that the free choice of the family was as much at issue as the choices by the principals of the marriage. Yet, in the first and third canons, the papal decretals had concentrated on the decision of the bride, pushing the matter much further than the petitioner (in the first case, a father, in the other, an uncle) might have desired. The same direction was taken by Gratian, whose question focused on the freedom of the woman and whose argument produced a stronger case for that freedom than his sources seemed to warrant. Yet this emphasis did not preclude his insistence on family consent. Perhaps his selection of the canons in question was calculated to present the freedom of choice by the daughter in a context in which she and her family would be in agreement. Whether this were the case or not, it is clear that the discussion of marriage in the *Decretum* presumes a world where family usually played an important role in the choice of marriage partners. Gratian's thinking on the matter is explicit in his gloss on *paterno* in C32 q2 c12: 'Where it is said "women are joined to their husbands by paternal choice," it is intended to be

---

prohibition to the undesired marriage rather than to the sins of the woman, is the more traditional and is in accord with the rules of the *cursus*. (For this last point I am indebted to my colleague Leonard Boyle, OP.) Such is Huggucio's understanding of the text in his *Summa*: 'contra preceptum apostoli, scilicet illud: nubat cui vult [1 Cor 7:39]' (Paris, BN MS Lat 3892 f 307r).

22 'Quorum unum futurum est corpus, unus debet esse animus: atque ideo nulla inuita est copulanda alicui.'

23 'His auctoritatibus euidenter ostenditur, quod nisi libera uoluntate nulla est copulanda alicui' (C31 q2 *dict. post* c4). On c4 see Noonan, 'Power to Choose' 421–2.

understood that paternal choice is desired in marriage, and that without it marriage is not legitimate, according to the words of Pope Evaristus: "Otherwise, unless [the bride] is given by the parents, the marriage is not legitimate."[24] It is true that, even in the context of the *Decretum*, the word "legitimate" might be read in terms of liceity rather than validity – as, in fact, it would be interpreted by later commentators. However, given the canons that follow, it becomes fairly certain that Gratian saw parental consent to be necessary for validity of the marriage.[25] Of the role of the lord in the choice of marriage partner he had little to say.

From another point of view, the author's insistence on parental consent seems illogical. Gratian demanded that marriage be publicly performed before the Church but admitted that the omission of formalities did not render the act invalid.[26] In the following century it was precisely this possibility of the clandestine marriage that was thought to undermine parental authority. It is hard to avoid the conclusion that Gratian was aware that the informality to which he objected, but which he permitted, negated his claim that paternal consent was necessary for marriage. Be this as it may, it was among the theologians that the freedom from parental control would become explicit.

Less than twenty years after the appearance of the *Decretum*, a theological synthesis on a comparable scale, *Libri IV Sententiarum*, was published by Peter Lombard. The volume was remarkable for its completeness, objectivity, and felicity of organization, if not for its originality, and summed up the accomplishment of the theologians and, to a certain extent, of the canonists of the previous fifty years. One of its more successful sections was the treatise on marriage. It is something of a commonplace that twelfth-century theologians were often dependent on the canonists, examining the same questions and frequently proceeding from their conclusions. The dependence of the Lombard on the *Decretum* is evident in almost every part of the treatise on marriage.[27] Yet he was able to present positions in radical disagreement with those of Gratian.

24 'VII Pars. Gratian. Cum dicitur: "paterno arbitrio feminae iunctae viris," datur intelligi; quod paternus consensus desideratur in nuptiis, nec sine eo legitimae nuptiae habeantur, iuxta illud Euaristi Papae: "Aliter non fit legitimum coniugium, nisi a parentibus tradatur."'
25 C32 q2 cc 13–16; C36 q2; cf C28 q1 *dict. post* c17.
26 C30 q5.
27 On Peter Lombard see *Magistri Petri Lombardi Parisiensis episcopi Sententiae in IV libris distinctae*, 3rd ed, Spicilegium Bonaventurianum 4–5 (Grottaferrata 1971–81) I pars 1, 5–45. The treatise on marriage is Bk 4, dist. 26–36, ibid II 416–75.

Thus on the crucial question of the mode in which the marriage bond was established he adopted the tradition favoured by some of his predecessors that present consent made marriage.[28] He stated the distinction between betrothal, or promise of marriage (consent *de futuro*), and the actual marriage (consent *de presenti*), maintaining that consummation was not necessary for creation of the permanent marriage bond. Furthermore, he taught that the consent of the principals was all that was necessary for the creation of that marriage bond; no essential role was reserved for third parties, be they family or lord.[29]

It has already been remarked that Pope Urban in the second decretal quoted and Gratian in his use of it based their judgments on the importance of the internal relationship between the principals of the marriage. The theologians' approach to matrimonial theory, one that, as has just been seen, was capable of considerable impact on marriage law, was characterized by a desire to explore the relationship between the couple. Peter Lombard had much to say of the life of charity that should grow between husband and wife so as to result in a relationship that was deeper and more permanent than sexual attraction.[30] His thirteenth-century successors were to go much further, teaching that the sacrament of marriage was a cause of grace in the couple and that this sacrament was administered by husband and wife to each other.[31]

Rather than to pursue later developments, however, it is important to reflect on the impact of the *Decretum* and *Libri IV Sententiarum*. They represent a major moment in the history of marriage theory. But the question must be asked whether their theories changed the notion of marriage that was functional in Western European society by creating an ideology that sooner or later would confront a view of marriage that saw the relationship in terms of wide social and political needs. The volumes in question were both products of the schools. Neither had official sanction. As has been seen, they disagreed on several important matters; the *Decretum* itself was far from being consistent. Yet, with all their limitations, they held the future. The *Decretum* was clarified, reinforced, and adjusted by gloss and commentary; eventually it became part of the regular instruction of canon lawyers. The *Libri IV Sententiarum* in turn

28 Dist. 27 cap. 3–10, 422–31.
29 Ibid cap. 3.
30 Dist. 30 cap. 2, 439–41. These notions were more developed in earlier theologians like Hugh of St Victor. See his *De sacramentis*, Liber 2, pars II (PL 176 476–520).
31 DTC 9 II 2217–23.

became a text of faculties of theology, and the presentation of a commentary on the *Sentences* became the final step in the training of the candidate for the master's degree. Thus it is clear that the ideas on marriage expressed by Gratian and Peter Lombard had a very long life indeed – so far as university circles were concerned.

Furthermore, between the advent of Alexander III in 1159 and the death of Innocent III in 1216, papal judgments in marriage cases gradually reduced the teaching of the schools to consistency and applied it throughout the Western Church. Lombard's position that the marriage bond was established by the simple exchange of consent was eventually adopted, and the general tendency to emphasize the role of the couple was vindicated, for their consent and the consent of no other was judged essential to their marriage.[32] The resulting relationship was seen essentially in terms of the good of the couple.

The same years saw the growing demand that marriage take place publicly within a religious ceremony. This was in accord with the growing emphasis on the sacred aspect of matrimony, but it was also seen as a protection of the rights of the couple. The private exchange of consent, inasmuch as it was without witness, was difficult of defence before the courts.[33] Furthermore, as the law of impediments was developed by canonists, it became clear that it was necessary to go beyond the information available to the couple, or admitted by them, to establish their freedom to marry. Early in the thirteenth century, the system of banns, a public announcement of the intention to marry made at mass in the parish church for several weeks before the event, was developed in northern France and England.[34] This method of control was adopted by the Fourth Lateran Council and applied throughout the Church.[35] It obliged parishioners to provide information to the parish priest if there were any reason to prevent the proposed marriage from going forward. This was the first

---

32 See Jean Dauvillier, *Le mariage dans le droit classique de l'Eglise depuis le Décret de Gratien (1140) jusqu'à la mort de Clément v (1314)* (Paris 1933) 55–142. Cf Charles Donahue, Jr, 'The Policy of Alexander the Third's Consent Theory of Marriage,' in *Proceedings of the Fourth International Congress of Medieval Canon Law*, ed Stephan Kuttner, Monumenta iuris canonici, Series C: Subsidia 5 (Vatican City 1976) 251–81. On the motives for the change see Noonan, 'Power to Choose' 427–34, and Donahue 270–79.

33 See *Decretum* C30 q5 *dict. post cc* 8, 9, 11.

34 See Dauvillier, *Le mariage* 104–5; cf n38, below.

35 Canon 51, *Conciliorum oecumenicorum decreta*, ed Josephus Alberigo et al, 3rd ed (Bologna 1973) 258.

general and organized system for negative control of the choice of marriage partner by powers other than the couple. It should be noted that it was intended to prevent the attempt of forbidden or impossible marriages and that its exercise was in the hands of the parish and the parish priest. Yet even here the unique role of the couple was respected: failure to obey the requirement that banns be published did not render their marriage invalid.

The regulation touching banns and the previously mentioned jurisprudence developed in papal decisions in marriage cases became part of the *Decretales* of Gregory IX, an official collection of law promulgated by the pope in 1234.[36] With its appearance, the medieval law of marriage was virtually complete. Theologians would continue to develop their understanding of the relationship of husband and wife, but the essential ideas and regulations, from the point of view of the present essay, were enunciated. They conveyed an ideal that was directly opposed to the current view of marriage. The question is whether they succeeded in permeating European society and, if so, by what means and at what rate?

Given the immediate and general use of the *Decretales* of Gregory IX in the schools and as source of the Church's law and given the ongoing exercise of papal appeal jurisdiction in marriage cases that applied this law, it can be presumed that the couple-oriented view of marriage was known at least within the upper levels of the court system of the Western Church and applied there.

Furthermore, it can be surmised that these ideas were carried further down the ecclesiastical structure by another instrument of dissemination, namely, local gatherings of the clergy such as the provincial council and the diocesan synod. The gathering of bishops of a region or province in a council and the smaller gathering of the clergy of a diocese in a synod was one of the characteristics of the reform period. This was especially true of the years after the Fourth Lateran Council, so much so that the thirteenth century is usually considered to be the most effective period of conciliar function in the history of the Church.[37] Sets of decrees and

36 *Corpus iuris canonici*, 2, ed A. Friedberg (Leipzig 1881; repr Graz 1955). Bk 4 treats of marriage and related topics.

37 Augustin Fliche, *La chrétienté romaine (1198–1271)*, Histoire de l'Eglise 10 (Paris 1950) 389–90; Marion Gibbs and Jane Lang, *Bishops and Reform, 1215–1272* (London 1939) 104–30. Canon 6 of the Fourth Lateran Council (1215) ordered annual provincial councils and diocesan synods, *Conciliorum oecumenicorum decreta*, ed Alberigo et al 236–7.

constitutions were published at these meetings; their analysis is a useful instrument for those investigating the problems that especially exercised the local Church at a given time.

These regulations survive in large numbers. Unfortunately, for some parts of Europe they are poorly edited, if edited at all. Thus it is not yet possible to employ this type of source systematically. The case of England is different. Not only was this ecclesiastical unit more homogeneous, but, for about half of the Middle Ages, good editions of its conciliar and diocesan regulations are available. The pattern that is revealed there can be set out briefly.[38] First, the bishops in council or in synod were much concerned with problems touching sexuality, celibacy, and marriage. Second, the question of consent does not loom large in this literature. In a context that implied that the regulation was self-evident, it was stated as early as 1175 that the agreement of the principals was required for marriage. Yet the canon went on to allow the marriage of a child who had not yet attained the age of consent, where the union served the common good. It was only towards the middle of the thirteenth century that it was stated – and then almost reluctantly – that consent made the marriage and that the formalities which the legislators sought to impose were not necessary for its validity. About the same time this legislation mentioned the questioning of the couple to establish the fact of their agreement to the union they were about to enter. Third, it was pointed out as early as 1214 that sexual union after betrothal constituted marriage. Though this position was stated again in several statutes, the main impression given by this legislation is of a powerful statement on the necessity of publicity and formality in marriage which overwhelms the quiet admission that these latter were not essential requirements.[39] Finally, the role of family and lord was virtually ignored. From the point of view of English conciliar and synodal regulations the only limitation to the free choice of spouse was imposed by the various impediments that rendered marriage impossible. Here the legislator turned not to the family but to the parish for information touching the kinship and the freedom of the prospective spouses. The only social control was a negative one, and it was exercised by the local community through the medium of the parish priest. It can

38 This matter is studied in detail in my article 'Marriage Theory and Practice in the Conciliar Legislation and Diocesan Statutes of Medieval England,' *Mediaeval Studies* 40 (1978) 408–60 (here pp 118–76).

39 Cf Juliette M. Turlan, 'Recherches sur le mariage dans la pratique coutumière (XIIe–XVIe s.),' *Revue historique de droit français et étranger* 35 (1957) 477–528.

be concluded, then, that the local law of England reflected the developing common law of the Church, though sometimes with a delay of as much as a generation. Furthermore, it reveals something of the difficulty of application of the new understanding of marriage even at the level of law.

During the Middle Ages, it was a regulation of some dioceses that the rector of each parish church possess a copy of local statutes and be familiar with them. At synods, he could expect to hear them read aloud from time to time. This arrangement would assist the spread of the information with which we are concerned here, but it would still remain somewhat remote from ordinary means of instruction. By the fourth quarter of the fourteenth century, there is ample evidence in the registers of local ecclesiastical courts to show that the revolutionary ideas touching matrimonial consent that began to assume consistent form in the *Decretum* were known even by the young. The records of cases that appeared before bishops' officials reveal a general understanding of the necessity of consent by the spouses for the validity of a marriage, the successful defence of a union against the prohibition of parents, the frequency of clandestine marriage, and clear evidence of young people making preliminary arrangements for marriage without parental involvement.[40] The scholar's problem is to bridge the gap between the period when the new ideas on matrimony were enunciated and those last years of the fourteenth century when court records reveal that to a considerable extent those ideas were understood and acted upon.

40 See Paul Adam, *La vie paroissiale en France au XIVe siècle* (Paris 1964); Jean-Philippe Lévy, 'L'officialité de Paris et les questions familiales à la fin du XIVe siècle,' in *Etudes d'histoire du droit canonique dédiées à Gabriel Le Bras* (Paris 1965) II 1265–94; R. Weigand, 'Die Rechtsprechung des Regensburger Gerichts in Ehesachen unter besonderer Berücksichtigung der bedingten Eheschliessung nach Gerichtsbüchern aus dem Ende des 15. Jahrhunderts,' *Archiv für katholisches Kirchenrecht* 107 (1968) 403–63; Karen A. Corsano, 'Custom and Consent: A Study of Marriage in Fourteenth-Century Paris and Normandy, Based on the Records of the Ecclesiastical Courts,' MSL thesis (Pontifical Institute of Mediaeval Studies, Toronto 1971); Michael M. Sheehan, 'The Formation and Stability of Marriage in Fourteenth-Century England: Evidence of an Ely Register,' *Mediaeval Studies* 33 (1971) 228–63 (here pp 38–76), and 'Marriage and Family' 205–14 (here pp 77–86); Richard H. Helmholz, 'Abjuration *sub pena nubendi* in the Church Courts of Medieval England,' *Jurist* 32 (1972) 80–90, and *Marriage Litigation in Medieval England* (London 1974); Charles Donahue, Jr, 'A Case from Archbishop Stratford's Audience Book,' *Bulletin of Medieval Canon Law* n s 2 (1972) 45–59, and 'The Policy of Alexander the Third's Consent Theory of Marriage.' Earlier, though less fully reported, examples are to be found in Gero Dolezalek, *Das Imbreviaturbuch des erzbischöflichen Gerichtsnotars Hubaldus aus Pisa, Mai bis August 1230* (Köln 1969) nos 15, 17, 47, and 51 (May–July 1230).

The gap in question can probably be bridged by examining the Church's instruments of teaching and by studying those records that indicate the mentalities of different groups in the period under study. With regard to the instruments of teaching there were, first of all, the pastoral manuals. They were intended to assist the priest in various aspects of his pastoral office, but with special reference to his role as confessor. The liturgy, too, was a method of instruction. Thus, while the text and formalities of the marriage ritual focused on the couple, they helped to educate the larger group who assisted at the ceremony. Sermons reached a still larger audience, so both the *exempla* and the sermons themselves must be analysed for their contribution to the point at issue. Similarly the liturgical drama and morality play may well repay detailed study. The drama would also be a sign of mentality as well as an instrument that assisted in its formation. In the same way, literature (*belles-lettres*) and the iconography of the graphic and plastic arts must be made to yield their evidence on any shift of accepted ideas on marriage along the lines suggested by theological and canonical thinking. Such a program of research, daunting though it be, must be undertaken if the impact on society of twelfth-century thinking on the free choice of marriage partner is to be known. As an indication of method as well as a suggestion of the conclusion that may well be forthcoming, it is proposed to look briefly at the early stages of the development of pastoral literature and to examine the liturgical forms of the late twelfth and early thirteenth centuries.

A new type of pastoral treatise, the compendium for confessors, began to take shape late in the twelfth century.[41] It was intended to put develop-

---

41 See Pierre Michaud-Quantin, *Sommes de casuistique et manuels de confession au moyen âge (XIIe–XVIe siècles)*, Analecta mediaevalia Namurcensia 13 (Louvain 1962) 7–33; and Josef C. Ziegler, *Die Ehelehre der Pönitentialsummen von 1200–1350: Eine Untersuchung zur Geschichte der Moral- und Pastoraltheologie*, Studie zur Geschichte der katholischen Moraltheologie 4 (Regensburg 1956) 3–33. Among more recent work on the pastoral *summae* see Leonard E. Boyle, OP, 'The *Oculus sacerdotis* and Some Other Works of William de Pagula,' *Transactions of the Royal Historical Society*, 5th ser, 5 (1955) 51–110; idem, 'A Study of the Works Attributed to William of Pagula, with Special Reference to the *Oculus sacerdotis* and the *Summa summarum*,' D.Phil. thesis (Oxford 1956); idem, 'Three English Pastoral Summae and a "Magister Galienus",' *Studia Gratiana* 11 (1967) 133–44; idem, 'The *Summa confessorum* of John of Freiburg and the Popularization of the Moral Teaching of St. Thomas and of Some of His Contemporaries,' in *St. Thomas Aquinas, 1274–1974: Commemorative Studies*, ed Armand Maurer (Toronto 1974) II 245–63; Hugh Mackinnon, 'William de Montibus,'

ments in the theology of the sacraments and recent canonical teaching at the disposition of those directly involved in the *cura pastoralis*. Six centuries earlier, its analogue had appeared in the hands of those religious leaders who adapted the penitential discipline of the early Church so that it became a means for spiritual direction as well as for the traditional forgiveness of sin. This was the *Penitential*, a treatise well described by its name, since it was a list of the penances that were to be accepted and performed by a penitent as part of the preparation for his return to the full Christian life. For various reasons, these treatises suffered eclipse during the Carolingian period. But they never entirely disappeared, so that they remained to provide the basis on which the new manuals could be constructed. These new treatises went much further than the Penitentials: intended for the simple priest as they were, they gave serious attention to instructing him in the dogmatic and moral aspects of his faith as well as in pedagogy.

Scores of these manuals were written; serious investigation of them has increased since the Second World War, and editions of a few of the earliest examples have now joined the older editions of the great *Summae* of the mid-thirteenth century and later. Several of the earliest manuals are of special interest from the point of view of the present investigation. The treatises written at the end of the twelfth century continued to emphasize the list of penances, but the pedagogical note, the desire to instruct the confessor, was sometimes evident as well. Thus the *Liber penitentialis* of Alan of Lille, a treatise completed 1198–1203, begins as follows: 'This book is called Corrector and Healer (*medicus*). It contains many healing corrections of bodies and souls, and it teaches any simple priest how he can help anyone, be he in orders or not: the poor, the wealthy, the child, the youth, the elderly ... at that time when the priest can and ought to

D.Phil thesis (Oxford 1959), 'William de Montibus, a Medieval Teacher,' in *Essays in Medieval History Presented to Bertie Wilkinson*, ed T.A. Sandquist and M.R. Powicke (Toronto 1969) 32–45; Thomas N. Tentler, 'The Summa for Confessors as an Instrument of Social Control,' in *The Pursuit of Holiness in Late Medieval and Renaissance Religion*, ed Charles Trinkaus and Heiko A. Oberman, Papers from the University of Michigan Conference (Leiden 1974) 103–26, 131–7 (with critique by Leonard E. Boyle, OP, 'The Summa for Confessors as a Genre, and Its Religious Intent,' ibid 126–30), and *Sin and Confession on the Eve of the Reformation* (Princeton 1977) xi–xxiv; Joseph Goering, 'The Popularization of Scholastic Ideas in Thirteenth-Century England and an Anonymous Speculum Iuniorum,' Ph.D thesis (University of Toronto 1977). In addition to recent editions of *summae* mentioned below, see 'The *Summa de penitentia* of Magister Serlo,' ed Joseph Goering, *Mediaeval Studies* 38 (1976) 1–53.

invite the people to him to do penance and, as a faithful healer, give help.'[42] The Introduction goes on to list the different types of source used by the author; they include the traditional citations of the Fathers and the older law, with *quaedam ex decretalibus*, that is, with some of the new canon law. Part of the second book is given to a discussion of the problems touching concupiscence and sins against marriage: the older moral approach to matrimony is clearly operative here. Though there is remarkable refinement in analysing responsibility of action, Alan of Lille is not concerned with a general theory of marriage nor with its implications.

About the same year as that which saw the appearance of Alan's treatise, a first version of a new work, still entitled *Liber penitentialis*, appeared. It went through several enlargements and adaptations, changes that reflected current scholarship and papal judgments, and assumed a final form between 1208 and 1215. Its author was Robert of Flamborough, probably a Yorkshireman, who by 1205 was canon-penitentiary of the abbey of St-Victor at Paris.[43] As *penitentiarius* he was confessor of the members of the religious house and of those penitents who came from elsewhere for absolution. Developments adumbrated in the treatise of Alan appeared in that of Robert. It reveals a growing conviction that 'confession and especially contrition were more important than the austerity of the penances.'[44] Some of the older canons and traditional penances remain, but most have been replaced by new material based on current theological and canonical thought and on pastoral experience. In fact, the volume quickly reveals itself as an interface between the writings of theologians and canonists on the one hand and, on the other, the pastoral man, dealing with the practical world of confession. It is clear that its author considers one of its main functions to be the instruction of the confessor.

Book One presents the procedure of confession in dialogue form. The penitent begins, 'Receive me, sir, sad sinner that I am,' and the priest

42 'Hic est Liber qui Corrector vocatur et Medicus, qui correctiones corporum et anima-
   rum medicinas plenius continet et docet unumquemque sacerdotem et simplicem,
   quomodo vel qualiter unicuique succurrere valeat, ordinato vel sine ordine, pauperi,
   diviti, puero, juveni, seni, decrepito, sano, infirmo in omni aetate, in utroque sexu,
   quo tempore presbyteri debeant vel valeant plebem sibi commissam ad poenitentiam
   invitare et tamquam fidelis medicus auxilium dare,' *Alain de Lille Liber poenitentialis*,
   ed Jean Longère, Analecta mediaevalia Namurcensia 18 (Louvain 1965) II 15.
43 Robert of Flamborough, *Liber poenitentialis: A Critical Edition with Introduction and
   Notes*, ed J.J. Francis Firth, Studies and Texts 18 (Toronto 1971) 8–9.
44 Ibid 10.

replies, 'It is that mercy that cannot be measured that receives you, my son. He who embraces all things in his arms extended on the cross receives you.' The dialogue continued in this manner, then a hard bit of canonical realism appears. The priest says, 'But before we go any farther, tell me, do you belong to my flock or not?' The answer: 'No, but my abbot gave me permission to come to you.' The dialogue then continues what is really a general instruction on the Christian life.

Book Two is given to marriage. Note the shift of emphasis: Alan of Lille was preoccupied by failure touching sexuality and marriage obligation. Robert of Flamborough would deal with these, of course, but only after giving a whole book, that is one-sixth of his treatise, to a general instruction on marriage based on recent conciliar and canonical regulations. The chapters of Book Two are entitled: 'What is marriage?,' 'What is the substance of marriage?,' 'What impedes marriage?.' Chapter Two lists three requirements for the substance of marriage: the first is a *consensus animorum*, that agreement in spirit of which Gratian made so much; the second is *consensus corporum*, agreement as to sexual union; the third is *personarum regularitas*, the suitability of the principals of the marriage with regard to age, freedom from vow, relationship, prior marriage, etc. Where one of these is absent, there is no marriage.[45] Only after these matters have been studied in some detail does the author turn to the penitential aspect or matrimonial jurisdiction.

The *Liber penitentialis* of Robert of Flamborough was copied through the thirteenth and fourteenth centuries. Thirty-seven manuscripts survive, and at least ten more are known to have existed in Czechoslovakia, England, France, Germany, Italy, Spain, and Switzerland. It was obviously an important text. But, when seen in long term, its main contribution seems to have been in shifting the balance of this type of treatise, so that much of it was given to positive instruction of the confessor as a preliminary to directing him in healing the effect of immoral acts. That the change was appreciated is immediately evident in a new treatise, the *Summa confessorum* of Master Thomas, sub-dean and *officialis* (ecclesiastical judge) of Salisbury and rector of Chobham, Surrey.[46] Work began on the treatise about 1210; it was probably published in 1216.[47] Again, the plan is significant. The first three articles are given to a general discussion

---

45 Ibid 64–6.
46 *Thomae de Chobham Summa confessorum*, ed F. Broomfield, Analecta mediaevalia Namurcensia 25 (Louvain 1968) xxvi–xxxviii.
47 Ibid xl–lxii.

of penance, sin, and the circumstances of sin. Article four deals with the qualifications of the confessor; it occupies 117 pages of the printed edition, almost one-quarter of the volume. The second distinction is concerned with what the priest should know. Chobham first lists and briefly describes the books with which the priest should be familiar, quoting Gratian's *Decretum* (D38 c5): the sacramentary, antiphonary, lectionary, baptism manual, calendar, book of homilies, and a volume entitled *Canones penitentiales*, a book, he says, in which it is shown what penance should be enjoined on a given sin. 'It is of this that we propose to treat principally in this volume,' he wrote.[48]

Chobham then turns to a second matter: 'It is necessary that priests know what a sacrament is, the number of the sacraments, and how they should be administered.' A sacrament is described in this context as a visible form of invisible grace or as a sign of a holy thing. One by one the sacraments are discussed; question seven is given to matrimony.[49] Chobham remarks that the sacrament is called *matrimonium* rather than *patrimonium* because the mother suffers greater distress in the bearing and feeding of children than does the father. He goes on to say that it can properly be called *coniugium*, 'because it pertains equally to the man and the woman.'[50] Chobham then proceeds to a second chapter entitled *'Solus consensus facit matrimonium.'* The point of the title is briefly discussed, and the chapter is concluded with the remarkable sentence 'Therefore it is clear that a man and a woman can contract marriage by themselves, without a priest and without all others, in any place, so long as they agree in a permanent way of life.'[51]

48 '"Canones penitentiales" vocat libellum quemdam in quod ostenditur que penitentia cui peccato sit iniungenda, et de hoc propositum nostrum principale est tractare in hoc opere,' ibid 88.

49 Ibid 144–93.

50 'Dicitur autem potius matrimonium quam patrimonium quia mater sustinet plures angustias in portando quam vir et generando et nutriendo parvulum. Proprie tamen potest dici coniugium, quia eque pertinet ad virum et ad feminam,' ibid 145.

51 'Patet igitur quod vir et mulier possunt contrahere matrimonium per se sine sacerdote et sine omnibus aliis in quocumque loco, dummodo consentiant in perpetuam vite consuetudinem,' ibid 146. The importance of consent is set out in the instruction on the inquiry in its regard in Richard of Wetheringsett's *Summa 'Qui bene presunt presbiteri'* (1215–30): 'Item plene et aperte et plane inquirendum est de mutuo censensu qui maxime necessarius est. Est enim causa efficiens matrimonii. Iuxta quod scriptum est in Gen.: Vocemus puellam et queramus eius voluntatem. Nec aliquo modo propter aliquorum minas et seditiones coniugant sacerdotes nisi sint consentientes' (London, BL MS Royal 9 A XIV f 86v). The text was made available by my colleague Joseph Goering.

In chapter three Chobham goes on immediately to teach that, in reverence for marriage, additions are made to the required consent for its
security and solemnity. Thus the banns ought to be read to ensure the
couple's freedom to marry, and their vows ought to be exchanged in a
liturgical ceremony so that the fact of their union be known and that
matrimony be held in due respect.[52] He goes on to show strong disap-
proval of any other mode of procedure, saying that, in the event that the
public and religious forms were not observed, the couple ought not to be
considered married until the ceremonies were supplied.

Thus in consecutive chapters we meet a statement of principle with
regard to the personal quality of the exchange of consent, and a strong
insistence on the importance of the public ceremony with the reading of
the banns, a convenient juxtaposition of two principles that were in
constant tension during the Middle Ages. Elsewhere, Chobham goes on
to consider some of the implications of the personal element in consent.
Noting that many doubts arise touching the marriage of serfs, he quotes
those who say that serfs cannot marry (*non possunt*) without the consent
of their masters, for a serf has no yea nor nay (*non habet velle vel nolle*)
except with the wish and the power of the lord. This is false, he says, for
serfs have the freedom of their own will as to the contracting of marriage.[53]

The *Summa confessorum* goes on to elaborate these matters at some
length. It is only in article seven, after some three hundred pages, when
he finally broaches the usual subject matter of the older Penitentials, that
Chobham treats of sexual sin, marital failure, and the penances suitable
in such cases. Yet even here a much more positive impression is created,
for the section on marriage ends with a remarkable chapter: 'Quod
mulieres debent esse predicatrices virorum suorum.' '*Predicatrix*' is a rare
feminine form of '*predicator*,' meaning 'preacher.' The chapter invites
women to be preachers to their husbands.

Thus many things are necessary to priests in imposing penances on married
persons. There are so many cases of doubt that one is scarcely able to unravel.
Women should always be urged in confession that they be preachers to their
husbands. For no priest can soften a man's heart as a wife can. Hence the sin
of a man can often be imputed to his wife if, through her neglect, the husband
does not mend his ways. When they are alone and she is in her husband's

52 *Thomae de Chobham Summa confessorum*, ed Broomfield 146–7.
53 Ibid 177.

arms she ought to speak to him soothingly (*blande*); and if he is hard and merciless and an oppressor of the poor she ought to invite him to mercy, if he is a plunderer to detest his plundering; if he is grasping, let her inspire generosity in him and let her secretly give alms from their common property as well as the alms he fails to give. For it is licit for a wife to spend her husband's money in useful things and pious uses even though he is unaware of her action.[54]

That the wife be instructed in this way is seen as the first concern of the confessor. Chobham then goes on to address the husband. He is to be induced to conduct himself with his wife and to do honour to her as to part of his own body. If she is dull (*stulta*), let him correct her moderately and discreetly and, if necessary, punish her. For he ought to be more careful about the care of his wife than about any worldly possession, because nothing should (*debet*) be more dear to him than his wife.

Thus far the *Summa confessorum* on matters touching consent and the relations between spouses. This is a question of a very important text that reached a wide audience in the medieval world. More than one hundred manuscripts remain; many of them can be shown to have been used in priories, *studia*, and colleges, where they would have been accessible to a large readership. A further indication of the popularity of the treatise is the fact that two editions were printed in the 1480s.[55] With manuals such as the *Summa confessorum* – it is important to remember that, in different forms, there were many more of them – our research brings us to the point where contact occurred between the parish clergy and the laity. It is clear that advanced thinking on marriage was diffused to the level of personal instruction by the early years of the thirteenth century.

This conclusion is reinforced by an examination of the liturgy of marriage. *Lex orandi, lex credendi* is a favourite dictum of the historian of

---

54 'Multa igitur necessaria sunt sacerdotibus in imponendo penitentiam coniugatis. Tot enim dubii casus emergunt in coniugio quod vix potest aliquis enodare. Mulieribus tamen semper in penitentia iniungendum est quod sint predicatrices virorum suorum. Nullus enim sacerdos ita potest cor viri emollire sicut potest uxor. Unde peccatum viri sepe mulieri imputatur si per eius negligentiam vir eius non emmendatur. Debet enim in cubiculo et inter medios amplexus virum suum blande alloqui, et si durus est et immisericors et oppressor pauperum, debet eum invitare ad misericordiam; si raptor est, debet detestari rapinam; si avarus est suscitet in eo largitatem, et occulte faciat eleemosynas de rebus communibus, et eleemosynas quas ille omittit, illa suppleat. Licitum enim mulieri est de bonis viri sui in utiles usus ipsius et in pias causas ipso ignorante multa expedire' (ibid 375).

55 Ibid lxxvi–lxxxviii.

theology; certainly much is to be gained towards a grasp of the medieval understanding of marriage by an analysis of the blessings and prayers of the ritual and the evolution of their internal arrangements. Furthermore, during the twelfth century it became a common practice to include in the *ordines ad facienda sponsalia* several rubrics that indicated the formalities of the ceremony and the role of the different individuals involved in them.[56] This last source of information is especially important from the point of view of this essay. Though there is still much to be done on the history of the liturgy of marriage, recent synthetic works by Korbinian Ritzer for the period prior to 1100 and by J.-B. Molin and Protais Mutembe for the twelfth to the sixteenth centuries make preliminary conclusions possible.[57]

Ritzer has set out in detail the secular process whereby the priest came to play an ever greater role in the preliminaries of marriage and in the matrimonial ritual itself.[58] He sees two fundamental motives for this development, namely, the family's desire, reinforced by many ecclesiastical regulations, that the union of the couple be blessed by bishop or priest, and the growing pressure from Church authorities that there be an investigation of the spouses' freedom to marry.

It had been the custom among the recently christianized peoples of northern Europe and Spain to invite a priest to bless the couple, the bridal chamber, and the marriage bed after the secular marriage rite had been completed in the delivery of dower and the transfer of the bride to her husband by a representative of her family. This usage was eclipsed by the spread of the Roman liturgy due to missionary activity and the Carolingian reform. Here the nuptial blessing was conferred in church before the communion of the mass. The secular ritual of marriage occurred later in the home. Anglo-Saxon liturgical books and those of Spain reveal, however, that the older blessings continued to be used.[59] Furthermore,

56 Sets of *ordines* are edited by E. Martène, *De antiquis ecclesiae ritibus* (Antwerp 1736–8) II 354–402 (henceforth Martène). Some dates are corrected by W. Lüdtke, 'Ordines ad facienda sponsalia,' in *Festgabe für Prof D. Dr. Richard Haupt* (Kiel 1922) 95–128, and in Ritzer, *Le mariage* 386 n609; *Manuale et processionale ad usum insignis ecclesiae Eboracensis*, ed W.G. Henderson, Publications of the Surtees Society 63 (Durham 1875) 24–40, 155*–69* [henceforth Henderson]; Ritzer, *Le mariage* 421–60; J.-B. Molin and Protais Mutembe, *Le rituel du mariage en France du XIIe au XVIe siècle*, Théologie historique 26 (Paris 1974) 283–318 [henceforth Molin].

57 See above, nn 5 and 56.

58 Ritzer, *Le mariage* 327–60 and passim; cf Molin 25–33.

59 Ritzer, *Le mariage* 310–12, 297–306, and 447–50, an example of Spanish influence in an *ordo nuptialis* of a tenth-century sacramentary from the diocese of Fulda.

there is evidence among the Anglo-Saxon documents that these blessings were developed so that they corresponded to the stages of the secular ritual of marriage, thus suggesting that it was taking on a religious dimension.[60] There was also a growing pressure, manifested in local legislation as well as in the writings of canonists, that all first marriages receive priestly blessings.[61] At the same time, serious reflection on the impediments of marriage led to several attempts to institutionalize inquiry into the couple's freedom and their desire for the proposed union.[62] Thus there were tendencies, on the one hand, to make the priest a principal agent in the ritual by which the nuptial bond was established and, on the other, to make him the judge with whom would lie the preliminary decision on the feasibility of a marriage.

Early in the twelfth century, by a process on which there is still much light to be shed, the secular rite of marriage, preceded by an inquiry directed by the priest, began to become an ecclesiastical ritual of which the nuptial mass and blessing were part. This assumed several forms. The most precocious seems to have been in that part of northwest Europe under Norman control or influence.[63] There the *ordines* reveal a redesigned ritual in which the inquiry as to the suitability of a marriage, the endowment and conferment of the bride, and the exchange of consent were completed before the community at the entry of the parish church; then followed the marriage mass and blessing. This usage spread so rapidly that by 1189 a secular legal treatise like Glanvill would refer to the transfer of dower during the marriage ceremony at the door of the church as an established practice.[64] It is in the articulation of these ceremonies

---

60 See Molin 29.

61 See the Anglo-Saxon cases cited by Ritzer, *Le mariage* 322–3. The Council of Winchester (1076) required the priestly blessing for the validity of a marriage: 'Praeterea statutum est, ut nullus filiam suam, vel cognatam det alicui absque benedictione sacerdotali; si aliter fecerit, non ut legitimum conjugium sed ut fornicatorium judicabitur' (*Concilia Magnae Britanniae et Hiberniae, 446–1718*, ed David Wilkins [London 1737] I 367). It should be remembered, however, that second and later marriages were not to be blessed.

62 See Ritzer, *Le mariage* 332–3, 340–50; and Molin 30–2.

63 Ritzer, *Le mariage* 385–97 followed Lüdtke in concluding that the new *ordo* was developed in Normandy in the last years of the eleventh century. Molin, pointing out that some *ordines* were later than Ritzer thought, dates the development in the first half of the twelfth century and leaves the question open as to whether the first steps were made in Normandy or in England; see 28–40.

64 'Dicitur enim dos vulgariter id quod aliquis liber homo dat sponse sue ad hostium ecclesie tempore desponsationis sue' (6 1, *Tractatus de legibus et consuetudinibus regni*

that much is to be learned of early twelfth-century thinking on marriage and on the ways in which it was expressed on a level and in a manner that all can be presumed to have understood.

A missal from Bury St Edmunds, dated 1125–35, begins the *ordo ad desponsandam mulierem* with the rubric 'Benedictio anuli ante hostium templi.'[65] Then follow the questioning of the couple as to their intention, the delivery of dower, the transfer of the bride to her husband, and the placing of the ring on her finger. After all this had been done, the priest led the couple into the church for the wedding mass. Another text from the abbey of St-Mélaine at Rennes in Brittany, probably of the final half of the twelfth century, begins, 'In primis veniat sacerdos ante ostium ecclesiae indutus alba atque stola cum benedicta aqua,' then proceeds as above.[66] Yet another *ordo*, believed to be from the diocese of Evreux and dated from the twelfth century, makes it clear that witnesses were present: 'Ante omnia veniant ad januas ecclesiae sub testimonio plurimorum, qui thoro maritali conjungendi sunt.'[67] Rituals of the same period from Cahors and Albi witness to the introduction of the ceremonies before the wedding mass in accord with the Anglo-Norman form, but held within the church, an arrangement that is to be related to older usages of the Spanish Church and was to continue through the Middle Ages.[68] In either arrangement a significant change had occurred. The ritual during which a couple became man and wife was removed from the family circle to a public forum, the place of meeting of the local community considered in its religious capacity. Leadership in the proceedings had been assumed by the head of that community, the parish priest. Thus an important element in the family control of marriage was diminished.

The *ordines* then go on to indicate the subject of initial inquiry. It is clear that it was especially concerned with impediments of consanguinity and affinity. Thus at Rennes: 'sacerdos ... quaerat quomodo parentes non sint'; at Cahors: 'sacerdos ... inquirat de parentela fortiter'; or in a pontifical of the archdiocese of Canterbury, now at Magdalen College, Oxford, and dated 1150×1200: 'inquirat sacerdos an sponsus et sponsa legitime

Anglie qui Glanvilla vocatur, ed G.D.G. Hall [London 1965] 58–9). Thus secular custom supported the marriage ritual in question.

65 Laon, Bibliothèque municipale MS 238 f 165v–167v: Molin no 5 289–91.

66 Paris, BN MS Lat 9439: Molin no 2 284–6.

67 The text (Martène no 3 356–9 [=Molin no 3 286–7]) is lost.

68 Missal of Mateus de Braga (presumed to be from the diocese of Cahors), Braga, Bibliotheca publica f 186v ff: Molin no 6 291–2 (see below, n74); Albi, Bibliothèque municipale MS 3 f 38v–43r: Molin no 7 292–4.

convenire possint, ne scilicet aut consanguinitate aut aliqua spirituali copula iuncti sint.'[69] Later *ordines* reveal a major development of this inquiry, one that would often relate it directly to the system of banns that was elaborated in the same region late in the twelfth century.[70] The essential from the point of view of the present investigation, however, is that it had found its place as a preliminary act of the marriage ritual before 1150.

The Magdalen College Pontifical continues with the remark that, the inquiry as to relationship being completed, the priest was to proceed to question the couple on their intention to marry. This element in the *ordines* would quickly grow into one of its most developed sections. Perhaps an indication of the importance of the change of mentality that it represents is provided by a note added to the margin of a twelfth-century pontifical of Rouen. The note – it is in a thirteenth-century hand – has been published by Molin and Mutembe: 'According to the law, their consent alone suffices; if it happens that it is lacking in a marriage, all the rest, even the public celebration, is void.'[71] The missal from Bury St Edmunds, having mentioned the blessing of the ring at the church door, continues, 'The blessing done, let the man be questioned by the priest whether he wishes to have that woman as his lawful wife'; the same question is then to be put to the bride.[72] In the Pontifical of Evreux, probably a few years later, the rubric is stated: 'First of all, let those who are to be joined in marriage come before the church doors with many witnesses; the consent of each is required by the priest.'[73] In the missal associated with the diocese of Cahors the opening stages of the ritual are set out as follows: 'On the day when the groom and the bride are to be married, let them come to the church at the third hour. Let the priest don

69 Molin no 2 285, no 6 291; Henderson no 4 160–1 = *The Pontifical of Magdalen College, with an Appendix of Abstracts from Other English MSS of the Twelfth Century*, ed H.A. Wilson, Henry Bradshaw Society 39 (London 1910) 202.
70 See Sheehan, 'Marriage Theory and Practice' 432–40 (here pp 145–54); cf Molin 54–5.
71 'Sufficit secundum leges solus eorum consensus; si solus in nuptiis forte defuerit, cetera omnia, etiam cum ipso coetu celebrata, frustrantur' (Paris, BN MS Nouv acq lat 306 f 213v: Molin 64 n3). Note that the reference is to the *leges* rather than to a canonical text; but see C27 q2 c2.
72 'Dic[ta] hac benedictione interrogetur vir a sacerdote si mulierem illam ille ad legitimam uxorem habere velit. Hoc idem requiratur a muliere' (Molin no 5 289).
73 'Ante omnia veniant ad januas ecclesiae sub testimonio plurimorum, qui thoro maritali conjungendi sunt: et requiratur consensus utriusque a sacerdote' (Molin no 3 286).

his holy vestments and firmly inquire as to the relationship of the couple and whether they love each other. If some relationship is found, let them not be married. If, however, they are in love and no relationship is discovered, let them be married.'[74] A consent-dialogue, already implicit in the rubric of the missal from Bury St Edmunds, was set out in some *ordines* within a few years.[75] Thus the Magdalen College Pontifical instructs the priest to address the bridegroom by name: '"N. do you wish this woman?" If he replied "I do," let the priest say to him, "Do you wish to keep her in the faith of God and in your own faith, in both health and sickness as a Christian man should keep his wife?"'[76] Similar questions are to be put to the bride. In a similar form, though with adjustment and addition, a dialogue establishing the fact that the principals consented to their marriage would spread throughout the Western Church, survive the upheaval of the Reformation and the Council of Trent and continue to the present.[77]

No doubt, in the twelfth century as in our own day, one or other party would occasionally withdraw from the marriage at the moment when the essential question was put.[78] However, it seems reasonable to conclude that, in most cases, given the momentum developed by the ritual, even a reluctant bride would be carried through to the completion of the cere-

---

74 'Die qua sponsus et sponsa iungendi sunt, hora IIIa veniant ad ecclesiam; et induat se sacerdos vestimentis sacris, et inquirat de parentela fortiter, et si est amor inter illos. Et si aliquam parentelam invenerit, non iungantur. Si autem amorem habent, et in parentela non inveniuntur, iungantur' (Molin no 6 291).

75 Cf Molin 64.

76 'interroget sacerdos sponsum per proprium nomen, ita. N. Vis hanc feminam? Si responderit uolo, dicat ei sacerdos. Vis eam seruare in dei fide et in tua et in sanitate et in infirmitate, sicut christianus homo debet suam sponsam seruare? Similiter interroget sponsam' (ed Wilson 202; see above, n69). The text has been translated literally; a version that would reflect the colouring provided by the context and the use of the verb *volo* might be 'N. do you consent to have this woman as your wife, etc?' Cf the Rouen Missal (122–50), Molin no 8 294.

77 Molin 66–70.

78 See the account of the life of St Oda in Molin 5–6 (cf Ritzer, *Le mariage* 393 n621): the saint, when asked during the marriage ceremony if she would accept a certain Simon as her husband, refused to speak. Her refusal ended the proceedings. She became a Premonstratentian nun and died in 1158, *Vita sanctae Odae* (PL 203 1364). In *Brauttradition und Konsengespräch in mittelalterlichen Trauungsritualen: Ein Beitrag des Geschichte des deutschen Eheschliessungsrechts* (Berlin 1910) 99–155, Otto Opet argued that the consent dialogue was an innovation in the religious ritual at this time. He saw it as derived from a similar dialogue in the older civil ritual of the Germanic peoples. See the discussion in Ritzer, *Le mariage* 393 n621.

mony. What is more important in longer perspective is that a proclamation of the importance of consent was made in this public context. Steady and effective pressure to bring couples to a church marriage can be demonstrated; in many cases the attendance would be large.[79] Thus it can be concluded that there were frequent occasions in the life of a parish when the Church's teaching on the necessity of consent was expressed.

It will have been noted that at each stage of the series of inquiries by which freedom from impediment and consent to the marriage were established, the *ordines* indicate that, if the answers of those involved revealed that a situation not in accord with the Church's teaching obtained, proceedings were to be stopped. This is especially clear in the rubric from the missal of the diocese of Cahors set out above.[80] It was the parish priest who made a judgment at each step in accord with the evidence made available to him. Whatever control lord or family may have played in the preparation of the marriage there was no sign of it here. In fact, pressures that they might have brought to bear on the bride and groom were subject to examination as well. In the final stages, it was the religious society in the person of the parish priest that exercised a negative control over the projected union.

The *ordines* also emphasize the role of the priest as the principal agent in the rites leading up to the exchange of consent. Thus, while those of the twelfth century that have been discussed here mention transfer of the bride after the investigation of the propriety of the marriage had been completed – and in most cases indicate that it was by her father or a member of her kin[81] – a different ritual appears in some French texts after 1200. In the missal from Rouen, which Molin considers to have made a decisive step in the evolution of the Norman ritual, the bride is transferred to the groom by a relative after the couple's freedom from impediment has been established. The groom then gives her to the priest, who proceeds to question him and her as to the freedom and substance of their consent. Satisfied on these matters, he presents her to the groom saying: 'On this condition I give her to you.'[82] Other *ordines* neglect to

79 See above, 28 (here p 112) and n67.
80 See n74.
81 A general practice in England during the Middle Ages: see Henderson 26, 166*, 167*; *The Sarum Missal Edited from Three Early Manuscripts*, ed J. Wickham Legg (Oxford 1916) 413, etc. In the late twelfth-century pontifical from Magdalen College, the priest and the bride's sponsor give her to the groom: 'sacerdos et patronus sponse dent ipsam sponso per dexteram' (ed Wilson 202).
82 'Tunc sacerdos tradat viro mulierem, dicens: *Hac conditione do eam tibi*' (Molin no 8

mention the family's role, simply stating that the priest joins the couple's hands and invites them to exchange consent.[83] The gift of the ring is connected with the joining of hands. In most of the twelfth-century examples it is the priest who places the ring on the bride's finger, though he occasionally does so with the assistance of the groom.[84] By the thirteenth century it was common for the priest to hand the blessed ring to the groom, who would place it on his bride's finger while reciting a formula through which he was led by the priest. Thus in the joining of hands, the point at which the exchange of consent occurred in many thirteenth-century *ordines*, and in the gift of the ring it was the priest who served as the assistant to the couple.

There are several theoretical problems touching the role of the parish priest in the ritual that has been described; it is not our intention to discuss them here.[85] For present purposes it is enough to note that those who witnessed the marriage ceremony could clearly see that the essential supporting role had passed to that person who, representing neither family nor lord, spoke for the larger religious community that had come to state the conditions in which a valid marriage could occur. Thus although, for reasons that are obvious, there was no attempt to give ritual statement to the notion that the couple was capable of marriage without or against the wishes of their kin,[86] there can be no doubt that the *ordines*

294). In the ritual of the cathedral of Albi (twelfth century) the bride was presented to the groom by her close relatives or friends in the ceremony before the mass. After the Postcommunion the priest blessed the couple, then handed her over to the groom: 'Post haec tradat sacerdos sponsam sponso dicendo: *Accipe eam in nomine Patris et Filii et Spiritus Sancti*' (Molin no 7 293). In the tenth-century sacramentary from the diocese of Fulda, cited above, n59, before the final blessing, the bride was transferred to the priest by members of her family, and he veiled and blessed her before handing her over to the groom: 'His expletis tradet sacerdos puellam uiro admon[en]s eos, ut pro sancta communione ea nocte se abstineant a pollutione. Tunc absoluet diaconus dicens: *Ite missa est*' (Ritzer, *Le mariage* 449). Cf Molin no 12 301, a pontifical from Arles (1300–50). Like the sacramentary from Fulda, these rituals from southern France were influenced by Spanish models.

83 See Molin no 10, a pontifical from Arras (late thirteenth century); no 13, a ritual from the abbey of St-Victor, Paris (early fourteenth century); no 14, a missal from Rouen (fourteenth century?).

84 The bride received the ring from the priest in Molin nos 4 and 6; from the priest and the groom in Molin nos 3 and 5 and in two late twelfth-century pontificals from Ely (Cambridge, Trinity College MS B 11 10 f 112v, and Cambridge, University College MS LI 11 10 f 81r), published in *The Pontifical of Magdalen College*, ed Wilson 222.

85 DTC 9 II 2202–7.

86 Cf Molin 67 for an Italian version of the consent-dialogue in which the bride's father as well as the couple were questioned on their agreement to the marriage.

not only underlined the necessity of consent by the principals of the
union but also assigned a diminished role to their families.

From this preliminary examination of two of several possible areas of
inquiry, it appears that important instruments existed for the spread and
application of a revolutionary theory of marriage. Furthermore, the
evidence suggests that these instruments gave expression to the new
theory shortly after it was enunciated and that they were of a type capable
of reaching the population at large.

Not only did the confessors' manuals, which began to appear about
1200, incorporate the new ideas of the mode of establishing the marriage
bond, but they also made them directly available to the priest at the parish
level and to his parishioners in a most explicit way. The orchestration of
the formalities of marriage in the ritual proved to be even more precocious. At the very moment when the notions of Gratian and Peter Lombard were being enunciated, some *ordines* assumed a form that instructed
both the officiating priest and all those involved in the marriage ceremony
– principals, family, and parish community – on the necessity of the
couple's consent to their union. Furthermore, they describe a ceremony
that emphasized social control of the marriage while de-emphasizing the
part in that control that fell to family and lord. For northwest Europe, at
least, it is clear that by the end of the twelfth century the new ideas on
marriage were being taught.

8

Marriage Theory and Practice in the Conciliar Legislation and Diocesan Statutes of Medieval England

The law codes and disciplinary treatises and collections of the late Anglo-Saxon period included an important body of regulations touching sexual discipline and the requirements of the celibate and the married states. Sexual activity was permitted only within matrimony. Regulations touching the marriage and celibacy of the clergy and the requirements of religious life were developed at some length. Finally, the requirements for true marriage were considered: here there were regulations on impediments and freedom to marry, precocious notions on the necessity of consent by the woman, and some consideration of the quality of the relationship between the spouses. These matters are known to have been among the objects of the reform movement associated with St Dunstan, but, with minor exceptions, the councils of his time did not leave a body of legislation in their regard. It was after a generation of war with Danish invaders and, in part at least, in response to the resulting religious and social dislocation that the regulations in question appeared in a series of royal laws and disciplinary regulations derived for the most part from the circle of Wulfstan of York.[1]

The following sigla are specific to this article. – Editor

Alberigo *Conciliorum oecumenicorum decreta*, ed Josephus Alberigo et al, 3rd ed (Bologna 1973)

P–C *Councils and Synods with Other Documents Relating to the English Church, 2: A.D. 1205–1313*, ed F.M. Powicke and C.R. Cheney (Oxford 1964)

Pontal *Les statuts synodaux français du XIIIe siècle, 1: Les statuts de Paris et le synodal de l'Ouest (XIIIe siècle)*, ed Odette Pontal, Collection de documents inédits sur l'histoire de France, Section de philologie et d'histoire jusqu'à 1610, vol 9 (Paris 1971)

Wilkins *Concilia Magnae Britanniae et Hiberniae, 446–1718*, ed David Wilkins (London 1737)

The Anglo-Norman Councils and Marriage

With the coming of the Normans the ecclesiastical council became once more a common vehicle of reform and of the instruction preliminary to reform.[2] In the period between Lanfranc's legatine council of 1070 and the end of the twelfth century, legislation was cast largely in a context of church order, with the concentration on the office and discipline of the clergy that would be expected. All of the regulations touching the topics under examination here, with a few important exceptions, were the work of legatine or primatial councils and applied to all of England.[3] The exceptions were Archbishop Hubert Walter's legatine council for the Province of York (1195) and his provincial Council of Westminster (1200).

General regulation of sexual abuse did not loom large in the canons of the Anglo-Norman period. A call to penance for sins of adultery, rape, and fornication was among the penitential decrees associated with the first council held under the new regime, over which Lanfranc presided in 1070,[4] and condemnations of perversion were included in the long-delayed council that Anselm was able to assemble as primate in 1102.[5] It was the sexual discipline of the clergy that was the main focus of interest. Prohibitions of acts forbidden all Christians were joined with a series of regulations denying marriage to those in major orders. As canon 7 of the Second Lateran Council became understood, the possibility of matrimony for these clerics was ended. By the beginning of the thirteenth century it seems to have been generally recognized that major orders and religious vows were an impediment to marriage.[6]

Legislation touching marriage itself developed more slowly, main progress beginning only as the canons on clerical celibacy assumed their

---

1 See Frank Barlow, *The English Church, 1000–1066* (London 1963) 143–5, 258–61, and passim; R.R. Darlington, 'Ecclesiastical Reform in the Late Old English Period,' *English Historical Review* 51 (1936) 385–428; Michael M. Sheehan, 'Marriage and Family in English Conciliar and Synodal Legislation,' in *Essays in Honour of Anton Charles Pegis*, ed J. Reginald O'Donnell (Toronto 1974) 205–6 (here pp 77–117).

2 See Heinrich Böhmer, *Kirche und Staat in England und in der Normandie im XI. und XII. Jahrhundert* (Leipzig 1899) 44–8, 91–7.

3 See M. Brett, *The English Church under Henry I* (Oxford 1975) 75–82; and the list of councils in *Handbook of English Chronology*, ed F.M. Powicke and E.B. Fryde, 2nd ed (London 1961) 549–50; cf C.R. Cheney, 'Legislation in the Medieval English Church,' *English Historical Review* 50 (1935) 195–6.

4 c12 (Wilkins I 366); cf Brett, *The English Church* 156 n2.

5 c29 (Wilkins I 383).

6 See especially the Councils of Westminster (1125) c13, (1127) c5, (1175) [c1] (Wilkins I 408, 410, 477) and 2 Lateran 7: 'Huiusmodi namque copulatione, quam contra

essential position. In the earliest Anglo-Norman councils the question of impediments loomed large. Thus the national council over which Lanfranc presided in 1075 forbade the marriage of those related within the seventh degree of consanguinity and affinity, a regulation repeated in the legatine council of John of Crema held at Westminster in 1125.[7] Canon 25 of Anselm's council of 1102 referred only to the relationship of consanguinity, again to the seventh degree, but it included a clause that was heavy with the future. It sought to bring the knowledge and pressure of society to bear on the enforcement of this regulation: those aware of a relationship that would make a marriage incestuous were bound to reveal it or be guilty of the same crime.[8] The prohibition would be expressed again at the provincial Council of Westminster (1200), canon 11, but – and the fact is significant – the forbidden degree was not specified.[9] In the same canon a further impediment was stated, that of spiritual affinity rising between a person baptized and all the children of those who baptized and sponsored him.

A regulation touching the establishing of the marriage bond also appeared quite early. Thus Lanfranc's Winchester council of 1076 decreed that it required a priestly blessing, going on to assume the extraordinary position that without this religious act the marriage was null.[10] The matter appeared again in the provincial Council of Canterbury at Westminster (1175), where an old canon, long associated with Pope Hormisdas and

---

ecclesiasticam regulam constat esse contractam, matrimonium non esse censemus' (Alberigo 198). Cf Mary G. Cheney, 'Pope Alexander III and Roger, Bishop of Worcester, 1164–1179: The Exchange of Ideas,' in *Proceedings of the Fourth International Congress of Medieval Canon Law*, Toronto, 21–5 August 1972, ed Stephan Kuttner, Monumenta iuris canonici, Series C: Subsidia 5 (Vatican City 1976) 207–27, especially 211–17.

7　Council of London (1075) [c6], Council of Westminster (1125) cc 16, 17 (Wilkins I 363, 408–9).

8　'Ne cognati usque ad septimam generationem ad conjugium copulentur, vel copulati simul permaneant. Et si quis hujus incestus conscius fuerit, et non ostenderit, ejusdem criminis se participem esse cognoscat' (Wilkins I 383).

9　Wilkins I 507; here the reference was only to affinity: 'Vir non contrahat cum aliqua consanguinea olim uxoris suae; similiter nec uxor cum aliquo consanguineo quondam viri sui.'

10　'Praeterea statutum est, ut nullus filiam suam, vel cognatam det alicui absque benedictione sacerdotali; si aliter fecerit, non ut legitimum conjugium sed ut fornicatorium judicabitur' (Wilkins I 367). Cf Korbinian Ritzer, *Formen, Riten, und religiöses Brauchtum der Eheschliessung in den christlichen Kirchen des ersten Jahrtausends*, Liturgiewissenschaftliche Quellen und Forschungen 38 (Münster 1962) 325–9.

included in the *Decretum*, forbade secret marriage.[11] It added that a public blessing by the priest should be included, but did not question the validity of the act when the blessing was omitted. Since there was provision for the three-year suspension of a priest who failed to obey this canon, it seems that it was already understood that the term 'secret marriage' could indicate an exchange of consent involving a blessing by a priest. The growing pressure for publicity in the whole procedure of marriage was expressed much earlier in the ruling of the Council of Westminster (1102), canon 23, touching betrothal: promises to marry made without witnesses were to be considered null if either party denied them.[12]

A further innovation, touching consent and an impediment based on its lack, appeared in a canon of the provincial Council of Westminster (1175).[13] The first part of the canon was ascribed to Pope Nicholas. It began with the statement that, without the consent of the parties, there could be no marriage. This rule seemed to have been taken as generally understood, for it was obviously intended to be the principle on which the ruling of the canon was based: when children had been given in marriage, nothing was effected until both, having come to discretion, gave their consent. In the Friedberg edition of the *Decretum Gratiani* the text reads as follows: 'Ubi non est consensus utriusque, non est coniugium. Ergo qui pueris dant puellas in cunabulis, et e conuerso, nichil faciunt, nisi uterque puerorum post, quam uenerit ad tempus discretionis, consentiat, etiamsi pater et mater hoc fecerint et voluerint.'[14] The last clause of this canon was expressed more strongly in the *Panormia* of Ivo of Chartres and in one tradition of the *Decretum*. It read: 'nec est coniugium nisi fiat utriusque consensus, etiamsi pater et mater hoc fecerint et voluerint.'[15] But in the Westminster version this last clause was omitted and a quali-

---

11 'Ex decretis Ormisdae papae. Nullus fidelis, cujuscunque conditionis sit, occulte nuptias faciat; sed benedictione accepta a sacerdote, publice nubat in Domino. Si quis ergo sacerdos aliquos occulte conjunxisse inventus fuerit, triennio ab officio suspendatur' (Wilkins I 478). The first clause, 'Nullus ... Domino,' is Gratian, C30 q5 c2. The second clause provided the penalty of three years' suspension that would be used in 4 Lateran 51. On the history of this canon see Christopher N.L. Brooke, 'Canons of English Church Councils in Early Decretal Collections,' *Traditio* 13 (1957) 471–80, especially 479.

12 Wilkins I 383.

13 c18 (Wilkins I 478–9).

14 C30 q2 c UN., *Corpus iuris canonici*, ed A. Friedberg, 2nd ed (Leipzig 1879; repr Graz 1955) I 1100.

15 *Panormia*, Liber 6 c122 (PL 161 1275); C30 q2 c UN., *Corpus iuris canonici*, ed Friedberg I 1100 n9.

fication added which undermined the principle on which the canon was based. While the point was made that the free choice of spouse by children was to be more protected in the future, it conceded that the unions of minors would be tolerated in urgent necessity to bring about peace: 'Hujus ergo decreti auctoritate inhibemus, ne de caetero aliqui, quorum uterque vel alter ad aetatem legibus constitutam et canonibus determinatam non pervenit, conjungantur, nisi forte aliquando, urgente necessitate, interveniente, pro bono pacis conjunctio talis toleretur.'[16] It was in this form that the canon would appear in the *Compilatio prima* and in the *Decretales* of Gregory IX.[17]

Most of these earlier regulations were assembled, rendered consistent, and developed in Hubert Walter's provincial Council of Westminster (1200), canon 11.[18] Prohibition of marriage between those related by affinity (without the specification of the seventh degree), and between those impeded by spiritual relationship resulting from baptism, was stated. Furthermore, procedure for providing adequate opportunity for social control appeared in the regulation that no marriage was to take place before it had been publicly announced three times in church. The marriage itself was to be solemnized publicly before the Church in the presence of the priest.[19] If the union were effected otherwise the principals were to be excommunicated with reservation to the bishop. Finally, in an interesting reflection on the legislator's determination that the couple should be together, it was ruled that separation should not be

---

16 Wilkins I 479. See below, 420–1 (here pp 132–3).

17 *Compilatio Ia* 4 2 4, *Quinque compilationes antiquae*, ed A. Friedberg (Leipzig 1882), 45; X 4 2 2.

18 'Vir non contrahat cum aliqua consanguine a olim uxoris suae, similiter nec uxor cum aliquo consanguineo quondam viri sui. Et susceptus in baptismo, non contrahat cum filia baptizantis vel suscipientis, ante, vel post genita. Nec contrahatur aliquod matrimonium sine trina denunciatione publica in ecclesia, neque si fuerint personae incognitae. Sed nec copulentur aliquae personae matrimonio, nisi publice in facie ecclesiae, et presente sacerdote; et si secus factum fuerit, non admittantur alicubi in ecclesia, nisi speciali auctoritate episcopi. Nulli etiam conjugatorum liceat iter remotum peregrinationis arripere, nisi mutuo consensu publicato. Salvo in omnibus, etc.' (Wilkins I 507).

19 The phrase 'in facie ecclesiae' is understood to mean the local community considered in its religious capacity. The phrase 'nisi speciali auctoritate episcopi' is understood to refer to the admission of the couple to church *after* the marriage contravening the canon and not to a dispensation granted the couple to marry without observing the regulation requiring the publicity of the act and the presence of a priest.

occasioned by a spouse's departure on pilgrimage unless mutual consent were publicly expressed.[20]

The Diocesan Statutes and Marriage

Canon 11 of the Council of Westminster marked an important moment in the growing regulation of marriage. Its compact and consistent presentation provided a sound base for later English developments and reveals something of that local experience and legislation that lay behind the constitutions of the Fourth Lateran Council (1215).[21] It also marked the last occasion on which councils of medieval England would make major innovations in marriage regulation. The new instruments of discipline and organization were to be the diocesan statutes, most of which were issued by bishops in their synods. It is well known that the fifty years after the publication of the Lateran constitutions were a time of unusual synodal activity throughout the Western Church; England was one of the leaders in this effort at reform. Many of the English synods saw the promulgation of sets of regulations that implemented general church law with the detail that was only possible on the local level and that, to a considerable extent, instructed the parish clergy in the theology that lay behind the rules which they were expected to enforce. These synodal regulations and other collections published directly by the bishops were to provide one of the major means by which important developments in the understanding and practice of marriage were implemented during the thirteenth century.[22]

The Council of Westminster provided the basis for the treatment of marriage and associated matters in the earliest set of episcopal statutes, those published by Archbishop Stephen Langton for the diocese of Canterbury (1213×14).[23] There, within a long series of regulations organized

---

20 Cf James A. Brundage, *Medieval Canon Law and the Crusader* (Madison 1969) 30–65.

21 Cf *Thomae de Chobham Summa confessorum*, ed F. Broomfield, Analecta mediaevalia Namurcensia 25 (Louvain 1968) xl–lviii; and Pontal lxvii–lxix.

22 See C.R. Cheney, *English Synodalia of the Thirteenth Century* (London 1941; repr 1968) v–x, 34–50, and 'Statute-making in the English Church in the Thirteenth Century,' in *Medieval Texts and Studies* (Oxford 1973) 138–57. For other means of implementation see below, n213.

23 Statutes to which frequent reference will be made are edited in P–C; the method of reference used there will be followed with minor changes. The first set of statutes for the diocese of Canterbury are cited as 1 Canterbury, the second set as 2 Canterbury, etc. Thus 1 Canterbury 2 refers to the second canon of the first Canterbury statutes.

loosely around the sacraments, the canons of 1200 were restated with some adjustment and development. The prohibitions of unions impeded by affinity (once again, without specific reference to the number of degrees), of marriage to an unknown person and without banns, and the refusal to allow clandestine marriage were repeated (cc 53, 54). The suspension of the disobedient priest reserved to the bishop was added, while the prohibition of the separation of married couples due to the pilgrimage of one of the spouses was omitted. Two important clauses were added in 1 Canterbury 55. First, in a regulation echoing that of Anselm's legatine council of 1102, parish priests were ordered to forbid private betrothal and to insist that it be before witnesses who would testify to the act were it called into question. Second – here we have the first recognition of a position long debated by canonists and theologians – it was stated that carnal union, following an agreement to marry, would be regarded as marriage by the Church, which would require it to be observed as such.[24]

Important as was this Canterbury collection, it was with the synodal statutes of Bishop Richard Poore for the diocese of Salisbury that the model for the new instrument of regulation and instruction was set.[25] Benefiting from the constitutions of the Fourth Lateran Council as well as from the impetus for reform that it provided, this set of regulations, clearly organized around the sacraments and on a scale hitherto unknown, would provide the impetus and the direction for more than a half

The different collections, their dates, and their pagination in P–C are as follows: 1 Canterbury (1213×14), 23–36; 2 Canterbury (1222×28), 165–7; Carlyle (1258×59), 626–30; 1 Chichester (1245×52), 451–67; 2 Chichester (1289), 1082–90; 3 Chichester (1292), 1115–18; Coventry (1224×37), 207–26; Constitutiones cuiusdam episcopi (1225×30?), 181–97; 1 Durham (1228×36), 201; 2 Durham (1241×49), 421–35; 3 Durham (1276), 817–20; Durham Peculiars (1241×49?), 435–45; Ely (1239×56), 515–24; 1 Exeter (1225×37), 227–37; 2 Exeter (1287), 982–1059; Lincoln (1239?), 265–78; 1 London (1245×59), 630–2; 2 London (1245×59), 632–58; London Archdeaconry (ca 1229×41), 325–37; Norwich (1240×43), 342–64; 1 Salisbury (1217×19), 57–96; 2 Salisbury (1238×44), 364–87; 3 Salisbury (1228×56?), 510–15; 4 Salisbury (1257), 549–67; so-called Statutes of John Pecham (1279×92), 1118–25; Synodal Statutes (1222×25?), 139–54; Wells (1258?), 586–626; 1 Winchester (1224?), 125–37; 2 Winchester (1247?), 403–16; 3 Winchester (1262×65), 700–23; 1 Worcester (1219), 52–7; 2 Worcester (1229), 169–81; 3 Worcester (1240), 294–325; 1 York (1241×55?), 483–98; 2 York (1259), 658–9.

24 'quia si talem fidem carnalis copula subsequatur, ecclesia pro matrimonio hoc habebit, et faciet tanquam matrimonium observari' (P–C 35). See the discussion of this text below, 430 (here p 143).

25 See Cheney, *English Synodalia* 51–89.

century of remarkable legislation. Marriage received successful regulation there and in the dozen or more statutes derived to a greater or less extent from it. A second period of progress was that between the statutes issued by Bishop Walter de Cantilupe in 1240 (2 Worcester) and those issued by Bishop William Bitton I about 1258 (Wells). From the point of view of the present study the great era of synodal production would end with the statutes for the diocese of Exeter issued by Bishop Peter Quivil in 1287. Regulations touching marriage would continue to be issued until the Reformation and beyond, but, inasmuch as the present state of textual study permits an opinion, it was to concentrate on a few points, namely, the prevention of the clandestine union and the regulation of the jurisdiction hearing marriage cases. Furthermore, by and large this legislation became once again the work of the provincial council.

The statutes provided regulation of those three elements that were in tension and slow adjustment during the Anglo-Norman period, that is, the Church's teaching on the exercise of sexuality, on the celibate state, and on the married state. The position that there was to be no sexual activity outside marriage, that adultery, fornication, and perversion were serious sins, was established. The main development in the statutes was the creation of regulations that dealt with unacceptable sexual practices in the public forum. Only in the case where the resulting situation touched the possibility of marriage itself, need it be investigated here.[26] It had been made clear that religious vows and major orders constituted an impediment to marriage. Regulations for the enforcement of clerical continence and for the protection of the clergy from the occasions of sin were the main topics of interest in this matter found in the legislation of the period; for present purposes it can be set aside. It was only with the spread of the ideas of John Wyclif and in the religious crises of the Tudor period that the question of the value of celibacy and its relation to marriage would be raised again. The development of the regulation of marriage that began with I Salisbury was a complex process spread over about seventy years. Rather than try to examine each set of statutes as a unit, it has been deemed wiser to isolate different aspects of marriage – theory, impediments, etc – and analyse their regulation in the statutes and conciliar legislation of the period between 1217 and the Reformation. This method would lend itself to a detailed study of the transmission of texts from one collection to another both within the country and between England and the Continent. However, no systematic research along that line

26 See below, 446–8 (here pp 161–3).

is intended here. This study must be seen less as an essay in the history of canonical texts than in the history of the pastoral care that they were intended to inspire and direct.

Theory of Marriage

With 1 Salisbury 15, 82, and 83, the broadened point of view of statute legislation immediately became evident; these regulations included instructions on the purpose of marriage and attempted to establish its place in the history of salvation. Canon 15 presented the sacraments in general; each of the seven was listed and its purpose specified. Following an ancient and very involved tradition which derived from 1 Corinthians 7, it was stated that in marriage the sin of fornication was avoided: 'in coniugio peccatum fornicationis vitatur.' These words were repeated in a similar context in five sets of statutes between 1217 and 1259[27] and, with minor variations, in two others between 1238 and 1287.[28] However, the view that saw marriage as a remedy for sin was refined in the short treatise *De informatione simplicium sacerdotum* that constituted canon 9 of Archbishop Pecham's constitutions issued at the provincial Council of Lambeth in 1281. Here again, the context was a general presentation of the seven sacraments. However, the point of view had changed. While the earlier regulation of 1 Salisbury 15 and its derivatives listed the sacraments and their purposes, Pecham's canon was concerned with the grace of each. At the end of the section where holy orders and matrimony, the two sacraments not required by all Christians, were described, it was pointed out that under the New Law marriage was for the imperfect. Then, in a significant statement reflecting theological discussion of the previous generation, the text added: 'et tamen ipsum ex vi sacramenti credimus largiri gratiam, si sincero animo contrahatur.'[29] This more positive

---

27 2 Canterbury, 1 Durham, 1 Exeter 14, Durham Peculiars 11, 2 London 1 (P–C 165–7, 201, 232, 440, 634).

28 2 Salisbury 4: 'peccatum fornicationis excusatur' – an unhappy phrase – and 2 Exeter 1: 'per matrimonium fornicationis vitatur vitium' (P–C 367–8, 987).

29 'however, we believe that, by the power of the sacrament, marriage bestows grace if it is received sincerely' (see P–C 905). Cf Peter the Chanter, *Summa de sacramentis et anime consiliis*, ed Jean-Albert Dugauquier, Analecta mediaevalia Namurcensia 4, 7, 11, 16, 21 (Louvain and Lille 1954–67) I 19: 'In quolibet septem sacramentorum confertur cumulus gratie, excepto coniugio quod institutum est ad remedium et non ad augmentum'; and *Thomae de Chobham Summa confessorum*, ed Broomfield 90–1. On the canonists' difficulties with the notion of marriage as a source of grace, see DTC 9 II (1927) 2207–14.

statement, which likened matrimony to the other sacraments in the giving of grace, would have considerable importance in the following centuries.[30]

The instruction on the purpose and role of the sacrament received further development in the section of the Salisbury statutes given to a detailed regulation of marriage. Statute 82 ordered the priest to commend the married state, to teach that it was the first of the sacraments, having been instituted by God in paradise, and to set out the goods of matrimony so that it would appear that 'in this life it is most desirable, good and privileged.' Finally, it was pointed out that only the children of a marriage were legitimate and worthy of ecclesiastical dignity and civil inheritance. This position was repeated in 2 Canterbury and 1 Durham and, with some adjustment of wording, in 2 London 42. Practical conclusions from these considerations were drawn in 1 Salisbury 83. This canon, entitled 'De reverentia matrimonii' and closely dependent on Paris 40, concluded that marriage should be celebrated with dignity and honour.[31] It not only excluded offensive behaviour and unsuitable location of marriage but also forbade mock weddings, often a prelude to seduction, lest the mockers find themselves bound by the obligations of the married state.[32] These regulations were repeated in the close derivatives of 1 Salisbury, namely, 2 Canterbury, 1 Durham, and Durham Peculiars 50 and, though in a shorter form more directly dependent on the Paris statute, in Synodal Statutes 39, where there was the significant addition that marriage should be by day and before the Church. A final, more developed version in 2 London 42 included special reference to the necessity of maintaining dignity in second and third marriages.

A somewhat different tradition was begun in 3 Worcester 22. Here the teaching on the place of marriage in the history of salvation received a more compact statement. The notion of the sacrament as a remedy for concupiscence that had appeared in 1 Salisbury 15 was placed in the context of the fall of Adam and contrasted with its role before the original sin. The dignity of matrimony, symbolic of the union of Christ and the

---

30 A Latin catechism based on Pecham's text was published at the provincial Council of York by Archbishop John Thoresby in 1357. In the English translation that was appended, the phrase was rendered: 'In remedi of syn, *and* getyng of grace. If it be taken in gode attent and clennesse of lif.' For these texts and the later Wycliffite translation see *The Lay Folks' Catechism*, ed T.F. Simmons and H.E. Nolloth, EETS o s 118 (London 1901; repr Millwood, N.Y. 1972) 68–9. Cf the constitution of Archbishop George Neville of York (1466) in Wilkins III 601.

31 Cf P–C 87 and Pontal 66–7.

32 'ne dum iocare se putat, honeribus matrimonialibus se astringat' (P–C 87).

Church, and the difficulties that arise from error in its regard were set out as the motives for the regulations that followed. The *bona coniugii* were not mentioned in the context of reverence for marriage, but appeared in statute 25, where the priest was ordered to instruct the people on these goods and to teach them to raise their children in the love of God. There were to be no imitators of 3 Worcester in precisely this arrangement of material, but the approach of statute 22 was developed in Wells 9 and combined with 1 Salisbury 82 to express the reason for the reverence due the sacrament, namely, the goods of marriage and the rights of legitimate children. In this form, the teaching on the function and dignity of matrimony appeared in Carlyle 9 and York 9 within the next few months. A compact and rather elegant derivative of the Wells canon appeared in 3 Winchester 26, and a slightly more diffuse form served as introduction to the major treatment of marriage regulation that is found in 2 Exeter 7.

Impediments to Marriage

It has already been shown that, in the rather limited efforts at the regulation of marriage in twelfth-century English councils, it was impediments – especially those flowing from relationship and from orders and vows – that were the main subject of legislation. The first matter that had to be considered was whether the principals of a projected union were free to marry. The restrictions on their freedom were much discussed by canonists and theologians during the twelfth and thirteenth centuries; and, as is well known, the Fourth Lateran Council, in a constitution with important social consequences, considerably enhanced the liberty of choice of spouse by limiting impediments based on relationship.[33] Yet, as will be seen, in the treatment of marriage in the conciliar canons and diocesan statutes of England after 1215, these impediments had a position of comparatively diminished importance. Were it not for the fact that, in the frequent setting out of regulations touching banns, impediments were mentioned in general terms or at least understood, it could be said that in most of these sets of regulations the impediments to marriage were ignored. In part this can be explained by the promulgation of the Lateran constitutions at the provincial Council of Canterbury held at Oxford in 1222.[34]

---

33 4 Lateran 50 (Alberigo 257–8) = X 4 14 8. See DDC 5 (1954) 266–84, s v 'Empêche-ments de mariage'.

34 See P–C 100, 104–6. The promulgation of the Lateran constitutions was explicit in 1

A list of six impediments derived from the Paris statutes of Eudes de Sully was included in 1 Salisbury 86, its three principal derivatives (2 Canterbury, 1 Durham, and Durham Peculiars 52) and in 2 London 48.[35] In each case it was stated that attempted marriage would result in excommunication, and in the Salisbury and the two Durham statutes it was ordered that a warning to this effect should be repeated in each parish. Furthermore, in a tract on penance attached to the statutes of Bishop Alexander Stavensby for Coventry and Lichfield, the confessor was instructed to enquire whether relationship or any other matter impeded his penitent's marriage.[36]

There was little specific reference, in the portion of synodal statutes that dealt with the sacrament of marriage, to situations where impediments derived from a person's state. The impossibility of marriage for those in vows and major orders was included in the lists of 1 Salisbury as just mentioned; this fact was understood in the rules touching religious and the clergy that paralleled the treatment of marriage in the various statutes.[37] The impediment following on the fact that an individual was already married was implied in the many regulations imposing the banns, but explicit mention of this very important restriction occurred only in Chichester 29.[38] As in the earlier period, it was regulations touching relationship that received the most careful attention. They were included in the general lists of impediments but would receive more detailed statements as well.

Winchester 1: 'Inprimis Lateranensis concilii secundi statuta in episcopatu nostro ab omnibus observentur' (P–C 126 and n1).

35 'In nuptiis semper prohibeatur sub pena excommunicationis sortilega fieri et maleficia, et sub tali pena teneantur omnes qui celant impedimenta matrimonii: votum, ordinem, consanguinitatem, affinitatem, disparem cultum, compaternitatem. Et hec tantum iiii^or personas excludit a matrimonio: compatrem, commatrem, filiolum, fratrem vel sororem spiritualem, scilicet, filium vel filiam patrini. Et ista comminatio in singulis parochiis frequenter recitetur' (P–C 88; also 166, 201, 444, 644). The last sentence of the canon was omitted in 2 Canterbury. Cf Paris 42 and the more developed list in *Synodal de l'Ouest* 67 (Pontal 66–8, 182–3).

36 'querendum est si credat legitimum esse matrimonium, scilicet quod ibi non sit compaternitas, consanguinitas, vel affinitas, vel aliquod aliud impedimentum' (P–C 221).

37 See above, 409 (here p 119).

38 'In nuptiis prohibeantur ... celatio legittimorum matrimoniorum et aliorum impedimentorum' (P–C 457). On the frequency of cases touching this impediment see Michael M. Sheehan, 'The Formation and Stability of Marriage in Fourteenth-Century England: Evidence of an Ely Register,' *Mediaeval Studies* 33 (1971) 261–3

It will be recalled that a canon of Hubert Walter's provincial Council of Westminster (1200) forbade marriages where the impediment from an unspecified degree of affinity existed between the couple or where a relationship resulting from baptism existed.[39] This canon reappeared in 1 Canterbury 53 and Constitutiones cuiusdam episcopi 57. The last-mentioned set of statutes was compiled at least a decade after the Fourth Lateran Council and included some of its constitutions. However, there was no attempt to integrate the Lateran limitation of the impediment of affinity to the fourth degree with the text derived from the Council of Westminster. It was only in canon 95, one of a series appended to the collection, that the new regulation found its place. On the other hand 1 Salisbury 87 had already adjusted the earlier text by the insertion of the phrase 'usque ad quartum gradum.' As will be shown in more detail below, the Salisbury statutes integrated the canons from the Canterbury tradition with the Paris statutes of Eudes de Sully and the much more developed constitutions of the Lateran Council. The result was neither neat nor perfectly consistent, but statutes of the next twenty years would provide the desired refinement. For the moment, the Westminster canon as adjusted in 1 Salisbury 87 would reappear in 2 Canterbury and 1 Durham but would go no further. Not only was 1 Salisbury 87 poorly drafted, but 1 Salisbury 86 and 90 dealt with the same problems in a more satisfactory manner. In the Canterbury tradition, the impediment of spiritual relationship (compaternitas) was said to lie between the baptized and a child of the minister or sponsor whether born before or after the baptism.[40] In the version of the text in 1 Salisbury 87, reference to the minister was omitted. However, in the previous statute, drawing on Paris 42, the Salisbury legislator had presented the impediment as excluding marriage with the godfather, godmother, other godchildren, and the natural children of the sponsors.[41] This statement of the impediment reappeared only in 1 Durham and Durham Peculiars 52. Aside from a more developed definition in 1 Exeter 24, the impediment of spiritual relationship would not occur again in the statutes.

The impact of the Lateran constitutions was explicit in 1 Salisbury 90. In this statute were set out the new regulations on consanguinity and

(here pp 74–6); and Richard H. Helmholz, *Marriage Litigation in Medieval England* (London 1974) 57–66, 76–7.

39 See above, n18.
40 'ante, vel post genita' (above, n18).
41 See above, n35. See DDC 3 (1942) 952–60, s v 'Cognatio spiritualis'.

affinity within the fourth degree, the reasons for the change, the fact that long duration of such relationship did not excuse it, as well as the removal of the impediments derived from the second and third kinds of affinity and from the relationship of a child of a second marriage with a relative of the first spouse. This canon, in its fullness, would be used only in 1 Durham. With the clauses dealing with the second and third kinds of affinity and the marriage of the child of a second marriage omitted, it is found in 2 Canterbury and the Constitutiones cuiusdam episcopi 95, where it served to bring the collection up to date. A few years later, 2 Salisbury 26 stated the restriction of the impediment of consanguinity and affinity to the fourth degree, repeated the statement that long duration of such a relationship would not excuse it, and, in a benign interpretation of 4 Lateran 50, declared that those descended in the fourth and fifth degrees from a common ancestor were permitted to marry.[42] It was only in 1 Exeter 24 that the different strains were brought together. There, in a well-developed analysis of the persons excluded by spiritual relationship, the rule that the *de facto* marriage involving such a couple be declared invalid was followed by the brief statement that marriage within the fourth degree of affinity was forbidden. The impediment of consanguinity was mentioned in passing as something requiring neither statement nor explanation. With minor verbal changes this regulation would reappear in 2 London 10.

It is significant that, though the statutes for Durham Peculiars repeated almost all of 1 Salisbury, the regulations touching the impediment of relationship were omitted. One has the impression that the diminished requirements in the Lateran statement on consanguinity and affinity were understood quickly and with ease. This tends to reinforce the suggestion that the omission of the degree of affinity in the Westminster canon and 1 Canterbury 53 implied that the limited prohibition, an example of the *specialem quorundam locorum consuetudinem* mentioned in 4 Lateran 51, already obtained in England.[43] It was only the specification of the list of persons excluded by the impediment of spiritual relationship that posed problems. It was nicely stated by the 1230s and was repeated only once.

The impediment of *crimen* was the subject of 1 Salisbury 79: priests were to teach that the adulterer might not marry the adulteress if, during the lifetime of her husband, he had promised to do so, nor could he

---

42 'Ceterum enim qui a stipite quarto gradu cum ea que ex alio latere quinto distat ab eodem, licite dicimus matrimonialiter copulatum' (P–C 377).

43 Alberigo 258; see above, 412 (here p 123).

marry her if he or she were involved in the death of that husband.[44] The impediment was repeated only in those statutes most closely derived from 1 Salisbury;[45] it would not appear again.

A final group of impediments touched cases where marriage was invalid because of lack of consent by the principals of the union. Although care to ensure proper consent was explicit or at least implicit in many statutes, it was only the impossibility of consent consequent on insufficient age and the resulting impediment that found a place in the regulations under examination here.[46] It will be recalled that the provincial Council of Westminster (1175), canon 18, citing the ancient dictum 'Ubi non est consensus utriusque non est coniugium,' forbade the marriage of minors. However, the canon allowed an exception where an urgent necessity such as the making of peace existed.[47] Two traditions touching this impediment would develop in the thirteenth century. The notion of limited dispensation appeared in 1 Winchester 60: 'Prohibemus ne quis inpuberes vel alium inpuberem atque alium adultum sine consensu nostro matrimonio copulare presumat.'[48] It will be noted that here the minor's incapacity of consent as the basis of the prohibition was ignored. Marriages involving one or two minors were simply forbidden without the bishop's permission. This position was repeated in 2 Salisbury 23.[49] On the other hand, Norwich 42 and 2 Winchester 59 refused to allow such marriages.[50] Neither form of this regulation would appear again in conciliar canon or diocesan statute, but the original statement of 1175, ascribed to Archbishop Edmund Rich, was included in the brief treatment

44 'Moneant et prohibeant sacerdotes ne quisquam cum ea contrahat matrimonium quam vivente marito suo polluit per adulterium; et hoc si adulter fidem dederit adultere de ea ducenda adhuc viro suo vivente, vel etiam si ipsa adultera vel adulter in mortem viri machinati sunt' (P–C 85–6). The first clause seemed to forbid any marriage between adulterers after they had been freed by the death of the spouse(s); cf Gratian, C31 q1 c1. However, were it so understood, the second and third clauses would have been unnecessary; see X 4 7 6.

45 2 Canterbury, 1 Durham, Durham Peculiars 53.

46 See below, 445–6 (here p 160).

47 See above, 411 (here pp 121–2).

48 P–C 135.

49 The position is somewhat refined in 2 Salisbury 24: 'Pubes cum inpubere copulatus, nisi autem carnalis copula intervenerit, tempus exspectet pubertatis, et tunc contractus confirmetur vel infirmetur' (P–C 376).

50 'Interdicimus quoque ne quis inter minores, quorum alter vel uterque ad annos canonibus vel legibus determinatos nondum pervenerint, nuptias audeat celebrare' (P–C 351–2). Thus 2 Winchester 59 withdrew from the position of 1 Winchester 60 after somewhat more than twenty years.

of marriage by Lyndwood in his *Provinciale*.[51] Thus it was the twelfth-century regulation on the impediment of insufficient age that was kept before the canonist's eye in late medieval England. A similar point of view found a place in what appears to have been the draft of a code of canon law for the Church of England prepared in the last years of the reign of Henry VIII.[52] Betrothal and marriage were forbidden to men and women who had not completed their sixteenth and fourteenth years respectively. The possibility of dispensation in the case of urgent necessity such as the making of peace was included at least for betrothal.[53]

The list of six impediments in 1 Salisbury 86, mentioned above, occurred in a regulation that excommunicated those who, knowing of an objection to a proposed union, failed to reveal it. This excommunication was also applied to those who used sorcery and spells in marriage.[54] It is presumed that such action was considered capable of influencing the spouses, thus limiting or destroying their freedom so that their marriage was impeded by lack of consent.[55] This regulation appeared in the close derivatives of 1 Salisbury, namely, 2 Canterbury, 1 Durham, and Durham Peculiars 52 and in 1 Chichester 29 and 2 London 48.

The Formalities of Marriage

It was pointed out above that the teaching on marriage that began to appear in English diocesan statutes with 1 Salisbury included the notion that the seriousness of the union between spouses as well as its sacramental character required that it be performed with dignity and in a religious setting. There were several other important reasons for this position. Though the examination of the role of consent was not extensively developed in these regulations, there were abundant signs that

---

51 *Provinciale (seu constitutiones Angliae)*, ed W. Lyndwood (Oxford 1679) 4 2, 271–2. Note the emphasis of the rubric: 'Ante tempus legitimum non contrahatur Matrimonium sine dispensatione pro bono pacis.'

52 The transcription of the proposed code derived from London, BL Add MS 48040 was generously put at my disposition by Professor Donald F. Logan, who is preparing an edition.

53 'Districtius inhibemus ne masculus qui sextum decimum, mulier vero que quartum decimum sue etatis annum non compleverit matrimonium seu sponsalia contrahat, et quod contra factum fuerit nullum esse decernimus nisi urgentissima aliqua necessitas interveniat, ut pote pro bona pacis sponsalia tantum inter minores tollerantur' (f 71r).

54 See above, n35; cf DTC 14 II (1941) 2409–11, s v 'Sorcellerie, diffusion'.

55 Cf Burchard, *Decretum*, Liber 19 c5 (PL 140 961, 971–2); see below, 454 (here p 169).

its importance was presumed and that the dignified setting of marriage was justified in part as a way of preserving a freedom of consent that could easily be lost in the riotous conditions of some unions. This same teaching also underlined the tragedy of the invalid marriage and saw in formal conditions a defence against the evil. Many marriages failed because impediments rendered them impossible. A *de facto* union came about because the ignorance, self-deceit, or dishonesty of the couple and their families all too often resulted in the ignoring of the conditions that stood in the way of validity. But the memory of the wider community that became involved in the marriage under public conditions was less likely to fail.

Canonists and theologians of the eleventh and twelfth centuries had discussed these problems at great length. The reflection on the nature of marriage that found its way into the diocesan statutes was but a faint reflection of the earlier activity, yet it served as a motive for and an introduction to the regulations touching the formalities by which a couple became man and wife. The older position according to which, with important local differences, the Church in the West had been content to support the observance of the formalities of marriage found in local law and customs, intervening, where it intervened at all, by blessing the couple or by other religious acts, had come to be considered inadequate. In the attempt to prevent the *de facto* unions of those between whom there was an impediment, conciliar legislation and diocesan regulations had moved beyond the mere support of civil formalities. The Church became involved in them, 'canonized' them, to use Korbinian Ritzer's phrase, and drew them into a religious and ritualist context in which the priest played a role.[56] The thrust in this direction emphasized the canonical formalities and on occasion saw them as necessary for the validity of marriage. In the thinking of those typified by Gratian, who saw marriage as a process completed by a series of acts, the traditional formalities and even a growing liturgical dimension given them easily found a place. On the other hand, the school of theological and legal thinking that was based on the Roman *consensus nuptialis* not only saw the marriage bond established by a single act in which the couple freely consented to enter into a marital relationship but also stood in the way of any position that would attach essential importance to legal formalities.[57]

---

56 See Ritzer, *Formen* 253–84.
57 See Gérard Fransen, 'La formation du lien matrimonial au moyen âge,' in *Le lien matrimonial*, Colloque du Cerdic, Strasbourg, 21–3 mai 1970, ed René Metz and Jean Schlick (Strasbourg 1970) 108–26.

By the period that is of interest to the present study, the theory of marriage had come to a balance of tendencies which, precarious though it was, would last until the decree *Tametsi* of the Council of Trent: this position condemned the clandestine union, established procedures and formalities to make it difficult to bring about, provided penalties for those involved in any way with such a union, yet admitted that the clandestine marriage was valid if the couple were not prevented by some impediment that would have rendered any marriage impossible.

As would be expected, given the limited treatment of marriage in twelfth-century English councils, there was but little reflection of this wider discussion by the Western Church. Yet there were some indications of it, and they were not without significance. It will be recalled that canon 25 of Anselm's Westminster council of 1102 moved beyond the mere prohibition of marriage within forbidden relationships, calling on members of the community to report any impediments and informing them that failure to act made them partners in the incest they had condoned. Here Anselm adopted that use of the local community's knowledge about the couple in the control of marriage that would appear again in Hubert Walter's Westminster council of 1200.[58] By this later date the procedure had been refined, and the regulation required the triple announcement in church before marriage that became known as the banns. But the limitation of this method of control was already indicated by the admission that further regulation was needed for the stranger whose past was unknown to the local community: 'Nec contrahatur aliquod matrimonium ... si fuerint personae incognitae.'[59]

Lanfranc's Winchester council of 1076 went very far in imposing a formality on marriage: the couple was to be blessed by the priest. Otherwise their union was invalid.[60] Almost a century later, in the Council of Westminster, canon 18, a similar regulation derived from a long continental tradition appeared.[61] This time, however, the rule was put in a different context. Clandestine marriage was forbidden; the acceptable alternative was 'public marriage in the Lord' with a priestly blessing. Even more important from the point of view of the present discussion, however, was the change that appeared in the sanction clause that was added to the canon in England. The formality was enjoined but no longer required for validity, and the priest who cooperated in such a clandestine

---

58 See above, 410 and 412 (here pp 120 and 122).
59 Wilkins I 507; see above, n18.
60 See above, 410 and n10 (here p 120).
61 See above, 410 and n11 (here pp 120–1).

union was to be suspended for three years. By a similar regulation of the Council of Westminster (1200), canon 11, the marriage was to be public, before the Church, and in the presence of the priest. Here not only was there a significant difference in the role of the priest – he was required to be present rather than to give the blessing – but the sanction was also carried to the couple, who were to be suspended from entry of a church with reservation to the bishop: '... et si secus factum fuerit, non admittantur alicubi in ecclesia, nisi speciali auctoritate episcopi.'[62]

There was only one reference to the fact that the process whereby a couple came to be united occurred in several stages. In the Council of Westminster (1102), canon 23, the engagement to marry was isolated, and the necessity that it occur before witnesses was implied.[63]

More detailed consideration of the formalities of marriage is to be found in the diocesan statutes of the thirteenth century. Here the problems and discussion of the previous period were more fully reflected. The compilers of the statutes undertook a difficult task. They had to reckon with a long and complex tradition on the formalities of marriage, a tradition that was still operative in the Church, still enshrined in some of the older texts that they tailored to their use. The theories of marriage expressed in the statutes were not always consistent nor well understood. Even the vocabulary at the disposition of the compilers – the terms *matrimonium* and *sponsalia* to mention but two – often had meanings that confuse the modern student and that may well have left even the most efficient archdeacon at a loss as to their sense.

About the middle of the thirteenth century, a clause of 2 London 43 set out the order to be followed in bringing about the proper canonical marriage: betrothal, the announcement of the intention to marry by the banns, the exchange of consent *de presenti* between the couple.[64] The sequence of acts set out in the statute will be adopted for the presentation that follows. This procedure will result in an ordered exposition that is to be found in no set of diocesan statutes nor in any English conciliar document, but it will have certain advantages: it will establish the chronology of the development by which the formalities of marriage came to be required, show something at least of the influences that were

---

62 See above, 411–12 and n18 (here p 122); the text is discussed below, 449–50 (here p 165).
63 See above, 410–11 (here pp 120–1).
64 'ante fidem datam de matrimonio contrahendo et ante hec tria edicta, nullus audeat aliquomodo per verba de presenti matrimonium celebrare' (P–C 643).

operative, and isolate the aspects of the regulations that were weakest and required most refinement and care in their implementation.

Betrothal

In bringing about the union of husband and wife, the initial legal act was betrothal. It was in the regulation of this act that the first set of diocesan statutes remaining to us, those of Stephen Langton for Canterbury, moved beyond the remarkable treatment of marriage in Hubert Walter's Westminster council of 1200.[65] This was but a beginning, for twenty-three of the thirty-three sets of statutes between 1213 and 1289 would include canons setting out the formalities and other requirements of betrothal.[66] The order for the priest to instruct the people on the conditions required for betrothal and on the consequences of the act was set out in 1 Canterbury 55. It would be repeated in eight sets of statutes up to the 1240s, then would disappear.[67] It was with the conditions in which the betrothal came about that the statutes were especially concerned.

Thus 1 Canterbury 55 ordered that the engagement be entered in public, before witnesses who could be counted on to give evidence should the fact of the betrothal be questioned. Specific reference to the publicity of the act was repeated only in three later sets of statutes.[68] A different point of view was revealed at Winchester, where the publicity of the tavern was rejected as destructive of the freedom of the principals,[69] and in the last important series of statutes, 2 Chichester 24, where 'fidei dationes domesticas' were permitted if proper witnesses were present.

The presence of witnesses at betrothal was an ancient practice in the different European traditions and was supported by custom and law. All the statutes of the group under discussion, except those of Coventry and

---

65 1 Canterbury 53–5; on the Council of Westminster see above, 411–12 (here pp 121–2).
66 1 Canterbury 55, 1 Salisbury 83, 1 Winchester 56, Synodal Statutes 41, 2 Canterbury 83, 2 Worcester 32, Constitutiones cuiusdam episcopi 59, 60, 1 Durham 83, Coventry 13, 3 Worcester 23, 28, 2 Salisbury 23, 2 Winchester 56, 2 Durham 46, Durham Peculiars 50, 1 Chichester 28, 1 York 25, Wells 11, Carlyle 11, 2 London 43, 2 York 11, 3 Winchester 27, 2 Exeter 7, 2 Chichester 24.
67 1 Salisbury 83, 1 Winchester 56, 2 Canterbury [83], Constitutiones cuiusdam episcopi 60, 1 Durham [83], Coventry 13, 3 Worcester 23, 2 Durham 46.
68 Constitutiones cuiusdam episcopi 60 and 1 Chichester 28, both close derivatives of 1 Canterbury 55 and Synodal Statutes 41.
69 2 Winchester 56 and 3 Winchester 27.

2 Salisbury, referred to them.[70] Occasionally their number was specified: three or four in 1 Salisbury and its close derivatives, four or five in 1 Winchester. What was more important were the regulations touching the quality of the witnesses; mere presence was not enough: they were to be formally invited (*testes vocati*), suitable (*idonei*), or worthy of belief (*fidei digni*).

Though the Coventry statutes did not mention lay witnesses, the presence of a priest was required. This significant step, whereby the canonical reinforcement of the witnessed betrothal was carried further to include the presence of a representative of the Church, was taken in 1 Salisbury 83. All of the collections regulating betrothal for the next generation except the Synodal Statutes included this requirement.[71] The later exceptions were 2 Winchester 56 and 3 Winchester 27 (which were, as was seen above, concerned with things to be avoided in the exchange of the promise to marry), 2 Salisbury, 1 Chichester, and Wells and its derivatives Carlyle and 2 York. That the priest in question should be parish priest or rector of the church was specified in 2 London 43, a position that was restated a generation later in 2 Exeter 7.[72]

A regulation that the principals of the betrothal should be fasting also contributed to the religious atmosphere which these statutes encouraged. It appeared in 1 Winchester 56 and was later included in 3 Worcester 23, Wells 11, Carlyle 11, 2 York 11, and 3 Winchester 27.[73]

The statutes not only regulated the conditions required for the betrothal; all of the twenty-three sets under discussion gave some evidence on the act itself and its manner of performance. It was usually presented as a promise (*fidei datio*) related to a marriage the futurity of which was

---

70   The reference in 2 Worcester 32 and 2 Winchester 56 is by implication.

71   Synodal Statutes 41: 'Item, prohibeant presbiteri frequenter in ecclesiis laicis sub pena excommunicationis ne dent sibi fidem mutuo de matrimonio contrahendo nisi in loco celebri et coram publicis et pluribus personis ad hoc vocatis' (P–C 146–7); this is closely related to Paris 41, two manuscripts of which read: 'ne dent sibi fidem mutuo de contrahendo matrimonio nisi coram presbytero et in loco celebri, scilicet ante januas ecclesie et coram pluribus' (Pontal 66 nn aa, bb). The reading of *presbytero* as *publicis* is suggested.

72   2 London 43: 'statuimus ut nullum matrimonium, nulla sponsalia sine presentia sacerdotis parochialis vel rectoris ecclesie et aliorum trium adminus fidedignorum contrahantur' (P–C 643); 2 Exeter 7 is virtually the same. In both cases *sponsalia* is understood to mean 'betrothal.'

73   The requirement was extended to those assisting at the betrothal in 3 Worcester 23; see the following note.

expressed in the words *per verba de futuro* or by the use of the gerundive.[74] A slightly different form, indicating an agreement between the couple, was used in 1 Winchester 56,[75] and 2 London 43 referred to betrothal as a contract related to the future entered into with or without a 'fidei datio.'[76] In no case was a role for family or lord stipulated or even mentioned.[77] A form of words whereby the act was effected first appeared in 2 Salisbury 23: 'Accipiam vel habebo te in me.' Another formula in the same text promised marriage unless the reading of the banns resulted in the revelation of an impediment that prevented the union, thus indicating what was considered to be the main barrier that had to be cleared before the marriage could take place.[78]

There may have been one further requirement. In the Paris statutes of Eudes de Sully it was stated that betrothal was not to occur until after the reading of the banns.[79] At first sight several of the English statutes seem to make a similar ruling. It is difficult to arrive at certainty in this regard, not only because the meaning of the terms *matrimonium* and *sponsalia* is sometimes unclear but also, at a deeper level, because the understanding of the acts they were intended to connote was changing. The twelfth century had seen the differentiation of several acts in the process by which a couple came to be man and wife.[80] The terms used to designate these acts and the understanding of their legal effects varied according to

74 Eg 3 Worcester 23: 'ne etiam sponsalia contrahant vel contrahentibus assistant fide data per verba de futuro, nisi ieiuna saliva' (P–C 302); 1 Salisbury 83: 'alicui fides detur de matrimonio contrahendo' (P–C 87).

75 'ne viri et mulieres aliquod pactum firment inter se de matrimonio contrahendo' (P–C 134).

76 'Ubi vero sponsalia contrahuntur per verba de futuro, sive per fidei dationem sive absque fidei datione' (P–C 643).

77 In the penalties set out in 2 Winchester 56 (see below, n82) there is reference to laymen in authority who were punished for their role in an improper betrothal.

78 'Ego te in meum, nisi notorium subsit impedimentum post primam denunciationem sub testimonio sacerdotis et aliorum fidedignorum contrahi sustinemus' (P–C 375–6). Cf 2 Exeter 7: 'Accipiam, vel habebo, te in meam, et: Ego te in meum' (P–C 998). Note that in both cases the second formula, 'Ego te in meum,' is not specific in its reference to the future. In fact, in both the Salisbury and the Exeter statutes the same form of words would be used for the contract *per verba de presenti*; see below, 445 (here p 160). Though the compiler of 2 Salisbury included the formula 'Ego te ... sustinemus' among those used in betrothal, it might easily have led to confusion, for it seems to express a conditional contract *de presenti*; see Sheehan, 'The Formation and Stability of Marriage' 238 ff (here p 48 ff).

79 c40 (Pontal 66–7).

80 DTC 9 II 2137–59.

different theories on the mode of establishing the marriage bond. In such a situation, it was to be expected that the term *matrimonium* might be used of any part or of the whole process whereby union was brought about. This was especially true of the context which saw betrothal as *matrimonium initiatum*. Where the engagement of the couple was so conceived, it was to be expected that the public scrutiny of an intended union made possible by the reading of banns would take place before the first step in bringing about the union was taken. This would explain the requirement of the Paris statute and would be in accord with the understanding of marriage expressed in the older layers of that collection.[81] Thus, in England, in the reference to the banns in the Council of Westminster (1200), 'Nec contrahatur aliquod matrimonium sine trina denunciatione,' where no distinction of the stages of the marriage was made, the term *matrimonium* may well have been intended to apply to the whole process that brought about the union of the couple. If such were the case, the reading of the banns would anticipate betrothal. The clause was repeated in 1 Canterbury 54, but, as was seen above, the legislator introduced a separate treatment of betrothal in the following statute. Even here, however, it is not unreasonable to suggest that the 'fidem ... de matrimonio contrahendo' of 1 Canterbury 55 was intended to be part of the *matrimonium* to which banns were related in the previous statute. However, since the second part of 1 Canterbury 55 strongly suggests that the legislator held that consent *per verba de presenti* established the marriage bond, the stronger opinion is that the Canterbury statutes did not require the reading of banns before the betrothal of the couple.[82] The matter was clarified in 1 Salisbury 84, where it was stated that marriage was contracted by the exchange of consent to which the banns were related.

A similar, though less difficult, problem occurs in the statutes' use of the term *sponsalia*. In many cases it clearly refers to betrothal. Occasionally the statutes require that the reading of the banns occur before *sponsalia*.[83] Though at first glance these seem to be references to the engage-

---

81 See below, 430 and n92 (here pp 142–3).
82 See below, 440–4 (here pp 154–8).
83 1 Winchester 55: 'Denuntietur publice in ecclesiis quod nunquam sponsalia *fiant* nisi presente sacerdote et congregatis parochianis suis, et per tres dies solempnes trina fiat denuntiatio'; 2 Winchester 51: 'Omnibus in super personis, vicariis, et capellanis curas parochiarum habentibus firmiter inhibemus ne alicui contractui matrimoniali vel sponsalium intersint vel auctoritatem prestent priusquam consuete et sollempnes denuntiationes in ecclesiis et parochiis contrahere volentium facte'; Ely 33: 'Inhibeant

ment of the couple, a more careful reading demands the translation 'wedding,' a meaning that fits the more common understanding of the order of the acts bringing about a marriage, namely, betrothal, reading of the banns, and expression of consent *per verba de presenti*.

A more difficult problem is posed by 2 Worcester 32: 'Prohibemus sub pena suspensionis ne sacerdotes intersint fidei dationi etiam per verba de presenti facte in contractu matrimoniali sine denuntiatione premissa. Item, ut nec sacerdos nec etiam laicus intersint fidei dationi facte per verba de futuro in contractu matrimoniali; quod si intersint, tam fide obligati quam illi qui interfuerunt fidei dationi gravi pena tam spirituali quam peccuniaria puniantur.'[84] Unless the word 'Item' at the beginning of the second sentence is taken to mean that the requirement of the reading of the banns, found in the first part of the statute, applies to the second part, the clause 'ut nec ... matrimoniali' imposes the impossibility of witnessing a betrothal. For the moment it seems best to conclude that, in the case of Worcester as at Paris, it was required that the announcement of the intention to marry should occur even before the betrothal. According to the statute, if this rule were not obeyed, all involved in the act including the priest were to be subject to grave spiritual and financial penalties.[85]

Although no sanction was included among the regulations in 1 Canterbury touching betrothal, it appeared within six years, in 1 Salisbury 83. One manuscript of this collection included a cancelled sentence in which it was stated that unless the required formalities were observed, the betrothal would be without effect.[86] The notion would appear again in the Constitutiones cuiusdam episcopi 59.[87] The Salisbury statutes maintained

---

... ut sine presbiterorum presentia et bannorum solempnitate matrimonia sive sponsalia contrahere ... presumant'; Wells 10: 'inhibemus ne, nisi trina denuntiatione premissa ... matrimonia contrahantur. Sacerdotes autem qui omissa denuntiatione huiusmodi contractui matrimoniali vel sponsaliorum intererint' (P–C 134, 410, 521–2, 597).

84 P–C 175–6.

85 At this point 3 Worcester 23, a more carefully drafted statute than its predecessor, added 'nisi ieiuna saliva.' If the phrase had been added after 'Item ... matrimoniali,' this tortuous reading of the statute would be unnecessary; cf P–C 176 n1.

86 Worcester, Cathedral Library MS Q 67 f 143v: 'Quod si secus actum fuerit, et fides pro nulla habeatur et carnalis copula etiam si sit subsecuta' (P–C 87 and n e).

87 'Nec fides de aliqua desponsanda detur nisi presente sacerdote. Quod si aliter factum fuerit, decernimus contractum non tenere et persone legittime puniantur' (P–C 190). This sentence was added at the end of a statute derived from 1 Canterbury 54. It

that those who did not obey the regulations touching the publicity of marriage – the requirements for betrothal seem to be included therein – would be denounced to the bishop and by him to the Apostolic See. This extraordinary sanction would reappear only in 2 Canterbury and 1 Durham. Excommunication of the couple and a fifty-day suspension of the priest who failed to make the regulations known were imposed by 1 Winchester 56. According to Coventry 13, the couple was to be sent to the bishop for punishment. Beginning with 3 Worcester 56, it became the general practice that the principals and all others involved in a betrothal that failed to obey the requirements of the statute were punished.[88] The prescription of 2 Winchester 56 against betrothal in taverns ordered that the couple be whipped three times and that laymen who exercised authority or consented to such betrothals were to be seriously punished.[89] Public penalties were imposed by 2 Chichester 24 on all laymen involved because of the scandal they had given.

One further contribution to the understanding and regulation of betrothal was made by 1 Canterbury 55. In a text illustrating the balance between the canonical desire for legal formality and the power of the position which maintained that the essential element in marriage was the free consent of the couple, the priest was ordered to warn his people that, if carnal union followed betrothal, the Church would hold the union to be marriage and require that it be observed as such: 'quia si talem fidem carnalis copula subsequatur, ecclesia pro matrimonio hoc habebit, et faciet tanquam matrimonium observari.'[90]

Before turning to the subsequent history of this doctrine, two points should be noted about the Canterbury text. First, the meaning of the words *talem fidem.* If interpreted strictly, they mean that the ruling of 1 Canterbury 55 applied only where the formalities of betrothal as set out in the statute had been implemented. It will be recalled that in one manuscript of 1 Salisbury and in Constitutiones cuiusdam episcopi the observation of formalities was required for validity.[91] Furthermore, the Salisbury text directly related the legal effect of sexual union to the validity

supplemented the regulation in c60 that followed, which, being a duplicate of 1 Canterbury 55, made no reference to the presence of a priest.

88 Thus 2 Durham 46, 1 York 25, 2 Exeter 7, 2 Chichester 24.

89 'Si quis contravenerit, sive vir fuerit vel mulier, trine fustigationis pene tribus locis publicis subiacebunt. Laici quidem qui talibus contractis consenserint vel auctoritatem prestiterint graviter puniantur' (P–C 411–12).

90 P–C 35.

91 See above, 429 and nn 86, 87 (here p 141).

of the previous betrothal. Other statutes did not legislate on the matter. In spite of some evidence to the contrary, it seems likely that the strict reading of *talem fidem* was not long applied, if applied at all. In this regard it is important to remember that the requirement was deleted from the only Salisbury manuscript in which it occurred. In more general terms, it was characteristic of canon law to keep formalities to a minimum; even when it imposed them under strict moral obligation, it did not often require them for the validity of an act. The history of the formalities of marriage in the Middle Ages provides ample demonstration of this fact. It seems best to conclude that, with the possible exception of local practice for a few years after the publication of 1 Salisbury, it was understood that, if there were agreement that a promise to marry had been made and sexual union had followed, then the couple were to be considered man and wife. The second observation touches the theory on the mode of establishing the marital bond implied by the phrase 'ecclesia pro matrimonio hoc habebit.' It will be noted that the text does not say that sexual union confirmed the marriage, much less that it caused it. Rather it is stated that the Church presumed the couple to be man and wife, an implementation of the theory of *matrimonium presumptum* enunciated by Huguccio and applied in the exercise of jurisdiction by Innocent III.[92]

The implied statement of *matrimonium presumptum* in the Salisbury manuscript aside, the regulation of 1 Canterbury 55 would appear only in its close derivative Constitutiones cuiusdam episcopi 60 and, about a generation later, in 1 Chichester 28.[93] However much the practice might

---

92 Jean Dauvillier, *Le mariage dans le droit classique de l'Eglise depuis le Décret de Gratien (1140) jusqu'à la mort de Clément v (1314)* (Paris 1933) 55–75. The author cited a text long associated with the Paris statutes of Bishop Eudes de Sully as an example of the older understanding of the legal effect of carnal union following betrothal: 'sequens carnalis copula cum illa cui fidem dedit matrimonium confirmavit' (58). As examples of the theory of *matrimonium presumptum* he cited two texts. The first, 'the synodal statutes of an unknown bishop,' he dated ca 1237, adopting the position of J.-D. Mansi in *Sacrorum conciliorum nova et amplissima collectio* (Florence and Venice 1759–98) 23 471. The second was a set of canons from an unidentified council that had been preserved in a Corbie manuscript and subsequently lost (ibid 22 730). The studies of Professor C.R. Cheney have shown that both texts are English, being, in fact, Constitutiones cuiusdam episcopi 60 and 1 Canterbury 55 respectively; cf P–C 23–24, 181–2, and the references cited there. On the Paris statute, see Pontal 88 n to c96.

93 'quod si talem fidem carnalis copula fuerit subsecuta, ecclesia reputabit ibi matrimonium' (P–C 457).

be interpreted by those who, like Huguccio, were exercised to maintain that consent *de presenti* created the marriage bond, it was a usage against which the Church had set its face. The main purpose of the statutes was not to teach that such a union established a valid marriage but to forbid it. Thus in most of the manuscripts of 1 Salisbury and in its close derivatives, 1 Durham, 2 Canterbury, and Durham Peculiars 50, sexual union after betrothal was forbidden until the scrutiny afforded by the banns had been completed.[94] In 3 Worcester 28 carnal union was forbidden the couple under pain of excommunication until after their marriage had been solemnized. The same sanction was invoked in 2 London 43, but it was specified that both the banns and the solemnization of marriage were to be completed before the marriage was consummated, a position adopted by 2 Exeter 7 with the important addition that punishment was to be imposed even if there were no impediment preventing the marriage of the couple. Earlier, 3 Worcester 28 had, in addition to the threat of excommunication mentioned above, imposed very severe penalties on those who, having disobeyed the statute, were brought before the ecclesiastical court.[95]

During the forty years after the first mention of betrothal in 1 Canterbury 55, the English synodal statutes came to express a fairly complete set of instructions and regulations on its purpose, on the role of witnesses and the clergy, on the nature of the act and the form of words by which it was effected, and on its sanctions. During the latter part of the century these regulations would be repeated and refined. After that, inasmuch as our present knowledge of the conciliar legislation and diocesan statutes of the later Middle Ages permits an opinion, little more attention was to be paid to betrothal.[96] It was to be the stage after the promise to marry that would be their special concern.

94 'ita quod nullatenus per verba de presenti contrahant nec post matrimonium per verba de futuro contractum carnaliter commisceantur nisi rite canonicis denuntiationibus premissis' (P–C 87 n e).

95 'quater in anno veniat ad ecclesiam cathedralem, tam coram atrio ecclesie quam in vicis precipuis civitatis disciplinam publicam recepturus. In aliis diebus feriandis totidem in parochia sua propria consimilem subeat disciplinam' (P–C 302).

96 For an example of a repetition of the older regulations see *Registrum Thome Bourgchier Cantuariensis archiepiscopi A.D. 1454–1486*, ed F.R.H. du Boulay, Canterbury and York Society 54 (Oxford 1957) 23, a monition to parish clergy and to preachers at St Paul's Cross to publish, among other matters, that both marriage and betrothal should take place in the presence of two or more witnesses 'per quos matrimonium hujusmodi probari possit si per aliquam parcium contingat id depost denegari.'

The Banns

The betrothed were not allowed to marry until their intention to do so had been published and there had been opportunity for a wider public than those present at their engagement to object to the proposed union. As has been seen, this practice was imposed on the Province of Canterbury by the Council of Westminster (1200).[97] The announcement was to be public, repeated three times in church. The canon added a further regulation: if the principals were not known there was to be no marriage. The addition removes any doubt there might be as to the purpose of the procedure: it was intended that the parishioners' knowledge of the couple and of any impediment that might prevent their union be drawn into play in a public, formal way. Since the next clause of the canon required that the marriage itself be public and before the Church, it is clear that mere publicity was not enough: the earlier announcement was intended to provide time for investigation of the couple's freedom to marry.

With minor changes the Westminster canon would be adopted in 1 Canterbury, the first set of diocesan statutes that remain to us. During the next seventy-five years, the regulation controlling the announcement of intention to marry was taken up and developed by all but eight of the thirty-three sets of statutes that survive.[98] Of these eight, only two – 1 Worcester (1219) and 3 Chichester (1289) – ignored the matter completely. Of the others, Lincoln 42, Norwich 39, and 2 Durham 46 included brief prohibitions of clandestine marriage, and Coventry 11, 1 York 24, and 2 Chichester 23 developed rules dealing with the stranger who sought to marry.

English regulation of the announcement of the intent to marry was much influenced by the constitution of the Fourth Lateran Council that appeared shortly after the publication of 1 Canterbury. This constitution (4 Lateran 51) was especially concerned to prevent marriages impeded by relationship.[99] For this reason it did two things: first, it sought to ensure publicity by reinforcing secular prohibitions of clandestine marriage, forbidding the priest to be present at such a union; second, the possibility of discovering impediments was enhanced in widening the circle of those

---

97 See above, 412 and n18 (here p 122).
98 The York mandate of 1238 likewise dealt with this matter, imposing penalties on those involved in a marriage without prior announcement of the couple's intention (P–C 259–60).
99 Alberigo 258.

who would be informed of the couple's intention to marry by the priests' publication of the fact in churches. In addition to this broadening of the conception of clandestinity, 4 Lateran 51 provided a technical advance in its regulations on the sequel to the announcement made in the banns. A period was established during which those who were aware of impediments were to make them known. In the interval, the priest was to carry on his own investigation. On the basis of the information acquired, he was to make a preliminary judgment; if it seemed probable that there was an impediment, he was to forbid the marriage until the question was resolved. Then followed a statement of the consequences for all involved in a clandestine or forbidden wedding, the children of the union, the priest, and the couple. Finally, those who impeded a legitimate union by their allegation of an impediment were to be punished. There was no question of the validity of the marriage on the basis of failure to observe regulations set out; it was rather a matter of punishing those who disobeyed them.

Within four years the Lateran regulations were to be combined with the older rule on announcing the promise of marriage from 1 Canterbury 54 in the Salisbury statutes. First, it was stated in statute 84 that before the exchange of consent there was to be a triple, public announcement in church of the intention to marry. The regulation went beyond 1 Canterbury 54 in ordering that the announcement be solemnly made and by forbidding the exaction of a fee. Special care was taken to explain what was to be done with the strangers whose marriage had been flatly forbidden in the Canterbury statute: if both principals were unknown, the priest was not to lend his authority to their union unless he had established their freedom to marry. A detailed procedure was prescribed for the more common situation where only one spouse was a stranger: the priest was to have testimonial letters indicating capacity for marriage and affirming that the triple announcement in its regard had been made. Finally, 1 Salisbury 91 returned to the announcement of the proposed marriage and, quoting sections of 4 Lateran 51 verbatim, set out the procedure to be followed after the reading of banns. Children were to be considered illegitimate where their parents proceeded to marry without banns even though they were ignorant of the impediment that rendered their union invalid. On the other hand, those who maliciously impeded a legitimate marriage by their objections were to be punished.

Thus by 1219 the fundamental set of English diocesan statutes had achieved an important synthesis of the Lateran regulations on the banns with the more developed rules of the local tradition; the latter stipulated the mode of announcement and developed a method for supplementing the procedure where the mobility of population had created a situation in which local information on the betrothed was inadequate to the task at hand.

In the years that followed, some of the regulations set out in 1 Salisbury saw further development. This was especially true of the elaboration of the procedure of the banns. The original ruling that there should be a public *trina denunciatio* was repeated with minor variations many times until the middle of the century.[100] Already in 1223, however, 1 Winchester 55 specified that the three announcements should be made on three solemn days;[101] and, about the same time, adopting a text from Paris 40, it was required by Synodal Statutes 40 that the announcement be made on three Sundays and feast days separated by an adequate interval.[102] Some fifteen years later 2 Salisbury 23 ruled that the interval between announcements be fifteen days and, about 1258, Wells 10 allowed a lapse of time of as little as a week, a ruling that was commonly adopted in the statutes that followed.[103]

The same years saw a more precise definition of the person who was responsible for the banns and the place where they were to be read. It is not unreasonable to presume that the 'presbyteros' of 4 Lateran 51 and 1 Salisbury 91, who announced the couple's intention and investigated their freedom to marry, were the pastors of the parish churches in question. A similar understanding undoubtedly is implied in the procedure set down

100 Constitutiones cuiusdam episcopi 58, London Archdeaconry 14; the 'sollempniter' of 1 Salisbury 54 is found in its close derivatives and in 1 Exeter 24, 3 Worcester 22, and 3 Salisbury 14; 2 Winchester 51: 'consuete et sollempnes denuntiationes.' In Ely 32 the term 'banns' first appears in the statutes: 'ne decetero sine bannorum editione' (P–C 522).

101 'et per tres dies solempnes trina fiat denuntiatio' (P–C 134); cf the prescription of banns in the decree *Tametsi* of the Council of Trent, Session 24 (11 November 1563), 'Canones super reformatione circa matrimonium,' ci: 'idcirco sacri Lateranensis concilii, sub Innocentio III celebrati, vestigiis inhaerendo praecipit, ut in posterum, antequam matrimonium contrahatur, ter a proprio contrahentium parocho tribus continuis diebus festivis in ecclesia inter missarum solemnia publice denuntietur, inter quos matrimonium sit contrahendum' (Alberigo 755–6).

102 'Item, in matrimonio contrahendo semper in tribus dominicis et festivis diebus a se distantibus quasi tribus edictis perquirat sacerdos' (P–C 146); also in 1 London 1 and 2 London 43; 1 Chichester 27: 'tribus diebus festivis a se distantibus' (P–C 457). Cf Pontal 66–7. The text of Synodal Statutes 40, ascribed to Archbishop Walter Reynolds, was included in Lyndwood's *Provinciale* 4 1 270–1.

103 'cum debitis adminus octo dierum interstitiis' (P–C 597); also Carlyle 10, 2 York 10, and 2 Chichester 7; 3 Winchester 26: 'debitis observatis interstitiis' (P–C 707).

in later statutes, but it was only in the last major treatment of the subject, that of 2 Exeter 7, that the requirement was specified.[104] Again, though the use of the plural term 'presbyteros' implied more than one church, the possibility that the reading of the banns for a single marriage take place in several churches became explicit only in 1241, interestingly enough in statutes intended for a city – London Archdeaconry 14 – where it was specified that if the principals lived in two parishes the announcement should be read in each of them.[105] The churches and parishes of those wishing to be married were mentioned in 2 Winchester 51, a phrase that would become 'the churches in the parishes' in Wells 10, its derivatives and 2 Exeter 7.[106]

Though the statutes just mentioned recognized the fact that both spouses did not always come from the same parish, the stranger posed a special problem, for – as it was expressed in 3 Worcester 24 – the banns were not effective in his regard: 'Nec extranea persona, de qua per denunciationem constare non potest an legitima sit ad contrahendum matrimonium ...'[107] We have already seen that, though it followed 4 Lateran 51 in its understanding that banns might be read in several churches by several priests, 1 Salisbury 84 ordered a different procedure where one or both principals were completely unknown (omnino incognita). This regulation would be repeated in the close derivatives,

---

104 'trina denuntiatio ... per presbyteros parochiales' (P–C 997).
105 'denuntiationem factam in una parochia vel in duabus parochiis si sine de diversis parochiis' (P–C 336); cf 3 Winchester 26: 'in parochiis ubi habitant copulandi' (P–C 707).
106 'in ecclesiis in quarum parochiis habitant' (P–C 597).
107 P–C 302. The term *extraneus* underlined the fact that the person in question had come into the parish from elsewhere. It appeared first in Coventry 11 and would be used in 2 Durham 48 as well as in this Worcester text. A similar notion was expressed in the *alienum parochianum* of 1 York 24 and 2 Chichester 23. In manorial court rolls *extraneus* referred to a person from another manor who, though he may have been well enough known, having resided in the village for some time, was not a member of a tithing and not a fully recognized member of the community; see J. Ambrose Raftis, *Tenure and Mobility: Studies in the Social History of the Mediaeval English Village*, Studies and Texts 8 (Toronto 1964) 130–8. The more common expression emphasized the fact that the stranger was unknown: *persona incognita, persona ignota*. It was used in the first statute dealing with the problem (1 Canterbury 54) and is to be found throughout the thirteenth century and later. It emphasized the fact that a person's past was unknown. This rather than the place of origin was the essential problem with which the statutes sought to cope. The two traditions were brought together in 2 Exeter 7: 'prohibemus ne aliqua extranea et ignota persona ad contrahendum matrimonium ... admittatur' (P–C 998). See below, n125.

namely, 2 Canterbury, 1 Durham, and Durham Peculiars 51, and, with some simplification, in 2 London 47.[108] The statutes of the years that followed defined the source of evidence vindicating the stranger's freedom to marry. Thus in Coventry 11, where it was a question of a previous union, the information was to be acquired from the priest of the village where the stranger lived, apparently by direct contact or by letter from a prelate of his place of birth or dwelling.[109] In 3 Worcester 24 a letter from the prelate in whose jurisdiction the stranger had lived was to inform the bishop, archdeacon, or their official of his freedom to marry. Similarly, 1 York 24 ruled that a careful examination was to be made and the results communicated by letter from the strangers' prelates, while 2 London 47 added that the prelates involved should know them.[110] The regulation received its final form in Wells 12, where the prelate was finally identified: banns were to be read in parishes where the stranger had lived, and the decision as to his eligibility that resulted from this examination was to be communicated by the bishop or his official, or by the archdeacon under whose jurisdiction the intended spouse had lived. The same regulation would be published in Carlyle 12, 2 York 12, and, with minor adjustments, in 2 Exeter 7.

As was seen above, the regulations of 4 Lateran 51 directing the action of the priest after the reading of the banns were adopted in 1 Salisbury 91. They reappeared in 2 Canterbury and 1 Durham but did not find a place in the third of the close derivatives, Durham Peculiars. By and large these regulations were not repeated in the statutes of the generation that followed 1 Salisbury. After the middle of the century the subject was taken up again, usually with some refinement of the earlier regulations. Thus, minor but significant adjustments were made in 1 London 1. By the time of its issue, the triple announcement spread over three Sundays and feasts provided the 'competenti termino' of the Lateran decree for the posing of objections. With this London statute the priest was to assign a term for

108 The simple prohibition of marriages of unknown persons in 1 Canterbury 54 was repeated in Constitutiones cuiusdam episcopi 58.
109 'Item, precipimus ne aliquis extraneus admittatur in aliqua parochia ad contrahendum matrimonium, nisi prius facto scrutinio si alias uxoratus est' (P–C 212). That the exposure of an earlier contract was one of the main purposes of the banns is evident from the cases reported in the fourteenth-century Ely register: see Sheehan, 'The Formation and Stability of Marriage' 235, 248–50, 261–3 (here pp 45, 59–62, 74–6); cf Helmholz, *Marriage Litigation* 57–66.
110 'priusquam habeat litteras testimoniales a prelatis suis qui earum notitiam habent' (P–C 644).

the objector to prove his allegation before a superior. He was also instructed to inform his superior immediately of any impediment that he
had found. The marriage was to be expressly forbidden until that superior
had decided what was to be done. Thus the earlier regulations were
refined by indicating the procedure for dealing with an objection and, at
least in general terms, the judge who was to bring in a verdict.[111] Even
before the London statutes had been issued, more developed regulations
on procedure had been made in 2 Salisbury 23. Here it was recognized
that banns might be announced in churches other than that at which the
marriage was to take place, for priests were ordered to communicate
information gained from their inquiry to those to whom the celebration
of the marriage pertained. If an impediment were alleged about which
there was no public rumour, 'lest those wishing to marry be impeded in
this way,' the objector was immediately required to swear that he was not
malicious in his action.[112] He was then given a term in which to appear
before the bishop's official to prove his position; in the mean time the
projected marriage was suspended. If the objector refused to proceed and
if there were no public rumour supporting his position, the marriage was
to be allowed so far as the objection in question was concerned. This
regulation would appear with minor adjustments in 2 Exeter 7, which
added the regulation of 1 Salisbury 91 ordering punishment of the person
who impeded a lawful marriage.[113]

It will be remembered that, in the London council of 1102 prohibiting
marriage within the forbidden degree, one of the usages that lay behind
the system of banns was revealed: it was made clear that anyone aware of
an impediment to the proposed marriage and who failed to speak would
be guilty of the same sin as the principals of the union. A similar point
of view, concerned with the omissions of the people of a region who knew
a couple rather than with the uncanonical acts of those involved in a
marriage without banns, appeared in Synodal Statutes 40. Drawing on

---

111 Further precision was provided by 2 London 46: 'Nullus sacerdos audeat perficere
matrimonium in casu dubio inconsulto episcopo vel eius prelato, set ad eos semper
referat omnes matrimonii dubietates' (P–C 643–4).

112 Note the delicate reference to the infringement of the rights of the betrothed in the
legatine Council of London (1268) c13: 'Coniugale fedus ab ipso domino institutum,
sicut potestati humane non subiacet, ita nullius temerario patere debet occursui,
quominus in conspectu hominum solempnitatem accipiat per quam, prout expedit,
omnibus innotescat' (P–C 764).

113 That the action was malicious was explicit in the Salisbury statute. This understanding of the regulation can be presumed at Exeter as well.

Paris 40, this statute ordered the priest to inquire of the people under pain of excommunication as to the freedom of the couple. This regulation, heavily underlining the responsibility of the parish community to respond to the banns, was to be repeated only towards the middle of the century, in 1 London 1 and 2 London 43.[114]

The more common penalties were intended to ensure the reading of the banns. They would be along the lines set out in 4 Lateran 51 and restated, though with some confusion, in 1 Salisbury 85, 91. Beginning with 1 Winchester 55 most statutes applied the three-year suspension to those priests involved in a marriage without banns or who had failed to prevent it. A harsher attitude appeared in 2 Salisbury 25, which repeated the penalty, adding that a more severe penalty could be imposed if it were warranted by the priest's fault. This regulation would be reissued in 1 London 2 and 2 Exeter 7. The statutes of the London Archdeaconry 14 had already instructed the archdeacon to punish the delinquent priest if convicted, and 2 London 43 warned the same officer and his official, under pain of suspension, not to relax, omit, or commute the penalty under pretext of some pecuniary advantage. This regulation would appear in Wells 10 and in its derivatives Carlyle and York.

The Lateran decree and 1 Salisbury 85 ruled that the principals of the clandestine marriage should be suitably punished.[115] This regulation was repeated in 2 Canterbury and 1 Durham, but later statutes would seek to define the penalty and, by the middle of the century, it would have been extended to those who assisted at the marriage. Thus the York mandate of 1238 ordered suspension and whipping of all those laity involved, a penalty that was to be made more severe as the situation required and of which parishioners were to be reminded each Sunday. Similarly, Ely 33 ordered public flogging of the principals and of those who by consent or authority were responsible for the union. Another direction was taken in 2 Salisbury 25: the laity involved were to be excommunicated and denounced as such. A similar though somewhat refined position was taken later in 4 Salisbury 24: the principals and those 'knowingly' involved were excommunicated; the statute was to be solemnly read in each parish church four times annually. The consequences of the Salisbury excom-

---

114 A slightly different form of the regulation appeared in 1 Salisbury 86: under pain of excommunication, the use of magic in marriage and the hiding of impediments were forbidden (see above, n35); also 2 Canterbury, 1 Durham, and Durham Peculiars 51.

115 It is explicit in both texts that the term 'clandestine marriage' included any union that had not been preceded by the banns.

munication were made explicit in 1 London 2: the principals were to be denied entrance to church for a year; should they die during that period, their bodies were not to enjoy ecclesiastical burial without the special licence of the bishop, his official, or the archdeacon.[116] If any layman or cleric, 'officium sacerdotis usurpans,' presided at such a marriage, the layman was to be under interdict for three years, and the cleric suspended from office and benefice for a similar period. Other laymen and clerics, witnesses to the act, were to be under interdict and suspension respectively until they had merited pardon from the bishop or his official.[117] Even more severe were the regulations of Wells 11 and its derivatives Carlyle 11 and 2 York 11: the principals and the witnesses of the marriage were to be flogged three times at the church door before the procession, and on three Fridays they were to fast on bread and water and be scourged in private by the priest.

Finally, there was the penalty that touched the child born of an impeded marriage made without banns. It was the rule of 4 Lateran 51 and 1 Salisbury 91 that, even though the parents were ignorant of the impediment that rendered their union invalid, the child was illegitimate. The regulation was repeated in 2 Salisbury 25 and 2 Exeter 7 as well as in the Salisbury derivatives 2 Canterbury and 1 Durham.

It was seen in the examination of the statutes concerning betrothal that the main work of definition and regulation was accomplished in the generation after 1 Salisbury. The case was entirely different with the banns. Perhaps the increasing severity of penalties analysed above provides sufficient evidence of the problem that remained. Regulations on procedure and the penalties for failure to observe it continued to be issued through the eighty years that saw the flowering of the diocesan statutes, and the preoccupation with the banns continued in the provincial councils of the centuries that followed. Thus a canon of the Council of London, held under Archbishop Simon Mepham in 1329, reaffirmed 4 Lateran 51 and ordered that it be explained to the people in the vernacular on several solemn days when a large crowd could be expected to be present. The penalty of three years' suspension of the priest was repeated with the reminder that it was still to be imposed even if, in fact, there were no impediment to the marriage.[118] The canon was to be assured a

---

116 There was no provision for leniency in 2 London 43.
117 These regulations were to be read on Sunday and major feasts and were to be written in the missal or some other book.
118 Wilkins II 554.

wide impact, for it was included by Lyndwood in his *Provinciale*.[119] Lyndwood also included the canon *Humana concupiscentia* from Archbishop John Stratford's provincial council of 1342.[120] This text, at once a tribute to the successful control of marriage afforded by the reading of the banns under proper conditions and of the various strategies employed to avoid it, was especially concerned with the conditions and formalities of the exchange of consent *de presenti* and will be examined below. In the present context it is important to note that it reaffirmed the regulations touching the reading of the banns before marriage. All persons involved in irregular solemnizations were excommunicated *ipso facto*, a penalty that was to be announced in the four annual readings of the list of excommunications. Delinquents were also subject to the other penalties of the law. A similar point of view appeared less than a decade later in the constitutions issued by Archbishop John Thoresby at the Convocation of the Province of York (1361).[121] He excommunicated all involved in marriages not preceded by a reading of the banns and, reaffirming the regulations of 4 Lateran 51, added some refinements to the process of dealing with objections made to a proposed union.[122] Finally, he reserved absolution of delinquents, except at the hour of death, to himself and to higher authority. Any judgments in causes of marriage or divorce that had been made contrary to this constitution were nullified. This regulation would appear again in canon 11 of the constitutions issued by Archbishop Wolsey for the Province of York in 1518. Here further precision was added touching the punishment of those solemnizing marriage without banns, those doing so before an objection to their union had been resolved, and priests who had taken part. All were excommunicated.[123]

A somewhat different point of view appeared among the petitions of the clergy at the Convocation of the Province of Canterbury in 1460.[124] It

---

119 4 3 1 266 (*sic* for 273)–74.
120 Wilkins II 707. Derived from the text *Sponsam Christi*, published in May 1343; see C.R. Cheney, 'William Lyndwood's *Provinciale*,' *Jurist* 21 (1961) 419. Cf *Provinciale*, ed Lyndwood 4 3 2 274–7.
121 Wilkins III 71–2; see *The Records of the Northern Convocation*, Publications of the Surtees Society 113 (Durham 1906) xlvii, 95.
122 Both judgment of the objection and dispensation of banns were mentioned: 'donec quid fieri debeat super eo, per judicem in hac parte competentem legitime fuerit declaratum, vel alias de superioris ordinarii licentia, cum contrahere volentibus, quo ad temporum interstitia, et bannorum editionem fuerit dispensatum' (Wilkins III 72).
123 Wilkins III 668; see *The Records of the Northern Convocation* 207.
124 *Registrum Thome Bourgchier*, ed du Boulay 92 (Wilkins III 579).

revealed that a procedure of dispensation from banns existed and indicated that it had led to abuse. The clergy complained that clandestine marriage had become a scandal to the Church and that the situation had been created by an excessive frequency of dispensation from banns. They asked that in future the archbishop and his suffragans not be able to dispense (*non valeant*) unless the banns had been read twice at proper intervals in the parish churches of the couple and a suitable examination had been made. Inferior judges were not to give such dispensations. The petition concluded with recommendations for dealing with strangers: even though they were well established in a parish, there should be careful inquiry about them and a reading of banns in parish churches where they had lived for major periods of their lives and where they were better known.[125]

The Exchange of Consent *de presenti*

The mutual exchange of consent by the couple established the marriage bond. From what has been seen, it will be clear that this third and essential element in the series of acts leading to marriage was to be delayed until the scrutiny by the local community had been completed. It will also be clear that, in practice, the solemnization of the exchange of consent was sometimes used to defeat that social control. It should not be surprising then to find that the rules governing the contract *de presenti* were designed to make it more and more difficult to avoid the public announcement of the intention to marry.

The regulation of the marriage contract in 1 Canterbury 54 was derived from the provincial Council of Westminster (1200), canon 11.[126] Three

---

125 'proviso semper quod si vagabundi veniant ad parochiam aliquam omnino inibi commorandi ut parochiani, et sic faciant se parochianos inibi, eo non obstante, hujusmodi banna edantur publice in ecclesiis parochialibus, in quibus pro majore parte prius moram habuerunt hujusmodi vagabundi sive noviter supervenientes, et ubi melius sunt agniti et noti' (ibid). Note that recent newcomers to the parish (*noviter supervenientes*) were included in the regulation. The term *vagabundus* was commonly used of a person without a domicile. Here it is allowed that, by the time of the proposed marriage, the *vagabundi* were established in the parish; whatever their past, their current position was considered to be stable. Yet it was precisely the past that was the clergy's concern, and it was to learn of it that enquiries were to be made 'ubi melius sunt agniti et noti.'

126 'Nec contrahatur matrimonium inter personas incognitas, nec sine trina denuntiatione in ecclesia publicata; nec clandestina contrahantur matrimonia sed publice in facie ecclesie et presente sacerdote. Si vero secus factum fuerit, non admittatur in

prohibitions were set out first: marriage was not to be contracted between unknown persons, nor without banns, nor was it to be clandestine. (The third forbidden quality, clandestinity, was not mentioned in the Westminster canon.) Then the Canterbury statute continued and, following its model, set out the positive requirements of the exchange of consent: it was to be public, before the local Church, and in the presence of the priest. Solemnized with these three elements of publicity, the marriage was not clandestine. In the sanction clauses, to be discussed below, it was implied that the presence of the priest, one of the elements precluding clandestinity, sometimes occurred at marriages that were illegal.[127]

It was seen in an earlier discussion that 4 Lateran 51 not only forbade the priest to take part in clandestine marriages but also extended the concept of clandestinity to include failure to announce the intention to marry by the banns.[128] The punishment of both priest and the principals of the marriage that was announced applied whether they failed to honour regulations on the banns or those touching the contract de presenti. As was the case in its regulation of betrothal, 1 Salisbury sought to integrate the rules of the Lateran constitution with the older, local tradition expressed in 1 Canterbury 54; a certain muddying of the waters resulted. Treating of clandestine marriage, 1 Salisbury 85 made no mention of banns but, following its Canterbury model in forbidding such unions, ordered that the act be public, before the local Church, and in the presence of the priest.[129] Even though 'clandestinity' seems to have been understood in the older, narrower sense, the Salisbury statute then went on to adopt the punishments that 4 Lateran 51 had imposed on the couple involved in a clandestine marriage and on the priest who had failed to forbid such unions or had taken part in them.

ecclesia nisi de speciali auctoritate domini archiepiscopi. Sacerdos autem qui contra statuti huius nostri formam aliquos matrimonio copulaverit, ab omni officio suspendatur nec relaxetur nisi de speciali mandato nostro' (P–C 34).

127 This notion had already appeared at the Council of Westminster (1175); see above, n11.
128 See above, 432–3 (here pp 145–6).
129 'De clandestinis matrimoniis. Prohibemus similiter clandestina matrimonia, precipientes quod publice fiant in facie ecclesie, presente sacerdote ad hoc vocato. Si vero secus actum fuerit non approbetur, nisi de nostra speciali auctoritate. Sacerdos qui tales coniunctiones prohibere contempserit vel talibus interesse presumpserit, vel quilibet alius regularis, secundum statuta concilii ab officio per triennium suspendatur, gravius puniendus si culpe quantitas postulaverit. Set et qui taliter copulari presumpserint, etiam in gradu concesso, hiis condigna penitentia iniungatur' (P–C 88). Note that the Salisbury statute goes beyond 1 Canterbury by requiring that the priest be invited to be present at the marriage.

The Salisbury regulations were reissued during the next few years in 2 Canterbury and 1 Durham; but in the third of its derivatives, Durham Peculiars 52, the parts drawn from the Lateran constitution were omitted, leaving only the older regulations derived from 1 Canterbury 54.[130]

The joining of the two traditions was nicely expressed about five years after the Salisbury statute in 1 Worcester 55: it was to be announced in church that there should be no wedding without the presence of the priest and assembled parishioners and the triple reading of the banns.[131] However, by and large, most of the statutes of the first half of the century ignored the requirements of the contract *de presenti*. Some, like 2 Worcester 32, expressed what seems to have been the main concern, that the priest avoid involvement in marriages that had not been preceded by a reading of the banns.[132] Other statutes simply forbade clandestine marriage,[133] while a few were silent.[134] About mid-century a statement of requirements began to appear in statutes once again. Thus Ely 25, 32, 33 forbade clandestine marriage of any kind and brought the reading of the banns and the presence of the priest together as requirements under penalty of whipping all persons involved.[135] Similarly Wells 10, 11, and their derivatives presumed the presence of the priest and witnesses, though the statutes were cast in terms of a prohibition of their participation in marriages that had not been preceded by banns. That the priest be the pastor of the parish church and that there be other legal witnesses were required by 4 Salisbury 4, and a few years later 2 London 43 would be even more specific, requiring that the pastor or rector of the church

130 Also Constitutiones cuiusdam episcopi 59.
131 'Denuntietur publice in ecclesiis quod nunquam sponsalia fiant nisi presente sacerdote et congregatis parochianis suis, et per tres dies solempnes trina fiat denuntiatio. Si quis vero sacerdos desponsioni aliter faciende consencerit, per triennium ab officio suspendatur' (P–C 134).
132 London Archdeaconry 14, 2 Winchester 51, 1 Chichester 27, 28, 3 Winchester 26; cf the constitution of Archbishop Simon Mepham (1329): 'quibusvis sacerdotibus etiam parochialibus vel non parochialibus, qui contractibus matrimonialibus ante solennem editionem bannorum initis, praesumpserint interesse, poenam suspensionis ab officio per triennium infligendo; et hujusmodi contrahentes etiam, si nullum subsit impedimentum, poena debita percellendo' (Wilkins II 554).
133 Lincoln 42, Norwich 39, 2 Durham 46.
134 Coventry, 1 Exeter, 1 York, 3 Salisbury.
135 'Clandestina quoque matrimonia districtius in ecclesiis solempniter inhibeantur, quolibet genere clandestini matrimonii' (c25; P–C 520). See *gloss. ad* X 4 3 3 *clandestina* (*Decretales d. Gregorii papae* IX [Lyons 1584], 1460); and DDC 3 799–801, s v 'Clandestinité'.

and at least three other witnesses be present.[136] The last of the developed treatments of marriage, 2 Exeter 7, was virtually the same. By and large, the statutes of the period implied that the priest was expected to be present at a marriage, so the main purpose of the legislation was to prevent his support of a union that had not been preceded by banns or that had become impossible as a result of their reading.

A similar preoccupation is evident in the councils of the later Middle Ages. Thus in 1342, by the canon *Humana concupiscentia*, Archbishop Stratford moved to 'deny the veil of apparent marriage' to those who sought to live together without that reading of banns that they knew would make their union impossible. He forbade priests to solemnize marriages of non-parishioners without the licence of those who had jurisdiction over them.[137] A few years later in constitutions for the Province of York, Archbishop Thoresby began a canon reinforcing 4 Lateran 51 with reference to clandestine marriages solemnized 'per capellanos Dei timorem et legum prohibitionem temere contemnentes,' and forbade such practice under pain of major excommunication reserved, except at the hour of death, to the ordinary.[138] This regulation was repeated by Archbishop Wolsey at York in 1518 with specific reference to chaplains solemnizing against the law and with the further intimation that they were sometimes forced to do so. Those involved in this case were also excommunicated.[139]

The statutes included some regulation of the place and time for the proper celebration of marriage. It will be recalled that the presentation of matrimony in several sets of statutes began with a discussion of its dignity and concluded that the sacrament should be received under conditions that were sober and decorous.[140] Statutes quickly came to

---

136 A monition of Archbishop Thomas Bourgchier to the parish clergy of the Province of Canterbury, 25 May 1455, required two or three witnesses to a marriage. See above, n96.

137 Wilkins II 707. The prohibition and penalty were extended not only to the principals but also to those who by force or fear caused such clandestine marriages to be celebrated in churches, oratories, or chapels and to others who were involved in such solemnizations.

138 Wilkins III 71–2.

139 Wilkins III 668.

140 1 Salisbury 83 and derivatives: 'non in tabernis, potationibus publicis seu commessationibus'; 2 London 42: 'in locis honestis et tempore congruo'; 2 Exeter 7: 'in locis honestis et tempore congruo cum omni modestia et maturitate; non in tabernis, potationibus et commessationibus, non secretis locis, latebris et suspectis' (P–C 87, 642, 996). 2 London 42 made special reference to the dignity of second and third

present this request in more precise and positive terms. The phrase *in facie ecclesie* had appeared in the London council of 1200; while it referred directly to the local community considered in its religious capacity, it would not be unreasonable to presume that the exchange of consent in question occurred at the building in which the community met for worship.[141] This point became explicit in 1 Winchester 57: 'Preterea districte prohibeatur ne aliquis cum aliqua contrahat per verba de presenti nisi apud ecclesiam, tunc scilicet quando sollempnitas ecclesie debet fieri ...'[142] It was only at the end of the great period of English statute-making that 2 Exeter 7 described the exchange of consent at the church door.[143] The councils of the fourteenth and fifteenth centuries were concerned to keep the solemnization of marriage in the parish church. Thus at the provincial Council of London (1329) Archbishop Mepham ordered that any priest who solemnized marriage outside a parish church or chapel of ancient parochial right, without the special licence of the bishop of the diocese, was to be suspended for a year.[144] Whatever uncertainties may have existed as to the meaning of this canon were removed when it was reaffirmed by Archbishop John Stratford in *Humana concupiscentia*.[145] A reflection of this preoccupation with the reservation of weddings to the parish church is evident in the petition of the clergy at the Convocation of the Province of Canterbury in May 1466, asking that it be forbidden the Brothers of Jerusalem to solemnize marriage in their chapels or to allow others to do so.[146]

marriages, a regulation that was all the more required given the fact that ordinarily only the first marriage received the blessing of the priest; see below, 456 (here p 172).

141 The phrase had appeared earlier in a text assigned by Wilkins to Richard, archbishop of Canterbury, and dated 1173: 'Non occulta fiant matrimonia, sed palam in facie ecclesiae' (c20; Wilkins I 474). On this clause as part of a draft of the canons of the Council of Westminster (1175) see Mary G. Cheney, 'The Council of Westminster 1175: New Light on an Old Source,' in *Materials, Sources, and Methods*, ed Derek Baker, Studies in Church History 11 (Oxford 1975) 61–8.

142 P–C 135.

143 'Cum autem matrimonium in facie ecclesie fuerit solennizandum, palam et in ostio ecclesie sacerdos interroget contrahentes si sibi invicem consentiant ab ipsis singillatim' (P–C 998).

144 Wilkins II 554.

145 Wilkins II 707.

146 *Registrum Thomae Bourgchier*, ed du Boulay 91. It was alleged in the Convocation of 1489 that chaplains of the Brothers of Jerusalem claimed the right to solemnize marriage and that they often did so, even while a case touching the marriage of one of the spouses was *sub judice*: 'ac etiam solemnizare matrimonium contra jus

The statutes included a few regulations on the time of solemnization of marriage. In the general presentation of suitable conditions for receiving the sacrament, Synodal Statutes 39 decreed that the ceremony be by day, a regulation that found its way into Lyndwood's *Provinciale* ascribed to Archbishop Walter Reynolds.[147] About the same time 1 Winchester 57, having ruled that the contract be made at the church, went on to say that it should be at a time when a church solemnity ought to be held. It is likely that the 'sollempnitas ecclesie' of the statute refers to the time of ordinary ceremonies such as the Sunday mass and not to the festive, as opposed to the penitential, season of the year.[148] Understood in this way, the Winchester text implies that marriage was to be celebrated during the day, the usual time of service. Given the fact that the rite of marriage often included a nuptial mass at which the parish gathered, it is highly probable that it was intended that the exchange of consent be held before noon on Sunday morning before the parish mass. Much later, 2 London 42 and 2 Exeter 7 referred to 'tempore congruo' for matrimony, a phrase that probably implied a time not conflicting with the prohibition of marriage during Advent and Lent.[149] Both notions of time appeared in the introduction to *Humana concupiscentia*, where one of the strategies of those who would avoid the banns was to solemnize marriage 'at an unsuitable hour, during an unsuitable season.'[150]

One small sign of the many superstitions about the proper time for marriage appeared in 2 Worcester 55, where the unwillingness to marry except when the moon was filling was mentioned as an example of that observation of 'times and moments' forbidden by St Paul.[151] The priest was to preach against such practices. The prohibition was taken up again in 3 Worcester 29 with the additional command that the priest repeat it every Sunday, warning offenders that they would be sent to the bishop for severe punishment.

---

divinum et canonicum; et multotiens, pendente lite inter unum eorum inter quos solemnizatur tale matrimonium, per partem absentem non vocatam, nec bannis matrimonialibus editis' (London, Lambeth Palace, Registrum Johannis Morton f 43r; cf Wilkins III 625).

147 'Matrimonium similiter sicut et alia sacramenta cum honore et reverentia de die et in facie ecclesie, non cum risu et ioco ne sic derisui et contemptui celebretur' (P–C 146); *Provinciale*, ed Lyndwood 4 3 270–1.

148 Cf Gratian, C37 q4 cc 8–10; X 2 9 4.

149 See above, n140.

150 'nec horis nec temporibus opportunis' (Wilkins II 707).

151 Gal 4:10; 1 Thess 5:1.

Mention was made in 2 London 54 of a 'librum qui dicitur manuale' that each parish priest was expected to have and which included the ritual of marriage.[152] It is presumed that formalities of the contract *de presenti* were set out there in detail.[153] Such a manual would be a necessary supplement to the statutes which, though they provided many regulations touching the conditions, the witnesses, the time and place of marriage, tended to be silent on the formalities by which it came about. However, they did provide some regulations in this regard. Thus 1 Salisbury 84 set out the form of words that was to be used in French and in English and in the meaning of which the priest was to instruct the people. The legally effective part of the formula was in the present tense: 'I (N.) accept you as mine.'[154] The following sentence clearly expressed the function of the words in establishing the marriage bond: 'In his enim verbis consistit vis magna et matrimonium contrahitur.' As usual these regulations of 1 Salisbury were repeated in 2 Canterbury, 1 Durham, and Durham Peculiars 51. It was not until 2 Salisbury 23 that further regulation of the ceremony in which *verba de presenti* were exchanged was made. The priest was instructed that on the day of the wedding he should openly question the couple before the Church, inquiring whether they consented to each other and whether that consent were brought about by force and fear. Then, if he were satisfied that there was no impediment, he was to instruct them in the vernacular that they accept each other in a form of words similar to that used in 1 Salisbury.[155] As proved to be so often the case in the regulation of marriage, 2 Exeter 7 followed 2 Salisbury closely; however, a few refinements were added: the ceremony was to be held at the door of the church, and the couple were to be questioned separately as to the freedom of their consent.[156] If there were any suspicion on the matter, inquiry was to be made whether force or fear had led to consent. Should both or either spouse admit that such was the case, the ceremony was to proceed no further.

The statutes included no direct reference to that priestly blessing which Lanfranc's canon of 1076 required for validity,[157] nor to the marriage

---

152 See P–C 1408, s v 'Books, service, orders for provision of'.
153 See 'Ordo ad faciendum sponsalia,' in *Manuale ad usum percelebris ecclesie Sarisburiensis*, ed A. Jefferies Collins, Henry Bradshaw Society 91 (London 1960) 44–55.
154 'Ego .N. accipio te in meam. Similiter et mulier dicat: Ego .N. accipio te in meum' (P–C 87).
155 'Accipio vel recipio te in meam, et Ego te in meum, per que vel per similia verba coniugalis contractus forma designatur' (P–C 376); see above, n78.
156 See above, n143.
157 See above, n10.

mass. But there are some indirect references to them. Thus it can be concluded from the prohibition of the blessing of second marriages in 3 Worcester 26, 2 Durham 48, and one manuscript of 2 Exeter 7[158] that the priestly blessing was expected in a first union. Similarly, the requirement of 2 Exeter 12 that every parish church and chapel of parochial status should possess a *velum nuptiale* among its set of vestments implied that the Eucharist was expected to be part of the marriage ceremony. The *velatio nuptialis*, a rite in which a veil was spread over the couple, occurred during the blessing that immediately preceded the communion of the nuptial mass.[159] By and large, however, the statutes and conciliar canons contained few regulations on formulae and ritual. Their main purpose was to assure that the contract *de presenti* was delayed until after the reading of the banns, that it should be solemnized in public, and, towards the end of the period of the statutes, that the principals' freedom of consent be clearly ascertained in the presence of the parish community.

The statutes included another form of words used to bring about a marriage under different circumstances. If the procedure is to be understood, it must be seen in relation to a movement of reform that sought to remove the scandal of those men and women who frequented each other's company, were free to marry, yet refused to do so. In several English dioceses a solution was sought by requiring the couple to agree that future sexual intercourse would entail marriage. This legislation has been investigated elsewhere, but in the present context it is of some interest to examine the contract that was used.[160] The earliest form of words available to us is probably that ascribed by 1 London 3 to Roger Niger, bishop of London (1229–41). There it is stated that the couple were to promise in each other's presence that, should they have further sexual union, they would marry, if the Church allowed them to do so: 'Iuro quod si decetero te cognovero carnaliter, habebo te in uxorem meam si sancta ecclesia permittit.'[161] It will be noted that the form of words indicates a

---

158 P–C 997 n q.

159 See J.-B. Molin and Protais Mutembe, *Le rituel du mariage en France du XIIe au XVIe siècle*, Théologie historique 26 (Paris 1974) 228–33. Discussing the problem of legitimization of children in Ep 24, Robert Grosseteste wrote of the child placed 'sub pallio supra parentes nubentes extenso,' *Roberti Grosseteste episcopi quondam Lincolniensis Epistulae*, ed Henry Richard Luard, RS 25 (London 1861) 96.

160 See Richard H. Helmholz, 'Abjuration *sub pena nubendi* in the Church Courts of Medieval England,' *Jurist* 32 (1972) 81–90; and Sheehan, 'The Formation and Stability of Marriage' 253–6 (here pp 266–8), and 'Marriage and Family' 208–11 (here pp 81–3).

161 P–C 631.

promise for the future closely analogous to that seen for betrothal.[162] This futurity was also expressed in several other statutes that described the transaction.[163]

A somewhat different point of view of the nature of the act was suggested by the words of agreement set out in 2 Salisbury 53. There it was decreed that, where the above-mentioned relationship existed between a couple, they were to be denounced to the dean by their rectors or curates, then presented by the dean to the chapter in the presence of the archdeacon or his official. Before the chapter, they were to swear to each other: 'Promitto tibi quod si te de cetero carnaliter cognovero, te tanquam in uxorem meam legitimam, nisi aliquid canonicum obsistat, consentio. Sic me deus adiuvet et sacrosancta ewangelia.'[164] In this statute *promitto* seems to imply a promise of a future act (the resemblance to betrothal is patent), but the use of the verb *consentio* in the present suggests otherwise; the legally effective part of the text can be translated: 'I promise you that, if I have further carnal knowledge of you, I take you as my lawful wife.' The uncertainty of the meaning of the text is not removed by a clause in the sentence that follows, '... ad quod per censuram ecclesiasticam ... *compellantur*,' since the antecedent of *quod* is difficult to establish. It seems best to conclude that the text meant that a couple who were not yet married would be compelled to do so, rather than that a couple who were already married would be compelled to live together. Thus the form of words can best be read as a promise for the future, though it was beginning to suggest a conditional contract *de presenti*.

Any doubt in the matter was removed in the formula in Wells 13: 'Ego accipio te ex nunc in meam, si decetero te cognoscam carnaliter ...' Here the form of words was clearly conceived as a conditional contract whereby

162 See above, 427 (here p 139).
163 1 Winchester 54: 'Laici ... desponsare vel sibi invicem fidem dare coram pluribus per sacerdotem suum conpellantur, sub hac conditione quod si carnaliter post hec coniuncti fuerint tanquam coniuges inperpetuum se habebunt'; 1 Winchester 58 returned to the problem: 'Si aliquis ad aliquem mulierem consuetudinem habeat et hoc fit publicum, sacerdos suus eum conpellat per excommunicationem ad alterum istorum: scilicet ut in presentia quatuor aut quinque testium eadem muliere presente fidem det quod eam pro uxore semper *habeat* si eam decetero carnaliter cognoverit, et mulier hoc idem ex parte sua promittat fide media' (the alternative was a fine); 1 Coventry 15: 'iurare quod inposterum non cognoscat quam cognoscere consueverat, indicatur talis pena ei si eandem cognoverit, quod eam desponset'; 2 Winchester 52: 'iuret vel fidem prestet de ea habenda in uxorem si ipsam decetero cognoverit' (P–C 134, 135, 213, 410).
164 P–C 385–6.

a couple became man and wife once the condition – in this case, sexual union – had been realized. The text included an interesting reflection on the role of each sex in carnal union[165] and added that a written account of the transaction should be kept for greater certainty. It was this under-standing of the act, one harking back to the older theory that saw consummation as the perfecting of a matrimonial bond that already existed, that appeared in Carlyle 13, in 2 York 13, in 2 Exeter 7, and, with minor variations that gave more exact expression to the woman's consent to the act, in 3 Winchester 29.[166] As a constitution attributed to Arch-bishop Robert Winchelsey, the Wells regulation was to appear in many manuscripts of the fourteenth and fifteenth centuries.[167] Thus the form of words revealed a most interesting evolution in the understanding of the act to which it gave expression, one that suggested a growing rigidity in the method used to control the sexual activity of the couples in question. In the statutes of the 1220s a promise of marriage was extracted from them. If there were further sexual relations it was expected that they would marry (efforts might even be made to force them to do so), but they would not yet be married. By the time of the Wells statute, the original act was seen as a conditional marriage. Once the condition had been realized, the couple were man and wife.[168]

The Council of Westminster (1175), canon 18, declared that a priest who participated in a clandestine marriage was to be suspended from office for three years.[169] A similar approach was taken in 1 Canterbury 54,

165 The active form of the verb *cognoscam* in the formula used by the man is replaced by the passive in the woman's words: 'Ego te in meum, si a te decetero fuero cognita carnaliter' (P–C 598). About the same time a minor but important adjustment of 1 London 3 appeared in 2 London 80. The words *ex tunc* implied that the uniting of the couple as man and wife occurred with their sexual union: 'Iuro quod si decetero te cognovero carnaliter, ex tunc habebo te in uxorem' (P–C 650).

166 2 Exeter 7 required that the union be solemnized before the Church: 'Quod si con-trahentes postea se carnaliter cognoverint, et super hoc fides facta fuerit in iudicio, compellantur matrimonium antea sic contractum in facie ecclesie sollempnizare infra certum tempus arbitrio iudicis moderandum' (P–C 999); 3 Winchester 29: 'Ego te in meum, si a te permisero me cognosci' (P–C 707).

167 Eg Wilkins II 283; see C.R. Cheney, 'The So-called Statutes of John Pecham and Robert Winchelsey for the Province of Canterbury,' *Journal of Ecclesiastical History* 12 (1961) 14–34.

168 See Sheehan, 'The Formation and Stability of Marriage' 255 (here pp 67–8), a case where John Smith admitted contract and subsequent intercourse with Roisey Rous but claimed that before intercourse he stated that he did not want her as wife; the court declared them married.

169 See above, 410 and n11 (here pp 120–1).

where, as was seen above, requirements were set out in more detail; the priest who failed to honour them was suspended. We have also seen that the sanctions of 4 Lateran 51 were stated on similar lines: the priest was suspended for three years if he took part in a clandestine union or failed to oppose it. But in the Lateran constitution the conception of clandestinity was enlarged to include failure to announce the intended marriage by the banns. Furthermore the penalties for clandestinity thus understood were applied not only to the priest but also to the principals of the union. They were applied in England and have been set out above in the discussion of the banns.[170] By and large, the same penalties applied to the exchange of consent which did not respect the requirements of the statutes. But there was another tradition, that of the Council of Winchester (1076), in which a marriage without the blessing of the priest was declared invalid.[171] Here the sanction touched the act itself rather than the persons who had failed to act in accord with the law. In the early thirteenth century this approach appeared once more.

After setting out the requirements for the exchange of consent the Council of Westminster (1200), canon 11, ruled that the principals of a marriage which disobeyed the regulations would be denied entry to a church: '... et si secus factum fuerit, non admittantur [i.e. aliquae personae] alicubi in ecclesia, nisi speciali auctoritate episcopi.'[172] When the clause reappeared in 1 Canterbury 54, it had undergone an important change; at first sight, at least, the validity of the act was called into question: 'Si vero secus factum fuerit, non admittatur in ecclesia nisi de speciali auctoritate domini archiepiscopi.'[173] Thus the sanction that was to be removed by the bishop was transferred from the principals to the act they performed. With the substitution of *approbetur* for *admittatur*, the same ruling appeared in 1 Salisbury 85 and in its derivatives 2 Canterbury, 1 Durham, and Durham Peculiars 51.[174] The likelihood that this clause was sometimes understood to mean that the contract was con-

170 See above, 437–8 (here pp 151–2).
171 See above, 410 and n10 (here p 120).
172 See above, n18.
173 See above, 440 and n126 (here p 154).
174 It should be noted that in five of the seven manuscripts of 1 Salisbury the plural form *approbentur* or *approbantur* was used. In Worcester, Cathedral Library MS Q 67, the basis of the edition in P-C, the original reading was *approbentur*; see P-C 88 n d. Thus most of the Salisbury manuscripts provided a reading similar to that of the Council of Westminster (1200) c11, where the plural verb seems to refer to the principals rather than to the validity of their act.

sidered to be invalid is made all the stronger by Constitutiones cuiusdam episcopi 59. In this statute the regulations for contracting *de presenti* and the sanctions against failure to observe them were adopted from 1 Canterbury 54. Then followed a sentence requiring the presence of a priest at betrothal. Attached to it was a clause which made it clear that the added regulations touched the validity of the act: 'Quod si aliter factum fuerit, decernimus contractum non tenere et persone legittime punientur.'[175] Since in this set of statutes as in 1 Canterbury the requirements for betrothal were to be set out in the statute that followed, it seems best to explain this awkward insertion by a decision on the part of the author that a text declaring the invalidity of a betrothal performed without due observation of formalities should be placed with a text understood to state the invalidity of a contract *de presenti* that was similarly incomplete. Thus it seems necessary to conclude that Constitutiones cuiusdam episcopi 59 required the formalities of the contract *de presenti* for the validity of the act. Such may well be the best interpretation of 1 Canterbury, 1 Salisbury, and its derivatives.[176] Yet the texts in question made no mention of correcting the situation created by 'unadmitted' or 'unapproved' marriages by repeating the exchange of consent under proper conditions. The situation was to be retrieved by the authority of the bishop, a point of view that suggests that the validity of the bond established between the couple was not in question, but that its acceptance in the public forum was understood to depend on an act by the bishop.

Beginning in 1240 the statutes reveal an entirely different point of view. Thus in 3 Worcester 22, where the punishment of the priest who violated the Lateran constitution on the reading of banns was ordered, the text went on to point out that this regulation applied not only to solemn weddings but also to those performed otherwise so long as there was a contract *per verba de presenti*. There was no question of the validity of the act.[177] The problem was placed in a much wider context about the same time in 2 Salisbury 33. The opening sentence stated the dilemma presented by a theory of marriage that saw the consent of the couple as the essential act in a world where practice insisted on the formalities attached to that act: 'Though true marriage is contracted by the legitimate

175 P–C 190.
176 Cf P–C 1429, s v 'Marriage, clandestine: invalidity of'.
177 'Hoc autem non solum intelligimus de matrimoniis solempniter celebratis, set etiam de hiisque aliter fiunt, dum tamen contractum fuerit matrimonium *per verba de presenti*' (P–C 301–2).

consent of a man and a woman, however, as far as the Church is concerned, words or signs implying consent *de presenti* are necessary ...' The text went on to say that without the judgment of the Church, presumably based on the public reaction to the reading of the banns, marriage was not to be contracted. Then followed the rather grudging admission that it was tolerated with permission if sometimes contracted otherwise.[178] Almost forty years later 2 Exeter 7 would repeat the text of 2 Salisbury 23; but, by changing the last phrase, it removed any doubt as to the validity of the informal contract *de presenti*: 'quamquam alias contracta propter hoc minime dissolvantur.'[179] That clarifying step had already been taken about 1258 in Wells 11. Here there was no attempt to present the problem in its wider terms. The proper sequence of acts leading to marriage was set out and punishments for the disobedient indicated. Priests were ordered to forbid clandestine unions and to explain the penalties imposed by the Lateran constitution. The statutes ended with the simple statement that, whether formalities were observed or not, the marriages were valid.[180]

Stipends

From one point of view, the conciliar canons and especially the diocesan statutes can be considered as witnesses to the process whereby the priest came to play an ever greater role in the preliminaries of marriage as well as in the solemnization of the act itself. It is not surprising, then, that this same legislation should include regulations touching stipends and the avoidance of simony.

The exaction of a stipend for the reception of the sacraments and other spiritual services was forbidden in the English legatine Council of Westminster (1125), canon 2, but it was only in the first canon of a similar council held at Westminster in 1138 that the list was enlarged to include

---

178 'Licet verum matrimonium per legitimum viri et mulieris consensum contrahatur, necessaria tamen sunt quantum ad ecclesiam verba vel signa consensum exprimentia *de presenti*, ex quo manifestissime apparet quod sine auctoritate ecclesie, cuius iudicio approbandus est contractus vel reprobandus, non sunt matrimonia contrahenda licet alias quandoque contracta ex permissione tollerentur' (P–C 375). The phrase *ex permissu* is understood to refer to an act by the ordinary after the marriage, not as a dispensation from formalities before the exchange of consent.

179 P–C 997.

180 'In utroque tamen casu matrimonia contracta tenent iuxta canonicas sanctiones' (P–C 598); thus Carlyle 11 and 2 York 11.

a specific reference to marriage: 'pro ... desponsatione mulierum.'[181] In the provincial Council of Westminster (1200), canon 8, the effect of 3 Lateran 7 was evident in a much developed treatment of simony. It included in its list of prohibitions the demand of a stipend for the burial of the dead and the blessing of spouses.[182] The regulation appeared in 4 Lateran 66 and as such was promulgated with the rest of the constitutions of that council at the provincial Council of Oxford in 1222.[183]

The prohibition would enter matters of detail in 1 Salisbury 16. Here the demand of a stipend for the burial of the dead and the blessing of spouses was forbidden, but there was also a specific rejection of a fee for making announcements and giving testimony regarding marriage and for solemnizing the union. As was seen above, 1 Salisbury 84 forbade the exaction of a stipend for the reading of the banns. This developed form of prohibition appeared in 2 Canterbury and 1 Durham and partially in Durham Peculiars and 2 London 45.[184] On the other hand, several sets of statutes followed 2 Worcester 19 in reverting to the prohibition of a required stipend 'pro exequiis mortuum aut pro benedictione nubentium.'[185]

It was with this group that a significant change occurred. Beginning with 3 Worcester 56, a regulation appeared that derived from the nicely balanced statement of 4 Lateran 66: there was to be no stipend for marriage, but the pious customs of the faithful were not to be impeded.[186] The reticence of the Lateran constitution was maintained and the customs were not described, though it is clear enough that an offering was meant. A similar statute appeared about the same time in 2 Salisbury 4, but its colouring was different: where the laudable customs existed, they were to be observed. This position was repeated in Wells 55, its derivatives, and 2 Exeter 38. Thus while English ecclesiastical legislation was rather early

---

181 Wilkins I 408, 415. On the general prohibition see P–C 1439, s v 'Sacraments, granted without fee'.

182 'aut sepeliendis mortuis aut benedicendis nubentibus ... aliquid exigatur' (Wilkins I 506).

183 On the general promulgation of the constitutions of the Fourth Lateran Council, see above, n34. Canon 31 of the Council of Oxford forbade the impeding of marriage because of money (P–C 116). The prohibition is in a context of clerical fees and has nothing to do with marriage settlements, dower, etc.

184 Durham Peculiars 12 omitted the part of 1 Salisbury 16 that referred to marriage in detail, but c51 reproduced 1 Salisbury 84; 2 London 45: 'pro matrimonio celebrando vel pro testimonio ferendo de legittimitate sponsi et sponse' (P–C 643).

185 3 Worcester 56, Norwich 71, Wells 55, Carlyle 53, 2 York 53, and 2 Exeter 38.

186 'pias tamen consuetudines fidelium quas sponte servare voluerint nolumus inpediri' (P–C 310); cf Alberigo 265.

in forbidding the exaction of a stipend for the assistance of a priest at any stage of a marriage, it was to be a generation after the more nuanced position of 4 Lateran 66 that statutes allowing for the free offerings of the faithful would appear.

The Married State

Once the marriage bond had been properly established, the main task of guidance and enforcement by the Church's legislation had been accomplished. However, there were a few regulations concerned with the course of the marriage itself. Thus late in the thirteenth century 2 Exeter 7 ordered husbands to follow the advice of St Paul in loving their wives, rendering the conjugal debt, and providing the necessities of life in accord with their wealth. They were warned that, if it proved necessary, they were to be compelled to do so.[187] The provincial Council of Westminster (1200), canon 4, included among its regulations on the sacrament of penance a delicate measure intended to protect the privacy of the couple: penance was to be so assigned to wife or to husband that the spouse would not be aware of any secret sin. This regulation passed in a similar context to 1 Canterbury 40. A few years later it appeared as a separate statute in 1 Salisbury 34, with the significant addition that the transgressor should receive sufficient punishment and adequate satisfaction should be imposed. In this form the rule would be reissued in several sets of statutes until about the middle of the thirteenth century.[188] The conscience of the wife came under direct influence in a series of statutes originating in 1 Salisbury 89 whereby the priest was instructed to teach his people in general and to forbid wives specifically to take vows without much deliberation, the consent of their husbands, and the advice of a priest. This regulation, too, was repeated several times until about the middle of the century.[189]

Though theologians and spiritual writers had much advice to give on the temperate use of the marriage right, the matter did not appear in the

187 'Ad quod cum oportuerit eosdem decernimus compellendos' (P–C 999); see 1 Cor 7:3.
188 2 Canterbury, 1 Durham, 1 Exeter 32, and Durham Peculiars 26; 1 Chichester 18 was slightly different: 'Coniugatis nulla iniungatur penitentia ex qua suspecti habeantur adinvicem' (P–C 455).
189 2 Canterbury, 1 Durham; Constitutiones cuiusdam episcopi 61 stipulated that she consult her own priest; 1 Chichester 30 omitted the reference to the wife's deliberation.

statutes. On the contrary, they opposed several practices and beliefs that inhibited its exercise. It appears that in Bishop Robert Grosseteste's time some priests in Lincoln diocese imposed an offering on women who had sexual relations with their husbands before they had been purified after childbirth. The practice was condemned in Lincoln 27 and later in Norwich 29.[190] A much more serious problem was the widespread belief that after one had received the sacrament of extreme unction he might no longer have conjugal relations.[191] The condemnation of such belief first appeared in 1 Salisbury 94, a text derived from Paris 48. Priests were instructed to teach their people frequently that the sacrament might be repeated in every illness where death was feared. The statute concluded as follows: 'Dicant etiam et denuntient confidenter quod post susceptum sacramentum licitum est reverti ad opus conjugale.'[192] Similar regulations appeared in many sets of statutes until mid-century.[193] The seriousness of the belief and the extent of the restrictions to which it led had already received statement in 3 Worcester 37; restrictions included carnal relations with one's spouse, the eating of flesh-meat, and walking barefoot.[194] The belief was condemned as contrary to sound doctrine, and priests were instructed to use ecclesiastical coercion if necessary to bring such people back from their errors. The seriousness of the resistance to the sacrament resulting from these notions was set out in Wells 8: extreme unction was so abhorred that some would scarcely receive it even at the hour of death. To meet the problem, priests were to instruct their people on the free use of the sacrament and teach them that, should they survive, they need not forego their conjugal rights. This form of the regulation was used in Carlyle 8, 2 York 8, and, with minor variations, 3 Winchester 25 and 2 Exeter 6. Finally, there were the spells and machinations of the sorcerer that might influence the sexual life of the married couple. As was seen above, such practice was condemned in the statutes.[195]

190 The clause was omitted in 2 Durham 37 and Ely 28, both closely related to Lincoln 27.
191 See *Catholicisme: Hier, aujourd'hui, demain,* ed C. Jacquemet, G. Mathon, P. Guilluy, et al (Paris 1948–) IV 996–7, s v 'Extrême-onction'.
192 P–C 91; cf Pontal 70–1.
193 2 Canterbury, 1 Durham, Durham Peculiars 55, Synodal Statutes 37, Constitutiones cuiusdam episcopi 55, 2 London 53; 2 Salisbury 18: 'sine coniugalis operis preiudicio'; 1 Chichester 32: 'nec propter illud vitetur thorus' (P–C 373, 457).
194 Also 3 Winchester 25 and 2 Exeter 6.
195 See 421 (here p 133).

It had been established in principle during the twelfth century that major orders and vows were impediments to marriage. Those in minor orders were allowed to take a wife; their clerical role was limited as a result. Thus the Council of Westminster (1175), canon 1, required married men in minor orders to surrender their benefices.[196] This regulation was repeated again at the legatine Council of London (1237) in a context where it was noted that many men who had been married secretly held benefices, sought to obtain new ones, and tried to receive holy orders.[197] With Lincoln 9 and 10 regulation of this matter entered the tradition of the diocesan statute. Here it was stated that those with benefices and those in holy orders were not to marry; if they had been married before ordination, they were not allowed to hold a benefice or to exercise their order. This regulation appeared in Norwich 9 and 2 Winchester 12 and, with the important addition that the limitation might sometimes be lifted, in 2 Durham 20.[198] A somewhat different and more refined form of the regulation is found in 2 Salisbury 37: married clerics were to be deprived of their ecclesiastical benefices, especially those to which the care of souls was attached. If the married state of the alleged cleric were disputed, he was to purge himself canonically, and if he failed he was to lose his benefice. The problem would appear again at the Council of Westminster (1273) as one of the heads of inquiry: 'De clericis uxoratis beneficiatis.'[199]

With 2 Durham 41, towards the middle of the thirteenth century, a further limitation of the married cleric appeared in the statutes. There, in a series of regulations dealing with parish staff, mention was made of a tonsured cleric to assist the priest of a small church: he was not to be married. A few years later in 2 London 35, it was ruled that the married cleric was not to serve at the altar except in urgent necessity. In 3 Winchester 40, the *clericus uxoratus* was likened to a layman: neither was to touch the sacred vessels nor minister in church in place of clergy.[200] Finally, in a more developed text that was at once a continuation of the

---

196 Wilkins I 477. The clauses dealing with the benefices of those in minor orders were included in *Provinciale*, ed Lyndwood 3 3 1 128.
197 Council of London c15 (P–C 252); cf ibid 98–9.
198 'Nullusque eorum uxorem ducat; et si antequam sacros ordines susceperit uxorem duxerit seu postea, si beneficium habeat, ipso privetur et ab executione sui officii suspendatur, nisi in casu a iure concesso' (P–C 427). Note that this statute considered the possibility of marriage after receiving orders.
199 P–C 805.
200 'Nulli insuper laici aut clerici uxorati vasa consecrata contingant nec alias in ecclesia loco clericorum ministrent' (P–C 710).

old regulation and evidence of certain changes in society, 2 Exeter 21 forbade married clerics to minister at the altar even if they were literate.[201] The special problem of the *laicus literatus* is evident more than a century later in a constitution of Archbishop Henry Chichele which seems to have been issued during his first convocation of the Province of Canterbury (1413): the exercise of ecclesiastical jurisdiction was forbidden under severe sanctions to laymen, married clerics, and bigamous clerics.[202] This constitution found a place in Lyndwood's *Provinciale* and thus remained before the working canonists of the later Middle Ages.[203]

If the married cleric became a widower, the limitation to the exercise of his order was removed. Such was not the case of the bigamous cleric.[204] The marital relationship into which he had entered made him irregular; while he might be dispensed from its consequences, the irregularity remained all through his life. Beginning with 1 Canterbury 1 and carrying through to 2 Exeter 8, a series of statutes dealt with this matter. In the earliest of them, policy towards bigamists who were already ordained was set out. Thus in 1 Canterbury 1 priests were told that if they knew themselves to be bigamists, they were not to exercise their office until they had consulted the archbishop. The purpose of the consultation became explicit in 1 Salisbury 1, where the bigamous cleric was included in the list of those who were irregular: it was necessary to approach the authority from whom dispensation could be obtained.[205] In 2 Worcester 61 a different approach was taken. Here it was a question of ordination: preliminary examination of the candidates included inquiry about irregularities of which bigamy was one. This approach was developed further in 2 Salisbury 19 with the statement that, until the irregular candidates had been dispensed, orders were not to be received and that, if they had benefices, they should expect to lose them. The problem of the

---

201 The motive was drawn from 1 Cor 7:33: in their desire to please their wives they would be unable to give all their attention to the worship of God (P–C 1020).

202 On the constitution *De clericis bigamis* (Wilkins III 369–70) see Cheney, 'William Lyndwood's *Provinciale*' 422 and n70.

203 3 3 2 128–30.

204 The *clericus bigamus* was one who had married twice or had married a widow whose earlier marriage had been consummated. On the history of this irregularity see DDC 2 (1937) 853–82, s v 'Bigamie, l'irrégularité de'; and Stephan Kuttner, 'Pope Lucius III and the Bigamous Archbishop of Palermo,' in *Medieval Studies Presented to Aubrey Gwynn, S.J.*, ed J.A. Watt et al (Dublin 1961) 409–54.

205 Thus 2 Canterbury, 1 Durham, and 1 Chichester 25. The possibility of reference to the Holy See for dispensation was stated in 1 Exeter 3: 'qui secundum canones summi pontificis vel saltem nostra indigent dispensatione' (P–C 228).

promotion of the bigamous cleric appeared again among the heads of inquiry at the Council of Westminster (1273): 'De bigamis promotis in prelatos.'[206] The two sets of regulations were finally brought together in 2 Exeter 8: all those under irregularity were suspended from the exercise of office and all were to remain without ordination to higher rank until they had been dispensed.

During the twelfth and thirteenth centuries it had been debated whether the bigamous cleric lost all the privileges of his order. That such was the case was decreed at the Second Council of Lyons (1274).[207] Thus the question of the individual's irregularity was important from several points of view. It explains at least one of the motives that lay behind the complaint to the king at the Council of the Province of Canterbury held at London and Lambeth in 1309: since the recognition of bigamy pertained to the ecclesiastical courts, secular judges should not entertain this matter to the prejudice of the liberty of the Church.[208]

The irregularity of the *clericus bigamus* can be traced to the ancient Christian preference that a man be married but once; the prohibition of the blessing of second and subsequent marriages was a vestige of the same teaching. In principle the marriage bond was permanent; if broken by death, second and even further unions were permitted but without enthusiasm. As has been seen above, the statutes provided some of the regulations limiting the solemnization of these permitted unions and the role the husband might play in the official life of the Church. There were other problems, too, problems touching the permanence of the marriage bond. The statutes and canons provided some direction in their regard.

The regulation, treated above, which limited the wife's freedom to make a vow was usually coupled with another which ruled on the ending of a couple's life together by the entry of one or both spouses into religious life. The possibilities of abuse in such proceedings does not require comment; as the propriety of separation for a higher religious purpose was established in the discussions of the twelfth century, so were the regulations that saw to its control. Thus 1 Salisbury 89 was the first of a series of statutes that ordered the priest to instruct the people and to

206 P–C 806. On the relation of this inquiry to the preparation for the Second Council of Lyons, see ibid 804.
207 c16 (Alberigo 323) = VI I 12 I.
208 c12 (P–C 1273). Cf the constitution ascribed to Archbishop John Stratford by Wilkins (II 677): it was claimed that when clerics were arrested by lay authorities the allegation that they were bigamists was used frivolously; once again it was insisted that a decision as to the defendant's status lay with the ecclesiastical jurisdiction.

forbid, under pain of anathema, married persons to enter religious life without the bishop's permission.[209] The prohibition and penalty were extended to those who received them into religious houses. During the next forty years these regulations were repeated in 2 Canterbury 89, Constitutiones cuiusdam episcopi 61, 1 Durham 89, 2 London 49, and, without the reference to those who received the spouses, 1 Chichester 30.

At other times, the couple might have had reason for judging their marriage to be invalid and wished to be free of each other. Or, though it was clear to them that they were indeed married, their union might have become intolerable to the extent that they sought a separation. In a world where the establishing of the marriage bond was often a private matter, it would not be surprising if some men and women saw the decision as to its existence or its continuance to be a private matter as well.[210] It was in opposition to this way of proceeding that 1 Winchester 59 insisted that decisions on their marriage were not to be made by the couple but by the judgment of a court.[211] The jurisdiction that decided whether a couple were free to marry when the banns were read maintained the right to judge whether a *de facto* union were a true marriage and to decide under what conditions the couple should be free of some of the obligations of their state.

Conclusions

One of the more remarkable processes discernible in European society of the twelfth century is a change in attitude to marriage. There were many causes and many manifestations of that fact. In a welter of traditions, at a time of renewed sensitivity in many aspects of human endeavour, through examination of sexuality, celibacy, and the married state by poet, lawyer, and theologian, European thinking about marriage began a change in direction that launched one of the major movements in the social history of the West. Many forces helped to give a certain coherence and consistency to this multi-faceted trend. One of them – to my present

209 'prohibeant sub anathemate ne alter coniugum transeat ad religionem, nec recipiatur, nisi per nos aud nostram licentiam' (P–C 89).
210 See Helmholz, *Marriage Litigation* 59–63. In my article 'Marriage and Family in English Conciliar and Synodal Legislation, (here pp 77–117) I examine the jurisdiction over marriage cases as regulated by English councils and synodal statutes.
211 'quoniam si separatio talis contractus fieri debet, oportet quod fiat per sententiam et non per compositionem. Preterea cum de inpedimento matrimonii orta fuerit questio, nulla penitus admittatur compositio sed per sententiam dirimatur' (P–C 135).

thinking it may well have been the key – was the long effort by canonists to give legal structure to the institution that resulted and to guide society in the secular process of accepting it.

An understanding of the essence, the consequences, and the modes of establishing the marriage bond was arrived at by the long process of which some of the stages and some of the remaining historiographical problems were set out at the Colloque du Cerdic in May 1970.[212] At the centre of the development was the understanding of the role of the principals of the marriage, the bride and groom. Stated in drastically simplified terms, this change can be seen in two steps. The first is manifest in Gratian, namely, that the principals of the marriage must consent to it if there is to be a marriage. The second step, that no other consent is necessary, was slowly clarified in a series of papal judgments. In consequence, if not in intent, a principle was enunciated which withdrew the choice of spouse from both family and lord, vesting it in the couple themselves. Of course there could be many reasons why the couple should not marry; they too were set out by the canonists. But since ignorance, self-deception, mutual deceit or collusion might have led the principals to escape these restrictions, a series of regulations was developed; they touched the indication of intent to marry by the banns and the due publicity and form of betrothal and marriage. Thus, while the personal nature of the consent was enhanced, the condition of its exercise was subjected to a certain control by a wider circle who provided the publicity for the individual marriage and the memory of its existence. It is significant that neither the family nor the lord, as such, was the instrument of this control; it was vested in the fellow parishioners of the couple, the local community to which they belonged.

As has been suggested, the consequences of this new understanding of marriage were, when seen in long term, immense. However, until recently, little attention has been paid to the process whereby a theoretical construction entered practice; that is, how the understanding of marriage just sketched spread to different provinces of the Church and worked down through different levels of population, and at what tempo. Many routes are currently being explored: literature, iconography, ritual and prayer forms, pastoral instruction by sermon and letter, treatises on moral guidance, letters, diaries, and several other kinds of evidence might be mentioned.[213] Here as elsewhere, the role of canon law as discipline and pastoral guide must be explored.

212 See *Le lien matrimonial*, ed René Metz and Jean Schlick (Strasbourg 1970) passim.
213 See 'Choice of Marriage Partner in the Middle Ages: Development and Mode of

It has been the purpose of this essay to examine one index of that role: to show how the local legislation of the medieval English Church reveals the rate at which the general canon law found expression at the level where it was available to the parish clergy. With the blossoming of the diocesan statute as the preferred instrument, the detailed regulation of marriage and a not inconsequential teaching on its meaning and end began. The statutes moved well beyond that general statement of the external rules of behaviour that had been typical of conciliar regulation and would remain so. Beyond doubt, the crucial event was the publication of the First Statutes of Salisbury by Bishop Richard Poore within four years of the Fourth Lateran Council. Due to the very widespread influence of his collection during the twenty years after its appearance and the subsequent influence of the Third Statutes of Worcester and the Statutes of Wells, all the dioceses of England except Rochester and Bath and Wells are known to have had access to an advanced and more or less detailed statement of the recently developed law of marriage. We know that pastors were required to have copies of these statutes and that at synods these regulations were read to the clergy in attendance. Thus it can be concluded that the first sixty years of the thirteenth century was the period during which this teaching became available in England at the parish level. Most dioceses are known to have had access to it by 1240.

The clear intent of this literature was to promote the true marriage. The free consent of the couple was essential to such a union. Yet this requisite did not loom large in English legislation. There are many signs that it was taken for granted – this as early as the Council of Westminster of 1175. Yet it was only towards the middle of the thirteenth century that statutes remark – almost with reluctance – that it was consent that made the marriage. Thus, though the statutes were prompt to teach that sexual union after betrothal was considered to be marriage and were precocious in the theory of the bond that they revealed, the main direction of their teaching was that there should be no union of husband and wife until its possibility had been exposed to the full scrutiny afforded by the banns and the public exchange of consent *de presenti*.

Whatever the theoretical priorities of the new conception of marriage might have been, it contained within itself the grave pedagogical problem of the act that is at once forbidden and possible. English legislation resolved it by a steady insistence on the publicity of marriage that completely overshadowed the quiet admission that such publicity was not

Application of a Theory of Marriage,' *Studies in Medieval and Renaissance History* n s 1 (1978) 1–33 (here pp 87–117).

essential to the union. The requirements for betrothal were set out quickly and clearly; legislation after 1250 had nothing to add in its regard. It was the reading of the banns and the public exchange of consent *de presenti* that were recognized as the essential controls. It is important to note that the solemnization of the exchange of consent in the presence of a priest was sometimes used to give the strength of the *fait accompli* to a union that had not been preceded by the banns. Like a Romeo and a Juliet, some couples sought their Friar Lawrence, an act that was a clear indication that the role of the priest was accepted and that the banns were an effective obstacle to the impeded marriage. The period between the end of the thirteenth century and the Reformation in England, as in the Church generally, was not to see original legislation touching marriage, but the councils of the period were to return again and again to reinforce the proper reading of the banns and to prevent the use of an unacceptable solemnization of marriage to circumvent it. This was the key to the system and, in a sense, its most vulnerable point; it was to its defence and perfection that statute and canon continually returned. The system of social control of marriage first outlined at the Council of Westminster in 1200 was to require further adjustment, but it continued to be effective and, as such, survived into modern times.

9

The Wife of Bath and Her Four Sisters: Reflections on a Woman's Life in the Age of Chaucer

During the past decade many study sessions, numerous papers and collections of essays, and several monographs have been devoted to women's history in general or, more specifically, to the history of women in medieval Europe.[1] Much of this work is worthy of high praise. It is, however, not unfair to say that part of this literature suffers from a tendency to generalize: sometimes one wonders whether the notions advanced are applicable to any woman who actually lived.[2] To what extent can one write the history of 'women' without further explication? In the description of attitudes, it is perhaps feasible to proceed in such general terms,[3] yet in several other areas of research, this approach is not entirely

---

This paper was presented as the B.K. Smith Lecture in History at the University of St Thomas, Houston, in March 1982, in a joint session with David Herlihy entitled 'Did Women Have a Renaissance?' An earlier version was read at the Caltech Invitational Conference, 'Family and Property in Traditional Europe,' in 1981.

1 For retrospective bibliography see Carolly Erickson and Kathleen Casey, 'Women in the Middle Ages: A Working Bibliography,' *Mediaeval Studies* 37 (1975) 340–59; and Joan Kelly-Gadol, *Bibliography in the History of European Women* (Bronxville, N.Y. 1976). For current work see *International Medieval Bibliography* (Leeds 1967–); since July–December 1976, General Index s v 'Women'. On possible tensions between the study of the history of the family and the history of women, see Barbara J. Harris, 'Recent Work on the History of the Family: A Review Article,' *Feminist Studies* 3 (1976) 159.

2 See the reflections of Ria Lemaire on the limitations of the conference 'La femme dans la société des Xe–XIIIe siècles,' held at Poitiers, September 1976, 'En marge du colloque ...,' *Cahiers de civilisation médiévale* 20 (1977) 261–3. For this and several other references my thanks to Sharon Ady.

3 Eg Bede Jarrett, ch 3: 'Women,' in *Social Theories of the Middle Ages, 1200–1500* (Boston 1926; repr New York 1966) 69–93; and, more recently, Georges H. Tavard, *Woman in Christian Tradition* (Notre Dame, Ind. 1973); Vern L. Bullough and Bonnie

successful. There has been a tendency to forget that the study of the history of women in medieval Europe is by and large a new field of activity, one still at the stage of data collection and preliminary analysis. Much encouragement should be given to those who adopt a prosopographical approach, who seek to describe and reflect on the lives of individual women, and to those who concentrate their research on groups whose homogeneity permits the possibilities and realities of the lives of the women in question to be presented without danger of serious distortion.[4]

The second suggested approach, the analysis of homogeneous groups, will be employed in what follows, using the oldest tool of the social historian, the examination of law and its applications. In doing so, however, it is important not to fall into that error of vagueness criticized above. The intention is to identify and examine the lives of five women who will stand for groups within the three estates into which medieval authors long considered their society to be divided – those who pray, those who defend and govern, and those who work with their hands – and a fourth class, the merchants, whose importance was finally coming to be recognized. Chaucer can be of assistance in this enterprise: models are to be found in *The Canterbury Tales*, and to the period of their composition – the last quarter of the fourteenth century – the following description applies.

First was the group whose law was the common law of England, the class that was landed and free. It extended through a wide spectrum of wealth and power, from the aristocracy, typified by Dorigen of the 'Franklin's Tale,' to a woman – the wife of the Yeoman, perhaps – whose husband possessed a little land and was free of the control of the manorial lord. But the Knight, whose Emily was the Dorigen of another age, was typical of that class. His wife – let us call her 'Eleanor Knight' – can serve as model of the group.

Bullough, *The Subordinate Sex: A History of Attitudes towards Women* (Urbana 1973); several essays in *Religion and Sexism: Images of Woman in the Jewish and Christian Traditions*, ed Rosemary Radford Ruether (New York 1974); Carolly Erickson, 'The View of Women,' in *The Medieval Vision* (London and New York 1975) 181–212; Marie-Thérèse d'Alverny, 'Comment les théologiens et les philosophes voient la femme,' *Cahiers de civilisation médiévale* 20 (1977) 105–29; and M.C. Horowitz, 'The Image of God in Man – Is Woman Included?' *Harvard Theological Review* 72 (1979) 175–206.

4 Much progress has been made in obtaining data on the lives of individual women, including those of the lowest classes; see David Herlihy and Christiane Klapisch-Zuber, *Les Toscans et leurs familles* (Paris 1978); for the English peasantry, see the work of J. Ambrose Raftis in Toronto and Rodney H. Hilton in Birmingham and their students.

Second were those women whose families provided the free burgesses, the citizens of the towns, a group that was growing in power in the period that is being examined.[5] Here, too, was a considerable spectrum of wealth and influence extending from the great merchant families down to those of the minor crafts; but all were citizens of the towns, and their lives were regulated by the customs of those towns. The Wife of Bath was one of them and, being involved in the cloth trade, enjoyed a position within the upper levels of urban society. Here it is not a question of those virtues that were especially her own and that would have propelled her to the head of any group, but of the advantages of the craft of which she was a member. She can serve as the model of the free townswoman.

Third were the women of the largest group in English society of the age, those whose rights and duties were stated in manorial custom. Two individuals can be isolated who would be typical of different classes among the peasantry. First was the wife of the Ploughman; let us call her 'Joan.'[6] If a little imagination is used, it is possible to say something of her. Since it was April, the heavy farm work of spring was finished, so the Ploughman could go on pilgrimage. There was still much to be done on the manor, and Joan was attending to it. She was married to a man who could afford to leave his land for a few days while he journeyed to Canterbury, who owned or had the use of a horse – not a very good one, but still a mount – and who was stoutly, if plainly, dressed. The Ploughman and his Joan can be seen as typical of the unfree peasants of some substance, tenants of a half or a whole virgate or even more, members of the group who constituted a third to a half of the village community.[7]

---

5 Although the population of London and a few other urban centres increased during the late fourteenth century, many English towns experienced serious decline, May McKisack, *The Fourteenth Century, 1307–1399*, Oxford History of England 5 (Oxford 1959) 380–1.

6 The Ploughman is seen here as the type of the substantial peasant, possessed of plough and team as well as land, rather than as the *famulus*, specializing in ploughing and attached to the demesne. Demesne farming was much reduced in the late fourteenth century, so there was little or no need for the ploughman in the older sense of *bovarius*, Michael M. Postan, *The Famulus: The Estate Labourer in the XIIth and XIIIth Centuries*, Economic History Review, suppl 2 (Cambridge 1954) 12; and Rodney H. Hilton, *The English Peasantry in the Later Middle Ages* (Oxford 1975) 21–3.

7 In the changing conditions of the period, the economic position of this group was improving: see Edwin B. DeWindt, *Land and People in Holywell-cum-Needingworth: Structures of Tenure and Patterns of Social Organization in an East Midlands Village, 1252–1457*, Studies and Texts 22 (Toronto 1972) 115–27, for the East Midlands; and Zvi Razi, *Life, Marriage, and Death in a Medieval Parish* (Cambridge and New York 1980) 147–9, for Worcestershire; cf Michael M. Postan, 'Medieval Agrarian Society

Other members of this class had a more difficult lot. They extend from the quarter-virgator through the cottar, who held a few acres, to those nameless members of society who found a place in the village as servants or migrant workers. Within this group can be placed the Poor Widow of the 'Nun's Priest's' Tale,' the woman who owned Chanticleer. The opening lines of the tale make her spring into life:

> · A povre wydwe, somdeel stape in age
> Was whilom dwellyng in a narwe cotage,
> Biside a grove, stondynge in a dale ...
> By housbondrie of swich as God hire sente
> She foond hirself and eek hir doghtren two.
> Thre large sowes hadde she, and namo,
> Three keen, and eek a sheep that highte Malle ...
> A yeerd she hadde, enclosed al aboute
> With stikkes, and a drye dych withoute,
> In which she hadde a cok, hight Chaunticleer.[8]

Joan Ploughman lived a much easier life than did a cottar like the Poor Widow; she could be expected to live longer, and more of her children would survive.[9] Even so, in terms of their positions within their respective families, they were possessed of similar rights and, bound by similar obligations, their lives were circumscribed within the custom of the manor. The Poor Widow, whom Chaucer has presented so well, can serve as the type of the peasant woman.

Fourth were the women of a similar, lowly estate, but who lived in the towns. The lives of the men and women of this group are the most difficult to describe. In London they were called 'foreigns.'[10] They might be English or even have been born in London itself, but they did not

in Its Prime: England,' in *The Cambridge Economic History of Europe*, I: *The Agrarian Life of the Middle Ages*, 2nd ed (Cambridge 1966) 630–2. On Chaucer's view of the Ploughman as the ideal labourer see Jill Mann, *Chaucer and Medieval Estate Satire: The Literature of Social Classes and the General Prologue to the 'Canterbury Tales'* (Cambridge 1973) 67–70.

8 Geoffrey Chaucer, *The Canterbury Tales*, in *The Works of Geoffrey Chaucer*, ed F.N. Robinson, 2nd ed (Boston 1957) 199 lines 2821–3, 2828–31, 2847–9.

9 Razi, *Life, Marriage, and Death* 140–9.

10 See *Middle English Dictionary*, ed Hans Kurath and Sherman M. Kuhn, Vol E–F (Ann Arbor 1952) 735 a–b, s v 'forein: 1'. I am indebted to Professor R.H. Robbins for this reference and for valued assistance and advice touching many parts of this essay.

possess the freedom of the city, and the very word used to identify them spoke of their alienation. No class of documents describes their role in society; we meet them when their activity threatened the business enterprises of the burgesses, in pleas of debt, and when they were involved in crime. It is estimated that in London they outnumbered adult members of the citizen class by three to one.[11] This group provided the porters, the hawkers, the innkeepers, the servants, and the working men and women of many of the crafts, yet they remain the most elusive of all. The nameless women in the background of the 'Cook's Tale' or of that world in which the Miller and the Pardoner were so much at home were members of this class. It will be difficult to say much of these women with certainty; perhaps the main accomplishment of this essay will have been to insist on their existence. One of them – 'Rose Foreign' is a suitable name for her – can stand for her class.

The fifth group, and the last to be identified, was never numerous in medieval England. They were the women who chose to change their state and become religious.[12] Women of any class could find a place within religious life; indeed, the four types who have been identified thus far might have been received as choir nuns or as lay sisters in the greater nunneries, or as sisters attached to hospitals and other charitable institutions. Choir nuns were usually drawn from the upper classes, and women of the noble and knightly families as well as those of well-to-do burgesses were the principal sources of vocations. The Prioress might well have been a relative of Eleanor Knight, although the reference to her affectations may have had a snobbish overtone, implying that the Prioress was born into a family rather lower on the scale within the free classes.

The Prioress, Eleanor Knight, the Wife of Bath, the Poor Widow, and that unnamed woman of the towns whom we have called Rose Foreign will be the types to which the description that follows will refer. They have been isolated and identified because different sets of custom and law described, at least in part, the frame in which their lives developed. Before going further, however, it is important to recall that another kind of law was of general application to all these women. For three centuries before the period under discussion, there had been a revival of speculation on

---

11 Elspeth M. Viale, 'Craftsmen and the Economy of London in the Fourteenth Century,' in *Studies in London History Presented to Philip Edmund Jones*, ed A.E.J. Hollaender and W. Kellaway (London 1969) 136, 140–2, 163–4.

12 Eileen Power, *Medieval English Nunneries, c. 1275 to 1535* (Cambridge 1922) 1–41; David Knowles, *The Religious Orders in England*, 2: *The End of the Middle Ages* (Cambridge 1955) 260–1.

man and woman and their respective roles, speculation that considered all levels of society. This was the work of theologians, philosophers, and lawyers. In time, some of their ideas came to be accepted as social norms or rules of moral guidance and, in greater or lesser degree, became enforceable regulations in the form of religious or canon law. Many of its rules were of universal application, so they touched the lives of the Poor Widow and Rose Foreign as well as the lives of their more wealthy sisters.[13] These sets of regulations were a force within medieval society pressing towards general and consistent usage, a usage that transcended differences of class.

One final distinction must be made. It makes little sense in an essay to refer to the rights and responsibilities of a woman without noticing where she is located along the path of life. Recall that in the 'Prologue' to *The Canterbury Tales* there are radically different expectations of the Knight and the Squire:

> A Knyght ther was, and that a worthy man ...
> And everemoore he hadde a sovereyn prys:
> And though that he were worthy, he was wys,
> And of his port as meeke as is a mayde.[14]

In contrast to this wise, responsible, grave, and rather dull man is the Squire:

> A lovyere and a lusty bacheler,
> With lokkes crulle as they were leyd in presse ...
> Embrouded was he, as it were a meede
> Al ful of fresshe floures, whyte and reede,
> Syngynge he was, or floytynge, al the day;
> He was as fressh as is the month of May.[15]

Yet, from the point of view of this presentation, the Knight and the Squire are the same person seen at different moments of a single life.

---

13 René Metz, 'Le statut de la femme en droit canonique médiéval,' in *La femme,* Société Jean Bodin pour l'histoire comparative des institutions 12 (1962) II 59–113; Michael M. Sheehan, 'The Influence of Canon Law on the Property Rights of Married Women in England,' *Mediaeval Studies* 25 (1963) 109–24 (here pp 16–30).
14 Chaucer, *Canterbury Tales*, ed Robinson 17–18 lines 43, 67–9.
15 Ibid 18 lines 80–1, 89–92.

Having made all the necessary distinctions, we will examine the women of England – somewhat more than a million individuals[16] living in an area one-fifth the size of the state of Texas – in terms of the regulations that applied to them about the year 1380. They are distinguished as four typical women within two traditional and one recently recognized lay group: *bellatores*, *laboratores*, and *mercatores*, and one typical of the status open to them all, that of *oratores*. Their rights and duties at each stage of life will be examined.

Birth

At birth all girl babies were allowed to live. The history of infanticide, especially female infanticide, is long, and there is evidence of it in various parts of Europe in the early Middle Ages.[17] Steady pressure to protect the life of the newborn was exerted by the leaders of society so that, well before the period that is the object of the present study, infanticide was forbidden and punishable in the courts. The research of Richard Helmholz and Barbara Hanawalt during the past decade provides strong evidence that, in fourteenth-century England, the life of the newborn child was successfully protected by society.[18]

16 In a volume that, in spite of much criticism, has remained the benchmark of demographic study, *British Medieval Population* (Albuquerque, N.Mex. 1948), J.C. Russell estimated the population of England in 1377 at 2,232,373 (146). In a review in *Revue belge de philologie et d'histoire* 28 (1950) 600–6, J. Stengers argued that numbers were considerably higher. Russell maintained that the population fell during the last quarter of the century (260–3), a position restated in *Late Ancient and Medieval Population*, Transactions of the American Philosophical Society, n s 48 pt 3 (Philadelphia 1958) 118–19. For recent work on population trends, 1350–1400, see Razi, *Life, Marriage, and Death* 114–16. The numbers of men and women for this period were about equal: see Russell 148; and Sylvia L. Thrupp, 'Plague Effects in Medieval Europe,' *Comparative Studies in Society and History* 8 (1965–6) 475.
17 Emily Coleman, 'Medieval Marriage Characteristics: A Neglected Factor in the History of Medieval Serfdom,' *Journal of Interdisciplinary History* 2 (Autumn 1971) 205–19, and 'L'infanticide dans le haut moyen-âge?' *Annales: Economies, sociétés, civilisations* 29 (1974) 315–35. See Russell, *Late Ancient and Medieval Population* passim.
18 Richard H. Helmholz, 'Infanticide in the Province of Canterbury during the Fifteenth Century,' *History of Childhood Quarterly* 2 (1975) 379–90; Barbara A. Hanawalt, 'Childrearing among the Lower Classes of Late Medieval England,' *Journal of Interdisciplinary History* 8 (Summer 1977) 1–22. The possibility that female infanticide is the explanation of the high sex ratios revealed in early fourteenth-century England and in London (1259–1330) is suggested by Russell, *British Medieval Population* 148–9, and by H.A. Miskimin, 'The Legacies of London: 1259–1330,' in

Childhood

Infant daughters of the free, land-owning, and bourgeois classes could inherit and be recipients of landed property immediately after birth.[19] Rights, in fact, were vested even in the unborn child. Thus, in the case of uncertain inheritance, decisions as to the devolution of property were delayed until an expected child was born.[20] Money or chattels that came to little girls of these classes was considered to be the property of their fathers. Such, at least, was the law, although family attitudes on this matter are unclear and the practice revealed in testaments suggests that some, at least, intended that small children be the owners of legacies left to them.[21] If the father of little Eleanor Knight had died and she were his heiress, she and her estate would have been in the wardship of her feudal lord. If she were not the heiress, it is likely that her mother or other members of her family would assume the role, seeing to her nurture, administrating her property, and, eventually, arranging her marriage. Guardianship of the Wife of Bath during her childhood would probably be in the hands of the person chosen by her father or, in some towns, was exercised by the borough administration.[22] In the rare instance when property came to a Poor Widow or a Rose Foreign during her childhood, it was probably in the control of her father or the head of the family who raised her.

We know little of the early care and socialization of infant daughters. In the landholding and bourgeois classes they were often put out to wet nurse; there is some evidence in Coroners' rolls that this was done among the peasants, as well.[23] At all levels of society it was expected that the little

---

The Medieval City: Essays in Honor of Robert S. Lopez, ed H.A. Miskimin, David Herlihy, and A.L. Udovitch (New Haven and London 1977) 220–1, though the latter points out that under-reporting is a plausible hypothesis. See Thrupp, 'Plague Effects in Medieval Europe' 474–83.

19 'Infant' is used to mean a very young child and not in the common-law sense of a minor. On the rights of the minor, see F. Joüon des Longrais, 'Le statut de la femme en Angleterre dans le droit commun médiéval,' in La femme, Société Jean Bodin pour l'histoire comparative des institutions 12 (1962) II 148–63.

20 Testaments of the period provide for the child with which a wife is pregnant, or make bequests that are to be withdrawn if the pregnancy results in the birth of an heir.

21 Grandchildren are sometimes legatees; they would often be very young.

22 See Borough Customs, ed Mary Bateson, Selden Society 18, 21 (London 1904–6) II 145–57.

23 Hanawalt, 'Childrearing' 14.

ones would have adequate care to protect them from danger. Episcopal statutes were especially exercised to prevent neglect.[24] The little girls of the upper classes were probably trained by their mothers and servants with emphasis on obedience to their fathers. Some evidence suggests that from about ages four to seven the little peasant girls accompanied their mothers to work.[25]

Girlhood

At about seven, children were considered to come to moral responsibility. This did not touch their right to control property, but it meant, among other things, that they might be involved in the first step towards their adult vocation. Thus, little girls of the class of Eleanor Knight or the Wife of Bath, whose engagements were often made early (even before birth, on occasion), might take part in a betrothal ritual.[26] The Prioress, who would be drawn from those classes, may have entered a convent at this age, perhaps as a young student, perhaps as a postulant. And in this period of life between responsibility and majority, the lives of the four types of women would begin to diverge, and the fifth possibility become open to them. Eleanor Knight may have been attached to the suite of a great lady in a household other than her own where, in addition to training in deportment, she may have had some opportunity for the study of letters.[27] Young women of the Wife of Bath's group might enter apprenticeship in one of the crafts, such as the Silkworkers, in which women played a major role, or she may have become involved in her father's business in

24 See the 'General Index' to Councils and Synods with Other Documents Relating to the English Church, 2: A.D. 1205–1313, ed F.M. Powicke and C.R. Cheney (Oxford 1964) II 1411, s v 'Children: safety measures for'.
25 Hanawalt, 'Childrearing' 18.
26 'A woman hath seven ages for severall purposes appointed to her by law: as seven years for the lord to have aid pur file marier,' according to Coke on the first age of woman, as cited by F. Pollock and F.W. Maitland, The History of English Law, 2nd ed (London 1898; repr Cambridge 1978) II 439 n3.
27 'Although the evidence of literacy among women is less conclusive ... it appears that the typical upper-class education for women included reading knowledge of the vernacular, whether French or English, or possibly both, but little or no knowledge of Latin or of writing,' J.H. Moran, 'Educational Development and Social Change in York Diocese from the Fourteenth Century to 1548,' Ph.D. dissertation (Brandeis University 1975) 235 n18. See her Education and Learning in the City of York, 1300–1560, Borthwick Papers 55 (York 1979) passim; and F.R.H. du Boulay, An Age of Ambition (London 1970) 118–19.

ways that were suitable for her.[28] The probability that she would take a place in the business world ensured that she would at least learn some mensuration; many city women were literate.[29]

In these years the future Prioress learned the round of convent life, including the recitation of the office in Latin, although probably by rote; her reading would be in the vernacular.[30] Young peasant girls like the Poor Widow's daughters found their places in the endless tasks of household and field; many became servants. It is clear from recent work by Judith Bennett that, on some manors at least, peasant girls maintained control of the money they had received so that, when it became time for their marriage, they themselves were able to pay the marriage fine (*merchet*) to the lord of the manor, rather than have it paid by their fathers or their future husbands.[31] Girls born into the foreign class of the towns, of whom Rose is the type, probably began to work as soon as they were able to be of use. Where their parents had established themselves as workers attached to but not possessing the rights of the craft guilds, they may have found a place by their side. A similar situation probably obtained where parents were innkeepers or offered food-services as hawkers. No doubt many were beggars and were already being drawn into prostitution.[32]

Majority

At age twelve, young women began to enter their majority. It is necessary to emphasize that this was but a beginning because, for them as for the young women of our own age, majority came in stages: valid marriage became a possibility with the completion of the twelfth year, but the age

28 See Marian K. Dale, 'The London Silk-women of the Fifteenth Century,' *Economic History Review* 4 (1933) 324–35; S.L. Thrupp, *The Merchant Class of Medieval London* (1948; repr Ann Arbor 1962) 169–70; Viale, 'Craftsmen and the Economy of London' 150–1; and Maryanne Kowaleski, 'Local Markets and Merchants in Late Fourteenth-Century Exeter,' Ph.D. dissertation (University of Toronto 1982) 194–209, 220–5.

29 See Thrupp, *The Merchant Class* 170–1.

30 Power, *Medieval English Nunneries* 237–89, especially 245–50.

31 'Medieval Peasant Marriage: An Examination of Marriage License Fines in the *Liber Gersumarum*,' in *Pathways to Medieval Peasants*, ed J. Ambrose Raftis (Toronto 1981) 193–246.

32 Viale, 'Craftsmen and the Economy of London' 141–3. See James A. Brundage, 'Prostitution in the Medieval Canon Law,' *Signs: Journal of Women in Culture and Society* 1:4 (Summer 1976) 825–45.

at which disposition of property was permitted was considerably later.[33] At any rate, the time had come to think of a state in life. Marriage was the lot of most medieval women, but medieval society provided several honourable alternatives. One was religious life, considered to be a suitable vocation for women of Eleanor Knight's class or for that of the Wife of Bath. Their families would be expected to provide a dowry, although it would usually be considerably less than that for marriage. At this stage of life the young woman who had entered a convent in her childhood was permitted to take her final vows. The possibility of becoming a nun was also open to a woman at later stages of her life.[34] The fact that convents were often used as niches for women who had little or no desire for religious life was a constant threat to the monastic ideal and a cause of scandal as well: visitation records and the literature of the time leave no doubt in this regard.[35] The lay sisters (*conversae*) attached to the greater convents and those women who served in hospitals and other charitable institutions have not yet been studied. It is probable that some of them at least were recruited from the lower strata of society, that a Poor Widow or a Rose Foreign may have found a place among them.

Another possibility for the woman entering her majority was the single life in the world. The spinster in medieval England has proved to be a very elusive person but her name, at least, gives a clue to her place there. Spinsters probably existed in significant numbers among the sisters of the Wife of Bath and the Poor Widow, though they have left little trace. Testaments survive that are clear evidence of the activity of these women and, as well as other documents, have made it possible for scholars to begin the study of this group within English society.[36]

33 On the different ages of majority see Pollock and Maitland, *The History of English Law* II 436–9; and Michael M. Sheehan, *The Will in Medieval England: From the Conversion of the Anglo-Saxons to the End of the Thirteenth Century*, Studies and Texts 6 (Toronto 1963) 239–41. On proof of age see Russell, *British Medieval Population* 92–117; and Sue Sheridan Walker, 'Proof of Age of Feudal Heirs in Medieval England,' *Mediaeval Studies* 35 (1973) 306–23.

34 Power, *Medieval English Nunneries* 38–41.

35 Ibid 25–38, 436–74, and passim; Sister Mary of the Incarnation Byrne, *The Tradition of the Nun in Medieval England* (Washington 1932) 165–74; Mann, *Chaucer and Medieval Estate Satire* 128–37.

36 Annette Koren, 'Provincial Women and Their Economic Status in Late Medieval England,' a paper read at the Berkshire Conference of Women Historians, Vassar College, 1981. See the discussion about Cecilia Penifader, a spinster of Brigstock, Northants (ca 1316–ca 1344), and her wide social network in Judith Bennett, 'Gender, Family, and Community: A Comparative Study of the English Peasantry, 1287-1349,'

Marriage

The woman who became a wife and the married period of her life have thus far been the principal areas of research in the social history of her sex. Her betrothal and wedding, her rights during marriage, and the property distribution when her marriage ended have proved to be of special interest. At the social level of Eleanor Knight, the marriage of a woman at the minimum age of twelve was probably not uncommon, although a first union in the mid- or late teens would be more usual.[37] It will be remembered that the Wife of Bath insisted on her first marital adventure at twelve. She has sometimes been taken, at least in this matter, as a paradigm of the women of her class, but recent work suggests that first marriage usually occurred about five years later.[38] The possibility of a peasant woman finding a spouse was related to her succession to her parents' property at their death or retirement or the availability of land to the man she married. In either case the opportunity must often have been slow in presenting itself. In the conditions that obtained after the Black Death, however, land was more available. Thus the age of first marriage seems to have fallen, especially for peasant women like the Poor Widow, whose families held but little land.[39]

As to Rose Foreign, little more than surmise is possible. The completion of her twelfth year would be a requirement for a valid union, of course. For the upper levels of her class at least, the possibilities were similar to those of the Wife of Bath. Her marriage was probably less related to possessions than was the case with the women of the other groups and, therefore, may have occurred when she was quite young; but in her case, as that of the others, the question must be examined with

Ph.D. dissertation (University of Toronto 1981) 108–13, 136 n63; and the earlier remarks of Eileen Power, 'The Position of Women,' in *The Legacy of the Middle Ages*, ed G.C. Crump and E.F. Jacob (Oxford 1926) 411–15.

37 See Russell, *British Medieval Population* 158.

38 See Thrupp, *The Merchant Class* 196.

39 Razi found that, in the post-plague period, sons usually obtained land in the lifetime of their fathers and were able to marry earlier than had been the case before that time. They married at about twenty. The small sample that was available indicated marriage of women between twelve and nineteen. See Eleanor Searle, 'Seigneurial Control of Women's Marriage: The Antecedents and Function of Merchet in England,' *Past and Present* 82 (1979) 3–43; and Chris Middleton, 'Peasants, Patriarchy, and the Feudal Mode of Production in England: A Marxist Appraisal, Part 2: Feudal Lords and the Subordination of Peasant Women,' *Sociological Review* n s 29:1 (1981) 137–54.

more circumspection than has often been the case in the past. The older stereotypes of very early marriage in each of the four groups under examination must be set aside until much research has been completed; there are indications that first marriage towards the end of the second decade of a woman's life will prove to be the more common pattern.

Of similar difficulty is the question of the different individuals and groups who were expected to be involved in the choice of a woman's spouse. It can be taken as axiomatic that the higher a woman's position within the class structure, the more her marriage was a choice involving a wide circle of advisers. Thus the betrothal and marriage of Eleanor Knight would be a more complex arrangement than that of the Poor Widow or Rose Foreign. Depending on the class of the bride, in most cases her parents and wider family, neighbourhood and parish, feudal and manorial lords might be expected to intervene. The twelfth and thirteenth centuries had seen a careful examination of the ways in which marriage was constituted. It resulted in a decision that is an example, as mentioned above, of a regulation that touched women of every class: the final say in establishing the marriage bond lay with the bridal pair. At the level of canonical theory it was insisted that, unless the couple consented to their union, that union did not occur. This regulation was implemented and enforced, often with serious consequences that touched dynasties and fortunes as well as the lot of the individuals concerned. Furthermore, the ancient usage whereby marriage could be a private act, that is, made by an exchange of consent by the couple without announcement and without witness, was still accepted. In fact, that kind of marriage, with all its possibility of mutual or self-deception, was to remain in force in England until the Marriage Act of 1753.[40] The motive for the 'free choice' of spouse was not necessarily romantic; many other intentions might be at play.[41] But the stereotype of the young woman forced to marry against her will does not stand. The way in which fourteenth-century English society resolved the claims of individual freedom and the wider interests of those

40 See Christopher Lasch, 'The Suppression of Clandestine Marriage in England: The Marriage Act of 1753,' *Salmagundi* 26 (Spring 1974) 90–109. The possibility of a secret but valid union must be kept in mind in the discussion of the marriage of all classes and in any analysis of the literature of the time; see K.P. Wentersdorf, 'The Clandestine Marriages of the Fair Maid of Kent,' *Journal of Medieval History* 5 (1979) 203–31, and 'Some Observations on the Concept of Clandestine Marriage in *Troilus and Criseyde,*' *Chaucer Review* 15 (1980) 101–26.

41 Cf Jean Leclercq, *Monks on Marriage: A Twelfth-Century View* (New York 1982) 1–9, where the importance of the element of love in marriage is presented.

with some claim on the persons or property of the couple is a problem that has exercised several scholars for more than a decade.[42] It still has many uncertain elements, but it must be understood that, if any of the four women under discussion were to be married, she would have to consent to that union for it to occur.[43]

If the preparations for the marriages of Eleanor Knight and the Wife of Bath followed the path that society preferred, there would have been agreement between their parents or guardians and the future husbands and their families regarding the property that each would bring to the new ménage and the settlement that would be made on the wife, were she widowed, and on the children born to the union. The women would be expected to bring a dowry (*maritagium*) to contribute to the household. In Eleanor's case this would likely involve some land and chattels as well. If she had no brother, her dowry might have been considerable indeed: potentially as much as her family inheritance. The Wife of Bath, too, may have brought tenements in the borough in which her family lived and other land as well, but chattels and money probably played a larger role in her case. Again, if there were no brother, to marry her might be to succeed to her father's estate and business. At the level of the peasantry a similar situation obtained, though the property involved would usually be much less. If a peasant woman had siblings, she probably brought some chattels – farm animals, linen, grain – to her marriage, and merchet would have been paid to the lord for her or by her. Once again, if she were an heiress, she would bring to her husband the parcel of land held by her parents. The Poor Widow's main contribution may have been her strong back and the ability to bear and nurture children.[44] As for Rose Foreign, once again records fail us. Presumably, if hers were a family that had found a place on the fringe of one of the trades, she would be expected to bring some dowry to her spouse; those of the poorest class

---

42 See Sue Sheridan Walker, 'Free Consent and Marriage of Feudal Wards in Medieval England,' *Journal of Medieval History* 8 (1982) 123–34. My thanks to Professor Michael Altschul for this reference and for other assistance in this essay.

43 See John T. Noonan, Jr, 'Power to Choose,' *Viator* 4 (1973) 419–34; and Michael M. Sheehan, 'Choice of Marriage Partner in the Middle Ages: Development and Mode of Application of a Theory of Marriage,' *Studies in Medieval and Renaissance History* n s 1 (1978) 8–11 (here pp 92–5).

44 Barbara A. Hanawalt, 'Women's Contribution to the Home Economy in Late Medieval Europe,' a paper read at the Berkshire Conference of Women Historians, Vassar College, 1981.

would contribute what they could, presumably money and chattels that they had acquired themselves.

All four women came under the guardianship of their husbands when they married. The land that Eleanor Knight brought as *maritagium* and any land that came to her from family or other sources during her marriage passed into the control of her spouse.[45] He was not to alienate it, although, as court records make abundantly clear, he frequently did so. In that case, if she survived him, Eleanor had an effective means of recovery at common law. If she died before a child were born, her land reverted to her family. If, as seems to have been Eleanor's case, a child survived its mother, her land was held by her husband during his life-time, then passed to their offspring – in this case, the Squire. If the woman died giving birth to her child and the baby died too, as long as there was adequate proof that the infant was born alive – its cry was heard between four walls – then, by the courtesy of England, the husband held the property for his lifetime. On his death, it reverted to his wife's family. Any mobile property that Eleanor brought to the marriage, or that came to her later, by common law belonged to her husband. If she died before him, an attempt to dispose of these goods by testament was ef-fective only inasmuch as he approved of it.[46]

The brutal simplicity of the property rights of married couples before common law was somewhat refined in the boroughs and on many manors. Thus, quite aside from the moral and perhaps physical authority that the Wife of Bath exercised over her husband, her position by right with regard to him was stronger than was Eleanor Knight's in regard to her spouse. Although her husband would usually speak for her in court, she and women of her class were sometimes in business for themselves and were considered legally capable of controlling funds required for their business and of answering for that business in borough court.[47] Further-more, she could acquire landed property jointly with her husband in some

45 Joüon des Longrais, 'Le statut de la femme' 163–83; Pollock and Maitland, *The History of English Law* II 403–28.

46 William S. Holdsworth, *A History of English Law*, 5th ed (London 1966) III 542–3. For a recent re-examination of the question see Charles Donahue, Jr, 'Lyndwood's Gloss *propriarum uxorum*: Marital Property and *ius commune* in Fifteenth-Century England,' in *Europäisches Rechtsdenken in Geschichte und Gegenwart*, Festschrift für Helmut Coing zum 70. Geburtstag, ed Norbert Horn (Munich 1982) I 19–37.

47 Thrupp, *The Merchant Class* 169–74; and Kowaleski, 'Local Markets and Merchants' 194–209, 220–5. See *Borough Customs*, ed Bateson I 227–8.

boroughs and, again depending on local custom, could bequeath chattels and even land.[48] Patterns of peasant life, revealed by the anthropologist, in which the wife plays a major role in family support, often working closely with her husband, obtained among fourteenth-century peasantry; there were similar consequences. In many manors, villein tenements of husband and wife coalesced into a common possession. Furthermore, like her more wealthy sister in the borough, the Poor Widow during the time of her marriage may well have been in business for herself. She would most likely have been a brewer and would have been responsible for purchases, payments, and the fines to which ale-wives were so often subject.[49] The testamentary right of the villein was much debated in the fourteenth century. It can be demonstrated, however, that on some manors they did exercise that right and that some married women were included among the testators.[50] The testament of a Poor Widow would distribute small bequests and would likely be principally concerned with a gift in alms and her funeral.

When difficulties developed in a marriage, all four women had access to a remedy. It was the role of episcopal courts to protect the marriage rights of spouses and the bond that united them. Where the bond did not exist or proved to be intolerable, it was for the courts to provide an equitable separation. It is usually taken as axiomatic that the more wealthy were better suited to benefit from the remedies made available by the ecclesiastical courts. A first impression formed by a reading of papal registers and even those of the bishop's official is that Eleanor Knight and the Wife of Bath had a distinct advantage over the Poor Widow and Rose Foreign in these matters. It is clear that the marriage of Eleanor, or of women of the higher aristocracy, was more likely to be considered in terms of its political consequences.[51] Yet it must be remembered that the jurisdiction in question functioned at the local level and that, by the time

48 *Borough Customs*, ed Bateson II 106–11.
49 See J. Ambrose Raftis, 'Social Structures of Five East Midland Villages,' *Economic History Review*, 2nd ser, 18:1 (1965) 91–2; DeWindt, *Land and People* 235 and n157; Hilton, *The English Peasantry* 103-6; and especially Bennett, 'Gender, Family, and Community' 141–91, 262–74, and 320–9.
50 Holdsworth, *A History of English Law* III 542 and n23; see n69, below.
51 'Ubi non est consensus utriusque non est coniugium ... nisi forte aliquando urgentissima interveniente necessitate pro bono pacis coniunctio talis toleretur.' This text, c19 of the Council of Westminster (1175), was included in the *Extravagantes* of Gregory IX (4 2 2). See *Councils and Synods with Other Documents Relating to the English Church, 1: A.D. 871–1204*, ed Dorothy Whitelock, Michael Brett, and

of interest to the present discussion, it was possessed of an efficient *ex officio* procedure. This meant that the hearing of cases touching marriage was not dependent on one of the parties being in a position to launch the case; hearings were often begun by the court itself when need was seen.[52] There is good evidence that assistance was available to men and women of the lowest levels of society.

Throughout their married years women would, in the ordinary course, be in charge of the day-to-day direction of their households and often, in the absence of their husbands, would see to its wider needs as well.[53] In these same middle years of life the women who followed the vocation of the Prioress would have settled into the monastic routine. Some of them would have begun to take on responsibilities as an obedientiary, in charge of a monastic department such as housekeeping, the cellar, or the sacristy or, as the Prioress herself, have accepted the charge of a nunnery.[54] Although Chaucer spoke rather lightly of her, it should not be forgotten that he gave the Prioress the most numerous suite in the pilgrimage. As a superior of religious women she exercised one of the most responsible roles open to women during the Middle Ages. Not only the direction of a major economic enterprise but also the spiritual care of her sisters and their dependents was in her hands.

Christopher N.L. Brooke (Oxford 1981) II 991, 967 n3; and the discussion in Michael M. Sheehan, 'Marriage Theory and Practice in the Conciliar Legislation and Diocesan Statutes of Medieval England,' *Mediaeval Studies* 40 (1978) 411 (here p 121). Dynastic and political aspects of marriage are well presented by Henry Ansgar Kelly in *The Matrimonial Trials of Henry VIII* (Stanford 1975).

52 Slightly less than half of the marriage cases before the official of the bishop of Ely, 1374–82, were *ex officio*. Several of them began because, at the reading of the banns of matrimony, objection was made to a proposed union. Learning of this, the court proceeded *ex officio* to investigate the case, Michael M. Sheehan, 'The Formation and Stability of Marriage in Fourteenth-Century England: Evidence of an Ely Register,' *Mediaeval Studies* 33 (1971) 256–62 (here pp 68–74). On this matter generally see Richard H. Helmholz, *Marriage Litigation in Medieval England* (Cambridge 1974); and 'Introduction,' in *Select Cases from the Ecclesiastical Courts of the Province of Canterbury, c. 1200–1301*, ed Norma Adams and Charles Donahue, Jr, Selden Society 95 (London 1981) 81–4.

53 See Eileen Power, ch 5: 'The Menagier's Wife,' in *Medieval People*, 10th ed (New York 1963) 96–119, and *Medieval Women* (Cambridge 1975) 9–34; and Hanawalt, 'Women's Contribution.' A remarkable sense of women's administrative activity may be gained from the correspondence of Agnes Paston (1440–79) and Margaret Paston (1441–84). See *Paston Letters and Papers of the Fifteenth Century*, ed Norman Davis (Oxford 1971–6) I 26–49 nos 13–34, II 16–18 nos 434–6 (for Agnes Paston), I 215–389 nos 124–230, II 336–68 nos 707–36 (for Margaret Paston).

54 Power, *Medieval English Nunneries* 42–95, 131–60.

Widowhood

With the deaths of their husbands, the women representing the four lay groups suddenly sprang into full legal personality as expressed in the class to which they belonged. For those who had been married in their teens this was birth into a new kind of civil existence; for those who had married after a period of full adulthood, it was a rebirth.[55] Eleanor Knight would normally receive one-third of the landed property that her husband held during their marriage; it was hers for life, and she could use it as she saw fit so long as she did not alienate it. In addition, all the property she had brought to the marriage, and any that had accrued to her by inheritance or gift since that time, came under her control. She would be required to surrender the principal house of her husband's estate to the heir within forty days. It was customary that she would also receive a third part – or half, if there were no children – of her husband's chattels. By the period that is of interest here, the customary division of chattels was weakening in southern England to the detriment of the widow's right, but, if the evidence of testaments can be trusted, wives were well provided for from the chattels of the household.[56] The Wife of Bath and her class usually enjoyed at least as generous a share of landed property, and, since in some boroughs husbands were allowed to bequeath land to their wives, they might receive much more.[57] The wife's share of chattels remained the custom in the boroughs well past the period that is being described. In many manors, the Poor Widow benefited from the system of community property as her more wealthy sisters did not. She continued to hold the property that she had shared with her late husband and did not have to pay an entry fine. Thus she excluded the heir until she died or chose to relinquish the estate.[58]

55 Joüon des Longrais, 'Statut de la femme' 183–235; Pollock and Maitland, *The History of English Law* I 482–5.
56 See Holdsworth, *A History of English Law* III 554–6; Michael M. Sheehan, 'The Family in Late Medieval England, Extended or Nuclear? Evidence from Testaments,' a paper read at the Fifth British Legal History Conference, University of Bristol, 1981.
57 *Borough Customs*, ed Bateson II cviii–cxv.
58 On the customary rights of the peasant widow and the acquittal of the obligations of her holding, see George C. Homans, *English Villagers of the Thirteenth Century* (1960; repr New York 1970, 1975) 184–8; J. Ambrose Raftis, *Tenure and Mobility: Studies in the Social History of the Mediaeval English Village*, Studies and Texts 8 (Toronto 1964) 36–42; Edward Britton, *The Community of the Vill: A Study in the History of the Family and Village Life in Fourteenth-Century England* (Toronto 1977) 20–2; and Hilton, *The English Peasantry* 98–100.

Thus the widow faced the future not only with the wisdom that experience had given her, but often with a considerable fortune as well. She was free to remain single or to marry; in the latter case the choice of spouse was her own, although, as was to be expected, she was often subject to much pressure in this regard. From many points of view, not least from that of wealth, the widow was an attractive candidate for marriage, and many of them entered into a second union soon after the deaths of their husbands.[59] On the other hand, it is clear that there were many widows at all levels of fourteenth-century society. Women like Eleanor Knight or a less matrimonially inclined Wife of Bath sometimes took vows and entered a convent. Others made a formal commitment to a life of continence and prayer while remaining in the world, even in charge of their own households. The study of this form of widowed life has only begun; it is impossible to state the numbers who chose this path, though it is unlikely that they were numerous.[60] Peasant women were usually allowed to maintain their property and remain unmarried as long as they were able to acquit their obligations to their lord. Often the best solution to the problems of a Poor Widow was to remarry, although it is clear that many did not do so.[61]

As those who remained in the world grew older and their powers failed, they or their families sometimes arranged that they enter convents or hospitals as pensioners. In a similar circumstance the Poor Widow might choose to surrender her little property with the understanding that it would be transferred to an heir, or even to a stranger, who would be responsible for her support and care during the years that remained. Manorial court rolls illustrate this method of provision for old age and illustrate as well that these courts saw to the honouring of the agreement

59 On the removal of the required interval of at least a year and a day between the death of a husband and the remarriage of his widow see Sheehan, 'The Influence of Canon Law' 112 (here pp 18–19).

60 A preliminary study of these women was presented by Sharon Ady in 'Vows of Chastity and the Medieval English Widow' at the Sixteenth International Conference of Medieval Studies, University of Western Michigan, Kalamazoo, 1981. See J.R. Shinners, Jr, 'Religion in Fourteenth-Century England: Clerical Standards and Popular Practice in the Diocese of Norwich,' Ph.D. dissertation (University of Toronto 1982) 334–5.

61 See Barbara A. Hanawalt, 'Widowhood in Medieval English Villages,' a paper read at the Sixteenth International Conference of Medieval Studies, University of Western Michigan, Kalamazoo, 1981. Razi notes that peasant widows seem to have found it more difficult to marry in Worcestershire after the plague (Life, Marriage, and Death 138).

between the generations.[62] Religious like the Prioress could expect to be cared for by their communities until the end.[63]

Death and Burial

The description of the lives of these five typical women can be brought to a close with the final expression of affection and preoccupation with matters of the next world in their wills. According to the general law of the Church, religious were forbidden to own property and under ordinary circumstances were not to make wills.[64] In the somewhat relaxed state of monastic life in the later Middle Ages, however, these rules often proved difficult to maintain. Nuns accumulated chattels and sometimes sought to control their future use by will.[65] When one thinks of the Prioress, it is to wonder, who next wore her brooch with the device 'Amor vincit omnia'?[66] If Eleanor Knight died during her husband's lifetime she had no right to make a will, since she owned no chattels and landed property was not disposable by legacy. Moral guides urged that she make a will for charitable purposes and for the good of her soul, and church courts would have given probate and would oversee its execution. They did not seek to exact that right from her husband.[67] If Eleanor were a widow, she had full control over all her chattels and could dispose of them as she wished. As was mentioned above, the Wife of Bath had a somewhat better chance of having a right to make a will during her husband's lifetime. As a widow she could sometimes bequeath both chattels and real estate.[68] By the last years of the fourteenth century, on many manors, the Poor Widow would

---

62 See Homans, *English Villagers* 144–6; Raftis, *Tenure and Mobility* 42–6; S.R. Burstein, 'Care of the Aged in England from Medieval Times to the End of the 16th Century,' *Bulletin of the History of Medicine* 22 (1948) 738–43; and Elaine Clark, 'The Quest for Economic Security in Medieval England,' in *Aging and the Aged in Medieval Europe*, ed Michael M. Sheehan, Papers in Mediaeval Studies 11 (Toronto 1990) 189–200.
63 Power, *Medieval English Nunneries* 57.
64 The religious superior posed a special problem in this regard; see Sheehan, *The Will in Medieval England* 250–3.
65 Power, *Medieval English Nunneries* 315–40; see Knowles, 'The Wage-System and the Common Life,' in *The Religious Orders in England* 11 240–7. For Bishop William of Wykeham's injunctions against the making of wills by nuns (1387) see Power, *Medieval English Nunneries* 337 and n6.
66 Chaucer, *The Canterbury Tales* ed Robinson 18 lines 158–62.
67 Sheehan, 'The Influence of Canon Law' 119–21 (here pp 26–7), and *The Will in Medieval England* 234-41. See n46, above.
68 See n48, above.

be allowed to dispose of her chattels by will.[69] Of the last will of Rose Foreign little can be said with certainty. The more general freedom of bequest that obtained in borough custom suggests that, if she did make a will, it probably received probate and was implemented.

Adults had the right to choose their place of burial, and many of them stated it in their wills.[70] Widows usually chose to be buried with their husbands; but some, like Margaret Paston, preferred to return to the family that gave them birth.[71] An Eleanor Knight might be buried in the church of an abbey with which her husband's family was associated. The Prioress would rest in the choir of her convent church. For most of the women of England, burial was in their parish: the Wife of Bath would likely seek a place within the church; the Poor Widow and Rose Foreign would find rest in the churchyard. Women of all groups, like their male counterparts, sought to arrange by their wills that surviving relatives and friends reach into the next life to assist them by their prayers. The date of death of the Prioress would be entered in the beadroll of her house so that each year her anniversary would be remembered in the liturgy and, possibly, by the distribution of a pittance in her memory to her sisters. If confraternity provided that suffrages for the dead were established between her convent and other houses, she would be remembered more widely. In addition to the masses and other prayers offered for Eleanor Knight and the Wife of Bath soon after their deaths, it is possible that they would establish a chantry or be included in one founded by their husbands or other family. There they would be remembered for years to come, perhaps until chantries were suppressed in the sixteenth century.[72] The Wife of Bath would also benefit from the suffrages offered on her

69 In the diocese of Rochester, 1347–8, the testaments of 127 men, 33 married women, 20 widows, and 5 women (who were probably spinsters) were probated in groups. Many of these were the testaments of the very poor; see *Registrum Hamonis Hethe diocesis Roffensis A.D. 1318–52*, ed C. Johnson, Canterbury and York Society 49 (Oxford 1948) II 923–6, 1000, and passim.

70 See Antoine Bernard, *La sépulture en droit canonique du Décret de Gratien au Concile de Trente* (Paris 1933) 85–104.

71 'First, I betake my sowle to God ... and my body to be beried in the ele of the cherch of Mauteby byfore the ymage of Our Lady there, jn which ele reste the bodies of divers of myn aunceteres, whos sowles God assoile' (4 February 1482), *Paston Letters and Papers*, ed Davis I 383 no 230.

72 See K.L. Wood-Legh, *Perpetual Chantries in Britain* (Cambridge 1965) 8–29 and passim; and R.M.T. Hill, '"A Chaunterie for Soules": Chantries in the Reign of Richard II,' in *The Reign of Richard II: Essays in Honour of May McKisack*, ed F.R.H. du Boulay and Caroline M. Barron (London 1971) 243–55.

behalf by her guild. Unless she had risen to a position where she belonged to some craft or parish guild, Rose Foreign was probably quickly forgotten after her death; there would soon be little sign of her passing in the busy town churchyard. The Poor Widow, buried in the cemetery that surrounded her parish church, the cemetery through which her friends passed every week, might not be forgotten so soon. Although it is unlikely that she would be remembered in an anniversary mass beyond the first year or two, the physical proximity of her place of burial would help to preserve her memory for a generation. The poorest women, as the richest, would be remembered in a general way on the feast of All Souls.

10

English Wills and the Records
of the Ecclesiastical and
Civil Jurisdictions

Wills survive in England in large numbers after the middle of the fourteenth century. They yield much information on the families and economic situation of testators and occasionally reveal something of their interior lives as well. Many institutions were involved in the supervision of the execution of wills. It is only by examining their records that it is possible to know to what extent the description of testators' possessions revealed in their wills corresponded to reality, or to identify and estimate the effect of obstacles that threatened to defeat testators' intentions for the future enjoyment of their property.

In the context of a set of essays examining the use of legal records for the history of the family, a discussion of the last will or testament, in relation to the law of the Church and that of the different civil authorities, presents certain difficulties of choice. Given the general theme, it is tempting to suggest means to exploit the many facets of the history of the medieval family that English wills reveal. The death of a property holder, especially of the head of a family, was a moment of major adjustment for that family, for its surviving members and for the relations between them. By that curious legal act called the 'will' the deceased could play a major role and, as the Middle Ages progressed, an increasing role, in directing the course that those changes would take.[1] The will, then, is a window

For this article the method of documentation used in the original has been altered in keeping with the requirements of the present collection. Unnumbered notes original-ly incorporated in the text have been mixed with the numbered footnotes, with the result that the sequence of numbers here is different from that in the original printing. – Editor

1 As the Middle Ages progressed, testators tended to assume a more complete control over the future enjoyment of their chattels. This began with an increased attention to

through which that process can be observed.[2] Through it the social historian can learn much about the functional network of close family, servants, friends, and neighbours, about the importance or unimportance of kinship; the historian of religion can gain insight into the piety of the testator[3] and of the books at his disposal;[4] the demographer can often obtain information on the survival of the ancestors, children and grandchildren of the testator; the economist can gather information on the amount of wealth stored in household and personal furnishings and on the important process of redistribution as property passed between generations;[5] the legal historian can learn much of the theory and practice of inheritance as well as of the will itself. Each of these areas of research – and several others as well – is active at the moment; one is tempted to give the time available to one or other of them.

On the other hand, in the present context it is more suitable to concentrate on legal records as such, to indicate the different types that contribute to an understanding of the will and its practical consequences in the lives of people. Furthermore, this procedure will remind the scholar of the play between the complementarity and the competition among the different jurisdictions operative in medieval England[6] and of the care that

the way in which the shares of wife and children were assigned and was to end with the denial that these dependents had a right to a portion of the testator's chattels. See Richard H. Helmholz, 'Legitim in English Legal History,' University of Illinois Law Review 3 (1984) 655–74.

2 M.L. Zell, 'Fifteenth- and Sixteenth-Century Wills as Historical Sources,' Archives 14 (1979) 67–74.

3 P. Heath, 'Urban Piety in the Later Middle Ages: The Evidence of Hull Wills,' in Church, Politics, and Patronage in the Fifteenth Century, ed R.B. Dobson (London 1984) 209–34. See also M.G.A. Vale, Piety, Charity, and Literacy among the York Gentry, 1370–1480, Borthwick Papers 50 (York 1976); and M.L. Zell, 'Use of Religious Preambles as a Measure of Religious Belief in the Sixteenth Century,' Bulletin of the Institute of Historical Research 50 (1977) 246–9.

4 S.H. Cavanaugh, 'A Study of Books Privately Owned in England,' dissertation (University of Pennsylvania 1980); and Joel T. Rosenthal, 'Aristocratic Cultural Patronage and Book Bequests, 1350–1500,' Bulletin of the John Rylands Library 64 (1982) 522–48.

5 J.M. Jennings, 'The Distribution of Landed Wealth in the Wills of London Merchants, 1400–1450,' Mediaeval Studies 39 (1977) 261–80; and H.A. Miskimin, 'The Legacies of London: 1259–1330,' in The Medieval City: Essays in Honor of Robert S. Lopez, ed H.A. Miskimin, David Herlihy, and A.L. Udovitch (New Haven 1977) 209–77.

6 J.M. Jennings, 'London and the Statute of Mortmain: Doubts and Anxieties among Fifteenth-Century London Testators,' Mediaeval Studies 36 (1974) 175–7.

must be taken in drawing conclusions from a will, for it is always necessary to distinguish between the intention of a testator and what was actually done with his estate. Again a choice is necessary: there is much to be said for proceeding immediately to a given set of records, for example, the 'C 1' series at the Public Record Office; they indicate the growing role of the equitable jurisdiction of the chancellor in testamentary disputes as the Middle Ages drew to a close. What is proposed, however, is to follow the will from the moment of its creation to the acquittal of the executors who administered it. The different administrative bodies and courts that might have intervened or have been asked to intervene, as the implementation of the testator's intentions proceeded, will be noted, and the documents they produced described.

The process can be divided into three stages. First, there was the drawing up of the will and its probate, events that usually occurred over a short space of time.[7] Here the records of the institutions that gave probate are most important for they not only inform us of probate and of the attacks on the will that might occur at this stage but also provide the best source for the texts of the wills themselves. The second step was the process whereby the value of the estate was realized: it involved the recovery of the testator's credits and other assets that were in the hands of a variety of persons (members of family, agents, servants, friends, etc), and the payment of his debts. At this stage, more jurisdictions were involved than in either of the others, and it is here that the greatest variety of legal sources is to be noted. Finally, there was the distribution of property according to the intentions of the deceased and, where necessary, a diminution of legacies when available property was inadequate to implement all the testator's bequests.[8] Here, once again, the institutions that gave probate exercised the principal supervision and enforcement, and it is in their records that most information is to be found.

The Will and Its Probate

The process began when the individual made a will. Normally it was written; but, where this final expression of the testator's intention for his property received only an oral statement, the witnesses presented the information to the officer giving probate and a written version of this

---

7 Michael M. Sheehan, *The Will in Medieval England: From the Conversion of the Anglo-Saxons to the End of the Thirteenth Century*, Studies and Texts 6 (Toronto 1963) 206.
8 Ibid 216–18.

nuncupative will was prepared and authenticated with the seal of that officer. Further copies of either type of document were prepared and sealed to be employed during the implementation of the will. Though there is abundant evidence of their use and value when disputes came into court (sometimes many years after the will was proved), comparatively few wills have survived either as originals or as probate copies.[9]

After the death of the testator, the executor presented the will to the proper ecclesiastical authority for probate. Some boroughs allowed the bequest of land; in such cases probate of the part of the will that pertained to this property was obtained from the borough authorities. It is in their records that the earliest probate enrolments are found. Thus, in London, wills appear in the Hustings Roll in 1258;[10] by the last quarter of the thirteenth century several other boroughs are known to have taken up the practice, a practice that increased until, by the end of the Middle Ages, borough enrolment of wills is to be found the length and breadth of the land.[11] Through the same years, manorial court rolls begin to yield information on the wills of the peasantry.[12] There is one serious limitation to the use of these records, however: usually only that part of the will that referred to the bequest of land was engrossed in the register or roll – from the point of view of family history a serious limitation indeed!

For the full text of a will, it is necessary to go to enrolments in the registers of the various ecclesiastical jurisdictions. Wills that for a variety of reasons were presented to the bishop for probate, perhaps as a function of his court of audience, appear first in bishops' registers. The earliest example, a will of 1269, is found in the first surviving Worcester register, that of Bishop Godfrey Giffard.[13] Rather large numbers of testaments

---

9 Some originals as well as probate copies are included among the documents in Public Record Office, *A List of Wills* (London 1968); and Michael M. Sheehan, 'A List of Thirteenth-Century English Wills,' *Genealogists' Magazine* 13 (1961) 259–65 (here pp 8–15).

10 *A Calendar of Wills Proved and Enrolled in the Court of Husting, London, A.D. 1258 – A.D. 1688*, ed Reginald R. Sharpe, 2 vols (London 1889–90).

11 Bristol 1261, Exeter 1263, Norwich 1298, Kingston-upon-Hull 1303, Lincoln 1320, etc. On the survival of urban wills see Norman P. Tanner, *The Church in Late Medieval Norwich, 1370–1532*, Studies and Texts 66 (Toronto 1984) 113–14.

12 Sheehan, *The Will in Medieval England* 253–4.

13 The will of William Beauchamp; a resumé is provided in *Episcopal Registers, Diocese of Worcester: Register of Bishop Godfrey Giffard*, 1: *1268–1273*, ed J.W. Willis Bund, Worcestershire Historical Society (Oxford 1898) 7–9. A *rotulus de testamentis* is mentioned in the register of Oliver Sutton, bishop of Lincoln, in April 1293 (*The Rolls and Register of Bishop Oliver Sutton, 1280–1299*, ed R.M.T. Hill, Lincoln Record

survive in this way from the fourteenth century. The most important series of this kind, one that has been a major source for study since it was edited by E.F. Jacob in 1938, is from the register of Henry Chichele, archbishop of Canterbury (1414–43).[14] In the mean time, with the improvement of office procedures in the bishops' consistories and the courts of the archdeacons, probate registers were kept, beginning at York in 1316, increasingly after 1350, and attaining a daunting scale during the fifteenth century. The great series of prerogative-probate registers of the archbishops of Canterbury and York begin in 1383 and 1389 respectively.[15] They provide a major source for the history of the wealthy families of medieval England. *Wills and Their Whereabouts*, published in 1939 by B.G. Bouwens and carried through subsequent editions by Helen Thacker and Anthony J. Camp,[16] supplemented by *Pre-1858 English Probate Jurisdictions*, published county by county by the Research Department of the Genealogical Society of the Church of Jesus Christ of Latter-Day Saints,[17] provide the best access to the principal archives where wills are to be found.

If the execution of the will proceeded without dispute – that is, if the debts of the deceased were paid and all his credits realized, if those who held his chattels and bequeathed lands released them to the executors without demur, and if the executors delivered movable and immovable goods to the satisfaction of legatees and kept or disposed of the residue as directed in the will – that will would leave no further official record beyond the commission to hear accounts and the act acquitting the

Society 52 [Hereford 1958] IV 79). Similarly, there is a reference to a *liber testamentorum* in the register of Bishop Dalderby in April 1317 (Lincoln, Lincolnshire Archives Office, Episcopal Register 2 f 366). In the following episcopacy, that of Henry Burghersh (AD 1320–40), material touching wills and their administration was assembled in one section of the register (Episcopal Register 5 f 60–82), a section that probably had been a separate cahier. The same practice was adopted by the administration of Bishop Thomas Bek (1342–7), and the texts of wills were included (Episcopal Register 7 f 209–20).

14 *The Register of Henry Chichele, Archbishop of Canterbury, 1414–1443,* 2: *Wills Proved before the Archbishop or His Commissaries*, ed E.F. Jacob and H.C. Johnson (Oxford 1938).

15 On prerogative probate see Sheehan, *The Will in Medieval England* 200–5. For access to these wills see 'Index of Wills Proved in the Prerogative Court of Canterbury,' ed J.C.C. Smith et al, *Index Library* 10, 11, 18, 25, 43–4 (1892–1912); and *Index of Wills in the York Registry, 1389–1514*, ed F. Collins, Yorkshire Archaeological Topographical Association Record Series 6 (York 1989).

16 Canterbury 1968–9.

17 42 vols, ser A 7–48 (Salt Lake City 1967–70).

executors that are sometimes found in probate registers.[18] The process would, of course, generate some documentation: in addition to the inventory that was usually required, receipts, letters of acquittal, etc were exchanged and deeds drawn up for the disposal of real estate. It is probable that this material has not survived on a large scale, though it has been assembled in a few cases and is found scattered through the different archives of England.[19] It would provide a valuable tool for establishing the real value of testators' estates.

At any stage of the execution of a will, there could be dispute. A will was sometimes suppressed by interested parties or simply misplaced.[20] When it was presented for probate, the authenticity of the document could be challenged, as could the freedom or sanity of the testator. Bishops' registers, the records of the bishops' official, and borough records occasionally reveal these problems and their resolution.[21] Ecclesiastical probate of a will was obtained before the document was presented to borough court, but it is clear that this court was not content to accept the decision of the Church's jurisdiction and proceeded, by the examination of the document and its witnesses, to satisfy itself on the validity of the instrument.[22]

18 *The Register of Henry Chichele*, ed Jacob and Johnson II 10, 29.
19 Early examples are published in Sheehan, *The Will in Medieval England* 316–23. This set of documents includes items from the execution of the will of Roger, son of Benedict (d 1287), preserved at the Lincolnshire Archives Office (Dij 50 II 4). A similar series (Dij 60 III 7) is related to the administration of the will of William Watterton (1302–3). Among many examples from the British Library, see Harl Ch 48 C 34, constitution of a proctor by an executor (AD 1258); Topham Ch 50, a receipt issued by an executor (AD 1271); Harl Ch 46 F 45, notice of sale of chattels by executors (AD 1275); Wolley Ch 10 41, a receipt issued to executors (AD 1275).
20 Sheehan, *The Will in Medieval England* 222.
21 Erasures in a will are noted in the Plea and Memoranda Roll of the London Mayor's Court in November 1364: see *Calendar of Plea and Memoranda Rolls Preserved among the Archives of the Corporation of the City of London at the Guildhall*, vols 1 (1323–64), 2 (1364–81), 3 (1381–1412), and 4 (1413–37) ed Arthur H. Thomas; vols 5 (1437–57) and 6 (1458–82) ed Philip E. Jones (Cambridge 1926–61) II 4–5. Forgery is mentioned in the roll of 1470 (*Calendar of Plea and Memoranda Rolls*, ed Jones VI 61–2). Evidence that changes in a will were made by the testator himself is given in a notification of 1279 (London, Guildhall Library, St Paul's Cathedral, Dean and Chapter Archives Box 68 79 2).
22 On the different offices of probate and relations between them see Sheehan, *The Will in Medieval England* 196–211. The requirement of witnesses by the London Court of Husting is stated in 1325 (*Calendar of Plea and Memoranda Rolls*, ed Thomas I 7–8). On the necessity that the testator's seal be appended see ibid II 189.

Resolution of Disputes over Debt

Model wills instructed potential testators to provide first of all for the payment of their debts;[23] it is clear from surviving documents that many followed this advice. Religious preoccupations, manifest in so many wills, logically led to such an attitude. On the other hand, some testaments suggest that it was the testator's intention that debts be paid after the legacies had been delivered, and it is clear from court records that this was sometimes done.[24] Testators also instructed their executors to collect the debts that were owed to them. Occasionally, individual debtors were named in the will, sometimes to be acquitted of their obligation.[25] The testator's credits and debts, their collection and payment, were the part of testamentary administration in which there seems to have been most dispute about claims. It was around this aspect of the will that the courts of various jurisdictions and their officers gathered, and it is here, too, that the widest variety of sources must be consulted.

Through the middle years of the thirteenth century, the royal courts came to recognize the executor as the active and passive representative of the testator.[26] Once that had been done, debt pleas in which the executor was defendant or demandant began to multiply before that jurisdiction. Furthermore, the courts of borough and manor can be shown to be acting in testamentary debt cases by about the same time.[27] The degree of completeness of the representation of the testator by the executor was to prove capable of considerable refinement; the Year Books and treatises of the age record reflection and decision as the matter was clarified. Thus the

---

23 Introduction to a model will of ca 1300: 'In testamenti cujuslibet exordio vel primordio duo sunt principaliter cuilibet testatori, antequam suum condat testamentum, consideranda, videlicet, debita in quibus aliis tenetur, et debita in quibus alii sibi tenentur' (Sheehan, *The Will in Medieval England* 315). For a similar example of ca 1477 see London, BL Add MS 12195 f 3.

24 See *Calendar of Plea and Memoranda Rolls*, ed Thomas II 50; sued for payment of their testator's debt, the executors answered that all the estate has been distributed except fifty pounds left to the testator's son. Saying that common justice demands payment of debt before all else, the court required that the son's bequest be used for the purpose. The executors were not bound to make up the difference.

25 See *The Register of Henry Chichele*, ed Jacob and Johnson II 864, s v 'Debts: remission of'.

26 Sheehan, *The Will in Medieval England* 225–8.

27 *Calendar of Early Mayor's Court Rolls Preserved among the Archives of the Corporation of the City of London at the Guildhall, A.D. 1298–1307*, ed Arthur H. Thomas (Cambridge 1924) 1, 6, 13, and passim.

rolls of the central courts as well as those of the justices in eyre and of boroughs and manors provide an important source for our understanding of the administration of wills, and of the degree of indebtedness of testators. Useful supplementary information is to be found in bishops' registers. Clergy were often involved in the administration of wills, and royal writs ordered their bishops to ensure their presence before the court dealing with testamentary debt. Copies of these writs abound in the bishops' records.[28]

Before the royal jurisdiction was willing to recognize the executor, those exercising probate jurisdiction within the ecclesiastical system had played a role in the collection of the debts and credits of the deceased. Evidence is provided by the fact that, once the central courts were opened to the executor, the writ of prohibition was used to prevent the reception of causes of testamentary debt by the courts Christian.[29] Nevertheless, once the records of the latter jurisdiction begin to survive on a significant scale towards the middle of the fourteenth century, it becomes clear that, in many cases, the principals in disputes over the debts and credits of testators preferred that the matter be settled in the ecclesiastical courts. In a brief but very important article, Richard Helmholz has recently shown that the eclipse of this jurisdiction, a commonplace in the historiography of English law, did not occur and that it continued to be active and presumably effective until the beginning of the sixteenth century.[30] After that time, testamentary pleas of debt virtually disappeared from the records of the ecclesiastical jurisdictions. Professor Helmholz suggests that the change is related to actions based on the Statute of Praemunire that began to be used against claimants in ecclesiastical court

28 An early example is the register of Walter Stapledon, bishop of Exeter (1308–26): see *The Register of Walter de Stapledon, Bishop of Exeter (A.D. 1307–1326)*, ed F.C. Hingeston-Randolph (London 1892) 413–45.

29 The prohibition *de debitis vel catallis nisi sint de testamento vel matrimonio* was available by 1219 (G.B. Flahiff, 'The Writ of Prohibition to Court Christian in the Thirteenth Century,' *Mediaeval Studies* 6 [1944] 277–9), implying that, before that date, the ecclesiastical courts had received cases of testamentary debt. However, as the executor's claim to the unacknowledged debts of the testator was received by royal courts, such debts were no longer considered to be *de testamento*. Bracton admitted, however, that prohibition did not lie 'if a testator bequeathes money owed him, provided the debt was acknowledged and proved in his lifetime, for sums of that kind are reckoned among the testator's goods and belong to executors' (f 407b): see *De legibus et consuetudinibus Angliae*, ed G. Woodbine, trans S. Thorne (Cambridge, Mass. 1977) IV 267.

30 Richard H. Helmholz, 'Debt Claims and Probate Jurisdiction in Historical Perspective,' *American Journal of Legal History* 23 (1979) 68–72.

in matters that pertained to royal justice. These actions, with all their attendant dangers, included testamentary debt.

Thus, for most of the period between 1250 and 1500, the *acta* and registers of the courts Christian are relevant for our understanding of the resolution of disputes touching testamentary debt. As is well known, only a small part of this body of records is available in print.[31] The inquiries of the Church Court Records Working Group promises to provide the basis of information that will soon make it possible to establish priorities and then, it is hoped, proceed to rectify the situation.

Testamentary debt and credit that touched the king's revenue was considered to be a special matter. In principle, the chattels of testators who were indebted to the king or were thought to be so indebted were seized until the matter was settled. If there were dispute, it was resolved by the Exchequer of Pleas. Similarly, where payment of the testator's creditor would enable that creditor to acquit his obligation to the king, the Exchequer could be counted on to assist in the process. As a complement to this, executors often obtained similar help in collecting their testator's credits so that they might the more readily discharge his debts at the Exchequer. As is well known, a like privilege was sometimes extended to officials of the Exchequer. Evidence in these matters is to be found in the memoranda rolls and in the records of the Exchequer of Pleas.[32]

Implementation of the Will and Dismissal

The executor was expected not only to recover the testator's credits and pay his debts but also to gain control of all his movable property, distribute it, and, in some cases, see to the delivery of bequests in land as well. Furthermore, during the period of administration, he had to protect this property from the claims, not to say the depredations, of those who desired it. Individuals often argued that legacies to which they were entitled had not been delivered; executors sometimes failed to recognize the customary claim to part of the property under their control; disagreement as to the meaning of a will was frequent. Executors might be accused of helping themselves to the property they administered – the epithet 'sticky-fingered executor' was surely not gratuitous – or of

31 E.B. Graves, *A Bibliography of English History to 1485* (Oxford 1975) 758–90 and 1091, s v 'Visitations'; D.M. Owen, 'The Records of the Established Church in England Excluding Parochial Records,' *Archives and the User* 1 (London 1970) 30–4, 36–45.
32 *Select Cases in the Exchequer of Pleas, 1236–1304*, ed H. Jenkinson and B. Formoy, Selden Society 48 (London 1932) xlv–xlvi, lv–lvi; Sheehan, *The Will in Medieval England* 223–5.

pocketing the residue.[33] They often disagreed among themselves; they might even deny that they were executors. These problems and many more led to confrontations in the courts. All the jurisdictions mentioned in the discussion of testamentary debt, above, intervened in one or other of these disputes.

General supervision of executors, decision as to the correctness of their actions, general protection of the estate during the time of their administration, and the resolution of claims to legacies of chattels pertained to the ecclesiastical courts.[34] Their records are rich in information on these matters. The various civil jurisdictions also intervened to resolve disagreement. Thus there are many pleas of trespass launched in the central courts and before justices in eyre, in which executors sought to recover chattels taken from them.[35] Claims to 'bairn's part' and 'wife's part,' based on custom, were made before the same jurisdictions and in borough court.[36] Many cases touching wardship – both the custody of the heir and that of the inheritance – occur in royal courts and, occasionally, in borough courts as well.[37] Furthermore, in boroughs like London, executors could be required to deliver legacies to the care of the mayor or others in whom the wardship of the orphan had been established by their testator's will.[38]

33 T.L. Kinney, '"Too Secuturs and an Overseere Make Thre Theves": Popular Attitudes towards False Executors of Wills and Testaments,' *Fifteenth-Century Studies* 3 (1978–80) 93–105.

34 Sheehan, *The Will in Medieval England* 220–30.

35 For example, *Select Bills in Eyre, A.D. 1292–1333*, ed C. Bolland, Selden Society 30 (London 1914) 73, 75–6 (AD 1292–3); London, PRO KB 27/35 m 16 (AD 1276), KB 27/94 m 2 (AD 1285–6), KB 27/95 m 9 (AD 1286–7), KB 27/170 m 24 (AD 1302), KB 27/171 m 38 (AD 1303), KB 27/184 m 52 (AD 1306); *Calendar of Plea and Memoranda Rolls*, ed Thomas I 228 (AD 1349). I am indebted to Professor Sue Sheridan Walker for the references to plea rolls here and in nn 36 and 39.

36 For example, claims of bairn's part: *Year Books of Edward II, 1: 1 and 2 Edward II, A.D. 1307–1309*, ed F.W. Maitland, Selden Society 17 (London 1903) 39–42 (AD 1307); *The Eyre of Northamptonshire, 3–4 Edward III, A.D. 1329–1330*, ed D.W. Sutherland, Selden Society 97–8 (London 1983) II 637–8 (AD 1330); *Calendar of Plea and Memoranda Rolls*, ed Thomas II 213 (1376); claim of wife's part: ibid 168–9 (AD 1373), 215–16 (AD 1375).

37 For example, the ward has been detained, this delaying the execution of the will (*retardationem executionis testamenti*): PRO KB 27/123 m 33 and 27/125 m 9 (AD 1290); discussion of whether a wardship is a chattel and thus bequeathable: *Year Books of Edward II, 10: 5 Edward II, A.D. 1311*, ed G.J. Turner, Selden Society 63 (London 1947) 252–6; defendant in a plea of wardship calls executors, from whom she holds it in lease, to warrant: *Year Books of Edward II, 25: 12 Edward II, Part of Easter and Trinity, 1319*, ed John P. Collas, Selden Society 81 (London 1964) 14.

38 *Calendar of Letter-books of the City of London, Letter-book H*, ed Reginald R. Sharpe

These same courts were willing to examine a defendant's claim that he was not an executor, to consider the authenticity of a will, to decide whether executors had indeed been acquitted of their office before a claim of debt had been moved against them – all of this with a singular willingness to ignore information that could have been supplied on these questions by the ecclesiastical jurisdiction.[39]

The bequest of land was permitted in many of the boroughs; as would be expected, disputes touching the exercise of that right by testators were heard in borough court. Sometimes a bequest of land or the allegation that such property had passed by will was challenged in royal courts by writs of mort d'ancestor or novel disseisin.[40] The same jurisdiction received pleas touching bequests of land held in gavelkind and, as was mentioned above, of land held by executors in virtue of wardship.[41]

Common law estate in land did not permit of its disposal by bequest. The development of the use during the reign of Edward III made it possible for a landowner to enjoy his property and yet, if all went well, arrange that it should pass at his death to the beneficiaries that he had chosen.[42] As this possibility became better understood, the use and the last will were often used to complement each other: the former to place the property in the hand of trustees, the latter to instruct them, at the moment the feoffor chose, as to its future enjoyment.[43] The weakness of the use in itself and in its combination with the last will is obvious: by its very nature it was not admitted to enforcement by common law, so there could be no recourse to that jurisdiction when feoffees failed to honour their trust. In a recent article, in which he demonstrates the truth of a

---

(London 1907) 3 (AD 1375); *Calendar of Plea and Memoranda Rolls*, ed Jones VI 11 (AD 1477).

39 Forgery of will: *Select Cases in the Court of King's Bench*, ed G.O. Sayles, Selden Society 58 (London 1939) III 73 (AD 1298); claim that administration had been completed before the action of debt was begun (the ordinary's quittance of the executors was not deemed sufficient); decision sought as to whether a defendant is executor: *Eyre of London, 14 Edward II, A.D. 1321*, ed Helen M. Cam, Selden Society 85–6 (London 1968–9) 316 (AD 1321); and *Calendar of Plea and Memoranda Rolls*, ed Thomas I 262 (AD 1363). (In both cases a jury was empanelled to decide.)

40 *The Eyre of Northamptonshire*, ed Sutherland II 472–3, 561–2.

41 For example, gavelkind: PRO KB 27/26 m 27d and KB 27/27 m 9 (AD 1276–7); lands held in wardship: LB 27/131 m 25d (AD 1292). See Sue Sheridan Walker, 'Violence and the Exercise of Feudal Guardianship: The Action of "ejectio custodia",' *American Journal of Legal History* 16 (1972) 329.

42 J.M.W. Bean, *The Decline of English Feudalism* (Manchester 1968) 148–79.

43 *Select Cases in Chancery, A.D. 1364–1471*, ed W.P. Baildon, Selden Society 10 (London 1896) xxxix.

suggestion made by Maitland ninety years ago, Richard Helmholz has shown that, by the late fourteenth century, a remedy was provided for this problem before the courts Christian.[44] At almost the same time, the jurisdiction of the chancellor in disputes where there was no remedy in common law began to be extended to the use. Helmholz suggests that, as the chancellor's remedy became known, enforcement of the use was withdrawn from the ecclesiastical jurisdiction. Almost immediately, that complementarity of use and will, mentioned above, can be seen to be operative: the will is advanced as evidence as to the true intent of the feoffor/testator, and the chancellor is asked to enforce it. From an examination of the first bundles of early chancery proceedings it becomes clear that a significant part of the surviving bills are concerned with the execution of uses and that in many cases the indication of the feoffor's intention is provided by his last will.[45] Thus, from one point of view, the action before the chancellor can be seen as one intended to enforce the delivery of a bequest of land.

Furthermore, as the fifteenth century passed, bills were presented touching an ever wider set of problems that arose from the administration of wills: the validity of the document itself, claims for or against the testator's estate, and embezzlement by the executors, to mention but a few of them.[46] Thus, with all their limitations, the Early Chancery Proceedings provide an ever more important source for the history of the will in the late Middle Ages. One has but to spend a few hours trying to untangle a case presented by a bill that involves a use or uses, a will, and a marriage agreement to realize that, in this body of records, there is much to be learned about the practice of testamentary execution and about the network of relationships and agreements that supported the families of those days.[47] It is a commonplace that there is need of extended research in this daunting set of documents. When it is done, the history of the English testament will be much better known.

44 Richard H. Helmholz, 'The Early Enforcement of Uses,' *Columbia Law Review* 79 (1979) 1503–13.
45 Eg London, PRO C 1 17/1–150: 59 items, more than a third, involve the use and usually a will as well (AD 1406–57).
46 Timothy S. Haskett, 'The Equity Side of the English Court of Chancery in the Late Middle Ages: A Method of Approach,' Ph.D. dissertation (University of Toronto 1987) 449–77. Some uses, by which all property, in chattels as well as in land, passed into the hands of trustees to be distributed according to the intention of the feoffor, became virtual replacements of the testament: eg PRO C 1 17/88, 147.
47 Eg PRO C 1 17/24 6. Cf W.E. Jones, *The Elizabethan Court of Chancery* (Oxford 1967) 400–17.

11

Theory and Practice:
Marriage of the Unfree and the Poor
in Medieval Society

About the year 1000, a Swabian serf named Heimrad asked freedom of the lady he had served as priest.[1] The request was granted, and he began a life of wandering that eventually led him to Rome and Jerusalem, thence back to Germany. Heimrad lived in extreme poverty, trusting in God for his daily needs. His prayer, his preaching, and his eccentric appearance and manners excited admiration in some, revulsion and fear in others. This way of life was, in fact, a foretaste of one that was to become rather common by the end of the eleventh century; but for the moment, as his biographer tells us, the limitations of believers who met him were such that he hid his light under a bushel.[2]

On his return to Germany, Heimrad so impressed Arnold, abbot of Hersfeld, whom he met at the monastery of Memleben, that he was invited to become a monk. Ever the individualist, Heimrad refused to take vows or wear the habit, though he did live with the community. One day he announced in chapter that he wished to withdraw. Asked for his reasons, he replied that he did not think that he could save his soul if he

---

In this study, I am much indebted to the insights of my late colleague, Reverend Arthur P. Gibson, whose assistance proved crucial in the reflections that follow. The essay was read in an earlier form at the Assumption University Symposium, Windsor, Ontario, 26–7 October 1979.

1 'cum esset in obsequio cuiusdam matronae ... ipse libertati se donari peciit,' *Vita sancti Haimeradi presbiteri auctore Ekkeberto*, ed Rudolf Köpke, MGH Scriptores 10 (Hannover 1852; repr Leipzig 1925) 599–601. The *Vita* is cited by Rosalind B. Brooke in *The Coming of the Friars*, Historical Problems: Studies and Documents 24 (London 1975) 40–4.

2 'sed propter credentium penuriam lucerna diu latebat sub modio' (*Vita sancti Haimeradi*, ed Köpke 599; cf Matt 5:15).

continued to live in the monastery. The abbot was furious; he kicked Heimrad and had him ejected. As he waited at the door of the guest house, Heimrad remarked that neither the monks nor the abbot had treated him with sufficient respect, given his birth. He asserted that his was a noble line and that he was brother of the emperor.[3] The monk who overheard the remark was not impressed, but he brought Heimrad back to the abbot, who had him flogged until he finally explained his meaning: had not St Paul taught 'sive servus sive liber, omnes in Christo unum sumus,'[4] and did Christ himself not seek to make us understand that we have one Father in heaven, calling all men brothers (Matt 23:9)? The abbot was no more impressed than the monk had been; Heimrad was brutally beaten and thrown out of the monastery.

Heimrad's sorrows were far from ended, though eventually he was able to find a bishop who understood him and would provide protection and peace. The happy ending, however, is not the part of the story that is important for the purpose of this article. It is, rather, Heimrad's self-evaluation as contrasted with others' judgment of him. Here one meets the problem of understanding how, at any given time in the history of mankind, members of the lowest classes were valued by themselves and by their 'superiors' and whether, in those cases where the said superiors maintained that certain rights and responsibilities pertained to all, they actually intended that the lowest classes should exercise them.[5] How was a peasant like Heimrad judged by his lord? How was he judged by his peers? How did he see himself within the social order? For the under-

---

3 'fertur interea in hanc vocem prorupisse, non recte se nec satis honorifice pro nata-
libus suis tractatum fuisse a monachis atque ab abbate, latuisse illos generis sui
nobilitatem, imperatoris fratrem se esse' (ibid 600).

4 Gal 3:28: 'Non est Judaeus, neque Graecus; non est servus, neque liber; non est
masculus, neque femina. Omnes enim vos unum estis in Christo Jesu.'

5 See the reflections of Marc Bloch, 'How and Why Ancient Slavery Came to an End,'
in *Slavery and Serfdom in the Middle Ages: Selected Essays by Marc Bloch*, trans William
R. Beer (Berkeley 1975) 10–12. 'Heightening of consciousness' is the current expression that seeks to describe this awakening to an awareness of the implications of
a theoretical position (the experience of Heimrad or, perhaps, of his biographer). The
tendency to avoid facing the consequences of one's position seems to be part of the
human condition: one might mention Aristotle's discussion of human nature and its
dignity in a society of which a large proportion was without rights; the reflections on
the rights of man by Thomas Jefferson, a slaveholder; more recently, public manifestations of surprise and horror over the death by freezing of a mother and her
children in London during the bitter winter of 1984–5, when Archbishop Runcie
pointed out that death in this manner was all too common among the elderly poor.

standing of the medieval period of European history, a period during which the majority of society were members of the unfree peasantry or poor dwellers in the town, much might be gained if criteria of judgment could be established that would assist in answering those questions.

The century during which Heimrad lived saw the beginning of rapid progress in the elaboration of the Christian ideal of marriage and its acceptance by a significant portion of society. In those years, too, it was recognized that marital questions should be judged by the ecclesiastical jurisdiction, a decision of major importance in the order of practice.[6] The ideal in question differed in several ways from the understanding of marriage that had governed the ménages of all classes in the past. And it was very demanding. It is the intention of this article to examine the questions suggested by Heimrad's experience as they apply to the implementation of this ideal among the lower levels of society in Western Europe during the period when it was finally given shape.

I

It is somewhat surprising, given the importance attached to the institution of marriage in sociology and anthropology, that, until comparatively recently, little attention had been paid to its history. Sociologists were long content to ignore the possibility that knowledge of the earlier stages of the institution they studied might lead to deeper understanding of contemporary structures.[7] Social historians, though much interested in the history of the family, paid scant attention to marriage except inasmuch as it was part of the system of family recruitment and property management. For many years it was largely the work of historians of law and, to a lesser extent, of theology that maintained interest in the history of marriage as such. Recently, especially with the period of major social change that

6 The claim was advanced as early as the Council of Agde (506), but its general acceptance was delayed until about 1100; see Pierre Daudet, *Etudes sur l'histoire de la juridiction matrimoniale: Les origines carolingiennes de la compétence exclusive de l'Eglise (France et Germanie)* (Paris 1933), and *L'établissement de la compétence de l'Eglise en matière de divorce et de consanguinité (France Xe–XIIe siècles)* (Paris 1941).

7 See John Mogey, 'Introduction' to *Changes in the Family* in a special number of *International Social Science Journal* 14:3 (1962) 411–24. Having presented the scholarly accomplishments of the years following the Second World War, he suggested lines of future work; the value of historical studies was virtually ignored. Contrast the essay, seventeen years later, by Michael Anderson, 'The Relevance of Family History,' in *The Sociology of the Family: New Directions for Britain*, ed Christopher C. Harris, Sociological Review Monograph 28 (Keele 1979) 49–73.

began after the Second World War, many disciplines have tended to come together in an ever deepening study of marriage and the family. In that rather exciting process several important matters have become clear. One of them is that the institution of marriage took a direction in the twelfth century, the implications of which are still being unfolded in our own day.

That development had many causes. One of the most important was the formation of a theory and ideal of marriage that not only was new in several aspects but had powerful institutions prepared to teach and, to a certain extent, to enforce it. Many distinct traditions were contributory to the development. They were derived from social and religious usages of different peoples. Christian thinkers slowly developed a broad theory of human sexuality in which marriage found its place. These notions were in relationship – sometimes of symbiosis, sometimes of conflict – with older traditions among the peoples to whom the Christian religion had spread. By the end of the twelfth century the theory was assuming a degree of completeness and consistency that was new, and it was becoming more and more recognized that it should be the ideal of society.[8]

In the anthropology that became generally accepted, human sexuality was seen as an imperious urge, one that especially revealed the damage done to the pristine order within mankind's appetites by the sin of Adam and Eve. The Christian ideal was to deny and sublimate the irrational element in that sexual appetite by a life of continence, a life usually within the framework of a religious order or the clerical state, or to channel the exercise of that appetite by the mutual service of husband and wife in marriage. Each of the three elements of this synthesis – the limited exercise of sexuality, the notion of the married state as the exclusive place of its exercise, and the view of the celibate state as a viable and honourable alternative to marriage – entered into conflict with tendencies of mankind and, more particularly, with the different social structures in which Christianity expressed itself. Yet, in principle, the ideal was to triumph. Though several aspects of this development have not yet been investigated, it is already clear that theologians, poets, lawyers, and moral

8 For the stages of this development see Gabriel Le Bras, 'Mariage: La doctrine du mariage chez les théologiens èt les canonistes depuis l'an mille,' in DTC 9 II (1927) 2123–2317; and, for a detailed examination of the earlier period, Korbinian Ritzer, Le mariage dans les églises chrétiennes du Ier au XIe siècle (Paris 1970); for a discussion in a broader context, see George H. Joyce, Christian Marriage: An Historical and Doctrinal Study, Heythrop Series I, (London–New York 1933). Cf Robert Fossier, Histoire sociale de l'Occident médiéval (Paris 1970) 124–7; and Philippe Ariès, 'Le mariage indissoluble,' Communications 35 (1982) 123–37.

guides analysed the nature of marriage, set out the conditions that made it possible, decided on the precise way in which the marriage bond was established, contributed to the design of the procedure of marriage preparation and the liturgies of the wedding itself, concluded that the relationship should be exclusive and permanent, and explored the love that should grow between the couple.[9]

Each of these elements is of considerable interest, but, for the present purpose, it is sufficient to consider two of them. First, the relationship was seen to be permanent and exclusive, one in which each spouse owed a sexual debt to the other, a debt not lightly to be denied. Second, the role of consent in establishing the marriage bond: the interest in the part played by the consent of the spouses led to a discussion in which it was finally decided that there was no marriage without their consent and that, when all was said and done, the consent of no other person or group was necessary. There was much encouragement of the traditional view that family and lordship should play their part in the choice of spouses and their endowment, but, by 1200, the principle had been stated that, if there were no impediment between a couple and they consented to marry, no one could prevent them from doing so.[10]

9 On the last point, much progress has been made during the last few years. See Philippe Ariès, 'L'amour dans le mariage,' *Communications* 35 (1982) 116–22; Johan Chydenius, *Love and the Medieval Tradition*, Societas scientiarum Fennica: Commentationes humanarum litterarum 58 (Helsinki 1977); Georges Duby, *Que sait-on de l'amour en France au XIIe siècle?*, Zaharoff Lecture for 1982–3 (Oxford 1983); Jean-Louis Flandrin, 'Contraception, mariage, et relations amoureuses dans l'Occident chrétien,' *Annales: Economies, sociétés, civilisations* 24 (1969) 1370–90; Fossier, *Histoire sociale de l'Occident médiéval* 131–2, 158–68; Jean Leclercq, 'The Development of a Topic in Medieval Studies in the Eighties: An Interdisciplinary Perspective on Love and Marriage,' in *Literary and Historical Perspectives of the Middle Ages: Proceedings of the 1981 SEMA Meeting*, ed Patricia W. Cummins, Patrick W. Conner, and Charles W. Connell (Morgantown, W. Va. 1982) 20–37, and *Love in Marriage in Twelfth-Century Europe*, University of Tasmania Occasional Papers 13 (Hobart 1978); *Love and Marriage in the Twelfth Century*, ed Willy Van Hoecke and Andries Welkenhuysen, Mediaevalia Lovaniensia, Series 1, Studia 8 (Louvain 1981); Fabian Parmisano, 'Love and Marriage in the Middle Ages,' *New Blackfriars* 50 (1969) 599–608, 649–60; Sylvette Rouillan-Castex, 'L'amour et la société féodale,' *Revue historique* 272 (1984) 295–329; and Hubert Silvestre, 'La prière des époux selon Rupert de Liège,' *Studi medievali*, 3rd ser, 24 (1983) 725–8.

10 See John T. Noonan, Jr, 'Power to Choose,' *Viator* 4 (1973) 419–34; Charles Donahue, Jr, 'The Policy of Alexander the Third's Consent Theory of Marriage,' in *Proceedings of the Fourth International Congress of Medieval Canon Law*, Toronto, 21–5 August 1972, ed Stephan Kuttner, Monumenta iuris canonici, Series C: Subsidia 5

This theory of sexuality, marriage, and religious life was developed at the time when Europe, led by the reforming religious element within it, was coming to a homogeneity of intellectual life unknown before, so that the notions and ideals sketched above were, potentially at least, applicable anywhere in the Latin Church. Part of the progress made in the research of recent years touching the history of the family and marriage has been in examining the mode of transmission of these ideas, the tempo and depth of their penetration of society, and the resulting practice.[11]

Even from the rather general and abstract presentation of the development that has just been made it will be clear that some of the elements of that synthesis would collide with the accepted usages of different parts of Europe. Furthermore, even if the ideal in question were intended to be universally applicable, the social structures of the areas in which it was applied varied greatly, so that the mode and degree of reception might be expected to be diverse. Recognizing this, Georges Duby examined the local understanding of family, marriage, and sexuality operative among the aristocracy of the Mâconnais during the eleventh and twelfth centuries, confronted it with the model developed by religious thinkers, and showed how older usages adapted to the new ideal.[12] In time, it is to be hoped, a similar procedure will be applied in the examination of the same process in other regions and among other social groups.

Among these groups are, of course, the peasantry and that large but virtually silent part of the urban population, the poor. Duby's emphasis on the necessity of local study is important here, for it is abundantly clear that custom varied not only between country and country, region and region but also (though less drastically) between manor and manor, town and town. Prior to these local studies, however, there are other, more fundamental problems to be addressed, problems of mentality, problems touching how the peasant and the poor were seen by those more educated classes who formulated the system that spread throughout Europe. Heim-

(Vatican City 1976) 251–81, and 'The Canon Law of the Formation of Marriage and Social Practice in the Later Middle Ages,' *Journal of Family History* 8 (1983) 144–58.

11 Michael M. Sheehan, 'Choice of Marriage Partner in the Middle Ages: Development and Mode of Application of a Theory of Marriage,' *Studies in Medieval and Renaissance History* n s 1 (1978) 1–33 (here pp 87–117). See Jack Goody, *The Development of the Family and Marriage in Europe* (Cambridge 1983) 103–56; and David Herlihy, *Medieval Households* (Cambridge, Mass. 1985) 79–88.

12 Georges Duby, *Medieval Marriage: Two Models from Twelfth-Century France*, trans Elborg Forster, The Johns Hopkins Symposia in Comparative History 11 (Baltimore 1978).

rad, an unfree peasant whose priesthood poses a question as to the application of the laws that forbade the ordination of members of the servile class, concluded that the Christian anthropology, based on the words of Christ and the writings of St Paul, had serious practical consequences that enhanced his personal value. In the century that followed many others were to draw conclusions touching social and political life as well as religious theory along similar lines. On the other hand, the behaviour of the abbot and monks at Hersfeld left little doubt that they disagreed with Heimrad. It might be said that the abbot's overreaction indicates a fear that Heimrad was right in his assertion, but the general impression created by the account is that the claim was considered to be nonsense.[13]

What is involved here is the general question whether the social consequences of a Christian anthropology, its demands and its assurance of rights – the ideal of marriage would be one of them – were considered applicable to all of society. Did the canonists, civil lawyers, and theologians who hammered out the ideal of sexuality with its marital and celibate components consider it to be suitable for the members of the lowest classes as well as for the knight or the citizen of a town? Duby assigned the source of the two models of marriage to members of the aristocracy on the one hand and members of the clergy on the other. The consequences of this difference have probably been exaggerated, however, since it cannot be too much emphasized that both groups came from the same families.[14] Members of the lowest classes rarely if ever played a significant role in the development of the new theory of marriage. Furthermore, those who developed that theory were members of the families and religious institutions that considered it their right to control larger or smaller segments of the lives of unfree peasants. Did they think that the high ideals of marriage that they had developed applied to those who ploughed their fields? Here we meet the difficult question of the extent to which the rules of the society were expected to apply to a subculture, a subculture often looked upon as a more or less criminal underworld.[15] Furthermore, even if society's leaders were in agreement

13 This point of view is nicely revealed in the revised *Butler's Lives of the Saints*, published by Herbert Thurston and Donald Attwater in 1956. The editors write: 'His biographer insinuates, let us note, that he *only* meant that he, like the rest of mankind, was a brother of Christ' (italics added). The feast of St Heimrad of Essingham is 28 June; see *Butler's Lives* (London 1956) II 661.
14 Cf Herlihy, *Medieval Households* 86.
15 See Fossier, *Histoire sociale de l'Occident médiéval* 145–7, 242–3, 258–60.

that such was the case, to what extent did members of the lower orders see marriage so understood as desirable? Were efforts made to convince them of this? Were legal and institutional controls devised to ensure compliance and, if so, to what degree?

II

By the late eleventh and twelfth centuries, when the new theory of marriage was assuming its full development, the last vestiges of slavery were disappearing in northern Europe.[16] Christianity had been born in a world familiar with that institution. As the new faith spread north and west to the tribes conquered by Rome, and later, when the barbarians streamed into the weakening Empire, it met slavery among them as well. The missionaries who penetrated the Celtic extremities of Europe, the German homeland, and the realms of the Slavs encountered a similar institution.[17] In the period before the birth of Christ and again in the third

16 Useful introductory discussions of this process are in Bloch, *Slavery and Serfdom*; cf Charles-Edmond Perrin, 'Le servage en France et en Allemagne au moyen-âge,' in *Relazioni del x Congresso internationale di scienze storiche, Storia del medioevo*, Biblioteca storica Sansoni 24 (Florence 1955) III 213–45; and Moses I. Finley, *Ancient Slavery and Modern Ideology* (New York 1980) 11–66, and 'Between Slavery and Freedom,' *Comparative Studies in Society and History* 6 (1964–5) 233–49. See János M. Bak, 'Serfs and Serfdom: Words and Things,' *Review* 4 (1980) 3–18; Jacques Boussard, 'Serfs et "colliberti" (XIe–XIIe siècles),' *Bibliothèque de l'Ecole des chartes* 107 (1947–8) 205–34; Pierre Dockès, *La libération médiévale* (Paris 1979) 16–22, 98–139; Philippe Dollinger, *L'évolution des classes rurales en Bavière depuis la fifin de l'époque carolingienne jusqu'au milieu du XIIIe siècle* (Paris 1949) 208–9, 253–63; Fossier, *Histoire sociale de l'Occident médiéval* 61–7, 161–8; Paul Ourliac, 'Le servage à Toulouse au XIIe et XIIIe siècles,' in *Economies et sociétés au moyen âge: Mélanges offerts à Edouard Perroy*, Séries études 5 (Paris 1973) 249–61; Pierre Petot, 'Evolution numérique de la classe servile en France du IXe au XIVe siècle,' *Recueils de la Société Jean Bodin*, 2: *Le servage*, 2nd ed (Brussels 1959) 159–68; Michael M. Postan, *The Famulus: The Estate Labourer in the XIIth and XIIIth Centuries, Economic History Review*, suppl 2 (London 1954); Werner Rösener, *Bauern im Mittelalter* (Munich 1985) 18–31; C. Van de Kieft, 'Les "colliberti" et l'évolution du servage dans la France centrale et occidentale (Xe–XIIe siècle),' *Tijdschrift voor Rechtsgeschiedenis* 32 (1964) 363–95; Charles Verlinden, *L'esclavage dans l'Europe médiévale* (Bruges–Ghent 1955–77) I 729–48, II 1 n2, 91–109, and passim; C.R. Whittaker, 'Circe's Pigs: From Slavery to Serfdom in the Later Roman World,' *Slavery and Abolition* 8 (1987) 88–122.

17 Francis Conte, *Les Slaves: Aux origines des civilisations d'Europe centrale et orientale (VIe–XIIIe siècles)*, L'évolution de l'humanité (Paris 1986) 89–93, 183–4, 265–6, 416, 422–6; Wendy Davies, *Wales in the Early Middle Ages* (Leicester 1982) 53–64; Carl

and following centuries, when military operations were endemic on the frontier of the Empire and even within its borders, there was a constant supply of slaves as the booty of war. They provided household servants and manned many of the larger enterprises of the time in agriculture, mining, and manufacturing. But, in a process lasting many centuries, the economic, political, and ideological structures of the region became less suitable for slavery. In different regions and at different tempos the slave supply diminished, the enterprises that had been able to make profitable use of slave gangs were no longer feasible, and a growing embarrassment that fellow Christians should be one's slaves lessened their attractiveness.[18] At the same time, certain liberties were acquired by custom and even by law so that the 'slave' was no longer the rightless one of the early Empire.[19] Many were established on lands over which they enjoyed a degree of control, a situation that encouraged them to establish a ménage that was their own.[20] At the same time, as the seigniory established itself in one or other of its forms, many of those among the lower ranks of

Koehne, *Die Geschlechtsverbindungen der Unfreien im fränkischen Recht*, Untersuchungen zur deutschen Staats- und Rechtsgeschichte 22 (Breslau 1888) 1–10; Niels Skyum-Nielsen, 'Nordic Slavery in an International Setting,' *Mediaeval Scandinavia* 11 (1982) 126–48.

18 See *The Cambridge Economic History of Europe*, 1: *The Agrarian Life of the Middle Ages*, ed Michael M. Postan, 2nd ed (Cambridge 1966) 246–55 and bibliography, 787–8; Bloch, 'How and Why Ancient Slavery Came to an End' 25; Georges Duby, 'Sur les voies ouvertes par Marc Bloch: Esclavage et servage au moyen âge,' *Annales: Economies, sociétés, civilisations* 12 (1957) 123–6; Jacques Heers, *Esclaves et domestiques au moyen âge dans le monde méditerranéen* (Paris 1981) 95–121.

19 See the discussion of the meaning of freedom in this context in Marc Bloch, 'Personal Liberty and Servitude in the Middle Ages, Particularly in France: Contribution to a Class Study,' in *Slavery and Serfdom* 66–91, 203–26; Pierre Petot, 'L'hommage servile: Essai sur la nature juridique de l'hommage,' *Revue historique de droit français et étranger* [henceforth RHDFE], 4th ser, 6 (1927) 86–7; Theodore J. Rivers, '*Symbola, manumissio, et libertas Langobardorum*: An Interpretation of *gaida* and *gisil* in Edictus Rothari 224 and Its Relationship to the Concept of Freedom,' *Zeitschrift der Savigny-Stiftung für Rechtsgeschichte: Germanistische Abteilung* 95 (1978) 57–78.

20 See Bloch, 'How and Why Ancient Slavery Came to an End' 4–6, 14; Boussard, 'Serfs et "colliberti"' 234; André Déléage, *La vie rurale en Bourgogne jusqu'au début du onzième siècle* (Mâcon 1941) I 552; Dockès, *La libération médiévale* 19–20, 140; Herlihy, *Medieval Households* 56–78; Postan, *The Famulus* 11–14. The process resulted in the creation of servile ménages, a situation that probably encouraged religious thinkers to reflect on the quality of the relationship. On the other hand, the fact that these unions came to be considered to be marriage tended to consolidate the servile household (see Bloch, ibid 14).

freemen became more and more dependent on their lords and lost their liberty. By the end of the eleventh century, they and those who in a variety of ways, either recently or in a remote past, had risen above their position as slaves coalesced into a servile peasant group, denoted by an embarrassingly varied set of terms but that can, for present purposes, be called serfs.[21] It is these serfs and many of those from among them who fled to the 'freedom' of the towns – groups that constituted a much higher proportion of the population than was ever the case with the slaves of the earlier period – that are the special object of this study.

The slave, in the older sense of the term *servus*, continued as a significant element in the population of the regions around the north shore of the Mediterranean.[22] Here, where there was a constant war with non-Christian peoples or when oriental Christians fled before Islamic armies, there was a source of captives and refugees that continued the slave class through the Middle Ages. Eventually the acceptance of the idea of slavery, and slaves themselves, would be carried by Iberian explorers to the worlds they discovered.

Christian thinkers and Christian thinking played a role in the process whereby, through most of Europe, slavery disappeared.[23] To the modern mind it is often a surprise, sometimes a scandal, that an institution which involved such a fundamental denial of human worth was not confronted directly by Christ and by his followers. By and large, their approach was very different.[24] The principle was that invoked by Heimrad: all men are

21 In the case of Anglo-Saxon England, an area in which slavery resulting from captivity continued to be practised, there is evidence of a significant slave population and slave trade up to and after the Norman Conquest. Within two generations, however, the slave had virtually disappeared (Postan, ibid). One indication of the change is the frequent mention of slaves, their rights and obligations in earlier councils and synods. After the condemnation of traffic in slaves at the Council of Westminster (1102) there was to be no further reference to them. See c39 in *Councils and Synods with Other Documents Relating to the English Church, 1: A.D. 871–1204*, ed Dorothy Whitelock, Michael Brett, and Christopher N.L. Brooke (Oxford 1981) II 681.

22 See Verlinden, *L'esclavage* I 246–629, 745–822, and II passim; Heers, *Esclaves et domestiques* 66–78.

23 See Bloch, 'How and Why Ancient Slavery Came to an End' 10–25; Verlinden, ibid I 31, 40.

24 See J. Kevin Coyle, 'Empire and Eschaton: The Early Church and the Question of Domestic Relationships,' *Eglise et théologie* 12 (1981) 75; John F. Maxwell, *Slavery and the Catholic Church: The History of Catholic Teaching Concerning the Moral Legitimacy of the Institution of Slavery* (Chichester 1975) 1–43 and the bibliography assembled there; and Raoul Naz, 'Esclave,' DDC 5 (1954) 448–54. Some writers did propose the end of slavery. Two late Carolingian examples are Smaragdus of St-Mihiel, in his *Via*

brothers; before God there is really no difference between slave and free. The immediate practical consequence was provided by St Paul in his Epistle to Philemon. Here there was no questioning the fact that Onesimus was a slave, but Philemon was urged to treat him as a brother. On the other hand, Onesimus returned to his master at Paul's bidding and, it can be presumed, was expected to accept his position as slave and serve his master with the generous spirit that both Paul and Peter recommended in their letters.[25] It was not to be a confrontation with the institution but an amelioration of the conditions of the slave's life which contributed to the fact that, in the end, he could no longer be considered to be a slave at all. One of the areas in which these principles were applied was that of slave marriage.

In Roman law, though under favourable conditions a slave might establish a stable, even a devoted, ménage, that relationship was at best a *contubernium*. The slave could not have *conubium*, the legal capacity for marriage in the full sense of the word (*matrimonium iustum*).[26] From what has been learned of Celtic and Germanic custom, the slave's situation was similar among them as well.[27] Even though a couple lived together and

regia (ca 825) ch 30 (PL 102 967–8), and Jonas of Orléans, in *De institutione laicali* II 22–3 (PL 106 213–18); see Fossier, *Histoire sociale de l'Occident médiéval* 43, 51, 65.

25 Eph 6:5; Col 3:22; 1 Pet 2:18.

26 Percy E. Corbett, *The Roman Law of Marriage* (Oxford 1930) 24–67; Arnold M. Duff, *Freedmen in the Early Roman Empire* (Oxford 1928; repr Cambridge 1958) 59–60. On the quality of the relationship in some ménages of slave and slave, free and slave, see Beryl Rawson, 'The Roman Family,' in *The Family in Ancient Rome: New Perspectives*, ed Beryl Rawson (Ithaca, N.Y. 1986) 26, 253–4. and 'Family Life among the Lower Classes at Rome in the First Two Centuries of the Empire,' *Classical Philology* 61 (1966) 71–83; Orlando Patterson, *Slavery and Social Death: A Comparative Study* (Cambridge, Mass. and London 1982) 186–9; Richard P. Saller, 'Slavery and the Roman Family,' *Slavery and Abolition* 8 (1987) 65–87; Richard P. Saller and Brent D. Shaw, 'Tombstones and Roman Family Relations in the Principate: Civilians, Soldiers, and Slaves,' *Journal of Roman Studies* 74 (1984) 124–56, especially 134–9; Susan Treggiari, 'Contubernales in CIL 6,' *Phoenix* 35 (1981) 42–69; P.R.C. Weaver, 'The Status of Children in Mixed Marriages,' in *The Family in Ancient Rome*, ed Rawson 145–69. I am much indebted to Professor Saller for his advice on this matter.

27 See William W. Buckland, *The Roman Law of Slavery* (London 1908) 75–6; T.M. Charles-Edwards, 'Naw Cynyweddi Teithiawg: Nine Forms of Union in Wales, Ireland, and India,' in *The Welsh Law of Women: Studies Presented to Professor Daniel A. Binchy on His Eightieth Birthday, 3 June 1980*, ed Dafydd Jenkins and Morfydd E. Owen (Cardiff 1980) 23–39; Elizabeth Eames, 'Mariage et concubinage légal en Norvège à l'époque des Vikings,' *Annales de Normandie* 2 (1952) 195–208; Edith Ennen, *Frauen im Mittelalter* (Munich 1984) 85–6; Koehne, *Die Geschlechtsverbindungen der Unfreien* 1–23.

brought children into the world, they had no power over themselves, each other, or their children, and the set of relationships that they had established could be destroyed at the wish of those who controlled their lives.

This was not acceptable to some Christian teachers.[28] The problem became apparent in an ill-tempered attack on St Callistus I, bishop of Rome, about 220, in which St Hippolytus accused him of recognizing the union of a free woman and a slave as marriage and of accepting a secret union as valid.[29] Just how widely this judgment was accepted within the Christian community of Rome or even further afield is unknown. (The voice of Christianity in the wider society was as yet a weak one.) But the case touched the marriage of the slave and the ease with which, from the point of view of a church leader, an acceptable union could be brought about. As such, it was heavy with promise for the future.

Christian teaching on marriage was to see a remarkable development during the first millennium. One aspect of that teaching is of special importance to the present analysis. It had appeared in St Paul's earliest discussion of the matter in a context where the celibate life was presented as an ideal. Here he did not consider the childbearing aspect of marriage but, recognizing the imperious quality of the sex urge, presented marriage as the means of assuaging it without sin (1 Cor 7:1–9).[30] The Pauline text leaves little doubt that its author considered this to be the usual human condition.[31] This notion was to play an important role in future dis-

28 Cf Ex 21:1–6. On the contribution of the Jewish tradition to this attitude see Joseph Freisen, *Geschichte des canonischen Eherechts bis zum Verfall der Glossenliteratur* (Paderborn 1893) 60–1 nn 9 and 11. See Louis M. Epstein, *Marriage Laws in the Bible and the Talmud*, Harvard Semitic Series (Cambridge, Mass. 1942) 34–66; Ze'ev W. Falk, *Introduction to Jewish Law of the Second Commonwealth*, Arbeiten zur Geschichte des antiken Judentums und des Urchristentums 11 (Leiden 1972–8) 11 263–9; Verlinden, *L'esclavage* 11 21.

29 Hippolytus, *Refutatio omnium haeresium*, ed Miroslav Marcovich, Patristische Texte und Studien 25 (Berlin–New York 1986) 355–6. See the discussion in Johannes Quasten, *Patrology*, 2: *The Ante-Nicene Literature after Irenaeus* (Westminster, Md. 1953) 204–6.

30 See Ariès, 'L'amour dans le mariage' 116–18.

31 Cf Ariès, ibid 119; and James A. Brundage, 'Concubinage and Marriage in Medieval Canon Law,' *Journal of Medieval History* 1 (1975) 3. This notion that spouses had a right to sexual access is the principle that underlay the requirement that the Crusader, who would usually leave his wife at home, was to obtain her permission before doing so. Only in a case of extreme necessity – Innocent III judged such to be the case at the time of the Fourth Crusade – was it concluded that this obligation must yield to the higher one of defending Christendom: see James A. Brundage, 'The Crusader's Wife: A Canonistic Quandary,' *Studia Gratiana* 12 (1967) 425–41.

cussions, especially after it had been expounded in detail in the careful analysis of the married state by St Augustine.[32] From this point of view, if a slave were considered a mature Christian, he had a right to marry where it was necessary to avoid sexual sin. The question remains – and this is but a restatement of the question with which this study began – whether Christian thinkers thought the members of the servile class to be of sufficient moral responsibility to make this argument a compelling one. The answer to this question is complex. It involves our understanding of both theoretical and practical reflection and the development of modes of implementation that went on simultaneously over many centuries. For purposes of analysis it seems best to distinguish three parts in the question so that they may be examined separately. It must be remembered, however, that the three processes involved went on simultaneously and that all, in fact, were parts of one multifaceted development. The questions are: first, the moral responsibility of the servile class; second, the possibility both theoretical and practical of a true Christian marriage between persons in whom a third party had rights; third, the consequences of the accepted mode of establishing the marriage bond.

1. The Moral Responsibility of the Servile Class

A basic principle of ethical theory is that there are degrees of responsibility in the act of any individual; medieval moral thinking was of considerable refinement on this matter.[33] To what extent was the slave considered liable for his actions? An examination of the discussion of the circumstances of a moral act found in the penitential books shows that it was

---

32 De bono coniugali, ed Josef Zycha, Corpus scriptorum ecclesiasticorum latinorum 41 5 pars 3 (Prague, Vienna, and Leipzig 1900) ch 1–10, 187–202; St Augustine, Treatises on Marriage and Other Subjects, trans Charles T. Wilcox et al, Fathers of the Church 27 (New York 1955) 9–25. Augustine situated this 'good' in the context of all the goods of marriage. A good summary of earlier patristic writing on the necessity of making marriage possible as a means to channel sexual desire is in Ritzer, Le mariage 97–9.

33 For remarkable examples dealing with the degrees of responsibility of those taking part in military operations, see Reginon of Prüm (ca 906), Libri duo de synodalibus causis et disciplinis ecclesiasticis, ed F.G.A. Wasserschleben (Leipzig 1840; repr Graz 1964) cap. CCCIV 142; a letter of Gregory V (998): see Gratian, Decretum C12 q2 c8; the penitential articles touching those who fought in the battle of Hastings, issued 1067×70 (Councils and Synods 1, ed Whitelock, Brett, and Brooke II 583–4). Cf Joseph Vogt, Ancient Slavery and the Ideal of Man, trans Thomas Wiedermann (Oxford 1974) 104–5.

agreed that the slave's responsibility was sometimes diminished. The general notion of limited moral responsibility appears in the *Penitential of Cummean* (ca 650), one of the earlier examples of the literature,[34] and direct reference to the condition of the slave in this regard appears in the *Penitential of Egbert* (ca 750). Here the reader is reminded that not all are to be judged in the same way, that distinctions must be made according to the sinner's wealth, whether he is free or slave, his age, and his status within the Church.[35] Towards the end of the eighth century a more definite conclusion in this regard is drawn in the *Paenitentiale Valicellianum* I: 'Understand this, brothers: when male or female slaves come to you seeking penance, do not oppress them, nor make them fast as much as the wealthy, because male and female slaves are not free agents; therefore impose half the usual penance on them.'[36] Thus the notion becomes explicit, that unlike those whose capacity to judge is reduced by poverty, ignorance, lack of experience, and fear, the slave is limited because his life is controlled by another. Penitential books of the ninth and tenth centuries repeat this judgment that the slave is not of full moral responsibility and should not be punished as though he were. The notion would continue in the canonical collections,[37] and would receive a remarkable statement in the *Summa* of Hostiensis (1253), where, after an extended discussion of the circumstances of a sin, the author concludes that quality

34 *The Irish Penitentials*, ed Ludwig Bieler, Scriptores latini Hiberniae 5 (Dublin 1963) 112–13, 116–17, 127–9.
35 'Non omnibus ergo in una eademque libra pensandum est, licet in uno constringantur vitio, sed discretio sit unumquodque eorum, hoc est inter divitem et pauperem, liber, servus, infans, puer, juvenis, aduliscens, etate senex, ebitis, gnarus, laicus, clericus, monachus' (*Die Bussordnungen der abendländischen Kirche*, ed F.G.A. Wasserschleben [Halle 1851] 232). A similar phrase occurs in the closely related *Penitential of Bede*, ibid 250. On these texts see Pierre J. Payer, *Sex and the Penitentials: The Development of a Sexual Code, 550–1150* (Toronto 1984) 16–17. Note that poverty is one of the causes of limited responsibility; see below, 478–83 (here pp 236–42).
36 'Et hoc scitote fratres, ut dum venerint ad vos servi vel ancille querentes penitentiam, non eos gravetis, neque cogatis tantum jejunare quantum divites, quia servi et ancille non sunt in sua potestate. Ideoque medietatem penitentie eis imponite' (*Die Bussbücher und die Bussdisciplin der Kirche nach handschriftlichen Quellen dargestellt*, ed Hermann J. Schmitz [Mainz 1883] 243). Cf *The Penitential of Halitgar* (817×830), *Die Bussbücher und das kanonische Bussverfahren nach handschriftlichen Quellen dargestellt*, ed Hermann J. Schmitz (Düsseldorf 1898; repr Graz 1958) II 292.
37 Eg Burchard of Worms, *Decretum* (1008–12) 17 32, 34 (PL 140 925); Ivo of Chartres, *Decretum* (1100) 9 90 (PL 161 682); *Decretum Gratiani* C22 q5 c2. Cf *De judiciis omnium peccatorum* 8 30 (*Die Bussbücher und das kanonische Bussverfahren*, ed Schmitz 501).

of person is the principal circumstance to be established in judging. The case of the *servus* who sins in executing his lord's command is used as the example of diminished responsibility and, therefore, of lesser punishment.[38] The meaning of the term *servus* in the context in which Hostiensis wrote is not clear: it may refer to a slave, or to a person of less restricted right, or to both, because both would be within his experience in the Italy of his time, and the principle of diminished responsibility would apply to each of them.[39] From all of this it can be concluded that, in those cases where the offence was caused at least in part by the situation in which his lord had placed him, the sexual sins of a slave or a serf would be seen as less serious than a similar action by a free man. As a consequence, the argument that the slave or serf was considered to have a right to marry so that he might avoid sin by channelling his sexual appetite in a suitable manner would lose some of its power.

Yet, however their limited responsibility was explained or justified, Christian slaves were not looked upon as persons incapable of moral acts.[40] Rights and duties flowed from that fact: they were expected to pursue a life of virtue. With the passage of time, the *servus*[41] was frequently discussed from this point of view in the writings of religious leaders. Regulations to ensure the possibility of the life of virtue were issued in councils and soon found their place in canonical collections. Some of these rules became part of Roman and barbarian law as well.[42] First, the slave's religious needs were to be respected: he was to be allowed Sunday

38 'Licet autem omnes circumstantie diligenter sint attendende, principaliter tamen considerande sunt qualitates personarum; nam si servus sit, et timore peccaverit obediendo domino in atrocioribus mitius puniendus est ... et tamen in talibus non tenebatur obedire' (*Summa, una cum summariis et adnotationibus* 5 60 [Lyons 1537; repr Aachen 1962] f 283vb). Note that the author points out that the *servus* is not bound to obey such an order.

39 In his treatment of the different penances assigned to *libri* and *servi* in the context of England or northern France (1208–13), Robert of Flamborough was clearly referring to serfs, *Liber poenitentialis: A Critical Edition with Introduction and Notes*, ed J.J. Francis Firth, Studies and Texts 18 (Toronto 1971) 229, 247.

40 J. Dutilleul, 'Esclavage,' DTC 5 I (1924) 457–519, especially 474–5.

41 For the remainder of this essay, where the meaning is uncertain, the term *servus/ servi* will be used, with purposeful indefiniteness, to describe those members of the lowest level of society to which the evidence under discussion refers. The term 'slave' or 'serf' will be used where the meaning of the original is clear.

42 See Dockès, *La libération médiévale* 117. For a detailed study of the place of the slave in legislation, see David A.E. Pelteret, 'Late Anglo-Saxon Slavery: An Interdisciplinary Approach to Various Forms of Evidence,' Ph.D. dissertation (University of Toronto 1976) 107–53.

rest and be free to attend mass that day; he was to observe fasts in their season. Efforts were made to protect the faith of the servile class: they were not to pass under the control of pagan or Jew. It became established that the *servus* should be allowed to control the movable property that he acquired under certain conditions; eventually, when he could properly be called 'serf,' that power extended to the giving of alms at death, and the long debate between church leaders and the seigniorial class over his right to make a will began.[43] Further evidence of the serious role of religion in the life of the slave is provided by his access to those rites – in time, they were identified as sacraments – which touched him personally, rites that enabled him to enter or re-enter the Church and to participate in its principal religious act, the Eucharist. The rites that had social consequences, however, were treated differently: the *servus* was not to receive orders for he did not have that control of his person which was deemed necessary for the clerical state;[44] similarly, his marriage, real though it was judged to be, was seen to be limited in some respects by the rights of his lord.

When the requirements of the Christian life are approached from the point of view of the avoidance of sin, the writings of the Fathers show concern with helping the slave avoid sexual temptation.[45] Furthermore, however careful the penitential books were to point out the limitation of the slave's accountability for evil acts, they did not absolve him of all responsibility. It was in this literature that the first developed Christian statement on sexual sin was made: there was a refined examination of extenuating circumstances, but it is clear that the principle from which the moralists proceeded was the acceptance of the notion that only heterosexual relationships were permitted and that they were to be within

43 See Michael M. Sheehan, *The Will in Medieval England: From the Conversion of the Anglo-Saxons to the End of the Thirteenth Century*, Studies and Texts 6 (Toronto 1963) 253–4. After 1102, this is the only matter touching slave or serf that is found in *Councils and Synods 1*, ed Whitelock, Brett, and Brooke; Bloch, 'Personal Liberty and Servitude' 43–4.

44 See Naz, 'Esclave' 3: 'L'esclave et les ordres sacrés,' DDC 5 453–4; see Gratian, D54 cc 1–24.

45 See the texts assembled by Paul Allard, *Les esclaves chrétiens depuis les premiers temps de l'Eglise jusqu'à la fin de la domination romaine en Occident* (Paris 1914) 251–60: Clement of Alexandria (ca 200) warns women to be modest in the presence of their male slaves and advises husbands to avoid embracing their wives in the sight of their slaves lest the latter become excited; John Chrysostom (ca 400) preaches that slave owners must arrange the marriage of slaves to assuage their sexual desire; etc.

marriage.[46] It is also clear that the slave was considered to be bound by this code. The insistence that the slave have access to a legitimate spouse is probably to be explained, at least in part, by the desire to protect him or her from the occasion of sin in the situation where sexual desire could not otherwise be assuaged in a morally acceptable way.[47] The caveat touching the limitation on the freedom of marriage resulting from the rights of lordship somewhat weakens this argument; but, as will be seen, that limitation was to be removed as the theology of marriage was given its full statement towards 1200. It was precisely at this point – the confrontation of marital and seigniorial rights – that the argument was located.

2. The Right to Marry

The process whereby it became established that a slave was capable of marriage, with rights and obligations as understood by the Church, was long and complex. The development was often local and rarely continuous; there were set-backs and inconsistencies. Its investigation has proved difficult not least because of the problems presented by the meaning of terms: the scholarly method of both canonist and theologian required the examination, interpretation, and rendering consistent of texts that came from the past. In many of those texts terms such as *servus, ancilla, servilis conditio,* etc undoubtedly referred to slaves in their original context. But their meaning in a treatise or business document of the high Middle Ages is often a problem for the modern reader as it was for medievals themselves.[48] Nevertheless the 'marriage' of the slave has long been of interest

---

46 See Payer, *Sex and the Penitentials* 19–54, 115–22. A useful assemblage of these texts is available in *Medieval Handbooks of Penance: A Translation of the Principal Libri poenitentiales and Selections from Related Documents,* ed John T. McNeill and Helena M. Gamer, Records of Civilization, Sources and Studies 29 (New York 1938); see 473–4, s v 'Slaves', 'Servitude'.

47 The Penitentials were especially concerned with the protection of the female slave: see preceding note.

48 Pascal II (1099–1118) reflected on this matter in a letter confirming the right of the serfs of the Church of Paris to witness in court against freemen: 'pro eo quod ipsius ecclesiae famuli, qui apud vos servi vulgo improprie nuncupantur' (cited by Dutilleul, 'Esclavage' 480). See John Gilchrist, 'Saint Raymond of Penyafort and the Decretalist Doctrines on Serfdom,' *Escritos del Vedat* 7 (1977) 303–7; and John W. Baldwin, *Masters, Princes, and Merchants: The Social Views of Peter the Chanter and His Circle* (Princeton 1970) I 237–8.

to scholars, and much progress has been made in its understanding.[49] It soon becomes clear that it is best to proceed by distinguishing two principal problems. Their solutions developed in somewhat different ways but, by and large, complemented each other. First, there was the question with which the marriage of the slave appeared in Christian literature, namely, that union of a free woman and her slave countenanced by St Cyprian. Second, there was the more straightforward question of the slave's capacity for marriage and, that being granted, whether he could, in fact, enjoy the full rights that were considered to belong to that state.

With regard to the first, the marriage that sought to cross the free-slave barrier, it is clear that, however much both Roman and barbarian societies were willing to permit such a ménage, there was no question of marriage between the principals. There was also a powerful current in the early Church against such a union.[50] The Pauline text touching the rejection of the slave-girl and her son by Abraham (Gal 4:31) was not without effect, whatever Pope Callistus may have decided. The possibilities of abuse were patent, and Christian thinkers were slow to agree that a concubine could be a wife.[51] But as the marital capacity of the slave became clarified in Frankish councils of the eighth and ninth centuries,[52] attention shifted to

49 Allard, *Les esclaves chrétiens* 247–75 (a good collection of texts; the author's interpretation is to be used with caution); Pierre Bernard, *Etude sur les esclaves et les serfs d'église en France du VIe au XIIIe siècle* (Paris 1919) 55–7; Jean Dauvillier, *Le mariage dans le droit classique de l'Eglise depuis le Décret de Gratien (1140) jusqu'à la mort de Clément V (1314)* (Paris 1933) 94–7, 185–8; Adhémar Esmein, *Le mariage en droit canonique*, ed Robert Génestal and Jean Dauvillier, 2nd ed (Paris 1929–35) I 350–70; Freisen, *Geschichte des canonischen Eherechts* 58–71; Andrés E. de Mañaricua y Nuere, *El matrimonio de los esclavos: Estudio histórico jurídico hasta la fijación de la disciplina en el derecho canónico*, Analecta Gregoriana, Series Facultatis juris canonici, Sectio B, I (Rome 1940); Fabien Thibault, 'La condition des personnes en France du IXe siècle au mouvement communal,' RHDFE, 4th ser, 12 (1933) 448–62; Charles Verlinden, 'Le "mariage" des esclaves,' in *Il matrimonio nella società altomedievale*, Settimane di studio del Centro italiano di studi sull'alto medioevo 24 (Spoleto 1977) II 569–601.

50 See Esmein, *Le mariage* I 356–8.

51 Freisen, *Geschichte des canonischen Eherechts* 58–91. See the important general discussion of the matter in Brundage, 'Concubinage and Marriage' 1–17; note the bibliography, 14–17.

52 Esmein relates this development to the improved status of the slave in Frankish society (*Le mariage* I 359). Writing on the subject ca 1138, Walter of Mortagne noted that in Roman law and in the practice of some churches *conjugium* was denied the union of *liber* and *ancilla* but that some churches had not received this regulation, 'sicut in multis ecclesiis Gallicanis fit frequenter libero retinente libertatem et servo servitutem' (*De conjugio*, published as Hugh of St Victor, *Summa sententiarum* [PL 176 165–6]; see Edward A. Synan, 'Walter of Mortagne,' in *New Catholic Encyclopedia* 14 [New York 1965] 790).

the question of the possibility of a marriage where, by intent or in ignorance, there was error as to the status of the spouses. Echoes of the more fundamental question touching the radical incapacity of the slave for marriage remained, but the principal discussion beginning with the eleventh century was about the validity of marriage where this error existed. Esmein has described how, at an earlier date when the Church's teaching on the indissolubility of marriage was only partially formed, such unions were sometimes terminated by divorce but, once the strict rules on the permanence of the marriage bond had been arrived at, another approach became necessary.[53]

Wrestling with the problem, Peter Lombard fell back on the notion that there was an intrinsic quality in the servile condition which somewhat limited capacity for marriage, a limitation that could be overcome if the spouses knew and accepted each other's status.[54] It was the notion that error of condition rendered a union invalid that was to hold the future, but such a position was not received without opposition. Thus Peter the Chanter, writing in the last decade of the twelfth century, admitted that canonists taught that there was no marriage where error of condition occurred, but held that it was valid. Noting that it would be worse to cohabit with a leper than with a person of servile condition and that error about leprosy did not invalidate a marriage, he insisted that he could not see how error of condition would do so either.[55] Thomas of Chobham, one of Peter's students writing a generation later, posed the same objection, but he returned to that older notion suggested by Peter Lombard, namely, that servitude was more intrinsic to human nature and was thus a greater impediment than other kinds of error. Chobham's conclusion disagreed with that of his master.[56] After much discussion, it was accepted in the

---

53 Esmein, ibid I 359–63; note the evolution of the thinking of Ivo of Chartres (ibid 360–2).

54 In Bk 4 dist. 34 cap. 1, discussing those legally capable of marriage, the Lombard notes that some are rendered 'nec plene legitimae, nec omnino illegitimae' for marriage 'per frigiditatem' and 'per conditionem' (*Magistri Petri Lombardi Parisiensis episcopi Sententiae in IV libris distinctae*, 3rd ed, Spicilegium Bonaventurianum 4–5 [Grottaferrata 1971–81] II 462–3). Later, Bk 4 dist. 36 cap. 1, he observes that, if the servile condition is known and there is consent, the marriage is indissoluble (II 473). See Esmein, *Le mariage* I 363–4.

55 *Summa de sacramentis et anime consiliis*, ed Jean-Albert Dugauquier, Analecta mediaevalia Namurcensia 4, 7, 11, 16, 21 (Louvain 1954–67) III 294–5.

56 'Ad hoc dicendum quod servitus magis est de statu hominis, et quasi de substantia hominis magis quam aliud accidens, et ideo error servitutis magis impedit quam alius error' (*Thomae de Chobham Summa confessorum*, ed F. Broomfield, Analecta mediaevalia Namurcensia 25 [Louvain 1968] 176).

jurisprudence of the thirteenth century that the union of free and unfree, whether brought about in error or by deceit, was invalid where the free spouse was the one misled.[57] This understanding of the marriage of slave and free would continue in Roman canon law until it was removed in the new code of 1983, a chilling reminder of the fact of slavery in the modern world.[58]

It is difficult to know to what extent the discussion at the beginning of the thirteenth century applied to the marriage of serf and free. The survival of the notion in the canon law of the modern Church is a strong indication that application to the slave was one of the intended meanings. It is clear enough that the *servus*, who was a serf, was no longer without rights, nor was he a chattel of his master even though he might be transferred to another lord with the land he worked. Some canonists make it clear that they consider the serf to be free of this restriction, a position that might be in accord with the position of Peter the Chanter, even though in the latter case it was question of the validity of the marriage of an *ancilla* whose status was erroneously perceived.[59] Chobham, writing in England, where slavery was virtually unknown in the thirteenth century, used the same term but opted for the impediment. The perennial question returns, whether he was referring to the situation that he observed around him or was simply dealing with an old problem and using old terms with their old meaning, namely, the marriage of a slave and a freeman. The answer to this question will be found in the records of the manorial and ecclesiastical courts and may well show local variations. Evidence available thus far suggests that the limitation did not apply to marriages involving the free and the serf, an impression reinforced by the understanding of the marital rights of the serf to which Christian thinkers had come by the beginning of the thirteenth century.

---

57 See Dauvillier, *Le mariage* 94–7; Esmein, *Le mariage* I 367–70; Friedrich Merzbacher, 'Die Bedeutung von Freiheit und Unfreiheit im weltlichen und kirchlichen Recht des deutschen Mittelalters,' *Historisches Jahrbuch* 90 (1970) 274–8.

58 See the *Code* of 1917, c1083 2: 'Error circa qualitatem personae, etsi det causam contractui, matrimonium irritat tantum: 1. Si error qualitatis redundet in errorem personae. 2. Si persona libera matrimonium contrahat cum persona quam liberam putat, cum contra sit serva, servitute proprie dicta' (*Codex iuris canonici* [Vatican City 1936] 297). (Note that 'serva' is interpreted as 'slave.') The new *Code* of 1983 is more subtle but still recognizes difference of condition: c1097 2: 'Error in qualitate personae, etsi det causam contractui, matrimonium irritum non reddit, nisi haec qualitas directe et principaliter intendatur' (*Codex iuris canonici auctoritate Iohannis Pauli II promulgatus* [Vatican City 1983] 213).

59 Above, n55. Note that he used the term 'ancilla' for the woman whose status was questioned.

Where it was question of two slaves, church leaders slowly developed the notion that they were capable of marriage as was any other Christian.[60] By and large, it was agreed that the consent of the owner of the slave was needed for the union to be accepted. But, even if the fact of the relationship were accepted, the possibility that the couple might exercise true marital and parental right, might live together, care for their children, etc was frequently denied.[61] By the Carolingian times it is clear that local councils were much concerned with this element of the marriage of *servi*, and, in the period when marriage law and theology were assuming their fully developed form, the period in which slavery disappeared in much of Europe, the final steps in doctrine on the matter were taken: much as the consent of the lord was desired, it was decided that the servile class was free to marry and live in the married state even where the lord was opposed to their doing so.

The discussion proved to be a complex one, and several decades passed before it came to a reasonably consistent resolution. As mentioned above (p 225), since the debate involved ancient texts and terminology connoting 'slave' rather than 'serf,' the matter is clouded for the modern student as it clearly was on occasion for the canonists and theologians of the time. The very texts of Scripture could be used to support various positions. Thus Peter's 'Servants, be submissive to your masters' assumed considerable importance (1 Pet 2:18). (The operative term in the Vulgate was 'servi' = slaves/serfs/servants.) At the same time the notion of the fundamental equality of men stated by Heimrad, when he quoted St Paul's Letter to the Galatians,[62] and the permanence of the marital

60 See above, n49.
61 Reginon of Prüm (ca 906), citing Roman law (Cod. Theod. II 25), noted in this regard that the position of the *servus* was worse in his time than it had been in the late Empire (*Libri duo de synodalibus causis et disciplinis ecclesiasticis*, ed Wasserschleben, Liber II cap. CXX–CXXII 261–2).
62 A nice example is provided by the reinforcement of a text of Justinian allowing the union of a man and a slave (*alumna*), whom he had freed: *Cod.* 5 4 26, purporting to be a letter to a Pope Julianus, resolves the ambiguity by allowing the marriage. When the text appears in the *Decretum* of Burchard of Worms (ca 1010), it is presented as a letter of Pope Julius (337–52), and the following, a tissue of texts that include references to Matt 6:1–9, 1 Cor 12:13, Gal 3:28, and Eph 6:8, is added: 'Omnibus vobis unus est pater in coelis, et unusquisque dives et pauper, liber et servus, aequaliter pro se, et pro animabus eorum rationem daturi sunt. Quapropter omnibus cujuscunque conditionis sint, unam legem, quantum ad Deum, habere non dubitamus' (9 18 [PL 40 818]). See Ivo of Chartres, *Decretum* 8 156, and *Panormia* 6 38 (PL 161 618, 1251); Gratian, C29 q2 cc 1, 3. Regarding this text and its appearance in 'Polycarpus' 6 4 8, see Jean Gaudemet, 'Le legs du droit romain en matière matrimoniale,' in *Il matrimonio nella società altomedievale* I 156–9.

relationship implied by Christ's words 'Whatever therefore God has joined together, let no man put asunder' (Mark 10:9) frequently played a part in the discussion. An important shift of perspective is soon evident. Whereas in Carolingian literature the thrust of conciliar canons was to state the right of the *servus* to marry and to protect his marriage from the massive claims of the lord, the general impression given by the literature discussing the matter after 1100 is that certain marital rights of the *servi* were taken as acquired. There was still a problem, but it was stated in a different way: how to reconcile two sets of rights that could easily come into conflict. Fortunately for the purpose of this study, much progress has been made in the analysis of the position of the married serf vis-à-vis his lord in articles by Peter Landau and John Gilchrist.[63]

Theologians of the mid-twelfth century had been precocious in stressing the freedom of children from the control of their parents in their choice of spouse.[64] As Landau shows, however, they were reluctant to assume the same position with regard to the serf's freedom from seigniorial control. The obvious question to ask was whether the lord's permission were necessary for the validity of the marriage. About 1138, in a discussion of servile marriage in his *De conjugio*, Walter of Mortagne, a theologian of the school of Laon, based his analysis of this problem on a text of the Carolingian council held at Châlons in 813. Citing Christ's words 'Quod Deus coniunxit, homo non separet' (Matt 19:6), the conciliar canon went on to say that, where there had been a proper marriage with the consent of the lord, the *servi* couple should remain married while rendering their services.[65] Walter asked whether the lord's consent were necessary for such a marriage. He concluded that, if the lord were unaware of the union and thus had not opposed it, it seemed reasonable

---

63 Peter Landau, 'Hadrians IV. Dekretale "Dignum est" (X 4 9 1) und die Eheschlies-
    sung Unfreier in der Diskussion von Kanonisten und Theologen des 12. und 13.
    Jahrhunderts,' *Studia Gratiana* 12 (1967) 511–53; John Gilchrist, 'The Medieval Canon
    Law on Unfree Persons: Gratian and the Decretist Doctrines, c 1141–1234,' ibid 19
    (1976) 271–301, and 'Saint Raymond of Penyafort' 299–327.
64 See Le Bras, 'Mariage: La doctrine du mariage,' DTC 9 II 2139–49, 2151–7; Fossier,
    Histoire sociale de l'Occident médiéval 158–9.
65 'Dictum est quod nobis quidam matrimonia legitima potestativa quadam praesump-
    tione dirimant, non attendentes illud Evangelicum: *Quod Deus conjunxit homo non
    separet* (Matt 19:6). Unde visum est nobis ut conjugia servorum non dirimantur,
    etiam si diversos dominos habeant; sed in uno conjugio permanentes dominis
    serviant suis. Et hoc in illis servandum est ubi legalis conjunctio fuit et per volunta-
    tem dominorum' (PL 176 166); cf Gratian, C29 q2 c8.

that the marriage should stand.[66] Though on other matters Walter's text was the basis of Peter Lombard's treatment of servile marriage in his *Sentences* (ca 1150), Peter came down firmly on requiring the lord's consent, merely reporting that 'it seemed to certain people' that, if the lord were ignorant, there would be a marriage.[67] Typical of the theological writers of the time, Gandulph of Bologna came to the same conclusion in his commentary on the *Sentences* (1160×70). But a limitation of seigniorial authority was provided by his additional question: if the lord can impose continence on his *servus* by forbidding his marriage, can he require him to assume the life of continence by entering a monastery, or can he force him to marry? Here the reply is in the negative. For the acts in question, the consent of the serf was required; the lord's power was not unlimited: he might stand in the way of marriage but he could not cause it.[68] (Note, too, that the choices were either continence or marriage; there was no question of an intermediate state suitable for the serf.) Among other theologians, the right of the lord to prevent the serf's marriage would be held well into the thirteenth century.[69]

At first, canonists assumed a similar position. Thus, in C29 of his *Decretum* (ca 1140), Gratian left no doubt that the serf could marry, but insisted on the necessity of the lord's consent. The second question opens with a canon ascribed to Pope Julius asserting the capacity of the *servus* for marriage. Remarking that the free and the slave have one Father in heaven and must render an account for their actions, the pope is made to state that the serf, like the freeman, cannot dismiss his spouse once he has entered into a marriage.[70] After a citation of other canons exploring

66 'videtur tamen rationabiliter quod inter eos possit fieri conjugium si ex communi consensu copulentur, quamvis eorum domini ignoraverint' (PL 176 166).

67 Bk 4 dist. 36 cap. 2 (*Sententiae* II 474).

68 'non tamen potest contra voluntatem servi ipsum compellere ... uxorem ducere, cum ista sine ipsius servi consensu ab eo fieri non possunt' (*Magistri Gandulphi Bononiensis Sententiarum libri quatuor*, ed I. de Walter [Vienna 1924] 561–2). This discussion was of practical importance, for lords sometimes applied pressure on their serfs to marry, at once evidence of the need that a servile tenement be held by a couple and of the acceptance of the notion that they should be married: see Elaine Clark, 'The Decision to Marry in Thirteenth- and Early Fourteenth-Century Norfolk,' *Mediaeval Studies* 49 (1987) 496–516; Rodney H. Hilton, *The English Peasantry in the Later Middle Ages* (Oxford 1975) 108; Richard M. Smith, 'Some Reflections on the Evidence for the Origins of the "European Marriage Pattern" in England,' in *The Sociology of the Family*, ed Harris 87–8.

69 See Landau, 'Hadrians IV.' 542–3.

70 The glosses on this canon are discussed by Gilchrist in 'The Medieval Canon Law on Unfree Persons' 290–2.

the problem of error of status in a marriage involving freeman and *servus*, the *quaestio* is completed by the text from the Council of Châlons quoted by Walter of Mortagne: married serfs are expected to serve their lords, but their marriage is a true marriage if their lords consent to it.[71] The first generation of decretists in their comments on these texts does not seem to have added anything of importance to Gratian's doctrine.[72] The practical problem of conflicting rights remained.

It was with the decretal *Dignum est* of Hadrian IV (1155–9) that the possibility suggested by Walter of Mortagne about twenty years before was realized. Quoting the Pauline text used by Heimrad, 'In Christo Jesu neque liber, neque servus est,' the pope stated that since neither freeman nor *servus* was to be denied sacraments of the Church, marriage between *servi* should not be forbidden. The decretal ended with a sentence that was to provide the main subject of the discussion for the next hundred years: though the lord should not prevent marriage of *servi*, the customary services to which they were obliged ought to be rendered to their own masters.[73] The practical problem faced by the ménage made up of *servi* of different masters was posed.[74] In the discussion that followed it becomes clear that the *servi* in question were serfs.

Dignum est quickly found its way into those compilations of papal letters known as the Decretal Collections[75] and was included in Bernard of Pavia's *Breviarium extravagantium* (1188×92). This, one of the early systematic collections and more commonly known as the *Compilatio prima*, provided the design and the basic set of texts for the great official collection, the *Decretales* issued by Gregory IX in 1234. In the latter, *Dignum est* is the first canon in Title 9, 'De coniugio servorum.' The change that had come about in the century since the publication of Gratian's *Decretum* is remarkable. Whereas Gratian's texts made it clear that, if the lord consented to the marriage of a *servus*, it was a true marriage, the first canon of the *Decretales* stated that the lord's consent was not needed for the validity of such a union.[76] Bernard of Pavia also wrote a *Summa* that glossed the *Compilatio prima*. In his commentary on *Dignum est*, he reinforced Pope Hadrian's argument for the serf's freedom

71 C29 q2 c8.
72 Landau, 'Hadrians IV.' 515.
73 'debita tamen et consueta servitia non minus debent propriis dominis exhiberi' (X 4 9 1). On the ascription of *Dignum est*, see Landau, ibid 514–15.
74 See Gilchrist, 'The Medieval Canon Law on Unfree Persons' 290–1.
75 Landau, 'Hadrians IV.' 515.
76 Cf Gratian, C29 q2 c1; and X 4 9 1.

to marry, referring to the moral necessity for the right implied by St Paul: 'But because of the temptation to immorality, each man should have his own wife and each woman her own husband' (1 Cor 7:2). As to the claim that the lord's consent to a marriage was required, he answered that it was fitting but not necessary.[77] Towards the middle of the thirteenth century, theologians such as Albert the Great and Thomas Aquinas would lift the discussion to a new level with the doctrine that the exercise of the appetite which continues the human species by generation pertains to the natural law. Since servitude is of positive law, it must yield to the former.[78]

By the time that the doctrinal dispute had been resolved, the examination of cases where rights of lord and serf were in conflict had long been under way. From the last decade of the twelfth century, the main point of discussion by both theologians and canonists was the right of the servile couple to live together as man and wife when it conflicted with the lord's right to their services. Was he permitted to separate them? Even when they were allowed to live together, did he have the right to make such demands of them as to make the mutual rendering of the marriage debt excessively difficult? Various ways for reuniting separated spouses were suggested. Peter the Chanter went so far as to say that, in the case where a serf had fled to the city and the lord refused to allow his wife to follow him, she ought to do so for the marriage bond is to be preferred to the bond of servitude.[79] As to the question of the rights of married serfs and those of the lord, the discussion fell back on the distinction between marriages with and without permission; but usually in the background was the Pauline dictum 'But because of the temptation to immorality, each man should have his own wife and each woman her own husband.' Where the lord gave permission for his serf to marry, his consent to uninterrupted marital life was implied. But, where the marriage occurred

---

77 'Hoc autem puto de honestate, potius quam de necessitate, cum etiam contradicentibus dominis possint ad invicem copulari' (*Bernardi Papiensis Summa decretalium*, ed Ernst A.T. Laspeyres [Regensburg 1860; repr Graz 1956] 154).

78 The texts are assembled by Landau, 'Hadrians IV.' 547–50.

79 Vol 3 pt 2a 295: 'ita uinculum matrimonii prefertur uinculo seruitutis. Unde ipsa tenetur si potest absque licentia domini fugere ad uirum.' Note that it is not simply that the wife *may* go, she *should* go. The moral dimension of the use of 'tenetur' is made all the clearer in the next part of the *casus*, where a serf marries a free woman and she flees to her parents. If she cannot be convinced to return to her husband and he fears that either of them will fall into sin ('et timeret de lapsu suo vel uxoris'), then he should leave his lord and join her (296).

without his permission, his demands were to be satisfied even though they made the marriage difficult, though not if they made it impossible. In most cases it was conceded that, if enforced continence posed the danger of adultery, the right of the lord was to yield before that of the marriage.[80]

3. Establishing the Marriage Bond

It might well be said that the concentration of discussion on the implementation of the serf's right to marriage by scholars, medieval as well as modern, has tended to focus attention too exclusively on the problems of the servile members of society. By the time that the fully developed doctrine on marriage was in place there was an ever increasing number of medievals who were considered to be free but the poverty of whose lives made marriage difficult to bring about.[81] It is in the reflection on the manner of establishing the marital bond that some thought was given to them.

The developing Christian theory of marriage manifested a surprising combination of qualities: it became rather easy to create the marital union, but its consequences became very serious. The opposite was the case in Roman law: the establishment of *matrimonium iustum* was hedged about with many restrictions, yet the union was rather fragile, depending to the extent that it did on the will of the principals.[82] The point of view of barbarian law was similar. The high seriousness of the commitment

80 See Landau, 'Hadrians IV.' 543–52.
81 It will be remembered that the penitential literature saw poverty as one of the causes of limited moral responsibility: see above, 468 and n35 (here pp 223–4). In 'The Ecclesiastical Code of King Aethelred' (1014) c6, the poor, be they slave or free, were seen to be in similar need: one-third of the tithe was for 'God's poor and poor slaves' (*Councils and Synods 1*, ed Whitelock, Brett, and Brooke I 391). It was noted above that after 1102 the slave disappears from the English conciliar texts; the poor become the growing concern (ibid II 1131, s v 'Poor, poverty'; and *Councils and Synods with Other Documents Relating to the English Church, 2: A.D. 1205–1313*, ed F.M. Powicke and C.R. Cheney [Oxford 1964] II 1404, 1430–5, s v 'Almsgiving', 'Mortuary', 'Offerings', 'Poor'). It is likely that, for much of Europe by the thirteenth century, poverty rather than servile condition was the more serious bar to marriage. See Fossier, *Histoire sociale de l'Occident médiéval* 241–5, 258–9 on the rise of rural and urban proletariats; and Jean Batany, 'Les pauvres et la pauvreté dans les revues des "estats du monde",' in *Etudes sur l'histoire de la pauvreté*, ed Michel Mollat, Publications de la Sorbonne, Etudes 8 (Paris 1974) II 469–86.
82 See Saller, 'Slavery and the Roman Family' 66–7.

required by the Christian ideal not only involved exclusive sexual rights, the *fides* of Augustine, but also was intended to be permanent. The actual implementation of such an ideal even within the rather small and highly motivated early Christian community was a slow and difficult matter. Within the group there are signs that the local community tended to exercise considerable control of the choice of spouse.[83] In addition, the bishop sometimes assumed a role in the marriage ritual.[84] After the peace of the Church, the reception of Christian teaching on the qualities of marriage by the population generally was even more difficult and dubious. Furthermore, it is clear that, in this wider context, Christian thinkers worked out the demanding consequences of the marital union before they gave serious thought to the manner in which the union was established. In fact it may well be that it was only after the consequences of Christ's words 'What God has put together, let no man put asunder' had been examined that the Church realized the necessity of establishing criteria to decide what unions had, in fact, been established by God.[85]

It was at that point that the question of the manner of establishing the marital bond became of paramount importance. One of the reasons for St Hippolytus' objection to the decisions of Pope Callixtus seems to have hinged on the lack of form in the marriages the latter was accused of accepting. This objection implied an expectation of formalities, and it is known that, in spite of the classical dictum that consent made marriage, much importance was attached to the contractual and formal elements of betrothal and marriage in Roman usage by the time of Callixtus' decision.[86] Similar insistence on formal processes of betrothal and marriage seems to have been common in regional customs of the various parts of the Empire and among the Germanic peoples as well.[87] As a rule, church leaders accepted such formalities as a suitable way to establish the marriage bond.[88] An important indication of their increasing interest in

---

83 Ritzer, *Le mariage* 81–90; Paul Veyne, 'The Roman Empire,' in *A History of Private Life*, 1: *From Pagan Rome to Byzantium*, ed Paul Veyne, trans Arthur Goldhammer (Cambridge, Mass. 1987) 263–5.

84 See Ritzer, ibid 110–21. For this and the following period see the dossier assembled by Cyrille Vogel in 'Les rites de la célébration du mariage: Leur signification dans la formation du lien durant le haut moyen âge,' in *Il matrimonio nella società altomedievale* I 397–465.

85 See Gaudemet, 'Le legs du droit romain' 143–50.

86 Ritzer, *Le mariage* 84–5. Cf *Cod.* 5 1–12, 14–15; *Dig.* 23 1–2.

87 Ritzer, ibid 220–2, 267–72.

88 Ritzer, ibid 91–2, 94–7. See the descriptions of marriage formalities, below, n92.

this matter is to be seen in the decree of the Synod of Ver (755) that all
lay marriages should be public.[89] By that time a Christian religious
element was increasing in importance in the marriage customs of many
parts of Europe.[90] Furthermore, and of major importance for the present
discussion, the Church began to interest itself in the appropriateness of
the proposed unions: were the couple free of previous marriage? were
they related within forbidden degrees?[91]

Without exception, the various general descriptions of marriage
formalities that are still extant, as well as the occasional accounts of
particular weddings, attach much importance to setting out the stages
whereby marital union was brought about.[92] Several of these occur in the
middle years of the ninth century. All set out the different steps of the

89 'Ut omnes homines laici publicas nuptias faciunt, tam nobiles quam innobiles' (cap.
    15, *Capitularia regum francorum*, ed Alfredus Boretius, MGH Leges II Capitularia
    [Hannover 1883] I 36).
90 See Ritzer, *Le mariage* 222–50, 273–84, 297–305, 307–25.
91 Daudet, *Etudes sur l'histoire de la juridiction matrimoniale* 45–50; Jean Fleury, *Re-
    cherches historiques sur les empêchements de parenté dans le mariage canonique des
    origines aux fausses décrétales* (Paris 1933) 144–240. In the late Anglo-Saxon descrip-
    tion of the procedure of betrothal and marriage described in the following note, there
    is provision for an examination of possible consanguinity between the couple.
92 General descriptions of the formalities of betrothal and marriage are included in a
    letter of ca 450 by Pope Leo I to Archbishop Rusticus of Narbonne (PL 67 288 [see
    the discussion of the text and critical problems related to it in Ritzer, *Le mariage*
    286–7 and n251; and Joyce, *Christian Marriage* 56–7]); descriptions of ca 850, among
    the Carolingian forgeries: one, among the *False Capitularies* of Benedict the Levite
    (*Benedicti Capitularia liber III*, cap. 463, ed D.F.H. Knust, in MGH Leges II, ed G.H.
    Pertz [Hannover 1837; repr Leipzig 1925] pars altera 132), and a second, ascribed to
    Pope Evaristus (AD 97–105), in Pseudo-Isidore, *Decretales Pseudo-Isidorianae et
    capitula Angilramni*, ed Paul Hinschius (Leipzig 1863) 87–8; the *responsa* of Pope
    Nicholas I to Boris, khan of the Bulgarians (AD 866): *Epistolae Karolini aevi*, ed
    Ernest Perels, MGH Epistolae 6 (Berlin 1925) Ep 99 568–600; a text of ca 1025,
    probably from the circle of Archbishop Wulfstan of York: 'Be wifmannes bewed-
    dunge' (*Die Gesetze der Angelsachsen*, ed Felix Liebermann [Halle 1903–16] I 442–4).
    A description of the formalities of an individual marriage survives for the marriage
    (and coronation) of Judith, daughter of Charles the Bald, to Ethelwulf, king of the
    West Saxons, at Verberie (Oise) in 856 (*Capitularia regum francorum*, ed Alfredus
    Boretius and Victor Krause, MGH Leges II Capitularia [Hannover 1893] II 2 425–7). In
    literature, the detailed description of the contractual and ritual elements of the
    courtship and marriage of the nephew of Ruodlieb and the daughter of the chate-
    laine, and the early stages of Ruodlieb's proposed marriage, are in Ruodlieb, ch 10–
    12, 14, 16–17 (*Ruodlieb: The Earliest Courtly Novel (after 1050)*, ed and trans Edwin H.
    Zeydel, University of North Carolina Studies in Germanic Languages and Literatures
    23 [Chapel Hill 1959] 102–17, 122–7, 130–9).

process in detail, and one of them underlines the importance of formalities, which made such marriages acceptable to the lord and guaranteed the legitimacy of children and their right to inherit.[93] Included among these documents is a section from a long letter of 863 from Pope Nicholas I to Boris, khan of the Bulgarians. There, a point of view not found in the other accounts appears.[94] The pope described the marriage rituals as practised by the Roman Church. He also mentioned Boris' reminder that the Byzantine Church required the marriage take place with formalities and in a liturgical setting.[95] But the pope insisted that, desirable as it might be that consent of the members of the principals' circles be obtained and that various familial and religious rituals be observed, none was necessary for the union to be acceptable to the Church. Only one thing was required: the consent of the couple.[96] This tension between what is to be desired in the process by which a couple is united and the minimum that is needed for the marriage to be valid would be a problem all through the Middle Ages. From the present point of view, it is important to note that Pope Nicholas emphasized the reason for the Roman usage: some members of the community were simply too poor to be able to provide for the more formal wedding.[97]

When descriptions of marriage were made, they usually envisioned, as would be expected, the unions of important members of society. Among the wealthy and powerful, the contractual and formal elements of marriage were important for personal reasons as well as for family strategies of longer term. Thus, in spite of the adage of Roman law that a dowry was not necessary, the formalities and fact of endowment were clearly of major importance. For the servile members of society such pressures would not be operative. Yet it is evident from what has been noted above that the expected permission of the lord or lords before the marriage of

---

93 'Taliter enim et domino placebunt et filios non spurios, sed legitimos, atque heredi-
  tabile generantur' (Decretales Pseudo-Isidorianae, ed Hinschius 87–8).
94 The phrase 'nisi voluntas propria subfragerit' may have been intended to provide a
  means to avoid the formalities described in the text attributed to Pope Evaristus, but
  Ritzer, Le mariage 351 rejects the interpretation.
95 On the requirement of formalities in the marriages of slaves and the poor in the
  Byzantine empire see Angeliki E. Laiou, 'Consensus Facit Nuptias – Et Non: Pope
  Nicholas I's Responsa to the Bulgarians as a Source for Byzantine Marriage Customs,'
  Rechtshistorisches Journal 4 (1985) 189–201; and Ritzer, ibid 170–1.
96 'ac per hoc sufficiat secundum leges solus eorum consensus, de quorum coniunctionibus agitur,' Epistolae Karolini aevi, ed Perels VI Ep 99 570.
97 'praesertim cum tanta soleat artare quosdam rerum inopia, ut ad haec praeparanda
  nullum his suffragetur auxilium' (ibid).

servi fitted well with the understanding that manifestation of wider consent should be one of the formalities of marriage. Probably it will not be possible to demonstrate the fact for *servi* of the ninth and following centuries; but, when there is more evidence touching the marriage of serfs and the poor, it becomes clear that endowment was considered to be of importance among them. Sometimes it appears as the only means of proof for the existence of the marriage bond in either the internal or the external forum.[98] Yet important as formalities – be they of the simplest sort – may have been for the marriages of the poor, the teaching of Nicholas I, that they were not essential, was to be remembered.

By the time that evidence of the importance attached to endowment by the poor becomes available, the developed theology and law of marriage had long since turned once again to insist that between a man and a woman, not restricted by relationship or previous marriage or vow, all that was needed for valid union was their consent.[99] Coupled with this was the teaching on the potential spouse's freedom and right to choose a marriage partner and the concomitant notion that no other consent was necessary. It is not surprising that, precisely at this time, the right of the serf to marry, to share rights and obligations with his spouse, and to control his children without the lord's consent and even against his wishes was finally established. It would be an error, however, to think that the various instruments of popular instruction that were brought into action to support the sacramental teaching of the late twelfth and following centuries emphasized the minimal requirement and the relative unimportance of all elements other than consent. Quite the contrary: they emphasized the importance of the ritual of marriage – a new religious ritual – as necessary for all.[100] But it is clear that the minimal requirement was under-

---

98 Thus in Burchard, *Decretum* 19 5, a confessor, enquiring about an alleged marriage, asks the penitent if he has not endowed his wife with at least a farthing: 'vel pretio unius oboli, tantum ut dotata fieret' (PL 140 958); on the use of the fact of endowment – even the gift of a kerchief – in ecclesiastical court as evidence of marriage, see Michael M. Sheehan, 'The Formation and Stability of Marriage in Fourteenth-Century England: Evidence of an Ely Register,' *Mediaeval Studies* 33 (1971) 246–7 (here pp 58–9).

99 See Gérard Fransen, 'La formation du lien matrimonial au moyen âge,' in *Le lien matrimonial*, Colloque du Cerdic, Strasbourg, 21–3 mai 1970, ed René Metz and Jean Schlick (Strasbourg 1970) 106–26.

100 On the development and reception of the full religious ritual of marriage for the high Middle Ages see Brian F. Bethune, 'The Text of the Christian Rite of Marriage in Medieval Spain,' Ph.D. dissertation (Toronto 1986); J.-B. Molin and Protais Mutembe, *Le rituel du mariage en France du XIIe au XVIe siècle*, Théologie historique

stood, and there is abundant evidence that many unions were established without an act which included the rites of the Church and that they were considered to be valid. Thus the informal union came to be accepted as a true marriage, with all the serious consequences of that relationship, so long as the required consent to live as man and wife was present when that union was established. Clearly, those theologians and canonists who had arrived at the fully developed theory of marriage saw it as realizable among all members of society, the free and the servile, the rich and the poor.

When information about individual marriages becomes available on a fairly large scale in the fourteenth century, it is discovered that there were many clandestine unions. There is no need to be surprised.[101] It is not so much a question of explaining the fact that there were so many informal marriages; rather the fact that needs explanation is that, once these unions were accepted as true marriages, such success occurred in leading the population to give them the public quality that the Church sought.[102] The whole weight of teaching by council and synod as well as the civil law of the twelfth and following centuries was to move members of all classes to establish their marital bond in a formal wedding before the Church, a liturgy that incorporated many of the older familial and civil rituals associated with marriage. It meant that a situation had been created in which it was easy for poorer members of society to establish an accepted union while, at the same time, instruments were developed to ensure that their unions moved beyond mere validity to that which was formal and public. The required formalities were intended both to ensure the couple's freedom to marry and to make it clear to the local ecclesial community that the union had taken place. Within those formalities there was no place for the lord to be involved. The peasant and the poor dwellers of the towns could marry if they wished; and, as will be seen, if they merely

---

26 (Paris 1974); Michael M. Sheehan, 'Marriage Theory and Practice in the Conciliar Legislation and Diocesan Statutes of Medieval England,' *Mediaeval Studies* 40 (1978) 408–60 (here pp 118–76).

101 It is important to note that, though many marriages were considered 'clandestine' in the canonical sense of the term, it need not follow that the union was brought about without formalities; see the discussion of this matter in Sheehan, 'The Formation and Stability of Marriage' 244–9 (here pp 56–60); Juliette M. Turlan, 'Recherches sur le mariage dans la pratique coutumière (XIIe–XVIe s.),' *Revue historique de droit français et étranger*, 4th ser, 35 (1957) 503–16.

102 Cf A. Lefebvre-Teillard, 'Règle et réalité dans le droit matrimonial à la fin du moyen-âge,' *Revue de droit canonique* 30 (1980) 41–54.

wished to live together, the religious society was organized to turn that union into a marriage.

Thus, when the different aspects of the Christian teaching on the marriage of the servile members of society are examined, it becomes clear that reflection on the moral obligation of all adult Christians, coupled with examination of the basis of the right to marriage and the theory of the essential element in creating the marital bond, led to the conclusion that it was not only possible but expected that the *servus* should be allowed to marry. That same reflection made marriage easier to achieve for those poorer members of society who enjoyed freedom but the condition of whose lives made the formalities of marriage difficult for them to fulfil. All in all, it is possible to discern from the third century onward a steady development of ideas and regulations, despite much variety and not infrequent inconsistency, that tended to enhance the completeness of the life of members of the servile classes and the poor. Though limitations to the moral responsibilities of these groups were recognized, there is clear evidence in the thinking of the time that, in principle, their exercise of sexual powers should be within the framework of a marriage that, essentially, was common to all Christians. This teaching was developed by the elements in society that were to produce the synthesis on sexuality, marriage, and the celibate life that was one of the principal achievements in the social thinking of the high Middle Ages. In answer to the first question, namely, whether the theory of marriage developed by the end of the twelfth century were intended to apply to the servile classes and to the poor, a clear affirmative must be given.

III

There is a second question, however: to what degree was the new theory of marriage actually implemented among the less fortunate men and women who constituted the vast majority of medieval society? One could expect resistance from slave owners or manorial lords (some of whom were the very persons who developed the theory in question), for an obvious threat to their prerogatives lay in this doctrine. In fact, there is abundant evidence of their efforts to maintain as many of their traditional rights as possible, while accommodating themselves to the new ideas on marriage. But the question exists at a more fundamental level: did *servi* and the poor desire, or could they be led to desire, to enter a relationship that was intended to be permanent and exclusive? It will be remembered how the disciples responded when Christ set out his doctrine on the indissolubility of marriage: 'If that is man's relation to his wife it is better not to marry' (Matt 19:10). Perhaps other arrangements were preferred: as has been seen above (p 241), there is much evidence on the frequency of informal unions among members of the lowest classes; how often were they ended with equal informality?[103] How important was it in the mind of the peasant or the poor townsman that he marry?[104] It was noted that one of the elements of the discussion of the marital rights of the *servus* was the notion that marriage was necessary to him if he were to avoid sexual sin. On the other hand, there is abundant evidence in literature and elsewhere of that age-old notion, so consoling to men, that the continence of lower-class women is not a very serious matter.[105] Yet it is clear that those in a position to control the instruments of opinion-forming and of formal teaching considered the matter very serious for all elements of the population.

First, it is evident from the confessor's handbooks which began to appear in large numbers early in the thirteenth century that a carefully enunciated code of sexual behaviour was becoming available to those whose duty it was to teach the people, that is, the parish clergy. Furthermore, this same literature, unlike the earlier Penitentials, which had concentrated on sin and its correction, presented a well-balanced and positive doctrine on the meaning and purpose of sexuality and marriage.[106] Sermon literature is presently coming under examination, and there is at least a suggestion that the doctrine on marriage was made available to parishioners on a regular basis.[107]

103 See the suggestions of Richard H. Helmholz, *Marriage Litigation in Medieval England* (Cambridge 1974) 74–6; and Lefebvre-Teillard, ibid 50–4.
104 See the important suggestions of Ariès, 'Le mariage indissoluble,' especially 133–4; and Fossier, *Histoire sociale de l'Occident médiéval* 96–7.
105 See Duby, *Medieval Marriage* 12–14; Saller, 'Slavery and the Roman Family' 72; and the discussion by J.H. Plumb in his review of David B. Davis, *Slavery and Human Progress* in the *New York Review of Books* 31 (17 January 1985) 32. The penitential literature was much concerned with the sexual abuse of the female slave: see *Medieval Handbooks of Penance*, ed McNeill and Gamer 463, s v 'Female slave'.
106 See Jacqueline Murray, 'The Perceptions of Sexuality, Marriage, and Family in Early English Pastoral Manuals,' Ph.D. dissertation (Toronto 1987); Sheehan, 'Choice of Marriage Partner' 20–5 (here pp 103–8); Josef G. Ziegler, *Die Ehelehre der Pönitentialsummen von 1200–1350: Eine Untersuchung zur Geschichte der Moral- und Pastoraltheologie*, Studien zur Geschichte der katholischen Moraltheologie 4 (Regensburg 1956).
107 For an introduction to this important literature see David L. d'Avray and M. Tausche, 'Marriage Sermons in *Ad status* Collections of the Central Middle Ages,' *Archives d'histoire doctrinale et littéraire du moyen âge* 47 (1980) 71–119; David L. d'Avray,

Furthermore, there is abundant evidence that pressures were brought to bear on all parish members to live in a proper nuptial relationship. (At the moment, because of the uneven publication of the texts of local councils and synods, this point can best be illustrated for England.) First, there was a series of episcopal statutes, beginning with the earliest set from Salisbury (1217×19), which required the priest to inquire carefully about the marital situations of parents when a child was presented for baptism, so that the legitimacy of the child could be recognized and, where necessary, fornicators punished. For the remainder of the thirteenth century, regulations of this sort appeared again and again.[108] Furthermore, it had long been the custom during visitation that inquiry be made about the public sins of parishioners.[109] When directives for archidiaconal visitation became available in England in the middle of the thirteenth century, it is clear that supervision of marriages was one of their tasks.[110]

'The Gospel of the Marriage Feast of Cana and Marriage Preaching in France,' in *The Bible in the Medieval World: Essays in Memory of Beryl Smalley*, ed Katherine Walsh and Diana Wood, Studies in Church History, Subsidia 4 (Oxford 1985) 207–24, and *The Preaching of the Friars: Sermons Diffused from Paris before 1300* (Oxford 1985), especially 69–70, 249–50, 257–8; Jean Longère, *La prédication médiévale* (Paris 1983) 215.

108 1 Salisbury 30: 'De inquisitione pueri (baptizandi). Diligenter querat sacerdos cuius sit puer baptizandus, quis pater, que mater, ut sic cognoscat et puniat fornicatores, et sic sciat qui legittimi, qui non ... Et quoniam propter multas causas necesse est sacerdotem huiusmodi facere interrogationem, precipimus hoc statutum diligenter observari; puero autem nunquam denegetur baptismus' (*Councils and Synods 2*, ed Powicke and Cheney I 70; similarly 1 Exeter 18 [1225×37], 2 Salisbury 8 [1238×44], Durham Peculiars 23 [1241×49?], 2 London 5 [1245×59], 2 Exeter 2 [1287]: ibid I 233, 369, 441, 635; II 988).

109 Thus the direction 'Deinde interrogandum de adulteriis et fornicationibus' in Reginon of Prüm, *Libri duo de synodalibus causis et disciplinis ecclesiasticis*, ed Wasserschleben 251 ff.

110 The question 'An incontinentes sine correpti per archidiaconum loci, et quoties unusquisque sit correptus et qualiter,' dated 1230 and ascribed to Hugh of Wells, bishop of Lincoln, in *Concilia Magnae Britanniae et Hiberniae, 446–1718*, ed David Wilkins (London 1737) I 627, is probably derived from the statutes of Robert Grosseteste: see *Councils and Synods 2*, ed Powicke and Cheney I 262 n2. Cf no 43, 'An adulteria, vel crimina publica laicorum sint rite per archidiaconum correcta; et si aliqua sint incorrecta?' (*Concilia*, ed Wilkins I 628). The articles of inquiry in the diocese of Lichfield listed in the Burton Annals for 1252 included 'An adulteria et alia crimina publica sint alicubi corrigenda,' and those for all of England in 1253 include 'An adulteria et crimina publica et notoria laicorum sint rite per archidiaconum correcta, et an aliquis contraxerit matrimonium in casu non concesso' (*Annales monastici*, ed Henry Richard Luard, RS 36 [London 1864] I 298, 309).

In these ways and as a result of *ex officio* proceedings in the bishops' courts, those found to be living together but of whose marriage there was no *prima facie* evidence were identified. They were subject to severe constraints to marry properly, if they were free to do so, or to separate. Those who refused to marry were sometimes threatened with a fine if they came together again. More drastic was the procedure by which those living in an improper union, though a true marriage was possible for them, were required to swear that further sexual relationship would constitute a marriage. This regulation began to appear in England in the statutes of Roger Niger, bishop of London (1229–41).[111] Thus it seems necessary to conclude that by the middle of the thirteenth century, in England at least, there were effective means for identifying the serf or any other member of society whose ménage was not judged a proper one and to require him to separate from his mate or marry her.

Several other arguments could be advanced in support of the proposition that procedures had been developed to educate the serf and the poor to an understanding of the new theory of marriage and to ensure that they embraced it. It will be enough to dwell briefly on but one of them, the one that, elsewhere, has been called the 'forbidden possibility.' Both the civil and the religious orders were agreed that the exchange of consent and endowments that accompanied marriage should be made in a public ceremony. The motives of the two orders differed: for the civil order it was to ensure the successful transfer of property and guarantee the legitimacy of the children of the couple; for the Church it was to ensure that local knowledge of the couple saw no reason why they should not marry and to ensure remembrance of the fact that the marriage had taken place. Furthermore, councils and synods insisted again and again on the importance of a public exchange of consent under conditions worthy of the event.[112] Yet, through the high and late Middle Ages, the Church never tried to deny that the simple, more or less private exchange of consent

---

111 See the discussion in Richard H. Helmholz, 'Abjuration *sub pena nubendi* in the Church Courts of Medieval England,' *Jurist* 32 (1972) 80–90; Sheehan, 'Marriage Theory and Practice' 446–8 (here pp 161–3) and n60. Cf Karen A. Corsano, 'Custom and Consent: A Study of Marriage in Fourteenth-Century Paris and Normandy, Based on the Records of the Ecclesiastical Courts,' MSL thesis (Pontifical Institute of Mediaeval Studies 1971) 122–4.

112 It is clear that some marriages benefited from a degree of formality and publicity but were not of the seriousness that was deemed suitable: see the discussion of marriages in alehouses, etc, in Sheehan, ibid 415–17 (here pp 126–8).

was a marriage. The Church might require those living in unions established in that way to exchange their vows *in facie ecclesie*, but it insisted that, if it could be shown that there was consent, the couple were man and wife from their first exchange of that consent. Thus, while there is much evidence that efforts were made to bring the wedding of the serf and of the poor to a level of formality that may have been unpleasant and too costly for them, at the same time the concept of marriage – indissoluble, exclusive, possessing rights that could override the claims of lordship – was applied to those humble unions which sometimes incorporated rituals that may well have come down from a time when the slave had little hope of establishing such a stable ménage, or consisted of nothing more than an exchange of consent.

Towards the end of the fourteenth century, a period for which records of the ecclesiastical courts are fairly common, it is clear that a high proportion of marriages were the private, simple acts that were possible to even the poorest adult. As described in the record, these unions are patently considered to be indissoluble by those summoned before the court. The essential elements of the ideal of marriage had been rather successfully applied among the lower levels of society. Thus it seems reasonable to conclude that the marital ideals and institutions, which were developed during the twelfth and early thirteenth centuries, were intended to assure that the new theory and practice would become the model for the populace at large.

12

The European Family and
Canon Law

With the publication of *The Oriental, the Ancient, and the Primitive*, Jack
Goody has enlarged the field of discussion that he opened in 1983 with
The Development of the Family and Marriage in Europe.[1] Both works reveal
the author's purpose to correct the Europocentric approach that has long
been characteristic of social history; both present historians and anthropologists with an exciting set of hypotheses that have been discussed since
the appearance of the earlier work and will be discussed for years to
come. In *The Development of the Family and Marriage in Europe*, Professor
Goody argued that, in the last years of the Roman Empire in the West,
society moved in the direction of exogamy and less stable family structures, that the same process occurred in Europe as it developed, and that
this change had major consequences for the development of the European family, the economy, and broader social structures as well. In *The
Oriental, the Ancient, and the Primitive* the author examines several cultures of the Far East and the Near East showing the considerable extent
to which the social structures of the Graeco-Roman world were similar to
them and how both groups differed from Africa in these regards. The
changes that began to occur in the late Empire are seen to have differen-
tiated the European family, not only from that which had obtained earlier
in the Mediterranean basin but also from the family in the Eastern
cultures that had been brought into the comparison. At the core of both
volumes lies the notion that changes in the recruitment and traditional

---

1 *The Development of the Family and Marriage in Europe*, Past and Present Publications
(Cambridge 1983); *The Oriental, the Ancient, and the Primitive: Systems of Marriage
and the Family in the Preindustrial Societies of Eurasia*, Studies in Literacy, Family,
Culture, and the State (Cambridge 1990).

guarantee of stability of the family came about due to pressures exerted by the Christian religion. Professor Goody suggests that the Church exerted this pressure in its search for the wealth needed for the support of itself and of its enterprises.

These remarkable studies, the summary of which gives but a weak indication of their complexity and of the sea of information that has been brought to bear in the formation of the author's hypothesis, have occasioned many discussions from which the historical enterprise has already benefited. What is proposed here is to continue that process by examining the changes in European society and the hypothetical motive for those changes from the point of view of canon law. The canons, after all, described and were intended to direct the activities of the Church, the implementation of whose policy, Professor Goody suggests, brought about the changes in the family that were of such important consequences.

I. Canon Law as a Legal System

Several aspects of canon law distinguish it from other legal systems of the Middle Ages. First of all, to an even greater degree than most other medieval legal systems, the canons were assembled and applied in a constantly changing historical context, adjusting their role and point of view accordingly. Thus in the early Church it is usually evident that the experience of local communities and the discussion of practical problems and Christian revelation by church leaders – a process that would eventually be called theology – were the principal sources of canon law. In that context the canons were not very numerous and were especially concerned with matters to which Christians were obliged or which were forbidden in the public forum. From the sixth to the eleventh century, a period for which there is very little that can properly be called theology in the Western Church, the collectors of canons and the occasional author who showed some capacity to reflect on their meaning assumed part of the mantle of the theologian. Thus, in certain areas of Christian thinking – sacramental theology for example – the canonists tended to function as theologians as well as jurists, because both religious and disciplinary issues were involved as they collected, correlated, and interpreted the rules by which the Christian lived. During those years, the regulations presented by canonists were often in the realm of counsel rather than obligation. It is only towards the end of the twelfth century, when theology had come into its own, that canon law becomes once again a legal system in the modern understanding of the term, a system that often drew on the conclusions of theology but that gave major emphasis to questions of obligation, judicial process, etc. From this point of view, then, the development of the canons touching the subject under discussion here should be seen in relation to religious and theological development. Second – this is implied by what has already been noted – canon law was an active, developing set of laws that, by the twelfth century, related to burgeoning administrative and judicial institutions. It not only preserved many of the regulations of the early Church in collections assembled all through the Middle Ages but also incorporated new legislation derived from the constitutions of councils or the decretals of the popes. Third, of special relevance to the present discussion, unlike most of the customals and codes of the time, the canonical system had a highly developed law of persons and was often surprisingly individualistic in its approach. Fourth, canonists were aware that the laws with which they were concerned were derived from sources of differing authority and, as such, were of different degrees of enforceability. This realization, coupled with the growing theory of papal authority, opened the way to a system of dispensation.[2] Related to this was the subtle notion – a notion that pertained at once to law and moral guidance – that, in certain cases, conditions required for the completeness of an act were not necessary for the act to be binding, a doctrine that would eventually be expressed in the distinction between liceity and validity, or between what was morally required and what was legally conclusive. Finally, medieval canon law provides an imperfect but comparatively good source for the social historian. Unlike the problem that the scholar faces in using many law codes of the past for the description and understanding of social usages,[3] there are several means whereby it is possible to judge whether a canon was a dead letter or whether it was an operative rule whereby society was expected to live. Evidence of this sort can be found in commentaries (from the eleventh century), in the registers of popes and bishops (beginning in the eleventh and thirteenth centuries respectively), and especially in the records of local ecclesiastical courts (from the thirteenth century).

---

2 See the review of *The Development of the Family and Marriage in Europe* by R.A. Houlbrooke, *English Historical Review* 99 (1984) 818.

3 See Goody, *The Oriental, the Ancient, and the Primitive* 409–15; and Richard P. Saller, 'European Family History and Roman Law,' *Continuity and Change* 6 (1991) 335–46.

II. Quaestiones disputatae

At the outset, the following discussion is premised upon this hypothesis: throughout its long history, with minor exceptions,[4] Christianity has had little to say directly about the family.[5] This silence, with its resulting flexibility, has been one of the Church's strong points as it made contact with various cultures. Of course, wherever Christianity has become established, it has had an impact, sometimes an important effect, on the local family.[6] But it is the Christian theory of sexuality, a theory developed into teaching on accepted marital and celibate forms of life, that has been the instrument of that impact.

The development of the special qualities of that position began from a rather small base, essentially a few remarks of Christ and a slightly more developed but still very limited teaching of St Paul. Christ taught a doctrine of permanence of marriage that was different from current practice and was so demanding that his disciples suggested that it might be better not to marry at all (Matt 19:3–10). He also presented a celibate life as preferable for those who could live it (Matt 19:11–12). Finally, he made two astonishing remarks about adultery. First, it could be forgiven (John 3:11); second, it could be committed entirely within the mind (Matt 5:28). St Paul also emphasized the indissoluble quality of marriage and returned to the possibility of the celibate life. In that context, however, reflecting on the power of the sexual urge, he presented marriage as the accepted way of channelling that energy (1 Cor 7:1–9). He also had several

4　Some communions, living in geographical isolation (Ethiopic Church) or living in a virtual ghetto among other Christians (Amish, Mennonites, etc), have tended to develop family usages that approach theological positions.

5　Since the end of the Second World War, Western Catholicism has been in the process of developing a theology of the family. The Roman Synod of 1982 on 'the family' marks a significant step in this regard and in part illustrates the problem created by the meeting of the Western European notion of the Christian family with the conditions and demands of the missionary areas of the Third World. Formal devotion to the Holy Family and dedication of churches under that title began in the nineteenth century; artists and sculptors explored the theme much earlier. This may be a case where religious art and the religious practice of Christians anticipated the reflection of their theologians.

6　As an example of the problem that the Church's position on marriage creates in the Third World and of the important, and sometimes bitter, discussion that has resulted, see Michael C. Kirwen, *African Widows: An Empirical Study of the Problems of Adapting Western Christian Teachings on Marriage to the Leviratic Custom for the Care of Widows in Four Rural African Societies* (Maryknoll, N.Y. 1979). Note the bibliography, 243–53.

recommendations touching the widow: if a celibate life for her were feasible it was to be preferred; but, and this is very important for the future, she was to be free to remarry as she saw fit and to the man she chose (1 Cor 7:39). These were recommendations that would be a basis for a development of immense social consequences.[7] Several other elements of Pauline teaching, elements touching the position of women within the family and within the Church, are seen as part of Jewish 'household codes'[8] and, though they have been the focus of much attention and some anger in recent years, are not pertinent to the present discussion. As the Christian doctrine of marriage and religious life was elaborated, Jewish, Roman, Germanic, and other usages were adopted in different areas and at different times. The Church had embarked on a complex, uneven, inconsistent, and sometimes contradictory development of its theory of sexuality in parallel marital and celibate forms,[9] one marked by a high degree of acculturation, but that, in the end, came to the rather well elaborated position of the late twelfth century that has been much discussed in recent years. Much of this synthesis came to be expressed in the law of the Church.

The changes discussed in Professor Goody's volumes touch two areas of major importance for the stability of the family. First, the possibility of endogamous marriage: it assisted the consolidation of family wealth and provided a larger marriage pool than was the case where exogamy was the rule. In regions of small population or where class endogamy lessened the choice of marriage partners, restricting the possibility of endogamy was of serious consequence, as both religious and secular leaders were to

7 John T. Noonan, Jr, 'Power to Choose,' *Viator* 4 (1973) 419–34; Michael M. Sheehan, 'Choice of Marriage Partner in the Middle Ages: Development and Mode of Application of a Theory of Marriage,' *Studies in Medieval and Renaissance History* n s 1 (1978) 8–14 (here pp 92–8).

8 See Edward C. Schillebeeckx, *Marriage: Human Reality and Saving Mystery*, trans N.D. Smith (New York 1965) pt 2, ch 5, cited by John F. Maxwell, *Slavery and the Catholic Church: The History of Catholic Teaching Concerning the Moral Legitimacy of the Institution of Slavery* (Chichester 1975) 29.

9 Not enough attention has been paid to this parallelism: thus the rituals of marriage and of entry into the virginal state developed at the same time from the fourth to the sixth century; regulations protecting the freedom of choice by the principals of a marriage and of one entering religious life developed in the late eleventh and twelfth centuries, etc; see Michael M. Sheehan, 'Sexuality, Marriage, Celibacy, and the Family in Central and Northern Italy: Christian Legal and Moral Guides in the Early Middle Ages,' in *The Family in Italy from Antiquity to the Present*, ed David I. Kertzer and Richard P. Saller (New Haven and London 1991) 168–83 (here pp 292–310).

remark. The wider marriage pool was also important in the provision of an heir, the second major element in family strategy. Polygyny, concubinage, and ease of divorce and remarriage also played a role in this regard, making it possible to have several sources of children. Each usage was thought to further the likelihood that an heir would be available. Where, for one reason or another, an heir was not forthcoming, adoption served as a further line of defence against the disappearance of a family. In each case, Goody argued, the developing position of the Church stood in the way of these solutions to the family's fundamental weakness and eventually sharply limited their use. Finally, there is the question of the Church's motive in taking its position.

The most obvious fact, of course, is that, by whatever means and for whatever motive, the Church was very successful in acquiring land, land that, in many cases, once belonged to families.[10] In part, the possession of this wealth is to be explained by the precocious, flexible, and consistent efforts on the part of ecclesiastical institutions to maintain their holdings, procedures carefully set out in canon law.[11] But the land was given to those institutions in the first place; and furthermore, in parts of northern Europe at least, the notion that land could be alienated from the family or even the larger kin group was probably developed so that the Church could be endowed.[12]

10 See the remarks of Rosaire Langlois, 'Orality and Literacy, Kinship and Marriage: Goody's Elusive Historical Materialism,' *Canadian Journal of Sociology* 14:1 (1989) 89–107, especially 98–9.
11 For preliminary bibliographical orientation on this important matter, see David Herlihy, 'Church property,' in *New Catholic Encyclopedia* 3 (1967) 849–53. Although Church property was not to be alienated, when there was danger of seizure by family or lord modes of 'alienation' by *donatio inter vivos* or testament were sometimes used to protect it: see the cases of Benedict Biscop (ca 690) and Bishop Hugh of Lincoln (ca 1200) discussed in Michael M. Sheehan, *The Will in Medieval England: From the Conversion of the Anglo-Saxons to the End of the Thirteenth Century*, Studies and Texts 6 (Toronto 1963) 93, 245–6. The prohibition of succession to ecclesiastical property by the sons of priests, and the withdrawal of benefices from those in minor orders who choose to marry, can be seen as part of the attempt to protect ecclesiastical property at a point where it was especially vulnerable; see Bernhard Schimmelpfennig, 'Ex fornicatione nati: Studies in the Position of Priests' Sons from the Twelfth to the Fourteenth Century,' *Studies in Medieval and Renaissance History* n s 2 (1970) 1–50.
12 See Lloyd Bonfield and Larry R. Poos, 'The Development of the Deathbed Transfer in Medieval English Manor Courts,' *Cambridge Law Journal* 47 (November 1988) 405–6. It is ironical that the tenure which allowed alienation of family property among the Anglo-Saxons was called *ius ecclesiasticum*; see Sheehan, *The Will in Medieval England* 84–5.

The present *quaestio*, however, is not whether the instability of families actually led to donation to the Church (a topic on which much detailed research is needed) but whether that instability was caused by the Church's positions on family formation and monogamy, and why it assumed those positions.

(a) Forbidden Degrees of Consanguinity and Affinity

It is evident that any limitation of marriage based on relationship diminishes the possibility of maintaining family property intact and of recovering it after alienation in dowry, in *maritagium*, or by other methods. On the other hand, almost all societies find it necessary to observe a certain limitation of marriage in this regard. The question here is the pattern of Christian development, its meaning, and its impact on family stability. Christian theologians found no revelation on the matter within the New Testament tradition, with the exception of St Paul's denouncement of the Corinthians for allowing one of their community to marry his father's wife (1 Cor 5:1), a denouncement that was in accord with the Old Testament. Positions on the matter were developed slowly and derived from Jewish law and custom (the words of Leviticus 18:6, 'Let no man approach a blood-relative for intercourse,' proved to be very important), from the law of Rome, and, as contact was made with various peoples outside the Mediterranean basin, from the customs of these groups as well.

It is very important to note the chronology of this development. Canonical prohibition of endogamous marriage is evident by the fourth century, the period when that turning in the history of the family began, as Professor Goody indicates. The broadening of the prohibition was gradual and uneven. The adoption of the fourth degree as the limit, the confusion between the Roman and Germanic systems that led to four degrees becoming seven, the hardening of opinion during the Carolingian period – often in the Carolingian forgeries – and several papal judgments in the tenth and eleventh centuries clearly moved in the direction of more extensive prohibition. But there were many decisions, especially in the case of the mission lands where conversion to Christianity was still taking place, in which a much reduced set of prohibitions was permitted.[13] The doctrine on the matter tended to become settled in the eleventh century: thus in the Council of Rome (1063) Alexander II, referring to the teaching of his predecessor, forbade marriage of blood relatives, and the signifi-

13 DDC 2 (1937) 233–6, s v 'Consanguinité'.

cance of the term was specified as within the seventh degree, that is, within the *parentela*.[14] The first two general councils in the West, 1 Lateran c5 (1123) and 2 Lateran c17 (1139), returned to the topic but were content to forbid marriage of blood relatives without further specification, a likely indication that the matter was judged to be sufficiently understood, though it is possible that room for a more generous interpretation was left intentionally.[15] Each added that such unions were forbidden by both divine and secular law. In the *Decretum* (ca 1140), Gratian held for the prohibition within the seventh degree, but he was careful to note that there were other opinions.[16] Just how widely the prohibition to the seventh degree was known and, even more critical from the point of view of the present discussion, the degree to which it was imposed will need much research before it will be possible to speak with authority.[17]

One thing is clear enough, however: within sixty years of the publication of the *Decretum* the extent of the prohibition was being diminished. The intolerable situation that had been created was indicated by Innocent III in a decretal of 1205.[18] Research on the councils of Normandy and England around 1200 suggests that the forbidden degrees were being limited and that the regulations which became a general law of the Church in 4 Lateran c50 (1215) were already being worked out there.[19] The Council's reduction of the prohibition from seventh to fourth degree, accompanied as it was by the removal of the impediments flowing from the second and third types of affinity, opened the way to a degree of reinforcement of kin ties and certainly enlarged the marriage pool to a

---

14 CII: 'Et ut de consanguinitate sua nullus uxorem ducent, usque ad septimam generacionem, vel quousque parentela cognosci poterit ' (*Sacrorum conciliorum nova et amplissima collectio*, ed J.-D. Mansi [Florence and Venice 1759–98; henceforth Mansi] 19 1026).

15 Mansi 21 283, 530–1.

16 *dict. post* C35 qq 2–3 c19.

17 See Constance B. Bouchard, 'Consanguinity and Noble Marriages in the Tenth and Eleventh Centuries,' *Speculum* 56 (1981) 268–87; and Aleksander Gieysztor, 'Le tradizioni locali e le influenze ecclesiastiche nel matrimonio in Polonia nei secoli X–XIII,' in *Il matrimonio nella società altomedievale*, Settimane di studio del Centro italiano di studi sull'alto medioevo 24 (Spoleto 1977) I 321–46.

18 Cited DDC 2 236.

19 See *Thomae de Chobham Summa confessorum*, ed F. Broomfield, Analecta mediaevalia Namurcensia 25 (Louvain 1968) xlvi–xlix; and Michael M. Sheehan, 'Marriage Theory and Practice in the Conciliar Legislation and Diocesan Statutes of Medieval England,' *Mediaeval Studies* 40 (1978) 418–20 (here pp 130–1); cf Etienne Diebold, 'L'application en France du canon 51 du IVe Latran d'après les anciens statuts synodaux,' *L'année canonique* 2 (1953) 187–95.

major extent. It is important to note in the conciliar texts that have been cited how often the notion that the regulation should implement the prohibition of marriage of blood relatives – the rule based on Leviticus – was repeated.

Given this fact, it is not unreasonable to argue that the implementation of this Levitical rule, a rule based on revelation and not on earthly legislation, was the principal purpose of those who developed the regulations under discussion.[20] On the other hand, it is important to note the preamble to the text of 4 Lateran c50; it implies that those who drafted the canon judged that the change it produced required an explanation, even a justification: 'It must not be deemed reprehensible if human statutes change sometimes with the change of time, especially when urgent necessity or common interest demands it, since God Himself has changed in the New Testament something that he had decreed in the Old.'[21] This preamble reinforces the notion that the older regulations had the high sanction of religious purpose. On the other hand, the point is made that, for sufficient reason, those regulations could be changed by the exercise of the authority that was vested in the Council.

As to the impact of the prohibition of endogamous marriage, there is abundant evidence that it was not without effect. On the other hand, it is important to remember that there was a consistent opposition to its extended form among Christian thinkers, especially in the eleventh and twelfth centuries, when, from the point of view of canon law, it came nearest to general application. Furthermore, there was the possibility of mitigating the prohibition by dispensation.[22] Thus, if this chronology is observed, it seems fair to suggest that too much has sometimes been made of the practical consequences of the prohibition of marriage between relatives, especially the seventh-degree rule, and that, when the Church produced an organized and consistent position on the matter, it

20 See the more developed argument along this line in Michael Mitterauer, 'Christianity and Endogamy,' Continuity and Change 6 (1991) 295–333.
21 'Non debet reprehensibile judicari, si secundum varietatem temporum statuta quandoque varientur humana, praesertim cum urgens necessitas vel videns utilitas id exposcit, quoniam ipse Deus ex iis, quae in Veteri Testamento statuerat, nonnulla mutavit in Novo,' Mansi 22 1035–6. See Charles Lefebvre, 'Evolution de la doctrine canonique du mariage en fonction des situations de fait et des requêtes des chrétiens,' Revue de droit canonique 29 (1979) 60–78.
22 It has been pointed out that dispensation was available only to the aristocracy, a small portion of society. That objection is not of consequence, however, because it is the devolution of the property of precisely this group that is under discussion here.

demanded a much diminished level of exogamy. The point has been made that the motive for the Church's position on exogamy was its understanding of revelation; this should not be interpreted to mean that no other motives for its policy could exist.[23] The conciliar canons referred to the agreement of civil law with their position, and it is likely that the experience and needs of the civil order were being considered in the preamble of 4 Lateran c50, discussed above.[24]

(b) Methods of Compensating for Failure to Provide Heirs

On the matter of a family's ability to provide an heir by birth, the complementary Christian teachings, that sexual powers should be exercised within a monogamous marriage and that no other exercise was permissible, imposed a serious limitation. The possibility of maintaining several spouses, whatever their status, was forbidden, and, important as the birth of children was considered to be, divorce of the sterile spouse and remarriage with the hope of producing a child was not accepted.[25] Once again, this Christian teaching became clear in the period of change indicated by Professor Goody. The tempo at which Christian teaching was adopted in principle by society and the degree to which it was lived in practice are not the question here. What is important is to realize that it was understood to implement the teaching of the New Testament.[26] These

23　On papal strategy in the grant of dispensation during its quarrel with the Hohenstaufens, see Hubert Kroppmann, *Ehedispensübung und Stauferkampf unter Innocenz IV: Ein Beitrag für Geschichte des päpstlichen Ehedispensrechtes*, Abhandlungen zur mittleren und neueren Geschichte 79 (Berlin 1937).

24　See the citation of the suggestions of Jean-Louis Flandrin and the more general discussion of this matter in Mitterauer, 'Christianity and Endogamy.' Furthermore, many ecclesiastics and ecclesiastical institutions enjoyed feudal lordship: the failure of a vassal family to provide an heir was not without benefit to its lord.

25　Thus St Augustine, who in listing the goods of marriage usually assigned the first position to children, insisted that divorce and remarriage for the purpose of engendering a child was not permitted; see *De bono coniugali*, ed Josef Zycha, in *Corpus scriptorum ecclesiasticorum latinorum* 41 5 pars 3 (Prague, Vienna, and Leipzig 1900) ch 15, 209–11. With the more developed examination of mode of establishment of the marriage bond, a declaration of nullity based on impotence became a possibility: see Jacqueline Murray, 'On the Origins and Role of "Wise Women" in Causes for Annulment on the Grounds of Male Impotence,' *Journal of Medieval History* 16 (1990) 235–49.

26　On other sources for these doctrines and their significance in the development of a different understanding of marriage, see Jean Gaudemet, 'Le legs du droit roman en matière matrimoniale,' in *Il matrimonio nella società altomedievale* I 137–79; and Peter

rules were indeed of significant effect in reducing the family's ability to provide an heir, but there is every indication that the motive for tenaciously holding to them for so long and against such powerful opposition was a religious one.

It is possible, on the other hand, to argue that the Church's doctrine of marriage sometimes served to increase the possibility of providing a legitimate heir. Although Christianity was opposed to concubinage, it helped to make it possible to turn some concubinal relationships into marital ones, with important consequences for the legitimacy of the children of the couple involved.[27] Related to this process, and to the validity-liceity distinction mentioned above, was the Church's reluctant willingness to recognize the clandestine marriage. This played a role in moving the civil order to accept marriages that crossed class lines or that lacked required formalities.[28] Furthermore, the Church eventually provided a means that, in some cases, could be used to make an heir available by the process of legitimization. Here there was not only legal theory but even a religious liturgy making it possible for the natural child to become an heir in the full sense of the term. In the thirteenth century this procedure – almost a necessary counterpart of the law that only the legitimate child could inherit – was accepted by much of Europe.[29] As is well known, the English development was different. The efforts by the bishops to make legitimization possible, led by Robert Grosseteste at the Council of Merton in 1236, were turned back by the lay aristocracy.[30] The problems of conscience and failures of succession that Grosseteste pointed out at the time were surely the result. The opposition to legitimization (it was not withdrawn until the twenties of the present century) had motives that are easy to understand, but the thrust of ecclesiastical

Brown, *The Body and Society: Men, Women, and Sexual Renunciation in Early Christianity* (New York 1988) 17–25.

27 See James A. Brundage, 'Concubinage and Marriage in Medieval Canon Law,' *Journal of Medieval History* 1 (1975) 1–17; and Michael M. Sheehan, 'Theory and Practice: Marriage of the Unfree and the Poor in Medieval Society,' *Mediaeval Studies* 50 (1988) 457–87 (here pp 211–46).

28 See the discussion of free choice of spouse below.

29 See X 4 17: 'Qui filii sint legitimi'; and Jan Piekoszewski, *La légitimation des enfants naturels simples par le mariage subséquent* (Paris 1952).

30 See Richard H. Helmholz, 'Bastardy Litigation in Medieval England,' *American Journal of Legal History* (1969) 360–83; and J.L. Barton, 'Nullity of Marriage and Illegitimacy in the England of the Middle Ages,' in *Legal History Studies, 1972*, Papers Presented to the Legal History Conference, Aberystwyth, 18–21 July 1972, ed Dafydd Jenkins (Cardiff 1972) 28–49.

policy remains clear: it was intended to confirm relationships that were informal but that might have been true marriages, and to provide legitimate status to the children born of them.

The procedure for providing an heir where a couple failed to provide one, a procedure well known to Roman law, was adoption. Professor Goody explains its mysterious 'disappearance' in medieval Europe by the Church's opposition to the practice.[31] There is indeed a problem here: it is clear that in parts of Europe there was no provision for adoption until the nineteenth century or, as in the case of England and other common-law countries, until the twentieth.[32] A few points need to be made here, however. First of all, the notion of adoption, understood in terms of Roman law, was well known to scripture commentators and theologians, for whom the exploration of the belief that the Christian was the brother of Christ and the adopted child and heir of God was a commonplace. Further, and more important in the present context, adoption did not disappear. There is evidence of its use during the Middle Ages in a wide band extending across northern Italy, southern France, and the northern part of the Iberian peninsula.[33]

As to the Church's position: while it is true that canon law pays little direct attention to the matter, it takes the possibility of adoption for granted. As is the case in so many other matters touching family, adoption is discussed in the context of marriage,[34] namely, the possibility of unions between the members of a reconstituted family where there is no blood relationship but where the element of public decency enters – a problem that still looms large in the law of adoption. A universal negative is always difficult to defend in the study of history, but it seems safe

31 See *The Development of the Family* 296, Index, s v 'Adoption'; and *The Oriental, the Ancient, and the Primitive* 433–4. In the latter volume, however, Professor Goody notes that in late Republican and early Imperial Rome little use of adoption was made (416); see Saller, 'European Family History and Roman Law' 335–46.

32 The tradition of fostering was well known and frequently practised. Much as the fosterling was drawn into the family, however, he did not become heir; on the other hand he contributed to the continuation of the family in some cases by marrying its heiress; see Goody, *The Development of the Family* 196–7, and *The Oriental, the Ancient, and the Primitive* 469.

33 See Roger Aubenas, 'L'adoption en Provence au moyen âge (XIVe–XVIe siècles), *Revue historique de droit français et étranger*, 4th ser, 13 (1934) 700–26. The article begins with a brief discussion of the 'accepted notion' that adoption was rejected by customary law.

34 *Decretum Gratiani* C30 q3 c6; X 4 2 1, 4 17 6. See DDC I (1935) 219–20, s v 'Adoption'.

to say that there is no indication of opposition to adoption in the general law of the medieval Church. Adoption has consistently been presumed as a possibility, and the canonist's treatment of it has been in terms of the impediment to marriage that might result.[35] Some other explanation must be found for the failure of parts of medieval Europe to allow adoption. The strong Germanic preference for inheritance in the blood line, expressed in the phrase 'only God can make an heir,' is probably one of the principal causes.[36] The opposition may also have had feudal roots: in the primitive form of feudalism the lord was expected to choose the vassal who suited his purpose, a practice that eventually gave way before the heir's claim to succeed to the fief. Failure of a vassal family to provide an heir gave the lord the right to recover the fief and assign it to whom he chose.[37] This surely is why bishops were such desirable vassals: they had no heirs!

(c) The Question of Free Choice of the Spouse

The possibility that the increased freedom of choice opened to spouses in the high Middle Ages had an impact on the development of those special qualities characteristic of the European family was not raised to any significant extent in the volumes under discussion. This development occurred too late to be of significance to the thesis that was presented as the essential explanation of the European phenomenon. Yet, the question of chronology aside, it is possible that the element of free choice among the changes in the manner of bringing about a marriage may have been

35 Glanvill knew that both canon law and Roman law provided the possibility of adoption (7 15): *Tractatus de legibus et consuetudinibus regni Anglie qui Glanvilla vocatur*, ed G.D.G. Hall (London 1965) 88 and nn 1, 3. The attitude to adoption found in the medieval *Corpus iuris canonici* reappears in the Codes of 1918 and 1983, *Codex iuris canonici* (Vatican City 1918) cc 1059, 1080, *Codex iuris canonici* (Vatican City 1983) cc 110, 877 3, 1094.
36 Professor Goody's observations on 'upper' and 'lower' families (*The Oriental, the Ancient, and the Primitive* 476–7) are significant here. On some English manors, peasants who did not have children could arrange for the succession to their tenement by the person they chose. Even more interesting, in cases where a child who would ordinarily have succeeded refused to promise to care for a father or mother who held the property, the tenant was allowed to arrange for succession by a stranger, to the exclusion of the heir by blood; see Bonfield and Poos, 'The Development of the Deathbed Transfer' 408–27; and Elaine Clark, 'Some Aspects of Social Security in Medieval England,' *Journal of Family History* 7 (1982) 307–20.
37 'Ultima heredes aliquorum sunt eorum domini' (Glanvill 7 17, ed Hall 91).

significant in the development of the 'European marriage pattern,' a concept that lies behind much of Professor Goody's reflection.[38] There is no need to open a detailed discussion of this matter here; for the moment, it will suffice to suggest several lines of exploration. First of all, when the question of the freedom of the spouse is approached through canon law it becomes clear that, for the free classes, the role of the lord was much diminished.[39] Not only was any claim of control that he might have exercised said to be irrelevant so far as validity was concerned, but after 1200 very little attention was paid to his claims at all. Family was another matter: the question of requirement for validity having been settled, there was constant reference to the involvement of family in the preparation of the marriage, in its choices, and even in the liturgy. Yet, looking back at the history of Europe during the last eight hundred years, one realizes that, while the controls of lordship were ephemeral in comparison to those exercised by the family, nevertheless even the latter, strong as they were, were much weakened by the insistence on the rights of the spouses. Family control of its members as well as of its property lost some of its strength. The consequences of this change still unfold in the West, consequences that the canonists who forged the theory in the first place and oversaw various attempts to implement it could never have dreamed of.[40] In fact, those changes can be demonstrated to have had significant effect in several parts of European society shortly before those qualities that Hajnal ascribed to the European marriage pattern have been observed.

III. Conclusion

Like theology, canon law never developed a position on family. From the point of view of the matter currently under discussion, the canons should

---

38 See *The Oriental, the Ancient, and the Primitive* 482. James A. Brundage, *Law, Sex, and Christian Society in Medieval Europe* (Chicago 1987), especially 229–416, discusses in great detail the evolution in the eleventh and twelfth centuries of canon law's position regarding freedom of choice: that is, the principle that intending spouses (in the absence of impediments such as pre-contract) were legally free to marry regardless of parental or seigniorial opposition.

39 The lord's right to an important role in servile marriage remained a major area of discussion until at least 1250. See Sheehan, 'Theory and Practice.'

40 See the conclusions to Michael M. Sheehan, 'The Formation and Stability of Marriage in Fourteenth-Century England: Evidence of an Ely Register,' *Mediaeval Studies* 33 (1971) 263 (here p 76).

be seen as primarily concerned with the two realizations of the Christian conception of sexuality, namely, marriage and religious life. It is ironical in the present context to note that within canon law was a developed doctrine and set of regulations on other *familiae*: the monastery and, to a lesser extent, the *familia* of the bishop. Inasmuch as there was reflection on the kin, on the extended family, or the nuclear group, this reflection was in terms of the relationship of the couples that were at the centre of these social units. The regulations that proved to be of such importance were concerned with the persons who were free to marry, how their union was to be brought about, and the qualities of permanence and exclusivity of their relationship.

Once the systematic canonical collections began to appear in the tenth century and the foci around which canon law was organized can be identified, the importance of marriage becomes evident. When one turns to the great monuments of medieval canon law, the *Decretum* of Gratian and the *Decretals* of Gregory IX, the fact is patent. Limitations based on relationship are cast in terms of the spouses' freedom to marry; opposition to those procedures that were expected to provide an heir – polygyny, divorce and remarriage, etc – was cast in terms of Christian revelation (specifically identified as such). Major interest was focused on the free choice made by the couple and on limitation of that choice due to ignorance, fear, or incapacity. Equally important from the point of view of the motive for the Church's position are the facts that adoption was not opposed and that the Church sought, by her doctrine of legitimization, to make it possible for some excluded children to enjoy the benefits of legitimacy – including that of being heir.

Finally, in terms of the ideas advanced in Professor Goody's volumes, it is suggested that more attention be paid to the implementation of the practice of consensual marriage and its extension to all levels of the population; the consequences of this development – to a considerable extent a canonical achievement – may prove to be significant in its contribution to that elusive social structure that is called the European family.

13

Maritalis affectio Revisited

One of the principal interests in the contemporary study of society is the analysis of relationships within the family. 'Family' in this context can be understood both in its nuclear and in its more extended form, though the emphasis in the discussion within the western world is primarily on the nuclear group. This analysis includes in its purview the various sets of relationships between the sexes. It understands that, with the passage of time, the quality of these relations varies and that, within the life span of a given group, they have their micro history. Furthermore, it has become abundantly clear that much is to be gained by studying the evolution of the quality of these relationships through the generations: they have a macro history that may well be important for our self-understanding.[1]

Within the broad field of social history, one of the areas in which there has been important progress during the last twenty years has been the study of marriage in Western Europe during the Middle Ages. It is interesting not only in itself but also because it enables us to observe how a developing Christian ideology was joined to powerful means of diffusion so that it came in time to exercise very serious pressures on marriage and, through it, on the family. (Implied in this statement is the notion that ideas run before social change, a position that social historians often tend to avoid or, at least, ignore.)[2] The family was forced to adjust to a much

---

1 Philippe Ariès, *Centuries of Childhood: A Social History of Family Life*, trans R. Baldick (New York 1962), where the child is seen in relation to adults, is an example of this approach.
2 The importance of the development of social ideas is fundamental to Georges Duby, *Medieval Marriage: Two Models from Twelfth-Century France*, trans Elborg Forster, The Johns Hopkins Symposia in Comparative History 11 (Baltimore 1978); and Jack Goody, *The Development of the Family and Marriage in Europe* (Cambridge 1983). The

more individualistic attitude to marriage. It is scarcely an exaggeration to say that the consequences of this change in the West still unfold before us.[3] In the large body of recent scholarly literature devoted to the analysis of this development within the history of marriage, there has been comparatively little study of the relationship between the spouses. Since so much of this research has involved the analysis of the role of consent in creating the marriage bond both in theory and in practice, it is something of a surprise to realize how little attention has been paid to the substance of that consent. On the other hand, this omission might well have been expected, for the answer, when it is finally available, will likely prove to be a very complex one. In a society such as that of medieval Europe to which so many traditions and so many cultures had contributed and in which there had been no attempt, by and large, to produce a homogeneous society, differences of expectation based on the nation, class, and age of family members were preserved. They have proved to be very tenacious, as is perfectly obvious even in America, where, in a transplanted European culture, that richness of background is still evident. The sources available for the investigation of the quality of the relationship that existed between spouses are daunting in their multiplicity and in their volume. The varied sets of documents associated with marriage agreements are obviously of prime importance, and more general information of a similar sort provided by collections of laws and legal treatises is contributory as well. Then there is the whole area of imaginative literature, on which so much scholarship has been lavished for more than a century. The list could be extended, but this is sufficient. Let it be said, however, that study of this material has tended to create an understanding of the spousal relationship that makes it secondary to those expected within the bloodline[4] or to those enjoyed, at least in imagination, by unmarried lovers. The spousal relationship thus understood can, not unfairly, be summed up in

common attitude of the social historian is different from that of the political scientist, who traditionally has seen development of political theory as the usual prelude to political change. Cf Michael Anderson, 'The Relevance of Family History,' in *The Sociology of the Family: New Directions for Britain*, ed Christopher C. Harris, Sociological Review Monograph 28 (Keele 1979) 49–73, where the socio-economic impact on the formation of these ideas is stressed. For this reference and for other valued suggestions I thank Professor Judith M. Bennett.

3 See Michael M. Sheehan, 'Marriage and Family in English Conciliar and Synodal Legislation,' in *Essays in Honour of Anton Charles Pegis*, ed J. Reginald O'Donnell (Toronto 1974) 211–14 (here pp 84–6).

4 Ibid 205 (here p 77).

the words of Kenelm Foster as 'a purely institutional and judicial state which only engages the personality in a relatively superficial way.'[5] It is very likely that such a description of marriage often obtained, but it must not be forgotten that the evidence is provided by a rather specialized set of documents and that they relate to a small part of medieval society.

The point was made earlier that the Church developed an ideology on these matters and was in a position to present it to – even impose it on – society. This ideology, as has been demonstrated in the discussion of the role of consent in establishing the marital bond,[6] was capable of application across a varied spectrum of cultural forms; and, although it would not oppose – much less eliminate – all local customary expectations on these matters, it could be expected to have a considerable influence. Thus there is much to be said for looking at Christian teaching on the relationship that should obtain between spouses. Beyond this lies the more difficult question, that of the degree to which this ideology was accepted by medieval society; but, first, an attempt must be made to describe that ideology.

It is proposed to study this question in the context of the large-scale discussion of questions touching sexuality, celibacy, religious life, and marriage that occurred during the two centuries following the Gregorian Reform. Often my purpose will be to suggest lines of approach, indicate serious or at least tentative progress that has been made recently, and, in a few cases, illustrate some of the conclusions that it is not unreasonable to expect to result from the enterprises that are currently under way.

The medieval discussion of relations between husband and wife was rooted in the Judaeo-Christian Scriptures. Those Scriptures provide a remarkably developed reflection on the matter at issue. There is a description of the creation of mankind and an explanation of the difference of genders in terms of the purpose of their relationship. Furthermore, that relationship had a history – a history in which there were two principal moments, namely the fall of Adam and Eve and the coming of Christ, after each of which sexuality and marriage and the relationship of spouses within marriage took on new meanings and new possibilities. Through-

5 'Courtly Love and Christianity,' in *The Two Dantes and Other Studies* (Berkeley 1977) 15–36. In this context it should be remembered that some canonists resisted the notion that marriage was a sacrament because the financial element involved in so many unions was redolent of simony.

6 *Le lien matrimonial*, Colloque du Cerdic, Strasbourg, 21–3 mai 1970, ed René Metz and Jean Schlick (Strasbourg 1970).

out the Scriptures there is much advice on the substance and quality of the relationship between the spouses, a quality of which the remark of Professor Foster, mentioned above, would not provide an adequate description. Those Scriptures were taken by the Fathers and interpreted in terms of the culture in which they lived and, as well, in terms of their own experience. When, in the period following the Gregorian Reform, the great intellectual enterprise that characterized the era was launched, it included the examination of this tradition, an ordering and interpreting of it and, occasionally, the rejection of parts that were not capable of being fitted into the syntheses created at the time. This enterprise was not based solely on the Christian tradition: it involved a huge intake of ancient ideas, some filtered through Arab scholars, some – and this element increased as the thirteenth century progressed – drawn directly from Greek authors.[7] These latter sources not only introduced ancient understandings of social organization and of human biology but, more especially, initiated an examination of the meaning of friendship that was to prove of considerable importance.[8] It was in this context that there occurred that large-scale reflection on marriage by Scripture scholar, theologian, philosopher, lawyer, artist, and poet the importance of which has already been mentioned. By and large, research in recent years, much as it has focused on this development, has paid little attention directly to the question that has been posed, that is, to the quality of the relationship between the spouses. The history of exegesis is only in its infancy: not surprisingly, there is as yet little to say of the texts that might be expected to help in this discussion. Similarly, while historians of theology have examined the role of the consent of the principals to the marriage in the creation of the bond and the sacramentality of matrimony, and while there has been an important discussion of abusive aspects of the marriage relationship, little is yet available about positive teaching on the life that spouses were expected to live. The recent work of Dom Jean Leclercq is an important

---

7 See Etienne Gilson, *History of Christian Philosophy in the Middle Ages* (New York 1955) 235–6.

8 Thus Thomas Aquinas in *Summa contra gentiles* 3 123, in a discussion of the indissolubility of marriage, wrote: 'Furthermore, the greater that friendship, the more solid and long lasting it will be. Now, there seems to be the greatest friendship between husband and wife, for they are united not only in the act of fleshly union, which produces a certain gentle association even among beasts, but also in the partnership of the whole range of domestic activity' (*On the Truth of the Catholic Faith: Summa contra gentiles* 3 2, trans Vernon J. Bourke [New York 1956] 148).

exception to this statement, and there are several other enterprises under way that can be expected to be helpful.[9]

Thus, while studies of theological speculation on the relationship between spouses are much to be desired, they have only begun. Significant progress has been made of late in areas more directly related to instruction and enforcement of the Christian life at both the level of moral guidance and that of practice. Among the instruments of instruction were confessors' handbooks, sermons, hymns, liturgical books, and suites of illustration and sculpture that commented on marriage in a variety of ways and had a certain amount to say about the relationship that was expected between the spouses. Other literature, notably the canons, was concerned with expressing the rules that the society could be expected to enforce; but, especially in its earlier stage, it often took on the mantle of moral guidance as well. Naturally enough, canon law, its jurisprudence, and the detailed information on decisions that the records of the ecclesiastical courts supply often tend to reveal marriage and human sexuality at the point where they pass beyond the acceptable. Thus canonical literature sometimes creates a foreshortening of vision that limits our understanding of what was expected in a positive way and, even more, of what was actually done in the society of the time.[10]

In their examination and enriching of the classical Roman concept of *maritalis affectio*, however, the canonists provided a much more positive

9 Jean Leclercq, 'The Development of a Topic in Medieval Studies in the Eighties: An Interdisciplinary Perspective on Love and Marriage,' in *Literary and Historical Perspectives of the Middle Ages: Proceedings of the 1981 SEMA Meeting*, ed Patricia W. Cummins, Patricia W. Conner, and Charles W. Connell (Morgantown, W. Va. 1982) 20–37; *Love in Marriage in Twelfth-Century Europe*, University of Tasmania Occasional Papers 13 (Hobart 1978); 'L'amour et le mariage vus par des clercs et des religieux, spécialement au XIIe siècle,' in *Love and Marriage in the Twelfth Century*, ed Willy Van Hoecke and Andries Welkenhuysen, Mediaevalia Lovaniensia, Series 1, Studia 8 (Louvain 1981) 102–15; *Monks on Marriage: A Twelfth-Century View* (New York 1982). Professor Pierre J. Payer is well advanced on a study, 'The Channelling of Desire: Ideas of Sex in the Later Middle Ages,' in which the thinking of the theologians of the high Middle Ages will be analysed in detail [*The Bridling of Desire: Views of Sex in the Later Middle Ages* (Toronto 1993) – Editor].

10 As was noted above, the canonical discussion of consent was of major importance both in itself and from the point of view of social developments. This and the other requirements for establishing the bond were the aspects of marriage that received the most detailed development. For canonical thought and its regulations on sexuality and the living of the sexual life see James A. Brundage, *Law, Sex, and Christian Society in Medieval Europe* (Chicago 1987); note the bibliography, 621–34, for a valuable selection of earlier literature.

approach to questions touching marriage. The fundamental examination of this concept appeared almost twenty years ago in an important article by Professor John T. Noonan, Jr.[11] It will be used to provide the base for the present discussion. Noonan showed how the notion was developed in Roman law as a means of defining a relationship distinguished from concubinage – a union the children of which were fit to inherit.[12] At first, it probably connoted nothing more than a legal intent, a willing. Implicit in the discussion was the notion that where marital affection had ceased, the marriage ended, but by the time of Justinian that possibility no longer applied. More important for the present discussion was the question of the relationship between marital affection and consent. Were the expressions synonymous? It is clear that both were required. 'Marital affection' defined the content of the consent, namely to have the other as spouse. Having discussed the meaning of the word *affectio* in this context, Noonan concluded that, by the time of Justinian, the term implied 'not simply a legal will but an emotion-coloured intent not far from love,' an implication that is important for this analysis.[13] The notion usually implied the intention to procreate and the understanding that the relationship was to be monogamous, exclude promiscuity, and enjoy a degree of permanence; but no intrinsic criteria were developed for judging whether that attitude existed. Roman law was content to fall back on an external expression of marital affection by proper registration, at least in the case of the well-to-do.

This notion was adopted by Gratian, the great canonist of the second quarter of the twelfth century. Collections like his *Decretum* were made up, for the most part, of canons taken from a wide variety of older sources. Gratian's volume had many of the qualities of a treatise, however, for it included an important discussion of the canons as his text progressed. It is in this discussion, the part most directly indicative of his thought, that the use of the term *maritalis affectio* is most common.[14] Like Justinian he used the term to identify a married union, but he went beyond Roman law, concluding that, where a relationship began with marital affection, the marriage persisted even though a spouse had become a prisoner or a slave. Furthermore, under the same conditions a marriage

---

11 'Marital Affection in the Canonists,' *Studia Gratiana* 12 (1967) 479–509.
12 On the question as to whether this notion were a Christian interpolation, see Noonan, 'Marital Affection in the Canonists' 482.
13 Ibid 488.
14 Ibid 489–90.

bond could be created between slaves. It was in this context that Gratian cited a text of Pope Leo to the effect that such a union was begun in God.[15] Thus he concluded that wherever there was marital affection the bond could come into being; and, once established, nothing short of the death of a spouse could cause it to fail.[16] He held that the concept need not include the intent to procreate. Thus in the case of the marriage of Mary and Joseph the relation was established by affection, an affection that was not procreative but completely faithful. On the other hand, marital affection could exist where the purpose was simply to satisfy sexual desire.[17] Furthermore, in his discussion of the first and very confused stage of the union of Jacob and Leah, Gratian introduced a distinction between consent and marital affection that was to prove of importance: to consent was to accept a given person as spouse, while marital affection referred to the quality of the relationship that, as a result, came into being between the spouses.[18] When it came to the criteria necessary for the law to recognize the existence of that bond and thus, where necessary, enforce it, Gratian fell back, as Roman law had done, on

15 'Ita illae quae in affectum ex Deo initum redeunt, merito sunt laudandae' (C34 q1 c1); see Noonan, 'Marital Affection' 492.

16 Ibid 499. Thus in his discussion (ca 1213) of the relationship that caused a cleric to be bigamous, Robert of Flamborough insisted that it was marital affection (*Liber poenitentialis: A Critical Edition with Introduction and Notes*, ed J.J. Francis Firth, Studies and Texts 18 [Toronto 1971] 162–5); in a case of 1381 the official of Ely enquired about the marriage of Pobert Puf 'super eo quod maritali affectione se invicem non pertractant' (Ely Consistory Court Register: Cambridge, University Library, Ely Diocesan Records D 2 [1] f 153v). In the Maddyngle case (1378) of the same register, marital affection is distinguished from other intentions of marriage: John's wife admitted their marriage but claimed that he was impotent. John countered: 'iurati sunt cohabitare et se mutuo maritali affectione pertractare et operam carnalis copule prestare' (f 91r).

17 C32 q2 c5, *dict. ad* IV. pars. See the letter of 1205 from Innocent III regarding the wife who, under much pressure, had allowed her husband of about twenty years to enter a monastery, then, when he left religious life, demanded that he return to her. The pope instructed his delegates that, if the woman were of an age that enforced continence might lead her to sin, then the husband was to be forced to receive her back as wife and treat her with conjugal affection ('ut eam recipiat eique affectum exhibeat conjugalem') (PL 215 593–4). Augustine tells us in his *Confessions* (2 3) that his mother wondered whether it would be possible for him to contain his sexual activity within the limits of conjugal affection: 'cohercere termino coniugalis affectus' (*Sancti Augustini Confessionum libri XIII*, ed Lucas Verheijen [Corpus Christianorum, Series latina 27 2]).

18 Gen 29:26–8; *Decretum, dict. ante* C29 q1. See Noonan, 'Marital Affection' 486–7.

external evidence: the agreed statement of the principals or the observance of visible formalities.[19]

With Pope Alexander III (1159–81), the notion of marital affection entered papal decretals. Here it was used as in the *Decretum*, but a further development is quickly discernible. The term was distinguished from consent, the act that created the marriage bond (the wedding). Marital or conjugal affection was expected to endure during the marriage. It was seen, in Noonan's words, 'as an active disposition which the spouses had a duty to cultivate.'[20] Thus a static notion was replaced by one implying the desirability of growth. With this in mind, and in accord with the Pauline exhortation that husbands love their wives, the pope was willing to command a certain behaviour during marriage. Thus a husband or wife might be ordered to take back a repudiated spouse and treat him or her with marital affection. The modern reader, at least one accustomed to the expectations of Western society, is tempted to judge that such action would hardly resolve the problem revealed. Yet it is clear that this solution was considered desirable, for there is abundant evidence in papal decretals and in the records of local ecclesiastical courts that both men and women often demanded the enforced society of their spouse.[21] This fact needs to be underlined, for it is an important indication of what some spouses expected of marriage, of what made it desirable and worth defending in court: a sexual partner even though another was preferred, a place in society, shelter and sustenance, etc. A somewhat different point of view is expressed in another of Pope Alexander's decretals exhorting the spouses of lepers (both husbands and wives) to accompany their sick partners and minister to them with conjugal affection. This was not likely intended to be a sexual service but the kind of mutual care that, the decretal implied, could be expected of those who were married.[22]

---

19 See the possibility suggested by Noonan, ibid 499.
20 Ibid 501.
21 Ibid 503–4. See the letter of Innocent III, above, n17: in the Poynant case (Ely Register, 1378) the marriage of John Poynant and Joan Swan had been declared null because of John's impotence. Joan married and John proved his sexual powers by less acceptable means, so the court declared the original marriage to be valid; and John and Joan were 'fore compellendos ut maritali affectione se invicem adhereant et pertractant' (f 142v). Joan at least seems to have been reluctant.
22 'ut uxores viros, et viri uxores, qui leprae morbum incurrunt, sequantur, et eis conjugali affectione ministrent' (X 4 8 1); Noonan, 'Marital Affection' 502–3 points out that the recommendation was not concerned with intercourse, a question dealt with in X 4 8 2. Note that husband and wife are equally obliged.

A similar understanding of marital affection as the quality that should characterize the relations between spouses during their life together was adopted by Pope Innocent III (1199–1216). He carried the notion considerably further, in the sense both of the substance of consent at the beginning of marriage and of the quality of the relationship that was expected to endure, in his discussion of the marriage and polygamy of pagan peoples. But with him, as with his predecessors, no attempt was made to define its essential qualities or to establish criteria that would make it possible for a court to decide whether marital affection existed or not.[23] The concept would continue to be used, especially as a means to describe external aspects of an ideal. Thus it was often employed against a certain type of behaviour (excessive correction of a spouse, mistreatment of a spouse, etc) as opposed to marital affection. More positively, husbands were ordered to provide suitable dress for their wives, to see to their proper nourishment, etc, as required by marital affection. Thus the concept can be seen to provide a set of rules expressing what was expected and what was not allowed; but the canonical system, especially in its more mature stage, when its role was to express rules that could be enforced, did not seek to become involved with the more intimate positive aspects of the affection that was called marital. No doubt, further research along the lines suggested will refine our understanding of this matter, but it will likely remain a description that rarely moves beyond the external aspects of *maritalis affectio*. The exhortation of Alexander III to the spouse of a leper, mentioned above, did indicate a more internal vision of its meaning; for further evidence of this sort it is necessary to examine other types of literature.

The confessor's handbook, a manual intended to instruct the priest who sought to form the consciences of his flock, correct their faults, and lead them to a life of virtue, seems a likely source where positive teaching on the meaning of marital affection might be expected.[24] This type of literature was derived in part from the ancient Penitentials, texts that had

---

23 Noonan also describes a different approach used in the time of Pope Gregory IX (1227–41), namely, the evaluation of a marriage in terms of the three goods discussed by St Augustine, *De bono coniugali*, ed Josef Zycha, *Corpus scriptorum ecclesiasticorum latinorum* 41 5 pars 3 (Prague, Vienna, and Leipzig 1900) 185–231. He suggests that here, too, they were 'objective touchstones'; see 508–9.

24 In this discussion of the *Summa confessorum*, I am indebted to the contributions of the members of my seminar, 'Marriage and Family in Medieval Europe,' especially to Jacqueline Murray, 'The Perceptions of Sexuality, Marriage, and Family in Early English Pastoral Manuals,' Ph.D. dissertation (University of Toronto 1987).

much to say of the abuses of sexuality and marriage but shed little light on the matter under present discussion.[25] These new manuals began to appear late in the twelfth century and rapidly increased in number and in the quality of their contents, especially after the Fourth Lateran Council (1215). At first, they were mostly given to instruction on the regulations of the Church, sins, and their penances; but as the years passed, they tended to provide instruction of a much more positive sort on the sacraments and on many of the practical problems of the Christian life. Though it remained very important, the legal element was reduced with the passage of the years; many of the notions developed by theologians received statement in a form that would be useful at the level of parish instruction.[26] Much use has already been made of this literature in the study of medieval marriage, especially with regard to the instruction on the requirements for the validity of the union.[27]

A preliminary examination of several of these *Summae confessorum* gives valuable insight into their authors' understanding of the spousal relationship. For example, in one of the earliest, the *Liber penitentialis* of Alan of Lille, completed 1198×1203, several indirect references to the causes of sexual excitement and its moral consequences are mentioned. Thus in a consideration of illicit unions, the confessor is instructed to learn whether the penitent was moved by lust or whether he purposefully set out to excite himself sexually.[28] Sin with a beautiful woman is less serious than with a homely one because her attraction diminishes the sinner's self-control.[29] To yield to passion after a single glance is a more serious offence than to fall as a result of prolonged social intercourse.[30]

---

25 See Pierre J. Payer, *Sex and the Penitentials: The Development of a Sexual Code, 550–1150* (Toronto 1984).

26 See Pierre Michaud-Quantin, *Sommes de casuistique et manuels de confession au moyen âge (XIIe–XVIe siècles)*, Analecta mediaevalia Namurcensia 13 (Louvain 1962); and Josef G. Ziegler, *Die Ehelehre der Pönitentialsummen von 1200–1350: Eine Untersuchung zur Geschichte der Moral- und Pastoraltheologie*, Studien zur Geschichte der katholischen Moraltheologie 4 (Regensburg 1956).

27 See Ziegler, *Die Ehelehre*; and Michael M. Sheehan, 'Choice of Marriage Partner in the Middle Ages: Development and Mode of Application of a Theory of Marriage,' *Studies in Medieval and Renaissance History* n s 1 (1978) 19–25 (here pp 103–9).

28 'Si non moveatur a concupiscentia, sed moveat concupiscentiam, majus peccatum est,' 1 25, Alain de Lille, *Liber poenitentialis*, ed Jean Longère, Analecta mediaevalia Namurcensia 17–18 (Louvain 1965) II 33–4.

29 'quia ille magis cogitur qui pulchram: ubi maior coactio, ibi minus peccatum' (ibid I 27; II 34).

30 'utrum uno aspecto in aliquam exarserit an paulatim inflammatus fuerit. Ille enim

There is nothing of great moment in these little insights, but they do suggest the reflection on the mechanisms of sexual attraction and the broad understanding of it that lay behind the moral guidance that this type of treatise sought to provide.

A similar awareness of the relations between spouses is suggested in an engaging passage from the *Summa confessorum* of Thomas of Chobham, sub-dean and *officialis* of the English diocese of Salisbury. The work, completed about 1216, marks a considerable progress on that of Alan of Lille. Its section on marriage, a major treatise on the subject, ends with a statement on the role of wives as preachers to their husbands – 'Quod mulieres debent esse predicatrices virorum suorum' – and leaves no doubt as to the author's judgment of when a husband is most likely to be moved by his wife's request. The confessor is instructed to urge women to take up this role, for no priest can he expected to soften a man's heart as a wife can. The text continues: 'Hence the sin of a man can often be imputed to his wife if, through her neglect, the husband does not mend his ways. When they are alone and she is in her husband's arms, she ought to speak to him soothingly, and if he is hard and merciless and an oppressor of the poor she ought to invite him to mercy; if he is a plunderer to detest his plundering ...'[31]

A considerably more developed reflection on these aspects of marriage is to be found in the *Tractatus de matrimonio* of John of Freiburg. The treatise is the fourth book of his *Summa confessorum*, a highly sophisticated compendium for the confessor published at the end of the thirteenth century.[32] In his definition he adopts the usual text from the

magis peccat qui solo aspectu seducitur, quam qui ex convicto inflammatur' (ibid I 29, 34).

31 'Mulieribus tamen semper in penitentia iniungendum est quod sint predicatrices virorum suorum. Nullus enim sacerdos ita potest cor viri emollire sicut potest uxor. Unde peccatum viri sepe mulieri imputatur si per suis negligentiam vir eius non emmendatur. Debet enim in cubiculo et inter medios amplexus virum suum blande alloqui, et si durus est et immisericors et oppressor pauperum, debet eum invitare ad misericordiam; si raptor est, debet detestari rapinam': *Thomae de Chobham Summa confessorum*, ed F. Broomfield, Analecta mediaevalia Namurcensia 25 (Louvain 1968) 375. The wider context of this instruction and the role of the treatise is discussed in detail in Sheehan, 'Choice of Marriage Partner' 22–5 (here pp 106–9); and Murray, 'The Perceptions of Sexuality' 141–81.

32 On the author and the significance of his treatise, see Leonard E. Boyle, OP, 'The *Summa confessorum* of John of Freiburg and the Popularization of the Moral Teaching of St. Thomas and of Some of His Contemporaries,' in *St. Thomas Aquinas, 1274–1974: Commemorative Studies*, ed Armand Maurer (Toronto 1974) II 246–7.

Decretum Gratiani: 'matrimonium eat viri et mulieris coniunctio individuam vite consuetudinem retinens' (C2 q2 c1), then goes on to state that the 'undivided companionship of life' implies mutual faith, mutual rendering of the marital debt, and 'mutuam exhibitionem,' which he defines as the obligation of both to provide the necessities of this life inasmuch as they can.[33] Furthermore, in the discussion of the consent that is necessary to create the marriage bond, he explicitly asked in what that consent consisted.[34] He replied that it could not be identified with cohabitation nor with carnal union. The latter need not be explicit in consent, though it should be implicit, since the communion necessary for conjugal society is not only of goods but also of bodies. The marriage of Mary and Joseph is seen as a touchstone for the understanding of matrimonial consent or conjugal society. This he says – and here John falls back on a traditional theme – is evident from the account of the 'formation' of Eve in Genesis 2:18–25: she is not taken from the head of man, lest she seem his superior; nor is she taken from his foot, lest she seem his servant. She is taken from his side, that he might have both a helper and an associate.[35] Furthermore, John followed the usual teaching that marriage was instituted by God for two reasons: before the Fall for the generation and education of children and, after the Fall, with an additional purpose: the channelling of sexual desire. He added that there could be other, secondary reasons for seeking marriage, such as wealth or a woman's beauty.[36] With regard to the rendering of the marital debt, the Pauline point of view was presented, as might be expected. Sexual

References to John of Freiburg's *Summa* in what follows are to book, title, and question, followed by the folio number of the Venice edition of 1568.

33 '& mutuam exhibitionem, scilicet ut uterque reliquo in necessariis huiusmodi vitae, si possit, providere' (Bk 4 tit 2 q1 f 217r). John had developed this statement earlier in his gloss to Raymund of Peñafort's *Summa de poenitentia et matrimonio*, gl. ad 'matrimonium', Bk 4 tit 2 q1 (Rome 1603) 510. The care of the leprous spouse, urged by Alexander III in virtue of marital affection, would be included in this 'mutua exhibitio.'

34 'Cum in matrimonio requiratur consensus, queritur in quod sit ille consensus' (Bk 4 tit 2 q12 f 218r).

35 Bk 4 tit 2 q12 f 218r. The text is taken from the *Summa Raymundi*, Bk 4 tit 2 q3 511–12, but in this case John refers it to the content of matrimonial consent, a point of view somewhat different from that of Raymund. See also Erik Kooper's discussion of the 'rib-topos' in *The Olde Daunce: Love, Friendship, Sex, and Marriage in the Medieval World*, ed Robert R. Edwards and Stephen Spector (Binghamton, N.Y. 1991) 44–56.

36 Bk 4 tit 2 q23 f 219r. In these matters John closely follows Raymund, *Summa de poenitentia*, Bk 4 tit 2 q6 514.

powers are to be exercised with restraint and with purpose. A practical reflection on the unselfishness and – if one may use an overworked word of the moment – the sensitivity that was recommended by this approach is evident in his adopting the observation made by theologians fifty years before: since women tend to be more modest than men in expressing their longing for sexual union, a husband should provide for his wife's wish not only when she asks but also when, though in her modesty she does not express it, there is some indication of her desire.[37]

It is hoped that, from peripheral remarks in the *Summae confessorum* such as these, further clues as to the meaning of that marital affection to which spouses consented will be gained in research projects currently under way. But there is a serious limitation to this literature: it was intended for those who were to instruct the laity at the local level, rather than for the laity themselves. Much that was personal, be it exhortation, warning, or command, was presumed; and, since there was no need to present it in these treatises, it appeared, if it appeared at all, on the fringe of major discussions.

Other modes of instruction were more directly intended for those to whom this discussion relates, namely the laity. One of the principal modes over the centuries has been the liturgy. Within it, the matrimonial rite, involving instruction of the principals as well as those present at the ceremony, had much to say of the Christian ideal of marriage.[38] Thus far liturgical texts have been analysed to establish the rate at which the necessity that spouses freely consent to their union became generally expressed. This has been done by exploring the questions put to them – a questioning that, in one case at least, included the enquiry whether there were love between the pair.[39] Similarly, the examination of a variety

---

37 'non solum quando expresse petit debitum uxori vir tenetur reddere: sed etiam quando per signa apparet eam hoc velle. Non tamen idem iudicium est de petitionem viri: quia mulieres magis solent verecundari petendo debitum quam viri' (John of Freiburg, Bk 4 tit 2 q40 439).

38 See Korbinian Ritzer, *Le mariage dans les églises chrétiennes du Ier au XIe siècle* (Paris 1970); J.-B. Molin and Protais Mutembe, *Le rituel du mariage en France du XIIe au XVIe siècle*, Théologie historique 26 (Paris 1974); and Cyrille Vogel, 'Les rites de la célébration du mariage: Leur signification dans la formation du lien durant le haut moyen âge,' in *Il matrimonio nella società altomedievale*, Settimane di studio del Centro italiano di studi sull'alto medioevo 24 (Spoleto 1977) I 397–472.

39 In a late twelfth-century Cahors missal: 'et inquirat de parentela fortiter, et si est amor inter illos. Et si aliquam parentelam invenerit, non iungantur. Si autem amorem habent, et in parentela non inveniuntur, iungantur' (cited in Sheehan, 'Choice of Marriage Partner' 29 and n74; here pp 113–14). On the source occur-

of graphic treatments of courtship, the wedding, and family life, especially in manuscript decoration, has begun to yield valued indications of the understanding of certain aspects of marriage.[40] But, even here, there does not seem to have been a study of this evidence from the point of view of the present essay.

Perhaps the last major area of medieval literature that has yet to be explored in a thorough way is the sermon. The first steps towards the easy accessibility of this literature have been taken during the last decade, and some important studies of the sermon and marriage have recently appeared.[41] Here we propose to devote a few paragraphs to suggest ways in which this literature may be expected to shed light on the question of the relationship between husband and wife that was seen as the norm among men and women of the time. An article by David d'Avray of Cambridge University, written in cooperation with M. Tausche, can be used for this purpose.[42]

Two principal types of marriage sermon have been identified. The first, much the more common, was related to the account of the marriage feast at Cana (John 2:1), read at the mass of the second Sunday after Pentecost. The second type was the *ad status* sermon, one of a series preached to different classes and groups – the married were included – within

rences of this text see Brian F. Bethune, 'The Text of the Christian Rite of Marriage in Medieval Spain,' Ph.D. dissertation (University of Toronto 1987) 102–21 and passim.

40 See the use of manuscript illustration by A. Melnikas, *The Corpus of Miniatures in the Manuscripts of Decretum Gratiani*, Studia Gratiana 16–18 (Rome 1975) III 887–1058, 1085–1172. It is the nature of manuscript illumination, essentially private art as it is, to be an indication of understanding rather than a means of instruction.

41 The fundamental work is by J.B. Schneyer, whose *Reportorium der lateinischen sermones des mittelalters für die Zeit von 1150–1350*, Beiträge zur Geschichte der Philosophie und Theologie des Mittelalters, Texte und Untersuchungen 43, 5 vols (Münster 1969–73) awaits but an index for completion. Among recent studies of sermons dealing with marriage, note especially N. Berious and David L. d'Avray, 'Henry of Provins, OP's Comparison of the Dominican and Franciscan Orders with the "Order" of Matrimony,' *Archivum fratrum praedicatorum* 49 (1979) 513–17; David L. d'Avray and M. Tausche, 'Marriage Sermons in *Ad status* Collections of the Central Middle Ages,' *Archives d'histoire doctrinale et littéraire du moyen âge* 47 (1980) 71–119; David L. d'Avray, 'The Gospel of the Marriage Feast of Cana and Marriage Preaching in France,' in *The Bible in the Medieval World: Essays in Memory of Beryl Smalley*, ed Katherine Walsh and Diana Wood, Studies in Church History, Subsidia 4 (Oxford 1985) 207–24, and *The Preaching of the Friars: Sermons Diffused from Paris before 1300* (Oxford 1985), especially 69–70, 249–50, 257–8.

42 d'Avray and Tausche, 'Marriage Sermons.'

medieval society. It is to the latter type that d'Avray and Tausche turn in
the article just mentioned. The authors see the sermon as a useful index,
not of the highest flights of theology but as a means 'to discover what sort
of ideas about marriage ordinary men and women were regularly exposed
to.'[43] Many of these ideas touched the relations between the spouses.
Thus, in a sermon of the early twelfth century, Honorius of Autun em-
phasizes the mutual love of the couple: 'Let husbands love their wives
with tender affection; let them keep faith with them in all things; let them
abstain from them on holy nights and on the nights of fasts, and at the
time when women suffer their natural infirmity ... In the same way,
women should love their husbands deeply ('Mulieres viros suos similiter
intime diligant'), fear them, and keep faith with a pure heart. Let them
agree in everything good, like a pair of eyes.'[44]

A more developed reflection on married love is found in an *ad status*
sermon of Guibert de Tournai, a Franciscan who seems to have been
active from ca 1235 to his death in 1284.[45] He writes, 'There is also a kind
of love founded on partnership, and this is the love which husband and
wife owe to each other, because they are equals and partners.'[46] Where so
many other authors pointed out that this equality referred only to the
equal sexual rights the spouses possessed, Guibert makes no such restriction, a fact that is in accord with the 'optimistic attitude to marriage'
that was typical of him. Later he says that husband and wife should, in
the words of Proverbs 17, be inseparable; as friends, they love each other
at all times.[47] They ought to have a feeling of love that makes separation
impossible; love is a guarantee of fidelity; spouses should be able to accept
criticism from each other.[48] The citation of this excellent article could be
carried much farther, but this should be sufficient to suggest the potential
of sermon literature as an indication of the relation of husband and wife
that was presented as an ideal.

43 Ibid 77.
44 PL 172 867. The translation is from d'Avray and Tausche, 'Marriage Sermons' 78.
   Note how Honorius has gone well beyond the instructions of St Paul (Eph 5:22–5;
   Col 3:18–19), where husbands were to love their wives ('Viri, diligite uxores vestras')
   and wives were to be subject to their husbands ('Mulieres viris suis subditae sint').
45 d'Avray and Tausche, 'Marriage Sermons' 74–5.
46 'Est enim dilectio socialis qua debent se coniuges diligere, quia pares sunt et socii'
   (ibid 114; the translation is drawn from the same source).
47 'Sit etiam inseparabilitas affectionis. Prov XVII. Omni tempore diligit qui est amicus'
   (ibid 115 and n23).
48 'Sit etiam liberalitas correctionis ut libere possit vir uxorem arguere, et ex dilectione
   illa recipiat, et e converso' (ibid 116–17 and n25).

These reflections are merely a series of probes into various kinds of literature that until recently have not yet been used at all for the study of medieval marriage; or, if they have been analysed, it has been with the purpose of gleaning their information on the marriage bond. Of the quality of that bond, they seem to have had little to say. Yet, from the brief presentation that has been made, it seems reasonable to hope that there is much to be derived from these sources and that a serious attempt should be made to master them. It has been suggested that the investigation of the conception of *maritalis affectio* (and probably of *coniugalis affectio* as well) in canon law and in the records of ecclesiastical courts will indicate the outer shell of accepted relationships; that the *Summae confessorum* will look more to the interior of the marriage but, because of an understanding that is presumed, will not turn to the problem directly, revealing the substance of that presumption only by the occasional remark in passing; that in the sermon, an instrument for the direct instruction of married people, a more fruitful source for the understanding of the ideals presented to the married couple will be found. Enough has been said already to suggest that the various types of literature that have been examined, when taken together and with due attention to their complementarity, present an understanding of the spousal relationship that cannot be described as one that 'only engages the personality in a relatively superficial way.'

14

The Bishop of Rome to
a Barbarian King
on the Rituals of Marriage

In its early stages, Christianity and the lean cultural vehicle that supported it stood somewhat apart from the societies of the Mediterranean basin. In time, however, it came to play a major role in the self-understanding of the region, influenced important developments and changes of direction in public and private institutions, and, eventually, became the religion of the Roman state. In the process, Christian faith and practice came to express themselves more and more in the languages, symbols, and social usages of that world. As the tendency for the Empire to divide along a north-south axis became more accentuated, the Church too became aware of a considerable degree of cultural variety within itself and, more seriously, of differences in theology and faith as well as in pastoral usages.

In the West especially it was the religious element in society that proved most vigorous in its meeting with the new peoples coming into the Empire from the north and east. Roman military and political institutions were eclipsed, but missionaries continued to carry the new religion of the Empire to the barbarians. Very often they brought not only Christian belief and practice but also much of the cultural vehicle in which Christian belief had come to express itself, so that it was not uncommon to see a confusion occur between the two orders, not only on the part of those to whom Christianity came but also sometimes among the missionaries themselves. These contacts produced profound changes in the lives of all involved. Now and then there were moments when the principal actors reflected on what was happening or sought advice from wiser men as to how they might best proceed in teaching the new peoples about Christianity. Sometimes they inquired whether place for barbarian customs of one kind or another could be found within Christianity, even though they were obviously incompatible with the practices of a more sophisticated sort in which the Church expressed itself in the Mediterranean basin. Those moments provide a precious view of life in that very agitated period and probably bring the historian somewhat closer to the actual state of affairs than do narrative histories and the various collections of laws that remain extant.

Among the most interesting are letters from the heart of a mission land in which an Augustine or a Boniface describes conditions and usages of the world to which they have come and seek advice as to the attitude to be adopted to them. The answers to these *consulta* have proved to be precious sources, providing information on differences of custom and the process of adaptation through which much of Europe was passing at the time. Perhaps the most famous of them is the exchange between Augustine of Canterbury and Pope Gregory I around 600, in which conditions in Kent were described, the Roman reaction indicated, and something of Roman practice of that moment revealed as well. These *consulta* have been the object of much analysis in recent years, and it has become clear that not all the information they contained when they found their place within Bede's *Historia ecclesiastica gentis Anglorum* (731) was part of the original exchange.[1] Yet even when interpolations are set aside they remain precious descriptions of Anglo-Saxon conditions and Roman expectations. They were to provide important norms for the centuries that followed.

On a much larger scale is a long letter of Pope Nicholas I sent in response to questions that came to him from the circle of Boris, khan of the Bulgarians, in 866.[2] These *responsa* manifest three, rather than the usual two, points of view: much is said of Roman practices – it was to learn of them that the *consulta* were sent – but beliefs and practices of the Greek Church and clear indication of some of the preoccupations of Bulgarian leaders are revealed as well. These were years of serious tensions within the Balkan peninsula, throughout the Eastern Empire and between the Churches of East and West. Iconoclasm had officially ended, but the divisions it had created were still evident within the Byzantine world, and there was resentment, by some at least, of papal intervention

---

1 *Bede's Ecclesiastical History of the English People*, ed B. Colgrave and R.A.B. Mynors (Oxford 1969) 78–102. See Paul Meyvaert, 'Bede's Text of the *Libellus responsium* of Gregory the Great to Augustine of Canterbury,' in *Benedict, Gregory, Bede, and Others*, Variorum Reprints (London 1977) X 15–33.

2 *Epistolae Karolini aevi*, ed Ernest Perels, MGH Epistolae (Berlin and Munich 1891–1975) VI Ep 99 568–600 [henceforth Ep 99].

in the quarrel. The see of Rome sought to re-establish its jurisdiction over the vicariate of Illyricum and had become involved in the dispute at Constantinople between Ignatius, the deposed patriarch, and Photius, his successor. Finally, Moravia and Bulgaria were subject to powerful religious and political pressures from both East and West, a situation in which they sought partial relief in alliances which presented a less immediate threat: Moravia with Constantinople and Bulgaria with the Franks. These arrangements involved the dispatch of Byzantine missionaries to Moravia and of Roman (and probably of Frankish) missionaries to Bulgaria. The latter mission received a serious set-back when the Bulgarians were defeated by Byzantine forces in 864. In the aftermath Boris was baptized according to eastern usages, even accepting the name of his patron, the Emperor Michael, and the area was opened to Byzantine missionaries. There must have been serious confusion as teachers representing East and West, and others of rather dubious allegiance, presented their versions of Christianity to those whom they had come to instruct. Within a short time Boris' military position was somewhat improved.[3] Perhaps the Byzantine failure to establish a Bulgarian patriarch was the main reason for his disappointment; no doubt many aspects of Christianity proved difficult to accept. At any rate, he sent a series of enquiries about the belief and practices of the Church of Rome, and Pope Nicholas replied in a long and important letter, the most recent study of which was published by Lothar Heiser in 1979.[4]

The language of Boris' *consulta* is unknown. Their contents can be deduced from the items treated in the *responsa*. The order of the replies is frequently without apparent rationale, though as a whole their organization is better than that of many of the legal collections of the time. Whether the papal letter follows the plan of the *consulta* has been much discussed, and the problem is probably incapable of solution.[5] It should be noted, however, that the first chapter of the *responsa* discusses the principal theological problem raised by Boris' *consulta*, and the point

3 See Francis Dvornik, *The Photian Schism: History and Legend* (Cambridge 1948) 91–131.

4 *Die Responsa ad consulta Bulgarorum des Papstes Nikolaus I (858–867)*, ed Lothar Heiser, Trier theologische Studien 36 (Trier 1979); see Richard E. Sullivan, 'Khan Boris and the Conversion of Bulgaria: A Case Study of the Impact of Christianity on a Barbarian Society,' *Studies in Medieval and Renaissance History* 3 (1966) 53–139.

5 See *Die Responsa*, ed Heiser 73–5; and Sullivan, 'Khan Boris' 59–60. On various opinions on the role of Anastasius the Librarian in the composition of the *responsa*, see Heiser 68.

is made that it was the first of his questions: 'Igitur optime ac laudabiliter in prima quaestionum vestrarum ...' The *responsa* begin with the statement that they are intended to be but a brief reply to Boris' questions – 'Ad consulta vestra non multa respondenda sunt ...' – because it is intended to send messengers (*missi*) and books for his instruction.[6] They prove, however, to be a major discussion that treats of one hundred and six items, some at considerable length. Over the years there has been much discussion of Nicholas' motive and of the attitude towards the Greek Church revealed in the *responsa*.[7] Some historians like Friedrich Kempf see an attack on '... the rites of the Greek Church, even exposing them to ridicule'; others emphasize the purpose to win Bulgarian allegiance to Rome.[8] It is true that during the years under discussion the see of Rome sought to extend its jurisdiction over the area occupied by the Bulgarians. It is important to remember, however, that, once Boris had requested instruction, the pope could hardly be expected to ignore him. Furthermore, when usages of East and West were in disagreement or when the pope judged Greek demands of their new converts to be unnecessary, he was to be expected to state the fact. The *responsa* note similarity of usage on occasion; and, where difference seems to have been revealed in Boris' *consulta*, the pope sometimes remarks that his reply is in terms of Boris' description, suggesting that the reality may be otherwise.[9] The quality of a simple pastoral reply to practical questions is apparent: given the usual rhetoric of the correspondence between Rome and Constantinople during Nicholas' reign, the tone of the *responsa* is remarkably restrained, almost irenic.

The *consulta* posed questions about many things: sometimes it is evident that further light was sought on demands being made by Greek missionaries. The Bulgarians clearly wanted to learn more of the customs of the Roman Church; some areas of special sensitivity are revealed. The replies can be grouped in two principal sets, one dealing with faith and cult, the other with morality and the practice of the Christian life.[10] The most developed single question, one to which the *consulta* seem to have

6 Ep 99 cap. 1 568.
7 See *Die Responsa*, ed Heiser 1–10.
8 Friedrick Kempf et al, *The Church in the Age of Feudalism: A Handbook of Church History*, ed Hubert Jedin and John P. Dolan (London 1969) III 179; Emile Amann, *L'époque carolingienne*, Histoire de l'Eglise 6 (Paris 1937) 476–83.
9 Eg 'Consuetudinem quem Graecos in nuptialibus contuberniis habere dicitis' (Ep 99 569 line 37) and 'quemadmodum Graecos vos astruere dicitis' (Ep 99 570 line 19).
10 See *Die Responsa*, ed Heiser 90–9.

referred again and again, is that of sexuality and marriage; nineteen of one hundred and six items treat of it.[11] This preoccupation is evident in other sources that give insight into problems faced by missionaries; Christianity had already developed a theory of marriage, and it was becoming clear that it touched the ways in which families recruited new members and reinforced their ties.[12] After Nicholas' initial discussion of faith and good works, the questions of relationship and the manner of establishing the marriage bond were addressed.[13] The pope had already been much involved in these matters. Both in replying to other, smaller *consulta* from bishops and in his correspondence generally, he had developed positions on various matters of uncertainty or dispute.[14] Similarly, he had intervened in the long quarrel with Lothair II, king of Lorraine, who sought to repudiate Theutberga – a quarrel in which Hincmar of Rheims also took part and in which they hammered out more precise thinking on the prohibition of divorce.[15] The text of the *responsa* to the Bulgarians is rather different. By and large it is not concerned with specific cases and hence does not offer solutions that must be enforced. It is true that it includes simple, clear statements of canon law on marriage and other topics, but its tone is more pastoral, more concerned to explain the reasons for the practices of the Church than to insist on the necessity that they be followed.[16] It is on one of its distinctions between the desirable and the necessary that this paper will principally reflect.

The third chapter, among the most extensive sections of the *responsa*, is an early description of the preferred steps by which marriage was brought about and a reflection on their significance.[17] Boris apparently

---

11 Persons involved in marriage: Ep 99 cap. 2, 29, 39, 51, 70, 71; endowment: cap. 49; marriage rite: cap. 3; time of marriage: cap. 48; end of marriage: cap. 87, 96; sexual activity: cap. 9, 28, 50, 52, 63, 64, 68; dress: cap. 59. It is presumed that in the last case, that of dress, sexual distinction was involved.

12 See Jack Goody, *The Development of the Family and Marriage in Europe* (Cambridge and New York 1983) 134–56.

13 Ep 99 cap. 2 and 3, 569–70. Did the original *consulta* place the questions of spiritual relationship and the rituals of marriage in these prime positions, or was it the decision of the author of the *responsa*? At any rate, their final position was established as of major importance. See the conclusion of this essay and the problem discussed there.

14 See *Epistolae Karolini aevi*, ed Perels Epp 141, 146, and 149 (respectively pp 660, 663, and 666); cf 'Nicolai I. papae epistolae spuriae et dubiae,' ibid 669–96.

15 See Amann, *L'époque carolingienne* 369–80.

16 Eg the explanation of spiritual relationship, Ep 99 cap. 2.

17 Ep 99 569–70. The text, the Roman tradition from which it is derived, and Greek

had sent a description of Greek custom as he perceived it,[18] and the pope proceeded to show how similar it was to the past and present usage of the Roman Church. The beginning of the chapter presents two serious problems to the modern reader. Thus, when the first sentence sets out the matter to be discussed, 'Consuetudinem ... in nuptialibus contuberniis ...,' it seems to run the risk of insulting Boris by the use of the term *contubernium*. In the Roman legal tradition – the pope had underlined the fact that the usages of which he wrote were traditional – *contubernium* referred to a ménage that, whatever its stability might have been, could not be considered a true marriage *(legitimum coniugium)*.[19] Isidore listed it last in a descending set of cohabitations and likened its stability to that of a tent.[20] A text from Pseudo-Isidore, written shortly before the *responsa* and almost certainly known in Rome, clearly stated that *contubernia* were not *coniugia* and presented itself as the teaching of Nicholas' predecessor, Pope Evaristus.[21] This understanding of the word was to continue through

usages to which it refers are discussed in detail by Heiser, 277–89. In addition see George H. Joyce, *Christian Marriage: An Historical and Doctrinal Study*, Heythrop Series 1, 2nd ed (London 1948) 47, 52, 105, 189, and passim; Cyrille Vogel, 'Les rites de la célébration du mariage: Leur signification dans la formation du lien durant le haut moyen âge,' in *Il matrimonio nella società altomedievale*, Settimane di studio del Centro italiano di studi sull'alto medioevo 24 (Spoleto 1977) I 397–65, especially 420–6; and especially Korbinian Ritzer, *Formen, Riten, und religiöses Brauchtum der Eheschliessung in den christlichen Kirchen des ersten Jahrtausends*, Liturgiewissenschaftliche Quellen und Forschungen 38 (Münster 1962) 127–34, 136–50, 157–80, and passim. Other early accounts of the stages by which marriage was brought about include that ascribed to Pope Evaristus by Pseudo-Isidore, *Decretales Pseudo-Isidorianae et capitula Angilramni*, ed Paul Hinschius (Leipzig 1863) 87–8; and 'Bewifmannes beweddunge,' a text of ca 1025, probably from the circle of Archbishop Wulfstan of York, *Die Gesetze der Angelsachsen*, ed Felix Liebermann (Halle 1903–16) I 442–4.

18 'Consuetudinem, quam Graecos in nuptialibus contuberniis habere dicitis, commemorare prolixitatem stili vitantes carptim morem, quem sancta Romana suscepit antiquitus et hactenus in huiusmodi coniunctionibus tenet ecclesia, vobis monstrare studebimus' (Ep 99 569 lines 37–40).

19 See *Vocabularium Codicis Iustiniani*, ed Robertus Mayr (Prague 1923–5; repr Hildesheim 1965) I 729, s v 'Contubernio', 'Contubernium'; and Adolf Berger, *Encyclopedic Dictionary of Roman Law*, Transactions of the American Philosophical Society 43 (Philadelphia 1953) 415, s v 'Contubernales', 'Contubernium'.

20 'Contubernium est ad tempus coeundi conventio; unde et tabernaculum, quod modo huc, modo illuc praefigitur,' *Isidori Hispalensis episcopi Etymologiarum sive originum libri xx*, ed W.M. Lindsay (Oxford 1911) I, Liber 9 VII 23.

21 'aliter vero presumpta non coniugia, sed adulteria aut contubernia aut stupra vel fornicationes potius quam legitima coniugia,' ed Hinschius 88. The text would appear in Ivo of Chartres, *Decretum* 8 4; *Panormia* 6 31 (PL 161 585, 1250); *Decretum Gratiani* C30 q5 c1; and in the canonical tradition generally. The reading is slightly

the Middle Ages and into modern times.[22] Nicholas seemed to employ *contubernium* in this pejorative sense in the second chapter of the *responsa* explaining why a sponsor was not allowed to marry a godchild; he noted that if those related by adoption were forbidden marriage, 'quanto potius a carnali oportet inter se contubernio cessare, quos per coeleste sacramentum regeneratio sancti Spiritus vincit?'[23] It will be noted, however, that *contubernium* is specified by *carnale*.

There was another usage of *contubernium* that referred to fellowship or close companionship but in which the heterosexual overtone was omitted. This had long been used of military comrades and found a place in the Vulgate translation of the Bible in Mark's account of the multiplication of the loaves, where Christ '... praecipit illis ut accumbere facerent omnes secundum contubernia super viride faenum' (6:39), and in the Book of Wisdom, where the loving relationship between God and Wisdom is shown to involve their presence to each other: 'contubernium habens Dei' (8:3). This understanding of the word, with its emphasis on companionship and common dwelling, was taken up by the Latin Fathers and can be found repeatedly through the Middle Ages.[24] Thus there was a traditional meaning of *contubernium* that expressed a variety of relationships extending from the mutual presence of God and the soul to the compan-

different in the present edition of Hugh of St Victor, *De sacramentis*, Liber 2 pars II cap. 5 (PL 176 486D): 'non conjugia, sed adulterina contubernia, vel stupra,' but the sense is unchanged.

22 See *The Oxford English Dictionary* (Oxford 1933) II 930B, s v 'Contubernal'.

23 Ep 99 cap 2 569 lines 30–1.

24 Eg Jerome, *Contra Rufinam* I 9: 'Ipse enim Eusebius, amator et praeco et contubernalis Pamphili,' *S. Hieronymi presbyteri opera*, Pars III, Opera Polemica I, ed P. Lardet, Corpus Christianorum, Series latina 79 (Turnhout 1982) 8; Peter Chrysologus, Sermon 6 3: 'Hinc est quod ille dominus deus est, qui fuit in cunabulis nostri capax, dulcis in gremio, mitis habitu, in nostro contubernio blandus,' *Sancti Petri Chrysologi Collectio sermonum*, ed Alexander Olivar, Corpus Christianorum, Series latina 24 (Turnhout 1975) 45 (for five similar uses see Sanctus Petrus Chrysologus, *Collectio sermonum*, Corpus Christianorum, Instrumenta lexicologica latina, Fasc 3, Series A–Formae [Turnhout 1982] 27, s v 'Contubernio', 'Contubernium'); Peter Damian, Sermon 383: 'Beatus vir Donatus ... Iuliano Caesari non solum in liberalium artium studiis contubernalis extitit,' *Sancti Petro Damiani Sermones*, ed Johannes Lucchesi, Corpus Christianorum, Continuatio mediaevalis 57 (Turnhout 1983) 57 (for nine similar uses see Sanctus Petrus Damianus, *Sermones*, Corpus Christianorum, Instrumenta lexicologica latina, Series A, Fasc 16 [Turnhout 1983] 28, s v 'Contubernalis', 'Contubernia', 'Contubernio', 'Contubernium'); Chaucer, 'Parson's Tale': 'for humble folk had been Cristes freendes; they been contubernyal with the Lord,' *The Works of Geoffrey Chaucer*, ed F.N. Robinson, 2nd ed (London 1957) 252 lines 758–60 (this example was supplied by Michelle Bull).

ionship of the least important of men. If carnal, this relationship was unacceptable; but if spiritual – and the nuptial relationship was spiritual – it was to be praised.[25] Whatever his intention may have been, Nicholas began his discussion of Christian marriage with the use of a term that prevented it from being identified with the unions of the aristocracy, a term that, potentially at least, could be applied even to the lowest members of society.

The second problem at the beginning of chapter three is that, having suggested the similarity between the customs of the two Churches but before describing Roman marriage, Nicholas proceeded to state what the Roman bridal couple did not do, namely wear a head-dress or crown of metal when they married: 'Nostrates siquidem tam mares quam feminae non ligaturam auream vel argenteam aut ex quolibet metallo compositam, quando nuptialia foedera contrahunt, in capitibus deferunt ...'[26] Since the place of the crown in the ritual was to be set out almost immediately, it is surprising that Nicholas saw fit to refer to it here. And there is a problem within the text itself: the meaning of *ligatura*. It may indeed have been intended to refer to the marriage crown, but a few lines later the term *corona* would be used in that sense. Elsewhere in the text, *ligatura* connotes 'binding' or 'bundle.' Thus in chapter sixty-six there is question of wearing a linen band on the head in church and in chapter seventy-nine of using an amulet to cure the sick.[27] Is it possible that reference here is not to the crown of the Greek ritual but to a head-dress to which the coins of marriage endowment were attached and which in some customs – those of the Bulgarians, perhaps – were worn during the rite of marriage?[28] Was it Nicholas' intention to make it clear from the beginning that no ritual of this sort was practised at Rome? Given the

25 Other examples in cap. 3: 'nuptialia foedera' (Ep 99 570 lines 1, 7–8), 'futurarum sunt nuptiarum promissa foedera' (line 2), 'iura nuptiarum' (line 16), 'in nuptiali foedere' (line 18) and 'in nuptiis' (line 22).

26 Ep 99 cap. 3 569–70.

27 Ep 99 cap. 66: 'Graecos prohibere vos asseritis cum ligatura lintei quam in capiti gestatis, ecclesiam intrare' (590); cap. 79: 'Perhibentes, quod moris sit apud vos infirmis ligaturam quandam ob sanitatem recipiendam ferre pendentem sub gutture' (594). See *Thesaurus linguae latinae* (Leipzig 1900–) VII 2, Fasc 10, 1380–2, s v 'Ligatura'.

28 Note that the text does not refer to the principals as a couple but states that neither men nor women wear the *ligatura*. See the discussion of the traditional meaning of the headband in marriage in Richard B. Onians, *The Origins of European Thought about the Body, the Mind, the Soul, the World, Time, and Fate*, 2nd ed (Cambridge 1954) 432, 446–8.

present knowledge of barbarian custom it is not possible to find evidence supporting this hypothesis. Thus, in spite of problems that remain, it seems best to conclude that Boris' description had laid much stress on the crowning in the Greek ritual and that the pope decided to emphasize the fact that it did not enjoy such a position in that of Rome – that, in fact, the crown was not worn during the actual marriage (*nuptialia foedere*) but afterwards.[29]

The pope then gave a remarkably complete description of the steps by which marriage was brought about. It is in two parts, the first inserted between the aforementioned statement of what was not done when marriage was contracted and the description of the marriage itself.[30] This first part consisted of three stages: first, there was the engagement (*sponsalia*), carefully identified as a promise of future marriage made by the couple and those in whose power they were. Then followed the giving of an earnest, a ring placed on the woman's finger by her fiancé. Finally, having come to an agreement as to the amount, the latter endowed his future bride and conveyed written evidence of the gift in the presence of witnesses invited by the two parties. It will be noted that these stages of the process are presented as entirely familial and civil, that there is no mention of dowry provided by the family of the future bride, and that no question is raised as to the quality of the obligation resulting from these acts, the penalty for withdrawal, or the procedure by which it might be done. It is a straightforward presentation of usage in a non-contentious situation with a single point of emphasis, namely, that betrothal is not marriage but a promise of future marriage. The description continues with the observation that, if the couple is of age – this is not specified –

29 Ritzer, who sees in this text a reference to the crowning (*stephanosis*) of the couple (*Formen* 136–7), suggests that the different metals used in the crown corresponded to the social position of the families involved. Given the fact that in its earlier stage the crowning of the couple by the bride's father was in a family context, it is likely that the crowns expressed family wealth. On the importance of this ceremony in the Greek tradition, see Ritzer 136–46; *Die Responsa*, ed Heiser 285–6; and Roger Béraudy, 'Le mariage des chrétiens: Etude historique,' *Nouvelle revue théologique* 104 (1982) 54–7.

30 'sed post sponsalia, quae futurarum sunt nuptiarum promissa foedera quaeque consensu eorum, qui haec contrahunt, et eorum, in quorum potestate sunt, celebrantur, et postquam arrhis sponsam sibi sponsus per digitum fidei a se anulo insignitum desponderit dotemque utrique placitam sponsus ei cum scripto pactum hoc continente coram invitatis ab utraque parte tradiderit' (Ep 99 570 lines 2–6).

they may proceed immediately to marry. But there can be a delay; indeed, in the case of those under age, it is required.[31]

Next follows the description of the marriage (*nuptialia foedera*), rituals in which the role of the priest was stressed.[32] First, in church and with offerings to God, presumably in the context of the Eucharist,[33] the priest blessed the bridal pair and covered them with a veil, acts that established the *nuptialia foedera*. The text notes the blessing of Adam and Eve and its promise of fecundity and the prayer of Tobias and his wife before the consummation of their marriage, references that apply to the blessing and the purity of relationship symbolized by the veil.[34] It is noted in passing that the ritual of the veil was denied those who marry a second time;[35] then the account goes on to note that when these rituals had been completed the couple left the church wearing crowns. Of the coronation itself, nothing is said, though we are informed that the crowns belonged to the church. It is presumed that they would be available to any couple whose union was blessed by the priest.[36] This description of the rites of marriage is brought to completion by a remark that placed the whole process within a religious context: having completed the nuptial festivities the couple was directed to take up their life together as God provided.

The central section of chapter three is an evaluation of the agreements and rites that have just been described, an evaluation the direction of which is anticipated by the pope's rather flippant remark that he has

31 'aut mox aut apto tempore, ne videlicet ante tempus lege diffinitum tale quid fieri praesumatur, ambo ad nuptialia foedera perducuntur' (Ep 99 570 lines 6–8).

32 George H. Joyce held that marriage occurred with the giving of the ring and the transfer of dower, while the blessing and veiling of the couple within the Eucharist were delayed until the couple was ready to begin conjugal life (*Christian Marriage* 47). As the ritual of marriage assumed form in northwest Europe during the eleventh century, the ceremonies of ring and endowment ceased to be associated with betrothal and became part of the marriage ceremonies at the door of and in the church. It is clear from the text of the *responsa*, however, that the rites described in n30, above, were completed before the *nuptialia foedera* took place; see L. Duchesne, *Origines du culte chrétien: Etude sur la liturgie latine avant Charlemagne* (Paris 1920) 449–51.

33 Early Cisalpine liturgical books like the Gelasian and Gregorian sacramentaries presume that the nuptial blessing occurs within the mass. See Ritzer, *Formen* 343–6.

34 Gen 1:28, Tob 8:4. See *Die Responsa*, ed Heiser 284.

35 'Verumtamen velamen illud non suscipit qui ad secundas nuptias migrat' (Ep 99 570 line 13). Since blessing and veiling were part of a single ceremony, it can be presumed that the denial of a second blessing is implied.

36 Cf n29, above.

described formalities as well as he can remember them.[37] Boris seems to have reported that he understood that all the rituals of marriage bound under pain of sin. The pope, noting that Boris claimed to have received this instruction from the Greeks, denied that ritual enjoyed such importance. He went on to point out that Roman law held that only the consent of the principals was necessary and gave the reason for this position: some were too poor to afford the formalities of marriage.[38] The pope continued, arguing that though all rituals were observed and the union consummated, there would not be a marriage unless the couple had consented. He seems to have been aware that his position confronted a strong movement within the Eastern Church, so he reinforced his argument by citing a text ascribed to one of the great teachers of that tradition, John Chrysostom: 'Matrimonium non facit coitus, sed voluntas.'[39] It would be an error to conclude from this part of his reply that Nicholas attached minor importance to the rituals that he had set out so carefully and that expressed consent to betrothal and to marriage, symbolized their meaning, and pointed out their consequences; the summing-up mentioned above makes this point clear.[40] At the same time, it must be

---

37 'Haec sunt iura nuptiarum, haec sunt praeter alia, quae nunc ad memoriam non occurrunt, pacta cuniugiorum sollemnia' (Ep 99 570 lines 16–17).

38 'peccatum autem esse, si haec cuncta in nuptiali foedere non interveniant, non dicimus, quemadmodum Graecos vos astruere dicitis, praesertim cum tanta soleat artare quosdam rerum inopia, ut ad haec praeparanda nullum his suffragetur auxilium; ac per hoc sufficiat secundum leges solus eorum consensus, de quorum coniunctionibus agitur' (Ep 99 570 lines 19–21). This consideration of the poor is evident in the *Ecloga* of Emperor Leo III (AD 717–40), where it is granted that, if because of poverty or humble condition, the couple cannot include the exchange of documents within their marriage (*gamos agraphos*), their consent and that of their relatives will suffice if it be expressed before witnesses or their union be blessed in church (Tit 2:8), J. Zepos and P. Zepos, *Jus Graecoromanum* (Athens 1962) II 22; cited by Béraudy, 'Le mariage des chrétiens' 55 n12. See Ritzer, *Formen* 112–13. Similarly, a text of Benedict the Levite, *Benedicti Capitularia liber II*, cap. 133: 'Nullum sine dote fiat coniugium; nec sine publicis nuptiis quisquam nubere presumat' (MGH Leges II, ed G.H. Pertz [Hannover 1837; repr Leipzig 1925] pars altera 80) appears in an interpolated form in Burchard, *Decretum* 9 6 (PL 140 816): 'Nullum sine dote fiat coniugium; iuxta possibilitatem fiat dos, nec sine publicis nuptiis.' In *Decretum* 19 5 (PL 140 958) a confessor, questioning a penitent about the formalities of his marriage, asks if he has not endowed his spouse with a farthing at least: 'vel pretio unius oboli, tantum ut dotata fieret.' The preoccupation with the poverty of the couple is evident in each case, but the requirement of some formalities remained.

39 *Opus imperfectum in Matt. 32.9* (PG 56 802). On the ascription of the text to a Greek Aryan bishop, see Ritzer, *Formen* 104.

40 'Et ita festis nuptialibus celebratis ad ducendam individuam vitam Domino dispo-

understood that he held resolutely to the position that consent alone was necessary and sought to lessen the possibility that lack of consent would be hidden or simply forgotten in the powerful momentum created by a sequence of ritual acts. The contrast between the *responsa* and the contemporary text of Pseudo-Isidore is significant. The latter also describes a series of steps leading to marriage, but it concludes by pointing out that where the rituals were not observed the union in question was presumed to be invalid.[41] In fact, even in this case the ménage could be preserved, though not easily. Such is not the tone of Nicholas' reply.

The first two parts of chapter three would enter the western canonical tradition and provide a powerful argument in support of public marriage ceremonies.[42] They also played a significant role in the long discussion of marital freedom contributing to the fundamental argument in its support, namely, that the consent of the principals alone was necessary, though, as the argument developed, it was the need of consent that was emphasized rather than the fact that there were no other essential requirements.[43] Pope Nicholas had explained why consent without formalities sufficed for Christian marriage – it was necessary since some were unable to observe the customary rituals because they were poor – but this part of his teaching was not remembered.

The final section of chapter three raises what at first sight seems to be a completely different question and provides a prompt answer: 'As to your enquiry whether, after the death of his wife, a man may marry another, be it understood that this is entirely possible.' The pope cites 1 Corinthians 7:8–9 with its preference for the celibate life but clear statement that marriage is acceptable: 'To the unmarried and the widowed, I say that it is well for them to remain unmarried as I am. But if they cannot

---

nente de cetero diriguntur' (Ep 99 570 lines 15–16). See Joyce, *Christian Marriage* 106.

41 See above, n21.

42 Eg *Decretum Gratiani* C30 q5 c5, where, though the 'peccatum autem esse' text (Ep 99 570 line 18) is included, the canon is entitled 'Nuptiae publice celebrari debent.'

43 Eg *Decretum Gratiani* C27 q2 c2. On the reluctance of English episcopal statutes of the thirteenth century to stress that consent alone sufficed for marriage, see Michael M. Sheehan, 'Marriage Theory and Practice in the Conciliar Legislation and Diocesan Statutes of Medieval England,' *Mediaeval Studies* 40 (1978) 459 (here p 175). On the other hand, Nicholas' words (Ep 99 570 lines 21–4) could be used as a limitation of the tendency to render ritual more precise: see the gloss on a twelfth-century pontifical from Rouen discussed in Michael M. Sheehan, 'Choice of Marriage Partner in the Middle Ages: Development and Mode of Application of a Theory of Marriage,' *Studies in Medieval and Renaissance History* n s 1 (1978) 28–9 (here p 113).

exercise self-control, let them marry.' (Boris was spared the final clause of the verse: 'It is better to marry than to burn.') The reply continues, probably going beyond the intent of the original query: 'A wife is bound to a husband as long as he lives; if he die, she is freed; let her marry whom she will, only in the Lord' (1 Cor 7:39). An interpretation follows; it shows how arguments in favour of a woman's freedom can be applied to that freedom for a man of which Boris enquired. Whatever is fixed for women is to be understood as applying also to men because, on the other hand, Scripture often speaks of man but is all the same understood to apply to woman.[44] The discussion is brought to a close with the citation of two verses from the psalms in which this equation of man and woman (*vir* and *femina*) is reinforced.[45]

The discussion of remarriage within chapter three seems to involve a serious lapse in the organization of the *responsa*. The question of the degree to which their plan follows that of the *consulta* comes to the fore at this point. If the juxtaposition were established by Boris it would appear that he saw the customary rituals by which marriage was brought about and the custom on second unions to be of similar nature and importance. On the other hand, there were other questions within the *consulta* to which an enquiry on second marriages might more suitably have been attached.[46] Alternately, if the questions were separated in the *consulta*, one wonders why Nicholas chose to bring them together. It is possible that, on the one hand, he regarded the matter of second marriages to be intrinsically unimportant and included it with the discussion of ritual because, as was noted earlier, second marriages did not include the ceremonial veiling of the couple. On the other hand the marshalling of Scripture texts to emphasize freedom to marry, and the developed argument showing that the text about second marriages referred equally to women and men and that in other matters as well they shared the same blessings, suggest that the pope had a more serious purpose. Chapter three of the *responsa* provides much information on the rituals and the understanding of marriage in ninth-century Rome and, upon reflection, reveals something of the practices of the Eastern Church as

---

44 'Quod enim de muliere sanxit, et de viro intelligendum est, quia e contra saepe sancta scriptura de viro loquitur, sed et de muliere nihilominus dicere subintelligitur' (Ep 99 570 lines 29–31).

45 'ubi non solum virum, sed et feminam ... beatam esse non inmerito credimus' (Ep 99 570 lines 32–4).

46 Eg cap. 51: 'Si liceat uno tempore habere duas uxores' (Ep 99 586 line 26).

well. These aspects of the text have been carefully analysed by several scholars. But there is another theme that appears again and again throughout this text. The use of the term *contubernium*, the discussion of crowning and the information that at Rome the crowns were the property of the church, the explanation of the essential formlessness of the process whereby the bond of marriage was established as a necessity because of the poverty of some members of the community, and, finally, the insistence not only that second marriages were permitted but also that in this matter as in others women were to be treated as men: all of these are examples of that theme. During the early Middle Ages, almost without exception, general regulations on betrothal and marriage, descriptions of individual ceremonies, and accounts of disputes related to marriage and its dissolution were concerned with the aristocracy.[47] The text from Pope Nicholas' *responsa* falls in large part into that pattern; but there is the recurring theme that would underline a fundamental equality in matters touching the freedom to marry. It would be an error to make of Pope Nicholas a leveller or a democrat; but it does seem that in his letter to Boris he tried to make that king understand that Christian marriage was open to all his people, men and women, rich and poor. Tradition seems to have ignored this part of the pope's message. We shall probably never know whether it was duly noted by Boris or by the *missi* from Rome who carried the letter to him.

47 See Pierre Toubert, 'La théorie du mariage chez les moralistes carolingiens,' in *Il matrimonio nella società altomedievale* I 241, 272–3; and Michael M. Sheehan, 'Theory and Practice: Marriage of the Unfree and the Poor in Medieval Society,' *Mediaeval Studies* 50 (1988) 457–87 (here pp 211–46). An important exception to the aristocratic bias of evidence on this matter has kindly been provided by Dr Carl Hammer: in his *Vita vel passio Haimhrammi* (ca 772) Bishop Arbeo of Freising describes the marriage of a slave in pagan Franconia, *Passiones vitaque sanctorum aevi Merovingici*, ed Bruno Krusch, MGH Scriptores rerum Merovingicarum (Hannover and Leipzig 1902) IV 512.

15

Sexuality, Marriage, Celibacy, and the Family in Central and Northern Italy: Christian Legal and Moral Guides in the Early Middle Ages

In the opening paragraph of his description of monastic organization, the sixth-century author of the *Regula Magistri* chose the domestic household as the model for the two 'divine households' of which he wrote: the local church and the monastery. His purpose was to provide a useful illustration of the hierarchical structure that he proposed to describe, yet the casual use of the comparison suggests a profound change that had occurred in sixth-century Italy.[1] He took for granted that two other structures which had appeared in the Roman world could be seen as parallels to and, to a certain extent, competitors with those households which, from the point of view of tradition and civil law, were the motor and substance of society. The spread of the ideology that contributed to that change and its implementation in the Italy in which the Master lived are the objects of analysis in this chapter.

As the patristic period, the first era of theological reflection in the history of Christianity, drew to a close in the early fifth century, it was clear that Christian thinkers had arrived at a well-developed and somewhat original conception of mankind, its nature, and its purpose. This

---

For this article the method of documentation used in the original has been altered in keeping with the requirements of the present collection. Unnumbered notes original-ly incorporated in the text have been mixed with the numbered footnotes, with the result that the numbers here are different from those in the original printing. – Editor

1 *La règle du maître*, ed Adalbert de Vogüé, Sources chrétiennes 105–7 (Paris 1964–5) II 8. The perception of a development of this sort a century earlier is suggested by the collecting of the *Consuetudines sirmondianae*: see *Theodosiani Libri XVI cum constitutionibus sirmondianis et leges novellae ad Theodosianum pertinentes*, ed Theodor Mommsen and P.M. Meyer (Berlin 1905) I 907–16, and the *Codex Theodosianus*, Bk 16.

conception was expressed with different nuances in different parts of the Church, but in general terms it was consistent. One of the more important aspects of this ideology was the notion that both the human race and its individual members had histories.

That humankind had a history was clear from the Old Testament. The appearance of the human race was related to the creation of the rest of the world, but it involved a special exegetical problem, having been described in two different ways. According to Genesis 1:26–9, the human race was created with an inherent gender distinction so that it could reproduce itself. The second account, Genesis 2:18–24, was more nuanced. It described the discovery of a need for adjustment within creation that became evident almost immediately. The first man needed a helpmate and companion; so a woman, a being similar to but distinct and somewhat different from him, was made from the first man himself. Furthermore, since the woman was both from and for the man there was to be both unity and hierarchy within their relationship. The first time that the couple was shown acting together, they made the tragic decision that produced an immense change. They became subject to a life of exhausting work and to death. In the sentence of the woman, the imperfection resulting from sin touched on both functions expressed in the accounts of her creation: because of her the human race would indeed increase and multiply, but at the cost of her suffering; she would bear the difficulties of her subjection to Adam because of her attraction to him (Gen 3:16).

The very difference that attracted the couple to each other – the difference of which they learned when they became aware of shame – was disturbed, so that it was at once delightful and problematic. Furthermore, since it was the couple's difference, namely their sexual powers, that allowed humanity to continue through time, the consequences of their original sin were seen to be passed on by that difference as well. Yet their prospect was not without hope, even in the Genesis account of the Fall. In time, the second or postlapsarian agenda was seen in a positive light, and the sad event that made it necessary came to be called a 'happy sin.' This was possible because of the arrival of a new Adam in the alternative agenda, Jesus Christ. He not only furnished the means whereby the evils consequent on the original sin could be removed, but also provided an interpretation of the meaning of life and a teaching on human behaviour that was to be implemented by all people. Some of this teaching touched the exercise of sexual powers.

First, Christ urged a self-discipline concerning sexual matters that reached even to one's innermost thoughts. Second, he suggested a way of life that did not involve the sexual bond, and presented it in such a way that it could be seen not only as honourable and desirable but also as superior to the life of the married. Finally, although his instruction on matrimony was not developed, the implications of his teaching were to require an adjustment of major importance to marriage and, eventually, to the general organization of domestic life. As his doctrine was developed by his followers, marriage took on the sacred character of a mystery like the union of Christ and the Church. Marriage was seen as indissoluble and monogamous and, though these elements developed slowly, was presented as open to all men and women and as depending on the free choice of the spouses themselves. Christ made it clear that the claims of domestic life, though it forms the background to his conception of society, were secondary to the greater personal good of inheriting eternal life. He did not give an abstract analysis of the operative domestic group but described it in simple terms: father and mother, wife and children, brothers and sisters, houses and lands (Matt 19:29). He went on to note that the choice for eternal life would cause strife within the domestic unit (Matt 10:34–6; Luke 2:51–3) and, in a rhetoric not our own, that the Christian might have to hate father and mother, wife and child, brother and sister to free himself to achieve his purpose. Furthermore, at that point in Mark's Gospel where Christ chose the Apostles, he insisted that a relationship based on doing God's will overrode any relationship based on blood: informed that members of his family were present and wished to see him, he asked, 'Who are my mother and brethren?' His reply made it clear that the most powerful and lasting relationship occurred between those who did the will of God (Mark 3:31–5). Thus the preparation of the soul to be with God after death was presented as the ultimate priority and criterion of judgment, a notion that drove right to the heart of a vision of humankind in which the good of the *domus* or the *civitas* was paramount.[2]

The history of the individual was seen to illustrate the application of the agenda of creation as adjusted by the Fall and by the coming of Christ. Each one began Christian life with the ritual of baptism, an act that introduced one into the Christian community and removed the essential damage resulting from original sin. The Christian could belong to any group in society, but from the point of view of the effect of

2 Michel Rouche, 'The Early Middle Ages in the West,' in *A History of Private Life*, 1: *From Pagan Rome to Byzantium*, ed Paul Veyne, trans Arthur Goldhammer (Cambridge, Mass. 1987) 548–9; Peter Brown, *The Body and Society: Men, Women, and Sexual Renunciation in Early Christianity* (New York 1988) 1–16.

baptism all were equal before God. The end of life was followed by a judgment in which all choices would be examined and their eternal consequences weighed. Between baptism and judgment was the period when the individual was expected to follow the teaching of Christ, a teaching that included control of all appetites, of which the sex drive was one. Here Christianity introduced or supported important changes of expectation in Roman society, changes that not only affected the development of the individual but also had important consequences in society itself. The Christian could choose between the married and the celibate state, and for those who chose marriage there were new rules regarding the individual, the couple, and the wider community. Later in the life course, further choice became possible: widowhood or candidacy for clerical office could require a decision to discontinue an active sexual life. Ideally, decisions were to be made in terms of the ultimate good of which Christ spoke, eternal life.

The impact of this ideology on the late Roman Empire has been much discussed.[3] That world was undergoing rapid political and social change. No doubt profound shifts in the composition of the population, the economy, and other aspects of society contributed to what occurred, but the impact of Christian ideas cannot be ignored. That new ideology, expressed by the best minds of the age and in a manner to reach all levels of society, was in place by the end of the fourth century.[4] Its adoption was evidently facilitated by other ideals and trends that were already operative in society, ideals that supported, even explicated those of the nascent Church.[5] But the slow evolution of attitudes to sexuality and to the married and celibate states in the West during the last two centuries of the Empire is generally seen as at least in part due to the influence of the Christian understanding of humankind sketched above. This not only touched individual decisions but also found expression in the *Codex Theodosianus* (438) and in the novels of the next generation.

Just as the patristic period drew to an end, and in part as the cause of this diminution of Christian reflection, Western Europe was subjected to a series of invasions that injected new peoples into the population,

3 Jean Gaudemet, 'Le legs du droit romain en matière matrimoniale,' in *Il matrimonio nella società altomedievale*, Settimane di studio del Centro italiano di studi sull'alto medioevo 24 (Spoleto 1977) I 139–79.
4 Peter Brown, 'Late Antiquity,' in *A History of Private Life*, ed Veyne I 251.
5 A.E. Hickey, *Women of the Roman Aristocracy as Christian Monastics* (Ann Arbor 1986) 1–11; Brown, 'Late Antiquity' I 247–51, 297–311; and *The Body and Society* 17–25.

especially into the dominant classes. Whether the Christian ideology, now shorn of its most successful exponents, was able to affect this group and continue to exert its influence on the older population, and, if such were the case, how it did so, are serious problems. By the beginning of the sixth century the Ostrogothic kingdom had been established in Italy. Towards the middle of the century the peninsula was subjected to the scouring of the Byzantine wars and then, when it was almost powerless, to the last major invasion, that of the Lombards. Their rather tense relationship with the Church would endure into the middle years of the eighth century, when Carolingian power appeared on the scene. By looking at the documentation extant from the two hundred and fifty years bracketed by the arrival of the Ostrogothic and the Carolingian armies in Italy, it will be possible to learn something of the moral guidance and ecclesiastical and civil legislation that show to what extent the Christian ideology, described above, continued to be presented to the peoples of the peninsula.[6] There is, of course, another dimension to the matter, that of the implementation of these ideals in the lives of the population. This difficult task will not be undertaken in a systematic way, though an attempt is made to suggest something of its impact on the lives of individuals and on domestic institutions.

The aspects of the Christian ideology that touched human sexuality continued to be taught at the pastoral level in Italy during the period under examination. There seems, however, to have been little of that development of theory and reflection on the meaning and purpose of sexual powers characteristic of the patristic era. Sexuality was to be realized principally in two forms, namely, the married and the celibate life. The latter, practiced in institutions that supported and protected it, was new and was to be important in its consequences. In the forms they assumed, both marriage and celibacy required adjustments to the traditional understanding and realization of the family, adjustments that

6 Compared with the literature of the age of the Fathers, it is inferior in quality and quantity. There are, however, a few collections of sermons, papal and episcopal letters, important liturgical documents, several collections of canon law, especially the *Dionysiana* assembled at Rome shortly after 500, and a remarkable group of monastic rules for both men and women. During the earlier part of the period in question, Provence was part of the empire of Theoderic the Ostrogoth. Not only were its ecclesiastical leaders among the most active of the time in preaching, writing, and issuing conciliar statutes, but they were also in close relation to Rome (Cuthbert H. Turner, 'Arles and Rome: The First Development of Canon Law in Gaul,' *Journal of Theological Studies* 17 [1916] 236–47). For this reason, it has been deemed suitable to include their writings in this discussion.

became more evident as the Middle Ages progressed and that can be seen as operative in Italian society.[7]

Sexuality

The documentation that survives from the sixth and seventh centuries gives some access to teaching on human sexuality and to guidance in its functioning. Sometimes these sources provide information that pertained to the external forum and its regulations. Occasionally an episcopal letter or a sermon shows community action on the matter in question.

One notion, fundamental to the understanding of sexuality, was the ancient one that sexual activity and contact with the divine are incompatible. Strict logic might have required that to be fully Christian a believer had to be celibate. But there was another principle, one that recognized the imperious quality of the sexual urge and provided for it, either throughout life or at certain periods along the life course. This was the notion of marriage as a means (*remedium*) of satisfying sexual desire. Its importance had been set out by St Paul in his discussion of the celibate life (1 Cor 7:1–9). Having received considerable development in the writings of the Fathers, this notion was to remain an important element in reflections on the married and celibate states by medieval theologians.[8] The degree of self-restraint that was required was seen as a function of the approach to the sacred that the individual sought. Thus attempts were made to ensure that bishops, priests, and deacons, because of their frequent contact with things divine, lived a celibate life. Those whose contacts were occasional, however, were allowed marriage but were urged to become celibate at those moments when contact with divine things occurred. It was in this context that the parable of the seed yielding one hundred-, sixty-, and thirtyfold came to be interpreted. Each yield was good; each was of different value. The virginal and the Christian married life were expressed by the hundredfold and the thirtyfold respectively. The sixtyfold was reserved to those between the extremes, who came to a life of celibacy after a time when they enjoyed the lesser good of marriage.[9]

---

7 See *The Family in Italy from Antiquity to the Present*, ed David I. Kertzer and Richard P. Saller (New Haven and London 1991).

8 Michael M. Sheehan, 'Theory and Practice: Marriage of the Unfree and the Poor in Medieval Society,' *Mediaeval Studies* 50 (1988) 467 (here pp 222–3).

9 G.J. Beck, *The Pastoral Care of Souls in South-east France during the Sixth Century*, Analecta Gregoriana 51 (Rome 1950) 223–4.

Thus the text from a Council of Carthage (419), which was widely read in Europe in the *Dionysiana* (PL 67 187, 191), the important canonical collection made at Rome early in the sixth century, required those who touched the mysteries to live a continent life.[10] The periodic abstinence required of those not in major orders is well illustrated in the writings of Caesarius of Arles. The late fifth-century *Statuta ecclesiae antiquae* required those whose marriage had been blessed to refrain from consummating their union during their first night together.[11] Caesarius went further, urging that their abstinence honour the model of Tobias and endure for three nights. He also mentioned a custom of the Church of Arles, according to which new brides 'should not presume' to appear in church for thirty days after their wedding, and suggested that husbands follow their example.[12] Those who were married were expected to avoid sexual union when important religious events were to take place. Thus married catechumens were to refrain from sexual activity before and after they received baptism, and all were expected to refrain during great feasts. Pope Gregory I (590–604), asked whether it was permissible to bathe on Sunday, said that bathing was in order so long as it was not preparatory to making love.[13] Both Caesarius and Gregory mentioned the personal problems, such as deformities in their children, that beset those who failed to abstain as required.[14] The penitent, too, was expected to live as a celibate, though Pope Leo (440–61) allowed that a dispensation could be given to those whose self-control was judged impossible without marriage (for example, the young), a decision that was included in the *Dionysiana*.[15]

10 That sexual union rather than marriage stood in the way of contact with the divine was underlined in a letter ascribed to Pope Pelagius I (556–61): a cleric who married a widow whose first union had not been consummated was not considered to have married bigamously and therefore was not bound by the impediment: see Cyrille Vogel, 'Les rites de la célébration du mariage: Leur signification dans la formation du lien durant le haut moyen âge,' in *Il matrimonio nella società altomedievale*, Settimane di studio del Centro italiano di studi sull'alto medioevo (Spoleto 1977) I 424.

11 *Les Statuta ecclesiae antiquae: Edition, études critiques*, ed Charles Munier, Bibliothèque de l'Institut de droit canonique de l'Université de Strasbourg 5 (Paris 1960) 100, c101. The *Statuta ecclesiae antiquae* was a private collection of regulations compiled in Provence during the last quarter of the fifth century, of which there is a substantial Italian manuscript tradition.

12 Beck, *The Pastoral Care of Souls* 232–3.

13 Gregory I, *Registrum epistolarum*, ed Dag Norberg, Corpus Christianorum, Series latina 140–140A (Turnhout 1982) II 991.

14 Beck, *The Pastoral Care of Souls* 234–5; PL 77 200–2.

15 PL 67 290.

Marriage, then, was seen as a lightning-rod whereby sexual energy was discharged.[16] Yet writers of the time were well aware that the permitted use of marriage did not solve all problems. It was successful only for those who were self-controlled. Both Bishop Caesarius and Pope Gregory emphasized the necessity to avoid evil thoughts.[17] On several occasions Gregory pointed out the connection between gluttony and sexual appetite: 'when the belly is extended, lust is aroused.'[18] Sermons and episcopal letters returned again and again to the dangers of heterosocial relationships. This was seen as especially significant for the clergy and for those celibate men and women living in the world or in monasteries. They were given not only general advice but also precise directions in letters that discussed the dangers of self-deception as well as other less worthy motives. It was all too evident that innocent contacts followed by the play of imagination could lead to masturbation, fornication, or, in the case of clerics required to live in continence, a return to an active sexual life with their spouses.[19] The special danger in associating with lower-class women was explicitly stated in this context.[20] The *Regula Magistri* instructed monks to observe personal modesty, for the sexual stimulation from touching their own bodies could easily lead to heterosexual desire and its consequences.[21] An extreme solution to sexual craving, occasionally referred to, was castration. Although a bishop who had been castrated by 'barbarians' was not held responsible by a canon of the Council of Nicea, which allowed him to continue his ministry, self-mutilation was clearly forbidden. Pope Gelasius (492–6) taught that clergy would lose their official function and that laymen would do penance, positions reinforced by earlier law and repeated in the *Dionysiana*.[22]

16 Thus the behaviour of those accused of homosexuality or bestiality was judged to be less worthy of excuse if they were married (PL 67 154).

17 Caesarius of Arles, *Sancti Caesarii episcopi Arlelatensis opera omnia*, ed Germain Morin (Maretioli 1937–41) 1 1 193; PL 77 109, 76 200–1.

18 PL 77 81.

19 Gregory's *Dialogues* are especially rich in examples of both wise and foolish behaviour in these regards; see the tale of Andrew, bishop of Fondi, and that of the priest of Norcia who, as he died, refused the ministrations of the wife he had avoided for forty years, with the words 'Go away from me, woman. The fire is still flickering' (PL 77 229–31, 336–7).

20 A similar notion is in cap. 62, *Edictum Theodorici regis*, ed Friedrich Bluhme, MGH Leges (Hannover 1875–89) V 158–9, which does not view sexual relations with a woman of the lowest class as adultery. See Sheehan, 'Theory and Practice' 467–71 (here pp 223–7).

21 *La règle du maître*, ed Vogüé II 30–2.

22 PL 67 143–4, 147, 307.

That the preference for the celibate life was not always based on a choice between goods, but instead resulted from a tendency to despise the sexual aspect of humankind in general and marriage in particular, was to be expected. The Christian community sometimes provided a place for men and women with these or similar attitudes.[23] But this was not acceptable: the *Dionysiana* brought to western eyes the powerful condemnation of the Council of Gangra (ca 345), which anathematized those who sought the virginal life not because it was good and holy but because they looked on marriage with horror.[24] Yet though church thinkers opposed such an extreme, they also agreed that human sexuality contained the disorder that resulted from the original sin of the first couple and should not be exercised without serious purpose. This attitude must be understood as the background to the teaching on the two states of life in which the Christian ideology was realized, the married and the celibate.

The Married State

One of the recurring patterns in the history of Christianity in ages marked by Manichaean thought has been the tendency to emphasize a positive view of marriage, and even to produce significant theological exploration of the institution. The Western Church of the sixth century had just come through a period of such dualist thinking; there are indications that it was judged important to insist that Christians should not contemn marriage. Thus in the prologue to the *Statuta ecclesiae antiquae* the matters on which a candidate for the episcopacy was to be examined included whether he despised marriage and forbade second unions.[25] A century later in his *Moralia*, Pope Gregory made it clear that he considered such an attitude to be heresy.[26] Yet another facet of his judgment of marriage in its day-to-day realization is expressed in the *Dialogues*. After narrating the difficult choice for the continent life made by Galla, the widowed daughter of Symmachus, Gregory remarked that whereas spiritual marriage often begins with suffering and leads to the joys of heaven, earthly marriage begins with joy but ends in sorrow.[27]

23 Hickey, *Women of the Roman Aristocracy* 15.
24 The council was reacting to the extreme asceticism of Eustathius of Sebaste (ca 300–ca 377), which provoked a local crisis in central Asia Minor. Included in the *Dionysiana* (PL 67 157–60), it became widely known in the West.
25 Ed Munier 77, 112.
26 PL 75 1125.
27 PL 77 340.

In theological terms, marriage had long been presented as a sacred relationship symbolizing the union of Christ and the Church. Yet this understanding, stated once again by Pope Leo in his letter to Rusticus of Narbonne and repeated in the *Dionysiana*,[28] must have been hard to maintain in the face of canons of the Council of Laodicea, also made available in the *Dionysiana*, urging Christians to behave discreetly at marriage banquets, suggesting that the clergy leave early, and prohibiting marriage celebration during the Lenten season.[29] Another development, however, reached closer to the comprehension of the laity and was to receive an ever greater importance as the Middle Ages unfolded, namely, the custom of giving public expression to the union of a couple in a religious ritual. Korbinian Ritzer and Cyrille Vogel have discussed this development in detail. For the present purpose it is sufficient to note that the blessing of the couple appeared in Rome in the fourth century and that by the middle of the sixth century the wedding was associated with the Eucharist itself, with blessing, prayer, and preface proper to the occasion.[30] This location of the marriage within an increasingly Christian ritual was not required – in some cases was not permitted – but, combined with the growing precision as to the times when it was suitably performed, represents an important turning in the presentation of the very delicate teaching that marriage was a good, a symbol of immense dignity, and a means to sanctification and at the same time contained tendencies that were uncontrolled and not worthy of God. Thus a use of ritual to reconcile seemingly opposite attitudes was developed in Italy in the period under consideration.[31]

However important the notion of marriage as an acceptable institution for the satisfying of sexual desire, its prime purpose was viewed as the begetting of children. Caesarius of Arles went so far as to state in one of his sermons that this purpose was expressed in the *tabulae nuptiales*.[32] In his discussion of marriage in the *Pastoral Care*, Pope Gregory underlined this purpose of marriage as well.[33] Such an understanding was one with

---

28 PL 67 288–9.
29 PL 67 165.
30 Korbinian Ritzer, *Le mariage dans les églises chrétiennes du Ier au XIe siècle* (Paris 1970) 222–6; Vogel, 'Les rites' 421–6.
31 A further indication of this point: clergy were expected to have their marriages blessed (Vogel, 'Les rites' 424–5).
32 Beck, *The Pastoral Care of Souls* 229.
33 PL 77 102.

which civil society would agree.[34] The points of disagreement between the Christian ideology and the worlds it confronted were areas in which dispute had begun well before the period of interest, namely, the qualities of marriage and, closely related to these qualities, the persons for whom marriage was permitted.

Christian marriage was to be monogamous, exclusive, and permanent. Roman law, expressed in the Theodosian Code, and barbarian law as well had much to say about the adultery of the wife and, though considerably less, of the husband. In the context of Roman law the concubine was always a possibility. Although Christian teachers allowed that, under certain conditions, a concubine could become a wife, she was forbidden to the married man.[35] The sermons of Caesarius of Arles reveal the scale of the problem and the vigour with which this bishop at least tried to deal with it. He makes it clear that some of his flock boasted and joked about their conquests, whereas others, perhaps with a wry reference to the remedium, pointed out that during their frequent separations from their wives on government affairs or business of their own no other mode of sexual release was available. Then there were soldiers who saw women as part of the booty of their trade.[36] Caesarius frequently confronted the double standard by which his hearers lived. He upbraided the men of his congregation for their inconsistency in expecting the same virtue in their wives that they destroyed in other women. Pointing out that at Rome men who maintained a mistress before marriage were not allowed the blessing of their new union, Caesarius imposed the practice on his own congregation. In the end, he hoped that the good example of some of his hearers would move the others to self-restraint.[37] The *Dionysiana* recalled both the teaching of the Council of Ancyra (314), that husband as well as wife was subject to penance for adultery, and that of Pope Innocent, who frankly admitted that a husband could more easily accuse his wife than she could accuse him, but insisted that adultery by either sex was equally condemned.[38]

---

34 See *Edictum Theodorici regis* 36 (ed Bluhme 154) and *Cod. Just.* 5 5 6; cf Rouche, 'The Early Middle Ages in the West' I 548–9.
35 On the apparent dispute between the positions of Augustine and Caesarius on the possibility of a concubine becoming a wife, see Beck, *The Pastoral Care of Souls* 226–8.
36 Ibid 237–8. On opposition to his sermons and the lengths to which Caesarius went to ensure that his flock remained and listened – including locking the church door – see ibid 142, 265–6.
37 Ibid 230–2.
38 PL 67 247.

Pertaining as it did to the external forum, the question of the permanence of marriage was a more obvious point of tension in society. Christian thinking on the matter probably played a role in the publication of Constantine's constitution of 331, which established a not inconsiderable limitation of divorce.[39] The year after the publication of his code, in a novel[40] that found a place in several of the barbarian codes as well as that of Justinian, Theodosius pointed out that for the good of children it should not be easy to dissolve a marriage. But civil law was reluctant to go further and forbid divorce.[41] The Christian communities had to be content with the moral pressure that they could bring to bear on their members. The *Dionysiana* quoted Pope Leo's judgment that marriage after divorce was adultery and included the rule and interesting suggestion of the Council of Carthage that when spouses dismiss each other they should be required either to remain single or to be reconciled, adding that the civil law ought to cooperate.[42] Several Gallic councils of the sixth century returned to this question, and one of them, the Council of Agde (506), indicated that on some occasions a marriage could properly be dissolved. The text continues with a casual remark that was heavy with the future, implying that it was for the bishops to make such a decision.[43]

A special problem, witness to the troubles of the age, was the second marriage of the woman whose spouse had been carried into captivity. The *Dionysiana*[44] included a series of directions from Pope Leo to Bishop Nicetas of Aquileia: if the husband was presumed dead, the woman was allowed to marry again; but should the husband return, the command of Christ 'What therefore God has joined together, let not man put asunder' was to be enforced. The woman would be required to return to her original husband. Secondary parts of the decretal confirmed that this was not always an easy solution.[45]

When marriage was approached by those free to enter the relationship, many obstacles presented themselves. Two of these, the seriousness of which would play important roles in the degree of endogamy in medieval

39 *Codex Theodosianus* 3 16 1.
40 12; see *Theodosiani Libri* XVI *cum ... leges novellae*, ed Mommsen and Meyer II 29.
41 Hickey, *Women of the Roman Aristocracy* 55–8.
42 PL 67 247–8, 215–16.
43 c25: *Concilia Galliae, A. 314 – A. 506*, ed Charles Munier (Turnhout 1963) 204; Beck, *The Pastoral Care of Souls* 228; Sheehan, 'Theory and Practice' 458 (here p 213).
44 PL 57 296–7.
45 These regulations were quoted *in extenso* in the *Responsiones* of Pope Stephen III during his visit to Gaul in 752: see *Sacrorum conciliorum nova et amplissima collectio*, ed J.-D. Mansi (Florence and Venice 1759–98) 12 562.

European society, are especially important to the present discussion: impediments resulting from an earlier marriage and those from relationship within unacceptable degrees. The previous discussion indicates the seriousness of the opposition to divorce by Christian leaders. Inasmuch as this opposition was effective, it involved the limitation of an individual's freedom to seek elsewhere for the wealth and children that were so important to the maintenance of family fortunes.[46] Given the frequency of divorce among the visible classes of Roman and barbarian society, the consequences of a limitation of the practice would have been of major proportions. Pressure towards achieving that end was essentially a moral one until those great confrontations between popes and bishops on one side and major political figures on the other, during the Carolingian period, caused an important shift in attitudes.

There were also unions deemed unacceptable because of blood or spiritual relationships. This rather surprising development in the Christian teaching on marriage was to be one of the principal forces moving European families towards a wider degree of exogamy. The beginnings were of limited application and, indeed, rather cautious. Canon 2 of the Council of Neocaesaria (314) forbade a woman's marriage to her husband's brother, and a late fourth-century oriental collection, the *Apostolic Canons*, denied ordination to anyone who married his wife's sister or his brother's daughter but did not mention its application to the marriages of the laity; both texts were brought to Western Europe by the *Dionysiana*.[47] Several imperial constitutions of the fourth century assembled in the *Codex Theodosianus*[48] applied restrictions in this area. More precise prohibitions and their extension were worked out in the Gallic councils of the sixth and seventh centuries against heavy opposition and only gradually found expression in the laws of the region.[49] The degree to which the papacy was involved in the process, let alone the extent to which the results were intended to apply to Italy, is difficult to ascertain.

It was in the eighth century, towards the end of the period of the present study, that an important series of Roman statements on relationship began. The first was in a council of Pope Gregory II, held at Rome,

---

46 Jack Goody, *The Development of the Family and Marriage in Europe* (Cambridge 1983) 31–3, 188–9.
47 PL 67 155, 143.
48 3 12 1–4.
49 Michel Rouche, 'Des mariages païens au mariage chrétien: Sacré et sacrement,' *Segni* 2 (1987) 857–61.

probably in 721. Among canons touching freedom to marry, several forbade union with a brother's wife, a niece, a mother-in-law, a daughter-in-
law, or a first cousin.[50] Then, after these precise prohibitions, a more
general canon forbade marriage with any relative or wife of a relative.[51]
There is no indication how far through the *parentela* this prohibition was
intended to apply.[52] Why it was deemed necessary to state the individual
prohibitions of the earlier canons is unclear. One might conclude that the
rule of canon 9 was intended as counsel rather than a strict prohibition,
but the addition of a penalty, a most serious penalty in fact, stands in the
way of this conclusion. Five years later, in a letter to St Boniface, the pope
adopted a somewhat different approach: pointing out that marriage was
forbidden within the fourth degree, he expressed the preference that those
aware of relationship of any kind should not marry.[53] In this case there
was no mention of anathema. Uncertainty on the matter was removed in
732 when Pope Gregory III informed Boniface that the prohibitions
extended to the seventh degree.[54] This large increase of forbidden degrees
must have posed many problems for Boniface. By 735 he had become
aware of the *Libellus responsionum*, a letter to Augustine of Canterbury
ascribed to Gregory I that somewhat hesitatingly permitted marriage of
second cousins.[55] In spite of various inquiries he was unable to find
confirmation of the texts in the Roman chancery, and Pope Zachary
finally replied in 742 that the information was erroneous.[56] This exchange
not only indicates resistance to the extended prohibition based on consanguinity and affinity but also shows that there was an earlier ruling,
thought to be of papal origin, that Boniface at least would have liked to

50 In a Roman council of 743, Pope Zachary stated that these regulations, which his
     council reaffirmed, were intended to apply to Italy: see *Concilia aevi Karolini*, ed
     Albertus Werminghoff, MGH Leges 3, Concilia 2 (Hannover 1906) I 19–20.
51 c9, PL 67 343.
52 In Rothair's publication of the Lombard law in 643, the *parentela* was defined as
     consisting of seven degrees (cap. 152, 'Edictus Rothari,' ed Friedrich Bluhme, in *Leges
     Langobardorum*, MGH Leges 4, ed G.H. Pertz [Hannover 1868; repr Leipzig 1925] 35).
53 *S. Bonifatii et Lullii epistolae*, ed Michael Tangl, MGH Epistolae selectae 1 (Berlin 1916)
     45.
54 Ibid 51.
55 Paul Meyvaert, 'Bede's Text of the "Libellus responsionum" of Gregory the Great to
     Augustine of Canterbury,' in *England before the Conquest: Studies in Primary Sources
     Presented to Dorothy Whitelock*, ed Peter Clemoes and Kathleen Hughes (Cambridge
     1971) 15–33.
56 *S. Bonifatii et Lullii epistolae*, ed Tangl 57, 90; *Concilia aevi Karolini*, ed Werminghoff
     I 20.

see retained. An indication of the pressure that the papacy was applying in this area at the time is seen in a 723 law of Liutprand, king of the Lombards: marriage to the wife of a cousin was forbidden, and Liutprand explained the change by stating that the bishop of Rome had urged him to impose it.[57] Liutprand's legislation also included the prohibition of marriage to spiritual relatives, that is, to a godchild or to the child's mother and between the godparents' child and the godchild.[58] Condemnation of marriage between sponsor and mother of the child had already appeared in the Roman council of 721.[59] St Boniface's correspondence after 735, strongly stating his objection to a Roman rule that seemed to stand in the way of reinforcing the spiritual bond established by baptism, suggests that the prohibition was recent. Thus in the period that saw a major increase of pressure to seek marriage partners outside the kin, regulations began to limit the reinforcement of spiritual kinship by marriage as well.[60] These limitations of the choice of marriage partner were to be of major importance, for they imposed significant restrictions on family strategies in the eighth century and thereafter.

The Celibate State

The Church's teaching on marriage was essentially a comment on and a criticism of the institution found at the centre of all the societies it met throughout the Mediterranean basin and beyond. Based on the Church's conception of humankind described above, it sought to adjust, improve, and occasionally change one or another aspect of marriage, but essentially the institution remained as before. The teaching on celibacy, however, was new; personally and socially it represented a major change in the understanding of the possibilities for an adult life. There were virtually no models. Between the late third and the fifth century many social forms were developed to support those who chose to live the celibate life; sometimes the results were chaotic. But gradually order was applied, and the celibates became organized for the most part around the local church or in a monastery, those two divine households of which the Master of the Rule wrote.

57 34 4: *Leges Langobardorum*, ed Bluhme 123–4.
58 34 5: ibid 124.
59 c4, PL 67 343; J.M. Lynch, *Godparents and Kinship in Early Medieval Europe* (Princeton 1986) 234–2; Goody, *The Development of the Family* 197–9.
60 For an important general discussion of the historiography of spiritual relationships, see Lynch, *Godparents and Kinship* 32–80.

Great effort was made to ensure that the higher clergy of the local church was celibate. Since many of them were already married, this rule, if implemented, required that they live apart from their wives. It is likely that many clergy suffered this loss because they wished to enjoy clerical office. The degree to which they saw celibacy as a good in itself is difficult to measure. The endless problems that conciliar canons and episcopal letters tell us about make it clear that the teaching was difficult to implement. There is much evidence that, in the centuries here discussed, the married clergy living as celibates was in decline.

Also attached to the local church were three groups of celibate women: widows, deaconesses, and dedicated virgins.[61] The enrolled widows of 1 Timothy 5:9 were the first group for whom celibacy was a requirement. They seem to have quickly assumed a role as assistants in such rituals as the baptism of women and are known to have instructed neophytes as well. The deaconess, as her name implied, was ordained for service. Whether celibacy was required of her at the beginning is not clear. Her function tended to be similar to that of the widows, and in fact her role in the Western Church was never an important one.[62] The dedicated virgins did not have a public role in the Church like their sisters the widows and deaconesses, but the future lay with them. All three classes of women received official recognition by the Church, expressed by rituals of reception and benediction. The virgin was a special case in the sense that her commitment was capable of several degrees. But if she did choose to receive official recognition, by the fourth century there was a ritual whereby the bishop blessed or gave her the veil, symbolic of her status, and by the middle of the sixth century the ceremony found its place in the Eucharist.[63] This development is parallel both in time and in form to that sacralization of marriage noted above. In the fifth century, it was already customary to consider this dedication permanent – in ideal, at least, under the image of marriage to Christ. Clearly the same ideology

---

61 Cuthbert H. Turner, 'Ministries of Women in the Primitive Church: Widow, Deaconess, and Virgin in the First Four Christian Centuries,' *Catholic and Apostolic: Collected Papers by the Late Cuthbert Hamilton Turner*, ed Herbert Newell Bate (London and Milwaukee 1931) 316–51; Jean Daniélou, 'Le ministère des femmes dans l'Eglise ancienne,' *La Maison Dieu* 61 (1960) 70–96.

62 Aimé-Georges Martimort, *Les diaconesses: Essai historique*, Bibliotheca ephemerides liturgicae, Subsidia 24 (Rome 1982) 197–217.

63 René Metz, *La consécration des vierges dans l'Eglise romaine: Etude d'histoire de la liturgie*, Bibliothèque de l'Institut de droit canonique de l'Université de Strasbourg 4 (Paris 1954) 96–100, 138–60.

that sought to move society to accept the permanence of the marriage bond was at play here. Domestic arrangements for the support of dedicated virgins varied. Many continued to live with their families. Early on in the movement, however, there was a tendency to seek some form of common life. It might have been nothing more than the occasional gathering for instruction and prayer, but by the end of the fourth century in Egypt, Syria, and Cappadocia the monastery for women had become the milieu to which many of those who wished to live a virginal life turned.

It was precisely in the region and at the beginning of the age presently being discussed that a remarkable period of monastic development occurred; and women's monastic communities found a place in it. These years saw not only Caesarius of Arles's publication of the first rule explicitly written for women[64] but also the composition of the *Regula Magistri* and the *Rule* of St Benedict. These texts were to have major influence on later rules and on monasticism as an institution throughout the Middle Ages and beyond. They also shed light on aspects of the development that are of special importance here.

In his *Life* of Anthony of Egypt, Athanasius describes the beginning of the saint's vocation not as a call to chastity but as a withdrawal from the world and its preoccupations with family and wealth.[65] Celibacy was involved, of course, but only as one element in the decision to leave all and follow Christ, a pattern similar to the process whereby Francis of Assisi found his vocation. Rules like the *Regula virginum* of Caesarius or that of Eugippius, with their incorporation of the *Rule* of St Augustine, are noticeably preoccupied with protection of the chastity of members and show a certain tension in this regard.[66] The rule Caesarius wrote for men and the rules of the Master and of St Benedict give a different impression. They were intended to create a place where men and women could grow in the love of Christ – a school of the Lord's service, as Benedict would express it. Concerned with those who seek to leave the world, they are designed to make clear to the monk that he has done so and to prevent the world from pursuing him into his place of withdrawal. This was achieved in part by the physical design of the monastery: it contained

---

64 *Césaire d'Arles, oeuvres monastiques*, I: *Oeuvres pour les moniales*, ed Adalbert de Vogüé and Joël Courreau, Sources chrétiennes 345 (Paris 1988) 68–9.

65 PG 26 835–978.

66 Caesarius, *Oeuvres pour les moniales*, ed Vogüé and Courreau 44–5; *Eugippii regula*, ed Fernandus Villegás and Adalbertus de Vogüé, *Corpus scriptorum ecclesiasticorum latinorum* 87 (Vienna 1976).

within itself much that was required – garden, mill, and so on – allowing members to live there without going beyond the walls. The development of rules of cloister in the *Regula virginum* was similarly intended to keep visits by outsiders to a minimum.[67]

The ritual by which a candidate joined a monastery was clearly intended to impress upon him or her a complete separation from an earlier form of life and entry into a new one.[68] By putting aside secular garb and assuming monastic dress, the candidate recognized that henceforth all the necessities for the physical support of life would be supplied by the head of the new household that he or she had entered. The different quality of the new life was enhanced also by the degree of ritualization in prayer, dining, conversation, and work.

The rules establish that members of a monastery were expected to cut family ties and to resist the endless attraction of family wealth.[69] It was understood that this was not easily achieved: Caesarius reminded the nuns of St-Jean of Arles that they should not let family considerations influence their choice of superior;[70] and, when Benedict warned his monks not to defend one another, he added that the prohibition applied even if they were closely related by blood.[71] The monastic communities described in the writings of the period, groups in which many men and women are known to have lived the celibate life, thus exhibited the qualities of inclusivity and exclusivity that are characteristic of vital communities in a time of major change. The monastery was presented as a society complete in every way except the power of reproduction, providing all the needs of its members, a society that recognized the necessity of excluding pressure even from the families that gave birth to its members and which might seek to lead them to withdraw from their original ideals.

Italian monasticism would pass into northern Europe in the seventh century. Though not without many problems, as the register of Gregory

67 Caesarius, *Oeuvres pour les moniales*, ed Vogüé and Courreau 70–84.
68 Giles Constable, 'The Ceremonies and Symbolism of Entering Religious Life and Taking the Monastic Habit, from the Fourth to the Twelfth Century,' *Segni* 2 (1987) 783–96.
69 André Borias, 'Les relations du moine avec sa famille d'après le Maître et S. Benoît,' *Regulae Benedicti studia: Annuarium internationale* 5 (1977) 13–25.
70 Caesarius, *Oeuvres pour les moniales*, ed Vogüé and Courreau 440–2.
71 69; *La règle de saint Benoît*, ed Adalbert de Vogüé and Jean Neufville, Textes monastiques de l'Occident 24–9 (Paris 1971–2) II 64–7.

the Great illustrates so well,[72] the movement was to be one of the Church's principal instruments in its pastoral, instructional, and missionary roles for the next five hundred years.

Examining the history of the family in central and northern Italy during the first three centuries of the Middle Ages in the context of the influence of Christian ideology suggests certain conclusions. First, there are good reasons for thinking that the effort to spread the Christian conception of sexuality and marriage and of the value of the celibate life, which had been stated in the early Church, was continued among older as well as new peoples of Italy during this period of major disturbance. At this stage of research, the impact of this teaching on the stability and fertility of the basic family unit cannot be gauged; much work remains to be done in this regard. Second, the gradual involvement of the Church in establishing the limits of relationships within which valid marriage was allowed proved to be very important, in terms not only of the choice of marriage partner but also of kinship and family strategy. The immediate practical consequences – the acceptance of a more exogamous type of kinship and the survival or disappearance of families – remain to be tested; but the long-term influence, as indicated in several of the chapters that follow,[73] is evident. Finally, the development of that other type of family, the monastery, proved to be rich in innovation and full of promise for the centuries that lay ahead.

72 Almost one quarter of the letters in his register are concerned with monastic problems; see Georg Jenal, 'Grégoire le Grand et la vie monastique dans l'Italie de son temps,' in *Grégoire le Grand*, ed Jacques Fontaine et al (Paris 1986) 147–57.
73 See n7, above. – Editor

16

The Bequest of Land in England
in the High Middle Ages:
Testaments and the Law

It is generally accepted that the more prominent members of society in the late Anglo-Saxon period controlled the devolution of at least some of their lands by bequest and that, a century later, these powers had been lost by their Norman successors.[1] Although the developing common law of England became more and more open to alienation during the lifetime of a landowner, it turned its face against the bequest of land[2] and adopted conveyancing procedures that made such an act powerless before the claims of the heir.[3] On the other hand, it is also clear that some local customs proved resistant to the restrictions of common law, preserving and developing the right to control the devolution of land at death. Of these customs, that of some of the boroughs was most noteworthy.[4] As will be seen, many landowners who did not enjoy the freedom of the boroughs in this regard found it desirable to seek ways around the restrictions of the common law.

Social historians are aware that the death of the head of a household and the subsequent devolution of the property controlled by the deceased reveal many of the social, legal, and political forces influencing the family at any given time and place. In the past (and, in different forms, in our

---

1 See J.C. Holt, *Feudal Society and the Family in Early Medieval England*, 1: *The Revolution of 1066*, Transactions of the Royal Historical Society, 5th ser, 32 (London 1982) 196–9, and the references assembled there.

2 On the reasons for adopting this position see Michael M. Sheehan, *The Will in Medieval England: From the Conversion of the Anglo-Saxons to the End of the Thirteenth Century*, Studies and Texts 6 (Toronto 1963) 266–70.

3 See S.F.C. Milsom, *The Legal Framework of English Feudalism* (Cambridge 1972) 121–7; and Sheehan, *The Will in Medieval England* 272–4.

4 Sheehan, *The Will in Medieval England* 274ff.

own day) the claims of lordship, of the kin, and of the smaller family group were all at play. These claims were expressed in custom as well as in law. But there were other, more personal forces that encouraged the householder to seek to direct the future use of property.[5] Similar tendencies were to be found among lesser members of society, who, though technically they owned little or nothing, nevertheless sought to direct the devolution of some of the movable or immovable wealth over which they had exercised a modicum of control. In much of Europe, as the Middle Ages progressed, these tendencies were manifest. In fact, the history of the Middle Ages could be written from the very specialized point of view of the desire of the individual to free more and more property from external controls and the development of usages and, eventually, of legal instruments – the testament was of prime importance here[6] – that, with greater or lesser degrees of success, could attain that end.

Since discussion can be limited in present circumstances to the persons who had the right to bequeath and the property that could be distributed by testament, the broad lines of medieval English legal development during the five centuries between the Norman invasion and the Statute of Wills can be set out briefly. First, as to those who were free to dispose of property at the end of their lives, only a small part of the population was guaranteed this right by law. Adult freemen were expected to make a will, but married women of that class, because their husbands controlled all their property, did not have this right; nor did the servile members of society.[7] Powerful pressure was brought to bear by the Church to reinforce the natural desire of the married woman and the serf to bequeath goods at the end of their lives. It can be shown that, in practice, that desire was often vindicated. But the general law denied this right, and bequest by married woman or serf could, in many cases, be

---

5 For a general discussion of this matter see E.F. Bruck, *Kirchenväter und soziales Erbrecht* (Berlin 1956) i–viii, 119; and Sheehan, *The Will in Medieval England* 5–7. The impact of Christian teaching in northern Europe played an important role in the development of the right of bequest; and, during the Middle Ages, the Church in England exerted a steady pressure to allow all adults to exercise at least minimal rights in this regard (ibid 234–41, 253–4).

6 Throughout this essay, the word 'testament' will be used as the equivalent of 'will,' namely, a legal act that appoints executors and instructs them on the division of the testator's property, or the document in which that legal act is described. In the context of English law, the testament did not create an heir.

7 See Sheehan, *The Will in Medieval England* 234–9, 253–4. Others were limited because of their state (minors, religious, etc) or because of special circumstances that restricted their right (ibid 239–53, 255–6).

defeated by its invocation.[8] Second, as to the property over which a power of bequest might be extended, the principal restriction applied to land: by the end of the twelfth century common law made the bequest of free tenures impossible, and manorial custom assumed the same attitude to servile land. As was mentioned above, there were significant derogations from these rules in many boroughs and also on royal and ancient demesne.[9] There was some restriction of the right to bequeath chattels as well, but, in principle, common law did not object to it. As a general rule, through the twelfth and thirteenth centuries, most of a householder's chattels were distributed according to a custom whereby a third was reserved to the wife, a third to children, and the remaining third bequeathed as the testator saw fit.[10]

As will be seen in what follows, testators in England applied steady pressure to break free from customary restrictions and to increase their control of the future use of their property. Soon it is possible to observe the ironical situation that has stated and restated itself in England from the thirteenth century until the present whereby the individual, having asserted his right against contemporaries who would restrict his control of property, tried to extend that control into the future. As a result, he denied to following generations the very freedom of alienation by act *inter vivos* or by testament that he had claimed for himself. As would be expected, this tendency was resisted by the individuals and groups mentioned above who considered themselves to have some claim on the family's property; and, under pressure from them, legal forms were developed that were intended to protect their rights. These developments have been set out at length in histories of English law and in reports of cases where attempts were made to circumvent the restrictions on the power of testation imposed by law. The reports on these cases provide an indication of the opposition of the living to the intentions of testators – a negative image, as it were, of what was done or what it was hoped could be done. It is proposed in the present essay to take a different approach,

8 Villein status would endure until the early years of the seventeenth century, by which time it had come to be meaningless; see William S. Holdsworth, *A History of English Law*, 5th ed (London 1942) III 507–8. The full testamentary right of married women had to wait until 1837 (7 William IV and 1 Victoria cap. 36). On the divergence of practice from the letter of the law see below and Sheehan, *The Will in Medieval England* 236–9, 254 nn 93, 94.

9 See Sheehan, *The Will in Medieval England* 274–9.

10 Where there were no children, the wife received half of the chattels. The divison varied in the boroughs. See ibid 282–3.

to seek direct access to what testators sought to accomplish by examining the texts of various instruments, principally wills, whereby they expressed their intention for the future enjoyment of their property in land.

The Problem of Sources

A few lines must be given to a discussion of sources. A rather extended search for documents reporting divisions of property at death, or evidence of such acts, for the period 1066–1300 in England has yielded only about two hundred items.[11] It is not until the second quarter of the fourteenth century that the survival of this kind of text, usually testaments in the original or in probate copy, increases notably.[12] Under these circumstances it is necessary to ask whether, for the earlier period, such instruments were used often enough to permit the conclusion that the attitudes they reveal indicate a common point of view of those who sought to arrange the division of their property after death. There is, however, evidence of a much wider use of the testament than the number of extant texts seems to indicate. A large proportion of the surviving texts are from the archives of the Dean and Chapter of St Paul's, London, and of Christ Church, Canterbury, and from the register of Bishop Godfrey Gifford of Worcester (1268–1302). Historical accidents explain the survival of many of the texts that have been found: the Dean and Chapter of St Paul's, living in London as they did, received many bequests of land, bequests of which they kept records; the Dean and Chapter of Canterbury kept copies of the wills to which they gave probate during the vacancies of 1278–9 and 1293; the bishop of Worcester decided to have many wills copied into his register. Had other jurisdictions done so, or had the records of other institutions survived as did those of St Paul's, the large-scale survival of testaments that begins after 1325 would have been much more precocious. An indication of the extent of the loss is provided by the wills of London. Of the two hundred documents mentioned above, only twenty-five are from London during the period 1258–1300. Yet, in the enrolments of the clauses touching the bequests of land contained within wills proved before

---

11 For lists of early wills see Michael M. Sheehan, 'A List of Thirteenth-Century English Wills,' *Genealogists' Magazine* 13 (1961) 259–65 (here pp 8–15); and Public Record Office, *A List of Wills* (London 1968).

12 See Michael M. Sheehan, 'English Wills and the Records of the Ecclesiastical and Civil Jurisdictions,' *Journal of Medieval History* 14 (1988) 9–10 nn 4, 5 (here pp 202–3 nn 13, 15).

the London Court of Husting during the same years, almost seven hundred are to be found.[13] Thus, though the survival of documents from the period prior to 1300 is small, it is not unreasonable to conclude that it represents a much larger documentation that has been lost. For the fourteenth and later centuries, the number of extant wills is embarrassingly large.

Anglo-Saxon Survivals

The period of the Norman Conquest witnessed major changes in the use of the testament in England. Of them, the most obvious was the virtual disappearance of the bequest of land.[14] There were, however, several practices and attitudes of the Anglo-Saxon period that survived and that are of significance for what is now to be examined. They are: the post-obit gift of a single property, the unitary attitude towards all the property of a testator that is manifest in the Anglo-Saxon form of the testament called the *cwide*, and the seeking of external support of a testator's intention from those in authority.

Sometimes the Anglo-Saxon landowner gave property to a beneficiary (usually ecclesiastical) in such a way that the beneficiary came to enjoy it only after the death of the donor. This, the post-obit gift, continued in use through the twelfth century and well beyond.[15] Different theories of gift lie behind this type of bequest. By the end of the twelfth century it probably involved a gift, completed by the giving of seisin followed by a life lease to the donor, or was simply the promise of a gift at death with the permission of those who might otherwise have made it impossible. A good example is provided by a document (ca 1225) of Richard Morin that is at once a testament and a charter.[16] It begins, 'Sciant presentes et futuri quod ego Ricardus Morin dedi et testamento legavi Deo ... et Ecclesie Rading' corpus meum ibidem sepeliendum.' Then follows a detailed account of gifts made or to be made to the abbey. The first employs the

13 Of the twenty-five London testaments, twenty-three include the bequest of land. Of them, only sixteen appear in the Husting enrolments. On the registration of urban wills in centres other than London see Sheehan, 'English Wills' 5 and 9 n2 (here p 202 n9).

14 See Sheehan, *The Will in Medieval England* 107–8.

15 See Holt, *Feudal Society* I 197–9; F. Pollock and F.W. Maitland, *The History of English Law*, 2nd ed (Cambridge 1898) II 263ff; Sheehan, *The Will in Medieval England* 19–20, 108–11, 273.

16 London, BL Add Ch 19615, printed in *Archaeological Journal* 22 (1865) 156–8.

common formula of a post-obit gift, 'Dedi etiam cum corpore meo ... totam terram quam Ricardus Bertram tenuit de me ...,' but adds that this has been done 'ex consensu heredis mei.' Finally, the text goes on to note that the donor and his heirs will warrant all the gifts and bequests mentioned: 'Ego autem et heredes mei warantizabimus predictis monachis omnia predicta.' This kind of document, and it is not unique, not only illustrates the continuance of the post-obit gift but also shows that the donor maintained the attitude that he should deal with his property including land at the end of his life and that he had adjusted to the limitations on the bequest of land by making earlier arrangements with those whose objection could deny his purpose.

Among the Anglo-Saxons, the post-obit gift was sometimes repeated in the document which called itself *cwide*, a document that was as much evidence of a group of legal acts as of a single will-making.[17] It presented the list of bequests of land and movable goods to be expected in a testament. But it also included confirmation of earlier transactions: sales or gifts of land, marriage arrangements, etc. Presumably the testator rehearsed these earlier acts when he made his testament. Thus he went well beyond stating arrangements for the future enjoyment of his estate to a general description of how he expected the persons and properties of his household to continue after he passed from the scene. Many wills of the post-Conquest period reveal this attitude as grants or sales of an earlier date are confirmed and new arrangements for distribution of property after death are united in a single act.[18]

Several *cwides* illustrate the third characteristic of Anglo-Saxon wills, namely, the fact that testators often sought the confirmation of those in a position to support their bequests. As we move into the thirteenth century the examples of bequests of land that could ordinarily be pre-

17 See Sheehan, *The Will in Medieval England* 39–45 and the references cited 39 n101.
18 Thus in the report of the last will of Gilbert de Gant, earl of Lincoln (1155×56), we are told that Gilbert rehearsed his previous grants to Bridlington Priory: 'quod dederat prius eidem ecclesie. Hec omnia confirmavit eidem ecclesie cum libertatibus que sunt in carta sua' (*Early Yorkshire Charters*, ed W. Farrer [Edinburgh 1915] II 456 no 1166). Amalric, son of Ralph, acted similarly (1180×86) regarding his gifts to Reading Abbey: 'quam carta sua confirmavit' (*Cartulary of Reading Abbey* f 38r–v: London, BL Egerton MS 3031). In a will of 1272, William de Dunwich chose to do so regarding a donation to St Giles Hospital, Norwich: 'in quadam carta mea feofamenti inde confecta plenius continetur' (Norwich, Norfolk and Norwich Record Office Case 24 Shelf B no 7); this example is especially important because, in Norwich, William could have bequeathed the property had he not granted it earlier. Many other examples could be given.

vented by an application of the law increase in frequency. In many cases the testament itself indicates that the testator was aware of the problem and intended to circumvent it by making prior arrangements to guarantee that his bequests be implemented.[19] On occasion the testator simply adds that, if the bequest is challenged, an alternative is to be provided.[20]

From all of this a preliminary conclusion suggests itself, namely, that there is evidence within the texts of wills that some testators continued to regard their whole estate as a unit and saw the testament as an instrument to include many and, in some cases, all the provisions that had been made for the future use of their property. This point of view does not fit well with the notion, common to histories of English law, that testators accepted the division of movable and immovable property and looked on chattels alone as the property to which their freedom of bequest extended.

How Testators Exercised Their Power to Bequeath

The desire of the English testator to control the devolution of his property more completely than custom permitted – and his growing success in this regard – is evident in the history of *legitim*. As was mentioned above, in the case of a testator who died with a wife and children, after debts had been paid, a third portion of the remaining chattels passed to the wife, a third to the children, and the remaining third was disposed of by the testator as he wished. Usually a large part of his portion went for the good of his soul, an intention with which the rise of the will had been associated from the beginning. As the thirteenth century progressed, the testator asserted more and more control over his chattels. In a first stage he proceeded to designate the individual to whom bequests were to be given, thus controlling the actual items that different members of the family and other beneficiaries would receive. Eventually, in many parts of

19 In a will of ca 1220, Agnes de Clifford gave land in Wicham manor to Holy Trinity Priory, Canterbury, 'una cum corpore meo per concessum et assensum domini mei' and assigned the income of a manor for a year to provide funds to implement her bequests, again with the assent of her husband (*The Registrum antiquissimum of the Cathedral Church of Lincoln*, ed C.W. Foster, Lincoln Record Society 27 [Hereford 1931] I 293–5). Among other examples, see the wills of John Cocus (before 1241), Chichester, Diocesan Record Office Liber Y f 182v; Ralph II, bishop of Chichester (1244), ibid f 162r; Beatrice (ca 1260), Oxford, Bodleian MS Ch Suffolk a 3 (200).
20 Thus in the will of Ivo le Moyne (1236×41) a message is given to Sawtry Priory: 'Ita videlicet quod si heredes sui voluerint dictum tenamentum a dicta ecclesia violenter auferre aut per legem terre repetere, solvant prius dicte ecclesie de Saltre dictas centum sexaginta libras' (London, BL Add Ch 34036).

England, this control was extended so that the amount received by wife and children depended on the will of their husband and father.[21] This disposal of chattels was extended even further to control, or at least exert pressure on, the lives of legatees after the testator's death. Thus in 1330, William de la Grave of Bristol bequeathed to his son Robert an additional ten marks if he released a tenement to the testator's daughter.[22] In those jurisdictions where the bequest of land was permitted, even greater control was possible. For example, in a London will of about 1200, Gregory, son of Gilbert, bequeathed rents to his mother 'quamdiu predicta mater eius sine sponso vixerit.'[23] Bequests of lands to wives that exceeded their grant in dower could be withdrawn if a widow remarried.[24]

21 See Richard H. Helmholz, 'Legitim in English Legal History,' University of Illinois Law Review 3 (1984) 665–74. Various patterns of distribution appear in the wills: in 1286, Sir Anthony Gurney bequeathed more than a third to his wife: 'Item Sibille uxori mee tertiam partem omnium bonorum et ultra haec x li' (Register of Godfrey Giffard f 295r: Worcester, Worcestershire Record Office MS 713); in 1290, Henry de Enfield made many bequests, then added: 'Item debitis prius solutis volo quod omnia bona mea dividantur in tres partes videlicet Alicie uxori mee unam partem, Johanni et Dyonisie pueris meis aliam partem, michi vero ad exequias meas faciendas et testamentum meum sup⟨p⟩lendum terciam partem' (Cartulary of St. Mary Clerkenwell, ed W.O. Hassall, Camden Society, 3rd ser, 71 [London 1949] 256–7); in 1300 William de Glovernia of London distributed his lands and many of his chattels to his wife and children, among others, then added: 'Et si quid residuum inventum fuerit in bonis et catallis volo quod in tres partes dividatur; de una parte sustentur honesti sacerdotes in London' pro anima mea celebraturi, altera pars detur Willellmine uxori mee, tertia pars inter pueris meis distribuatur iuxta ordinationem executorum meorum' (London, Guildhall Library, St Paul's Cathedral, Dean and Chapter muniments Box A 66 no 30); in 1342, John de Beauchamp distributed his jewels, plate, and armour in detail to wife, son, other family, and friends and divided the residue in thirds, one for his debts, one for funeral expenses, and one for his wife and son (London, BL Add Ch 40616).
22 London, PRO C 146/5912. In his will of 1349, William de Pontefract ordered that the service of an apprentice to his wife was to be withdrawn if she remarried. She was also to lose the guardianship of their children (London, BL Harl Ch 58 G 32).
23 London, Guildhall Library, St Paul's Cathedral, Dean and Chapter muniments Box A 66 no 21.
24 Gilbert, son of Fulk, had given his wife a dower of five marks rent, but by his will (ca 1210×19) gave her much more property 'quamdiu sit absque viro sibi lege maritali copulato.' If she chose to marry she was to be content with the original dower (London, PRO E 40/11559). Most wills do not mention the matter, though that of Nicholas Batte (1258) listed the properties his wife was to receive and added 'utrum recipiat virum vel non,' an indication of expectations at the time (Cok's Cartulary f 327v: London, St Bartholomew's Hospital Archives).

Wardship of children and their properties were bestowed on wives and others by will in London and other towns.[25] Often this office and its emoluments were denied wives who chose to marry again.[26] Given this steady pressure by testators to direct the devolution of chattels and rights after their death, it will not come as a surprise when they are found exercising similar pressure to control the devolution of land as well.

Attempts to Control the Devolution of Land after Death

Late in the twelfth century, writing of the prohibition of the bequest of land that was hardening in his time, Glanvill judged that it was necessary to explain why this limitation had been imposed.[27] Little more than half a century later, Bracton took this state of affairs for granted, choosing rather to explain why the bequest of land was possible in areas like the boroughs. He suggested that the need for liquid resources that was common to merchants made it necessary that land as well as chattels should be available to them when they arranged for the future of their estate at the end of their lives. This point of view is vindicated in scores of borough testaments, where executors are instructed to sell land and houses to provide the money that is required to implement the wills they administer.[28] The same position was adopted in the Statute of Wills (1540), where the prologue pointed out that such freedom was necessary to all for the good of their families and that they might play their proper role in society.[29] Actually some testators had learned well before that it

25 Thus in the will of Roger Bevyn of London, 1277 (Hospital of St Thomas of Acon, Register of Writings I f 26v–28v, London, Mercer's Company). In a will of 1349, William de Newenham, attorney in the royal exchequer, made his illegitimate daughter Agnes guardian of his other children, including a legitimate son (Chartulary of the Hospital of St Thomas the Martyr, Southwark, f 148v–149r: London, BL Stowe MS 942).

26 Thus the will of Henry de Frowick of London (1284): 'quod Isabella uxor mea habeat custodiam predictorum [sons and daughters] cum domibus et redditibus usque ad eorum etatem legitimam et discretam dum tamen se tenuerit in sua viduitate' (London, Guildhall Library, St Paul's Cathedral, Dean and Chapter muniments Box A 66 no 8.) Many more examples could be given.

27 See Sheehan, *The Will in Medieval England* 270–4.

28 This point is clearly stated in the will of Juliana Wyth (1282): 'Et quia non habeo pecuniam in promptu ad perficienda legata, uolo quod omnes reditus meos quos habeo in uilla Oxonie ... uendantur secundum disposicionem exsecutorum meorum, prout melius uiderint expedire, ut testamentum meum compleatur' (*Cartulary of Oseney Abbey*, ed H.E. Salter [Oxford 1929–36] I 412–13).

29 'his said obedient and loving subjects cannot use or exercise themselves according to

was impossible for them to provide the movable property required if they were to make the bequests that they deemed suitable. Thus as early as 1210, in a case before the royal courts, the practice of assigning land to a legatee, until the value of a bequest had been recovered, is revealed;[30] and, about ten years later, Agnes de Clifford found it necessary to devote the income of a manor for a year to provide the cash needed to implement her will.[31] Even Henry III and Edward I ordered that the income of their lands be used for this purpose.[32] Others, who were in a position to obtain royal permission for this arrangement in their testaments, are often found doing so.[33] But this solution to the problem created by the division between the movable and immovable property of an estate was a special and difficult one, similar to the procedures of testators mentioned above who arranged for the success of bequests of land by obtaining the permission of those who could defeat their purpose in court. During the last half of the thirteenth century two more direct attacks on the prohibition of the bequest of land were made.

The first was an attempt to withdraw lands from the category to which the prohibition applied. Charters of the late twelfth and thirteenth centuries were used to create a variety of limited estates according to the

their estates ... or to bear themselves in such wise as that they may conveniently keep and maintain their hospitalities and families, nor the good education and bringing up of their lawful generations ... but that in manner of necessity, as by daily experience is manifested and known, they shall not be able of their proper goods, chattels, and other moveable substance to discharge their debts, and after their degrees set forth and advance their children and posterities' (32 Henry VIII, cap. 1, cited in K.E. Digby, *An Introduction to the History of the Law of Real Property*, 3rd ed [Oxford 1884] 308).

30 See the discussion of this case in Cyril T. Flower, *Introduction to the Curia Regis Rolls, 1199–1230 A.D.*, Selden Society 62 (London 1944) 104.

31 Note that, in this case, the testator obtained permission from her husband: 'Et ad hoc testamentum meum perficiendum dominus meus Walterus de Clifford mihi concesssit omnes exitus manerii de Caveneby per unum annum integrum post obitum meum' (see above, n19).

32 Henry III made a will in 1252 while preparing to journey to Gascony. It includes the following: 'Et de debitis meis sic volo et ordino, quod regina mea ⟨et⟩ heredibus meis infra etatem et in custodia ipsius regine existentibus cum predictis terris meis debita mea acquietet quatenus potest de exitibus predictarum terrarum' (London, The College of Arms, Arundel 48 f 139r). In a will made at Acre, 18 June 1272, Edward I instructed his executors to acquit his obligations, adding, 'E por ceo ke nus savoms ben ke noz moebles ne purrent pas suffire a ceo,' they were to draw on the income of his estates (Liber munimentorum, Liber A f 341r–342v: London, PRO E 36/274).

33 Sheehan, *The Will in Medieval England* 286.

doctrine of *forma doni*. Thus land was granted to a recipient, his heirs, assigns, and legatees. The addition of the reference to legatees was intended to change the nature of the tenure so that not only could the property in question be alienated by donation or sale *inter vivos* (transactions to which the common law did not object), but its devolution could also be controlled by testament. Late in the thirteenth century, however, the courts turned back this attempt.[34] It was not until the Statute of Wills that a change of tenure would be the means used to widen the possibilities of the bequest of land.[35]

The second attempt to control the devolution of land at death was less direct. It fell back on the device that had been key to the success of the testament from the beginning: placing the testator's property and his intentions for its future enjoyment in the hands of a person of trust.[36] This device is commonly called the 'use,' and the trustee, who provided the essential service, is called the 'feoffee to uses.' Its background is complex, as is the realization that it could be employed to achieve the control of property after death.[37] As early as 1250 Bracton saw the possibility of the divisibility of land that it implied. An early example of this same period is provided by two documents, a grant of land and a notification, in the *Registrum antiquissimum* of Lincoln cathedral.[38] In the first charter, Master William of Southwell, canon of Lincoln, grants a messuage with buildings and a garden to the dean and chapter; they are to render due service to the lord. In the second document the dean and chapter give notice that William will have possession of the properties for the remainder of his life at two shillings a year and that, when he dies, they, with good faith ('bona fide'), will sell his properties and put the income to the use of the will of Master William as decided by his executors.[39] William's testament has not been discovered, but it is safely

---

34 See ibid 278–9.

35 See Digby, *An Introduction to the History of the Law of Real Property* 299–300.

36 J.L. Barton, 'The Medieval Use,' *Law Quarterly Review* 81 (1965) 562–77.

37 See S.F.C. Milsom, *Historical Foundations of the Common Law* (London 1969) 169–80; J.M.W. Bean, *The Decline of English Feudalism, 1215–1540* (Manchester 1968) ch 3; T.F.T. Plucknett, *A Concise History of the Common Law*, 5th ed (London 1956) 575–87; Pollock and Maitland, *The History of English Law* II 228–39.

38 *The Registrum antiquissimum of the Cathedral Church of Lincoln*, ed Kathleen Major, Lincoln Record Society 67 (Hereford 1973) nos 2784 and 2785, X 118–19. The documents are dated 1273.

39 'pecunia quae recepta de eisdem convertatur integraliter in usus eisdem magistri secundum suum voluntatem et executorum suorum disposicioni' (*Registrum antiquissimum*, ed Major X 118–19).

presumed that in it he instructed his executors how the income from the sale was to be used. Such a device had a fundamental weakness: if the trustee proved not to be a person worthy of trust, the intentions of the donor/testator were defeated. Common law could provide no remedy. The transfer of land to the trustee was either real or fictive. If it were real, then the land belonged to the trustee; the intended beneficiary had no recourse. On the other hand, if it were claimed that the transfer to the trustees was fictive, that the property remained with the testator until death, then his heir had the right to succeed to it. But an answer to the dilemma was found outside the courts of common law. It soon became clear that the trustee could be forced by the chancellor to fulfil his promise.[40] Employed in combination with a will, whereby the feoffees were instructed how to dispose of the land they held in trust, the use provided a testamentary control of land that was denied by common law. Some indication of its success is provided by the fact that occasionally a whole estate, chattels as well as lands, was distributed in this fashion.[41] When the use was made illegal by the Statute of Uses (1532), reaction by those who wished to employ it to control the devolution of their lands was so strenuous that the Statute of Wills was introduced to restore their option.[42]

A similar device was employed by peasants to dispose of land, after their death, in alms or for other purposes. Since seisin of villein lands was vested in the lord, his permission had to be obtained; such permission was granted on some manors during the fourteenth and following centuries.[43] But the lord, or his manorial official, went further. He

40 On the enforcement of the use see Richard H. Helmholz, 'The Early Enforcement of Uses,' Columbia Law Review 79 (1979) 1503–13; and T.S. Haskett, 'The Equity Side of the English Court of Chancery in the Late Middle Ages: A Method of Approach,' Ph.D. dissertation (University of Toronto 1987).

41 London, PRO C 1 17/147: Robert enfeoffed Richard Smyth in 'all his godes and catallis.'

42 See A.W.B. Simpson, An Introduction to the History of the Land Law (London 1966) 163–94. On later adjustments of the law of wills see Digby, An Introduction ch 8.

43 See A. Elizabeth Levett, Studies in Manorial History, ed Helen M. Cam et al (Oxford 1938) 218–22 for discussion and edition of early peasant wills, including wills of land. See other examples in F.G. Davenport, The Economic Development of a Norfolk Manor, 1086–1565 (Cambridge 1906) lxxvii–xc; Alan Macfarlane, The Origins of English Individualism: The Family, Property, and Social Transition (Oxford 1978) 84–8; and R.M. Smith, Women's Property Rights under Customary Law: Some Developments in the Thirteenth and Fourteenth Centuries, Transactions of the Royal Historical Society, 5th ser, 36 (London 1986) 174.

became, in the eyes of the peasant, a trustee that resembled the trustee employed by the testator who sought to control the future enjoyment of freehold by the use. The manorial procedure involved surrender of the property held by a villein to the lord or his officer. After the death of the tenant, he was expected to deliver the land in question to the legatee, who had been indicated, or to the executors, who were to assign it according to their instructions.

Reflecting on this small sample of evidence, drawn for the most part from testaments, a few points can be made. First, while it is clear that the devolution of chattels and property in land was carefully distinguished in common law and that this legal development led the individual to see his estate in two distinct parts, there were increasingly powerful pressures that led him to act as though they were a unity. Second, the desire to control chattels to an ever greater extent is manifest. It is also clear that many testators found that the liquid resources at their disposition were not sufficient to pay their debts and provide bequests as they saw fit. It was to be expected that many of them would seek to escape the limitation imposed by law, and that the freedom of testation that was being asserted regarding chattels would be desired for land as well. Third, some testators sought to achieve their end by support of the king or by the agreement of those who would ordinarily have succeeded to property after the testator's death. This method, of course, was awkward and not available to many. Finally, a more suitable solution was found in another version of that trusted representative that lies behind most systems of bequests, in this case, the feoffee to uses. He could be controlled by the testator, who thus came to enjoy a virtual power of bequest over his property in land. Thus more than a century before the Statute of Wills, many English landowners had found a way to control the devolution of their lands after their death.

Bibliography of
Michael M. Sheehan, CSB

Compiled by Mary C. English and James K. Farge

Books (authored or edited)

The Will in Medieval England: From the Conversion of the Anglo-Saxons to the End of the Thirteenth Century. Studies and Texts 6. Toronto: Pontifical Institute of Mediaeval Studies 1963.

The Condition of Man. Michaelmas Conference Papers. Ed Michael M. Sheehan, CSB, with R.W. Keyserlingk. Montreal: Palm 1965.

Family and Marriage in Medieval Europe: A Working Bibliography, comp Michael M. Sheehan with the assistance of Kathy D. Scardellato. Medieval Studies Committee, Faculty of Arts, University of British Columbia. Vancouver 1976; repr 1978.

Aging and the Aged in Medieval Europe: Selected Papers from the Annual Conference of the Centre for Medieval Studies, University of Toronto, 25–26 February and 11–12 November 1983. Papers in Mediaeval Studies 11. Ed, with a foreword and an afterword, Michael M. Sheehan, CSB. Toronto: Pontifical Institute of Mediaeval Studies 1990.

Domestic Society in Medieval Europe: A Select Bibliography. Comp Michael M. Sheehan, CSB, and Jacqueline Murray. Toronto: Pontifical Institute of Mediaeval Studies, 1990; repr 1995.

Articles (in books, journals, and encyclopedias)

'The Papal Order of the Day.' *Benedicamus* 1 (1948) 4–5.

'The New St Michael's College School.' *Benedicamus* 3 (1950) 27–9.

'A List of Thirteenth-Century English Wills.' *Genealogists' Magazine* 13 (1961) 259–65.

'The Church and Secular History.' *Basilian Teacher* 6 (1961) 23–5.

'Report of a Thesis Defended at the Pontifical Institute of Mediaeval Studies.' *Mediaeval Studies* 23 (1961) 368–71.

'Considerations on the Ends of the Canadian Catholic Historical Association.' *Canadian Catholic Historical Association Report* 30 (1963) 23–31.

'The Influence of Canon Law on the Property Rights of Married Women in England.' *Mediaeval Studies* 25 (1963) 109–24.

'New Areas of Christian Charity.' *Basilian Teacher* 9 (1964) 58–71.

'A Current Bibliography of Canadian Church History.' *Report, Canadian Catholic Historical Association* 31 (1964) 51–63.

'Canon Law and English Institutions: Some Notes on Current Research.' In *Proceedings of the Second International Congress of Medieval Canon Law* (Boston College, 12–16 August 1963). Monumenta iuris canonici. Series C: Subsidia 1. Ed Stephan Kuttner and J. Joseph Ryan. Vatican City 1965. 391–7.

'A Current Bibliography of Canadian Church History.' *Report, Canadian Catholic Historical Association* 32 (1965) 81–91.

'A Current Bibliography of Canadian Church History.' *Study Sessions, Canadian Catholic Historical Association* 33 (1966) 51–67.

'Discussion on Consensus.' *Basilian Forum* 2 (1966) 74–5.

'Annates.' In *New Catholic Encyclopedia*. New York: McGraw-Hill 1967. I 556b–557a.

'Asylum, right of.' In *New Catholic Encyclopedia*. New York: McGraw-Hill 1967. I 994a.

'A Current Bibliography of Canadian Church History.' *Study Sessions, Canadian Catholic Historical Association* 34 (1967) 77–93.

'History: The Context of Morality.' In *The New Morality: Continuity and Discontinuity*. Ed William Dunphy. New York: Herder and Herder 1967. 37–54. Spanish trans 'El contexto histórico de la moral.' In *La nueva moral: Continuidad o discontinuidad*. Trans José L. Alvarez. Salamanca: Ediciones Sigueme 1972. 17–33.

'Necrology.' In *New Catholic Encyclopedia*. New York: McGraw-Hill 1967. X 296a–297a.

'A Current Bibliography of Canadian Church History.' *Study Sessions, Canadian Catholic Historical Association* 35 (1968) 117–35.

'A Current Bibliography of Canadian Church History.' *Study Sessions, Canadian Catholic Historical Association* 36 (1969) 79–101.

'Ius matrimoniale in Anglia in saeculo quartodecimo, exemplum dioecesis Eliensis.' In *Acta Conventus internationalis canonistarum*, Romae, diebus 20–5 mai 1968 celebrati. Vatican City 1970. 674–8.

'Canon Law and Criticism of the System.' Distributed in spirit-duplicated
    format. Pp 17. Toronto ca 1970.
'A Christian Approach to Living Longer: Time as Opportunity for Growth in
    Christ.' In *Strategy for Tomorrow's Living*. Ed Sr Margaret Forguson. Pem-
    broke, Ont. 1971. 50–3.
'The Formation and Stability of Marriage in Fourteenth-Century England:
    Evidence of an Ely Register.' *Mediaeval Studies* 33 (1971) 228–63.
'A Guide to the Stained Glass Windows, St Michael's Cathedral, Toronto.'
    Distributed in multilith format to cathedral visitors. Pp 7. Toronto 1973.
'Marriage and Family in English Conciliar and Synodal Legislation.' In *Essays
    in Honour of Anton Charles Pegis*. Ed J. Reginald O'Donnell. Toronto:
    Pontifical Institute of Mediaeval Studies 1974. 205–14.
'Old English Literature and the Social Historian: Possibilities for Further
    Study.' Distributed in spirit-duplicated format. Pp 12. Toronto 1974.
'Choice of Marriage Partner in the Middle Ages: Development and Mode of
    Application of a Theory of Marriage.' *Studies in Medieval and Renaissance
    History* n s 1 (1978) 1–33.
'Marriage Theory and Practice in the Conciliar Legislation and Diocesan
    Statutes of Medieval England.' *Mediaeval Studies* 40 (1978) 408–60.
'Bertie Wilkinson.' Citation for the degree of Doctor of Letters, *honoris causa*.
    In *Memory and Promise*. From the Special Convocation upon the Fiftieth
    Anniversary of the Pontifical Institute of Mediaeval Studies, 20 October
    1979. Ed J. Ambrose Raftis. Toronto: Pontifical Institute of Mediaeval
    Studies 1980. 11–13.
'Dispensation.' In *Dictionary of the Middle Ages*. New York: Scribners 1982–9.
    IV 216a–218a.
'Family and Marriage, Western Europe.' In *Dictionary of the Middle Ages*. New
    York: Scribners 1982–9. IV 608a–612a.
'"Study Sessions" of the Second Fifty Years.' *Study Sessions, Canadian Catholic
    Historical Association* 50 (1983) 59–71.
'Christian Marriage: An Historical Perspective.' In *Christian Marriage
    Today: Growth or Breakdown? Interdisciplinary Essays*. Ed Joseph A.
    Buijs. Symposium Series 16. Lewiston, N.Y.: Edwin Mellen Press 1985. 15–
    32.
'Religious Life and Monastic Organization at Alahan.' In *Alahan, an Early
    Christian Monastery in Southern Turkey: Based on the Work of Michael Gough*.
    Ed Mary Gough. Toronto: Pontifical Institute of Mediaeval Studies 1985.
    197–220.
'The Wife of Bath and Her Four Sisters: Reflections on a Woman's Life in the
    Age of Chaucer.' B.K. Smith Lecture, University of St Thomas, Houston

(March 1982). *Medievalia et Humanistica: Studies in Medieval & Renaissance Culture* n s 13 (1985) 23–42.

'English Wills and the Records of the Ecclesiastical and Civil Jurisdictions.' *Journal of Medieval History* 14 (1988) 3–12.

'Theory and Practice: Marriage of the Unfree and the Poor in Medieval Society.' *Mediaeval Studies* 50 (1988) 457–87.

'Archbishop John Pecham's Perception of the Papacy.' In *The Religious Roles of the Papacy: Ideals and Realities, 1150–1300.* Ed Christopher Ryan. Papers in Mediaeval Studies 8. Toronto: Pontifical Institute of Mediaeval Studies 1989. 299–320.

'Jubilee 1989: Convocation.' *Jubilee 1989: Pontifical Institute of Mediaeval Studies: Foundation 1929 – Papal Charter 1939.* Ed Martin Dimnik et al. Toronto: Pontifical Institute of Mediaeval Studies 1989. 89–96.

'George Bernard Cardinal Flahiff, CSB (1905–1989).' *Mediaeval Studies* 52 (1990) v–viii.

'Special Buildings with Special Meanings: The Cathedrals of Canada.' *Catholic Register.* Special Supplement (18 May 1990) C 2–3.

'Hommage à Dom Jean Leclercq.' With Edouard Jeauneau. *Studia Monastica* 33 (1991) 379–88.

'The European Family and Canon Law.' *Continuity and Change* 6 (1991) 347–60.

'*Maritalis affectio* Revisited.' In *The Olde Daunce: Love, Friendship, Sex, and Marriage in the Medieval World.* Ed Robert R. Edwards and Stephen Spector. Albany: State University of New York Press 1991. 32–43, 254–60.

'The Bishop of Rome to a Barbarian King on the Rituals of Marriage.' In *In iure veritas: Studies in Canon Law in Memory of Schafer Williams.* Ed Steven B. Bowman and Blanche E. Cody. Cincinnati: University of Cincinnati College of Law 1991. 187–99.

'Sexuality, Marriage, Celibacy, and the Family in Central and Northern Italy: Christian Legal and Moral Guides in the Early Middle Ages.' In *The Family in Italy from Antiquity to the Present.* Ed David I. Kertzer and Richard P. Saller. New Haven and London: Yale University Press 1991. 168–83.

'The Bequest of Land in England in the High Middle Ages: Testaments and the Law.' In *Marriage, Property, and Succession.* Ed Lloyd Bonfield. Comparative Studies in Continental and Anglo-American Legal History 10. Berlin: Duncker und Humblot 1992. 326–38.

'The Future of Medieval Studies: A Retrospective Introduction to the Issues.' In *The Past and Future of Medieval Studies.* Ed John Van Engen. Notre Dame Conferences in Medieval Studies 4. Notre Dame, Ind.: University of Notre Dame Press 1994. 6–15.

'Illegitimacy in Late Medieval England: Laws, Dispensation, and Practice.' In
Illegitimät im Spätmittelalter. Ed Ludwig Schmugge. Schriften des Historis-
chen Kollegs. Kolloquien 29. Munich: Oldenbourg 1994. 115–21.
'Foreword.' *Artistic Integration in Gothic Buildings*. Ed Virginia C. Raguin,
Kathryn Brush, and Peter Draper. Toronto: University of Toronto Press
1995. ix–x.
'Widows and Widowhood.' In *Medieval England: An Encyclopedia*. Ed Joel T.
Rosenthal et al. New York: Garland, forthcoming.
'Wills and Testaments.' In *Medieval England: An Encyclopedia*. Ed Joel T.
Rosenthal et al. New York: Garland, forthcoming.

Reviews

Joseph Gill, SJ, *Eugenius IV: Pope of Christian Unity* (Westminster, Md. 1961).
In *Catholic Historical Review* 48 (1962–3) 242–3.
Roland H. Bainton et al, *The Horizon History of Christianity* (New York [1964]).
In *Basilian Teacher* 9 (1965) 311–12.
Gaines Post, *Studies in Medieval Legal Thought: Public Law and the State, 1100–
1322* (Princeton, N.J. 1964). In *Catholic Historical Review* 51 (1964–5) 84–5.
Henri Platelle, *La justice seigneuriale de l'abbaye de Saint-Amand: Son organi-
sation judiciaire, sa procédure, et sa compétence du XIe au XVIe siècle* (Paris
and Louvain 1965). In *Catholic Historical Review* 54 (1968–9) 118–19.
Hans J. Margull, ed, *The Councils of the Church*, trans Walter F. Bense, Jr
(Philadelphia 1966). In *Church History* 37 (1968) 211.
F.R.H. du Boulay, *The Lordship of Canterbury: An Essay on Mediaeval Society*
(New York 1966). In *Speculum* 44 (1969) 277–80.
Paola d'Ancona and Erardo Aeschlimann, *The Art of Illumination: An Anthology
of Manuscripts from the Sixth to the Sixteenth Century*, trans Alison M.
Brown (London 1969). In *Liturgical Arts* 38 (1970) 74–5.
The Très riches heures of Jean, Duke of Berry, Musée Condé, Chantilly, intro and
legends by Jean Longnon and Raymond Gazelles (New York 1969). In
Liturgical Arts 38 (1970) 107–8.
Georg Gerster, *Churches in Rock: Early Christian Art in Ethiopia* (New York
1970). In *Liturgical Arts* 39 (1971) 80–1.
H.G. Richardson and G.O. Sayles, *Law and Legislation from Aethelberht to Mag-
na Carta* (Chicago 1967). In *Catholic Historical Review* 56 (1970–1) 715–17.
Paul Hair, ed, *Before the Bawdy Court: Selections from Church Court and Other
Records Relating to the Correction of Moral Offences in England, Scotland, and
New England, 1300–1800* (New York 1972). In *Catholic Historical Review* 61
(1975) 610–11.

Jane E. Sayers, *Papal Judges Delegate in the Province of Canterbury, 1198–1254: A Study in Ecclesiastical Jurisdiction and Administration* (New York 1971). In *Catholic Historical Review* 61 (1975) 73–4.

Richard H. Helmholz, *Marriage Litigation in Medieval England* (Cambridge 1974). In *Speculum* 52 (1977) 983–7.

Charles R. Young, *Hubert Walter, Lord of Canterbury and Lord of England* (Durham, N.C. 1968). In *Journal of the Canadian Church Historical Society* 19 (1977) 210–12.

Richard H. Helmholz, *Marriage Litigation in Medieval England* (Cambridge 1974). In *Catholic Historical Review* 64 (April 1978) 307–8.

Henry Ansgar Kelly, *The Matrimonial Trials of Henry VIII* (Stanford 1976). In *Renaissance and Reformation / Renaissance et Réforme* n s 4 (o s 16) (1980) 105–7.

Georges Duby, *Medieval Marriage: Two Models from Twelfth-Century France* (Baltimore 1978). In *Catholic Historical Review* 66 (October 1980) 647–9.

Ralph Houlbrooke, *Church Courts and the People during the English Reformation, 1520–1570* (Oxford and New York 1979). In *American Journal of Legal History* 25 (1981) 363–4.

'Christianity and Homosexuality.' Review article of Michael Goodich, *The Unmentionable Vice: Homosexuality in the Later Medieval Period* (Santa Barbara and Oxford 1979); Peter Coleman, *Christian Attitudes to Homosexuality* (London 1980); and John Boswell, *Christianity, Social Tolerance, and Homosexuality: Gay People in Western Europe from the Beginning of the Christian Era to the Fourteenth Century* (Chicago 1980). In *Journal of Ecclesiastical History* 33 (1982) 438–46.

Norma Adams and Charles Donahue, Jr, eds, *Select Cases from the Ecclesiastical Courts of the Province of Canterbury, c. 1200–1301* (London 1981). In *Speculum* 59 (1984) 106–9.

Cicely Howell, *Land, Family, and Inheritance in Transition: Kibworth Harcourt, 1280–1700* (Cambridge and New York 1983). In *Albion* 16 (1984) 410–12.

Zvi Razi, *Life, Marriage, and Death in a Medieval Parish: Economy, Society, and Demography in Halesowen, 1270–1400* (New York 1980). In *Catholic Historical Review* 70 (1984) 293–4.

Dorothy Whitelock, Michael Brett, and Christopher N.L. Brooke, eds, *Councils and Synods with Other Documents Relating to the English Church, 1:I A.D. 871–1066; 1:II A.D. 1066–1204* (Oxford 1981). In *Speculum* 59 (1984) 215–17.

Jean Gaudemet, *La formation du droit canonique médiéval* (London 1980). In *American Journal of Legal History* 28 (1984) 82–3.

Jack Goody, *The Development of the Family and Marriage in Europe* (Cambridge 1984). In *Catholic Historical Review* 73 (April 1987) 264–5.

Caecilia Davis-Weyer, *Early Medieval Art, 300–1150: Sources and Documents* (Englewood Cliffs, N.J. 1985). In *Canadian Catholic Review* 5 (1987) 314.

Philippe Ariès and Georges Duby, eds, *A History of Private Life,* 2: *Revelations of the Medieval World,* ed Georges Duby, trans Arthur Goldhammer (Cambridge, Mass. 1988). In *Catholic Historical Review* 75 (1989) 474–5.

James A. Brundage, *Law, Sex, and Christian Society in Medieval Europe* (Chicago 1987). In *Catholic Historical Review* 76 (1990) 334–6.

Elisabeth Vodola, *Excommunication in the Middle Ages* (Berkeley 1986). In *Journal of Ecclesiastical History* 41 (1990) 294–6.

Richard H. Helmholz, *Canon Law and the Law of England* (London 1987). In *American Journal of Legal History* 36 (1992) 209–10.

DATE DUE

GAYLORD			PRINTED IN U.S.A.